POLITICAL THEOLOGY ON EDGE

TRANSDISCIPLINARY THEOLOGICAL COLLOQUIA

Theology has hovered for two millennia between scriptural metaphor and philosophical thinking; it takes flesh in its symbolic, communal, and ethical practices. With the gift of this history and in the spirit of its unrealized potential, the Transdisciplinary Theological Colloquia intensify movement between and beyond the fields of religion. A multivocal discourse of theology takes place in the interstices, at once self-deconstructive in its pluralism and constructive in its affirmations.

Hosted annually by Drew University's Theological School, the colloquia provide a matrix for such conversations, while Fordham University Press serves as the midwife for their publication. Committed to the slow transformation of religio-cultural symbolism, the colloquia continue Drew's long history of engaging historical, biblical, and philosophical hermeneutics, practices of social justice, and experiments in theopoetics.

Catherine Keller, *Director*

POLITICAL THEOLOGY ON EDGE

Ruptures of Justice and Belief in the Anthropocene

CLAYTON CROCKETT AND
CATHERINE KELLER, EDITORS

FORDHAM UNIVERSITY PRESS ❦ NEW YORK ❦ 2022

Copyright © 2022 Fordham University Press

All rights reserved. No part of this publication may be reproduced, stored in a retrieval system, or transmitted in any form or by any means—electronic, mechanical, photocopy, recording, or any other—except for brief quotations in printed reviews, without the prior permission of the publisher.

Fordham University Press has no responsibility for the persistence or accuracy of URLs for external or third-party Internet websites referred to in this publication and does not guarantee that any content on such websites is, or will remain, accurate or appropriate.

Fordham University Press also publishes its books in a variety of electronic formats. Some content that appears in print may not be available in electronic books.

Visit us online at www.fordhampress.com.

Library of Congress Cataloging-in-Publication Data available online at https://catalog.loc.gov.

Printed in the United States of America
24 23 22   5 4 3 2 1
First edition

CONTENTS

Introduction: Political Theology on Edge
| *Catherine Keller and Clayton Crockett* 1

PART I: POLITICAL THEOLOGY
AND THE ANTHROPOCENE

1. The Anthropocene as Planetary Machine
   | *William E. Connolly* 19

2. Anthropocenic Journeys | *Michael Northcott* 35

3. Resisting Geopower: Political Theologies
   of the Anthropocene | *Austin Roberts* 57

PART II: DESTRUCTION AND SUICIDE

4. The Tradition of Destruction
   (Kafka's Law) | *Gil Anidjar* 79

5. Suicide Notes (In Remembrance
   of David Buckel) | *Winfield Goodwin* 91

6. Catachresis in the Margins:
   Notes on Theologico-Political Method
   | *Lawrence E. Hillis* 109

PART III: AFFECTIVE AND AXIOMATIC
INTERVENTIONS

7. Doing Theology When Whiteness
   Stands Its Ground | *Kelly Brown Douglas* 139

8. Paul between Protagoras and Rancière:
"On the basis of equality, . . . that there
may be equality" | *Larry L. Welborn*   149

9. Listening for the Power of the People:
A Political Theology of Affect
| *Lisa Gasson-Gardner*   165

PART IV: GLOBAL POLITICAL THEOLOGIES

10. Undressing Political Theology for an
Animal-Saint Redress | *Balbinder Singh Bhogal*   183

11. What Is Political about Political Islam?
| *Mehmet Karabela*   214

PART V: FROM GENOCIDE TOWARD
A SACRED POLITICS

12. #BlackLivesMatter
and Sacred Politics | *Seth Gaiters*   237

13. Genocide and the Sin of Identity
| *Noëlle Vahanian*   254

14. Mystic S/Zong! | *J. Kameron Carter*   272

Acknowledgments   313

List of Contributors   315

POLITICAL THEOLOGY ON EDGE

Introduction:
Political Theology on Edge

CATHERINE KELLER AND CLAYTON CROCKETT

I

What is political theology? The modern conversation around the notion of political theology revolves all too famously around the book by that name by Carl Schmitt. It focuses on the concept of sovereignty, who in personalist terms is the one "who decides on the exception."[1] He traces this idea of sovereignty from a Christian theological conception of God, developed in the European Middle Ages, as the ultimate source of power and authority. For Schmitt, sovereign power, even if it appears divided, is a unifying force to decide what constitutes an exception to the normal situation. How do we decide who is excluded from "our" religion, community, nation, race, species, or planet? And how is that decision to be policed and enforced? Authority retains a link with divinity, however implicit. As with sovereignty, political theology finds that most of our modern political concepts have roots in theology, which means that our secular world remains deeply theological in its workings.

Over the last few decades we have witnessed around the globe the resurgence of political, literalist, and fundamentalist forms of religion in a way that challenges the modern secularist hypothesis that predicted religion's demise. In addition to the repudiation of secularism, we are seeing signs around the world of the collapse of the modern liberal European order, including the American empire that succeeded it. This is what Schmitt calls the "International Law of the *Jus Publicum Europaeum*" in *The Nomos of the Earth*, and it applies not just to Europe but to our inheritance of European traditions of liberalism and market capitalism.[2] And at our moment of this *saeculum*, we face not just political but also ecological crises, as we confront the sharpening edges of global warming framing the new geological order some call the Anthropocene.

If our shared political and ecological crisis counts at the same time as a theological crisis, a crisis in and of theology, it is because theology inhabits all of our politics in eschatological terms. If eschatology signifies the teaching of end things, what now appears as the end of all of our efforts and actions? What is happening in light of this end, to bring about, to redirect, or to postpone this eschaton? During the twenty-first century, Drew University has been the site of annual Transdisciplinary Theological Colloquia that have engaged with the most current and cutting-edge issues confronting our world, its meaning and its telos, in theological, political, and ecological terms. Political Theology is no exception. But how we think about political theology must and does change in light of the urgent challenges of our time, including anthropogenic climate change, global religious conflicts, the ongoing fires of racial injustice and the Black Lives Matter movement, not to mention the global pandemic in the form of COVID-19.

Along these edgy threats of various ends appear no easy answers. There is no theoretical trick/action/practice, no spiritual somersault, no miraculous brinksmanship that will rescue us from the political precipice of this time. What is "this time"? Ill-coordinated with schedules of publication or journalistic timeliness, the moment of this volume takes place at the time of multiple intersecting crises. These collective and collecting crises do not reveal the End of Time. They do however—from the point of view of the present conversation—mark a civilizational brink: There is nothing that has predetermined that we must go over it. Nor do we (the authors) guarantee that if you (the readers) will only put our theory into practice, we (the species) won't go down. This tense present—irreducible to any future-trumping US regime, indeed to any exceptionalist power—finds itself at multiple, shifting edges.

The intersecting politics of race and immigration, of gender and sexuality, of democracy and economics, of movements and parties—indeed of the religious and the secular—seem to converge along the eerie edges of the Anthropocene. Here the human and the nonhuman reveal (*apocalyptein*) their planetary relation as unsustainable. The End after all? Or rather a strange mingling of ends? One million species currently on the brink of extinction, not to mention the unthinkable millions of humans whose doom will be sealed by unmitigated global warming, might lead us to join Christian fundamentalism in collapsing revelation into termination. But we recall that eschatology, mistranslated as a simple "doctrine of The End," means actually teaching on the *eschaton*, the "edge," as rim or verge, spatial as well as temporal.

Political theology, inasmuch as it attends to a collective present edged with a precarious future, has always already been political eschatology. Yet whatever hope, faith, or love abide—for the new heavens/atmosphere and earth of a collective transformation, a new Jerusalem sparkling with always open gates—no honest eschatology can mistake hope for guarantee. And, anyway, theology's promises, social or supernatural, have hollowed out, have grown thin to the point of collapse. The failing of old Christian institutions converges with democratic failure, both limned upon the planetary horizon of ecosocial collapse. From the viewpoint of theological transdisciplinarity, the edginess of this moment pertains most intimately to the precarity of theology itself. So there is no snug theological vantage point from which to read the apocalypses of the political and the terrestrial. We have to do with a triple eschaton. In its edginess the material conditions of the planet are no longer patiently standing by for human civilization to morph into the peaceable kingdom, let alone for any religion to take the lead.

In its multireligious and irreligious transdisciplinarity, theology does not hope to transcend the precarious condition of its world. It aims to transgress the sovereign Christian exceptionalism that extracts itself from the world that it at the same time dominates. Or used to. Or does still, in ghostly secularizations, vulgar reactions of and against unification, and economic liquidations. These secularizations, as of sovereignty itself, constitute the grist of the "political theology" mill. Anything that calls itself political theology is practicing attention to the incarnations and transformations of religion into secular structures. In this it does not escape its "anti-Schmittian" (in the words of Gary Dorrien) association with Carl Schmitt, who at the cutting edge of a coming fascism declared the key concepts of modern politics to be secularized theological ideas. He read sovereignty as the secularization of the most exceptional power, that of divine omnipotence.

This volume is no exception to the current conversation *around* political theology. But it is not tightly contained *within* "political theology." None of the essays march under the banner of Schmitt. So in addition to essays that pick up on cues from such critics of Schmitt as Derrida, Badiou, and Agamben, several firmly avoid engagement in the largely Continental theorizing of political theology, let alone of Schmitt himself. Political theology as such, as the discourse that appropriated the title of Schmitt's 1922 *Political Theology*, has had a galvanizing effect on a particular set of conversations on the left, or at least on that progressive scholarship that has for decades been oscillating between a presumptive secularism and an emergent postsecularism. Perhaps we might call that vibrant between-space *secularreligious*. All of the essays here share that space. All of them work from within rich traditions of thought and activism that recognize the bi-directional flow of theology and politics.

For of course in a certain sense theology, at least in its Abrahamic force field, has never not been "political." This is true even when it denies its political implications, when it refuses to explicate any socioethical good beyond that of its own temples, churches, mosques. Then the silence speaks. The history of Christianity can be curated as one long convulsive struggle between the active theology of the Empire, the acquiescent theology of otherworldly reward, and the activist theology of the *basileia theou*, the Kingdom of God. More recently activisms of the right vie with the liberation movements of the left. The tradition that flows from the exodus from Pharaoh's empire can bifurcate into a politics of the wall, blocking out the echoes of Deuteronomy 10:19: "Love the stranger, for you were strangers in the land of Egypt." More recent theorizations have exposed the political theology behind the early twentieth-century radicalization of nationalism into fascism, while at the same time the movements for democratic socialism cannot conceal the input of religious socialism, as the work of Gary Dorrien has shown.[3] In other words, if theology has always been political, it recognizes with and beyond "political theology" that politics—imperial, national, liberal, neoliberal, socialist—has no history separate from theology.

If the volume does fly the flag of political theology as such, it does so in order to strengthen the secularreligious engagements that can energize and empower wider coalitions. It presumes with William Connolly that a full-spectrum multi-movement coalescence for the sake of a socioeconomically just and ecologically livable world demands—now—more insistently pluralist democratic collaborations. It suspects that without more vital cooperation between religious and secular publics, "aspirational fascism" will prevail.

So the essays here aspire to a movement more effectively resistant to the white straight masculinity of current sovereignty—political and economic. They may focus on race, or on religious difference, or on climate change. But by explication or by implication, they all participate in an attunement to the intersections of multiple vectors of planetary precarity. Language may crack in the effort to materialize an alternative broad and particular enough to resist the "new international" of multiple nationalisms, which constitutes the anti-planetary globalism of neoliberal capitalism. But the cracks do not inhibit these voices: on the contrary they open into the "Mystic S/Zong!" as elaborated in the contribution by J. Kameron Carter, of a language that may call itself theological or atheological. And so they each contribute to an intersectionalism that refuses every sovereign exceptionalism—even for their own articulate priority, their primary focus. And like the Black feminist originators of intersectionality, to refuse a single issue silo is not to back away from the urgency of race. Or of gender. Or of sexuality. Or of class. Or of the planet thus intersected. Rather, it is to intensify the urgency as complexity. And so, as the 2016 book *Intersectionality* concludes, "The central challenge facing intersectionality is to move into the politics of the not-yet."[4] So we find ourselves now, again, as ever again, at the eschaton, on edge, perhaps even—on the verge.

What causal force in the material world such vocalizations as *Political Theology on Edge* may muster remains of course inevitably uncertain. We do not forget that theology itself remains in question as a discourse. In its transit across and beyond academic disciplines, it finds itself on edge, right there at the multiple edges of our historic moment. That does not, however, necessarily reduce the force of materialization with which such essays move and breathe and have new embodiments.

II

On what edge are we perched? The year 2020 has launched an unprecedented global pandemic, COVID-19, that has brought much of the world to a standstill. This deadly rider of the fourth pale horse of Revelation has not (as we write) brought the massive numbers of dead dreamt about in apocalyptic disaster scenarios, but it has profoundly disrupted business as usual.[5] Ironically, the almost total shutdown of the global economy in spring 2020 temporarily reduced greenhouse gas emissions between 10 and 30 percent.[6] Unfortunately, this reduction is unlikely to slow down the progress of climate change, especially if we return to the fossil fuel–fired economic paradigm without significant transformations.

During the summer of 2020, the Black Lives Matter movement surged back to take center stage, in the wake of the murder of George Floyd at the hands of Minneapolis police. The protests that then erupted spanned the United States and the world, focusing attention on the brutality of policing and its racist effects on ethnic minorities, as well as the ways that nations and their weapons value and protect property at the expense of people. The authoritarian priority of Law and Order reinforces the racist structure of society and preserves and protects the massive transfers of wealth from poor to rich, as titans such as Amazon CEO Jeff Bezos became multibillionaires at a time when so many people were struggling to work, live, and take care of fragile others.

Our social order is strained to the breaking point, as is our planet in so many respects, to accommodate what Naomi Klein calls our contemporary disaster capitalism. Capitalism and Liberalism constitute twin pillars of the modern Eurocentric world, and we cling to these in a collective suicidal death spiral. The religion of capitalism believes in the necessity and possibility of unlimited growth, despite the physical limits of the material resources of our planet. The faith in liberalism, which in its current form is called neoliberalism, consists in believing that this market-fueled growth, limited in minor ways to ensure prosperity, will ensure a better world for most people.

As we reach the global limits to growth, first glimpsed by the environmental movements of the 1970s, faith in capitalism shreds along with our world. Liberalism morphed in the 1980s and 1990s into a brutal economic neoliberalism with a thin veneer of multiculturalism, and in this century a reactionary neofascism with cynical appeals to ethnonationalism has emerged. The politics of our sovereign leaders, at least in the most powerful nations, has become more explicitly authoritarian in the persons of Putin, Xi, and Trump, who tried to stage an insurrection despite his electoral loss. Alongside the political exceptionalisms we witness the comparable surge of theologies of blind complicity, of simplistic reaction, of supernatural escapism, and of profound climate denialism, even as the most promising liberationist theologies are marginalized to the point of inexistence.

We need to cultivate a liberationist ecotheology that takes account of what is happening along these sharp edges. In his book *Down to Earth*, Bruno Latour offers a mapping of our political reality in the new climatic regime.

Latour argues that the only way we can make sense of what is going on politically today is to understand how the ongoing deregulation of global capitalism, the explosion of inequalities, and the amplification of migrations around the world are all connected to climate change. He argues that "it is as though a significant segment of the ruling classes . . . had concluded that the earth no longer had room enough for them and for everyone else."[7] The denial of climate change by the elites who know better constitutes the incredible nonsense that characterizes our political discourse.

Globalization is losing its appeal as these inequalities and catastrophes mount. There is no more land that could support this globalization, because Earth does not possess sufficient resources to maintain the growth that capitalism requires. Political discourse has become more and more detached from reality, and Latour argues that the only way to comprehend this is to understand that the ruling elites have decided to *"stop pretending, even in their dreams, to share the earth with the rest of the world."*[8] The traditional oppositions between liberal and conservative, right and left, global and local, have completely broken down. "Everything has to be mapped out anew, with new costs."[9]

Latour offers a schema to visualize his analysis and to help us understand what is at stake. He argues that the elites are supporting an "Out-of-This-World" mentality that pushes people to fantasize about other worlds or non-earthly realities. In contrast, he offers another attractor, a "Terrestrial" attractor that would work to bring politics, society, and human activities *down to the real earth*. He posits the Terrestrial as a *"new political actor."*[10] A Terrestrial return to earth opposes the Out-of-This-World scenario that our ruling elites are promoting—often in cahoots with theologies of otherworldliness—with varying degrees of success. This Terrestrial attractor also avoids the oppositions between right and left (as well as local and global) that so many people continue to get hung up on.

The politics that is being served to us by the Trump administration and others is "Out of This World," because it denies the existence of our shared existence and our physical limits.[11] Our space odysseys, raptures, and other fantasies of planetary escape play into this scenario. The ruling elites promote a politics that "rejects the world that it claims to inhabit."[12] Modernity has failed, because it is premised on the notion of indefinite growth, which is impossible given a finite resource base. Latour argues that most of our visions of ecology have also failed, because ecological thinking and practice is incapable of doing more than resisting the demands of economic and technological development in the name of some nostalgic return to a planet that never existed.

Globalized Capitalist Modernity has failed, but so have contemporary environmental and ecological movements that rely on technical fixes or a return to nature. We need new visions—new ideas and practices—of alliance among people who are Earthbound and across Terran species and complex systems. We need to generate planetary alliances of solidarity among Terrans in the formation of new kinds of kinship. The genesis of a Terran community cannot be merely human community; we are embedded in too many entanglements with other nonhuman organisms and inorganic entities to survive alone.

We must rethink what it means to be in community, and take on the task of making kin beyond any form of familial kinship. This is what Donna Haraway advocates in her book *Staying with the Trouble*. She says that "the task is to make kin in lives of inventive connection as a practice of learning to live and die well with each other in a thick present."[13] Rather than an Anthropocene or even a Capitalocene, Haraway suggests that we are living in the Chthulucene, a name that indicates a thick presence for earth-beings. Chthulucene names "a kind of timeplace for learning to stay with the trouble of living and dying in response-ability on a damaged earth."[14]

What old forms of sovereignty must be rejected in the making and remaking of new kin here on Earth? We cannot afford the sovereignty of the global elites, who are sacrificing all of us—some more and sooner than others, to be sure—in their exceptionalist drive to enrich their wealth and power. What new forms of political theology can emerge, what vital ways of configuring the sacred might be possible on the verge of a new planetary age? We need to attend to the resources of philosophy, ecology, our religious traditions past and present, and an awareness of the "sacred humanity" (Carol Wayne White) that persists in oppressed Black lives to reanimate our politics and our experiments to live together—all of us earth-beings—at the end of the capitalist regime.[15] The chapters that make up this book help us open up and consider some of these vital issues.

III

What lies within the edges of this volume? The chapters that make up this book divide into five distinct but overlapping parts. Part I situates political theology firmly within the context of the Anthropocene. In Chapter 1, "The Anthropocene as Planetary Machine," William Connolly provides an overview of the conditions of our Anthropocenic world as well as a way to better comprehend it. An abstract machine is a philosophical term from Deleuze and Guattari, and it functions as an interlocking assemblage, a complex system composed of interacting elements to form an abstract but actual whole. Connolly applies this and other concepts from Deleuze and Guattari's important work to better articulate our contemporary climate crisis. Capitalism is not the only factor in the working of this machine, but it is a key driver of the process of planetary climate change. Connolly offers historical context and geopolitical overview of this complex situation, in hopes that more connections can be made for a critical intervention into this abstract machine.

Michael Northcott gives us another overview of the Anthropocenic in Chapter 2, but his reflections are less scientific and more personal and episodic. "Anthropocenic Journeys" supplies a concrete discussion of particular concepts and geographies in terms of how they are affected by and contribute to the planetary situation of the Anthropocene. As he does so, the author of *A Political Theology of Climate Change* attends to the shifting nature of some Christian theological imaginaries that better reflect and engage the urgent ecological in which we find ourselves.

In Chapter 3, "Resisting Geopower," Austin Roberts shows how dangerous our assumptions of a quick fix are, because we are tempted to think that more of the same can overcome the problems that modern industrial and postindustrial capitalism has created. Roberts engages with the problem of planetary sovereignty in the Anthropocene, the idea that some unified sovereign power is required to address the significance of the problem of global warming. This planetary sovereignty perpetuates the same form of political theology that was put forth by Schmitt, because it would and must be a sovereign exception. And we must refuse this alternative.

Part II, "Destruction and Suicide," engages the devastating effects of this ecological crisis that hits at so many levels, including the philosophical, religious, political, and personal. Gil Anidjar sharpens our conceptions of destruction and forces us to confront the limits of our desires for survival and redemption in social, political, and theological terms. Chapter 4, "The Tradition of Destruction," focuses on Kafka's *The Trial*, where the law is essentially reduced to nothing. This tradition of destruction as read through

Kafka lies between the interpretations of deconstruction, law, and the messianic that are proposed by two of the main philosophical influences on political theology, Derrida and Agamben. By returning us more directly to Kafka, partly as read by Walter Benjamin, Anidjar pushes against our tendencies toward social, political, and religious redemption that animate us but also perhaps continue to imprison us.

In Chapter 5, "Suicide Notes," Winfield Goodwin begins with the ecological suicide of David Buckel, who set himself on fire to protest the ecological destruction of the Earth. Buckel, a political rights attorney and LGBTQ activist who turned to environmentalism, performs an ecocide that Goodwin reads as a spectacular death in contrast with the myriad forms of "slow death" that are killing our planet. This singular ecocide raises new questions about what Walter Benjamin, already referred to in connection to Kafka by Anidjar, calls *Gewalt*, force or violence. The memory of Buckel's act forces us to consider new relations between Gewalt and time, and disrupts our assumptions about what political theology is and can be.

In Chapter 6 Lawrence Hillis analyzes the tradition of political theology as a form of catechresis, using Anidjar, Agamben, and Derrida, and concluding with Benjamin's notion of *Gewalt*. A catachresis is literally a kind of mistake, when someone uses an incorrect word or metaphor. At the same time, this mistake can have creative resonances and generate new interpretations and understandings. Political theology is catachrestic in its joining of the political and the theological, but this mistake is deeply significant for both traditions. In Chapter 6, "Catachresis in the Margins," Hillis concludes that what Benjamin calls divine violence is itself a kind of catachresis in a way that mirrors and distorts what we mean by political theology. He says that "as a counter-imperial catachrestic figure, 'divine violence' presents the Western theologico-political tradition with an inverted mirror of its torqued structural naming practices. In doing so, the reader is invited to consider *why* such incomprehensible language is *required* to perform an effective critique of power, authority, and violence."

We need new language to understand and effectively critique the violence that we are, that inhabits, animates, propels, and destroys us. And this violence is at once completely political and absolutely theological, even as it distorts both of these concepts. Part III of this volume, "Affective and Axiomatic Interventions," reconsiders in light of the catachrestic and overwhelming elements of force and violence to which we are subjected. In

Chapter 7, "Doing Theology When Whiteness Stands Its Ground," Kelly Brown Douglas returns us to the Black body, that intrudes into our social, political, and theological discourse despite the attempts of whiteness to "stand its ground" and keep it out. White identity is not innocent, but it is the formation and expression of a profound violence, because whiteness is constituted over against what is not white, paradigmatically Blackness. White bodies come together to form a white supremacy in the face of Black bodies' appearance onto the social and political field, erasing and in many cases destroying them. Here is the color line in the twenty-first century. Douglas draws on the theology of James Cone as well as some of her own experiences to help her reflect on what it means to have a Black theology where Jesus (a man of color who has been appropriated as white) says NO to white supremacy.

Douglas intervenes into Christianity to theologize Jesus as antagonistic to white supremacy. Analogously, Larry L. Welborn offers a scholarly interpretation of Paul that figures this Apostle, who appears to authorize a certain paradigmatically violent form of Christianity, as a preacher of equality. Drawing on biblical criticism and contemporary philosophy, Welborn uses Jacques Rancière to help argue that Paul affirms an equality of persons amid the inequality that pervaded the ancient Greek and Roman world. Our own world is becoming increasingly unequal in material and economic terms, and we desperately need more equality, whether we are Christian or not. Welborn reads "Paul between Protagoras and Rancière" in Chapter 8, and concludes that Paul may be a significant resource for us today. He argues that particularly in Corinthians Paul extends "the principle of 'equality' into the sphere of economic relations between Christian believers [that] builds upon and develops egalitarian and democratic impulses that were already at work in the earliest Christian communities." This extension of equality empowers the marginalized peoples who were rendered invisible in the Empire, giving them a voice.

For Lisa Gasson-Gardner, we need religion and political reflection, including the resources of political theology. But we also require more affect, and she draws on and employs affect theory, specifically music, to intervene into the discourses of political theology to recover a kind of truth that resists racial, political, and anti-environmental authoritarianism and extremism. In Chapter 9, "Listening for the Power of the People," Gasson-Gardner argues that we need to critique and repudiate the concept of sovereignty, but still retain the idea of an exception, including the exceptional power of the people to fashion their truth. She has us listen to the words of Jonelle Monae, whose song "Americans" performs a counter-sovereign inclusivity that voices truth.

From these reflections on justice, equality, affect, and violence from the standpoint of certain strands of Christian faith, we shift to a global expansion of what political theology is and can be. Part IV, "Global Political Theologies," considers two important political theologies that exceed the Schmittian and the Christian frameworks and transform our understandings of sovereignty. In Chapter 10, "Undressing Political Theology for an Animal-Saint Redress," Balbinder Singh Bhogal sketches a decolonial work to undo the European colonialism at the heart of political theology. He mines Indian religious traditions, particularly Sikhism, to conceptualize sovereignty differently. Beyond egoistic rationalism, a form of ahuman affective knowing links what we call the animal and the saint. Rather than the Western sovereignty of the One, Bhogal asserts a double and doubled sovereignty in Sikhism that is horizontal rather than vertical in its operation. There is an "internal, co-dependent sovereignty" in everyone, "a pluriversal sovereignty within all beings" that undresses political theology in its Western guise.

Following Bhogal's decolonial deconstruction of political theology, Mehmet Karabela, in Chapter 11, "What Is Political about Political Islam?," draws on Schmitt's analysis more explicitly to interrogate and understand how Islamic and Western scholars have conceptualized an "apolitical" Islam that could then be politicized. He applies Schmitt's friend/enemy distinction as characteristic of the political to the study of Islam and shows how Islam has always been political and religious at the same time in this context. Liberalism posits a separate realm of religion and politics that it charges Islam and other political religions wrongly mix, but there is no intrinsic separation of politics from religion in a postsecular context, and we have many lessons to learn of and from Islam. Rather than the modern nation-state, which is the locus for Schmitt, the polity of Islam is situated on the Muslim community, which is less determinate and defined. Every community, particularly every religious community, is potentially political in the Schmittian context.

These expansions of political theology beyond European Christianity, and what we designate as the West, open up political theology to new horizons. More important, they trouble political theology in its Schmittian,

Western, and Euro-American iterations. The contributors to this book are not comfortable with any stable understanding of political theology as such, so the chapters in it acknowledge and contest the Schmittian origin of political theology, as well as verge beyond it in important ways. The book concludes in Part V, "From Genocide toward a Sacred Politics," with three chapters that shift our perspective. In Chapter 12, "#BlackLivesMatter and Sacred Politics," Seth Gaiters offers a counternarrative to the predominant understanding of the Black Lives Matter movement. Here he engages with the form of the memoir, specifically the memoir by Patrisse Khan-Cullors, *When They Call You a Terrorist: A Black Lives Matter Memoir.* This emphasis on the personal, affective memoir carries through an attempt of this volume to contest and expand what counts as a political-theological discourse, which can also be seen in the last two chapters. In addition to the genre of the memoir as a source of knowing, Gaiters attends to the distinctively sacred element expressed in and by it, as well in the Black Lives Matter movement generally. Specifically, this text and this movement evince a vector of the sacred "that names a fundamental commitment to realize a new world where the last will be first and the first will be last." Gaiters attends to how Khan-Cullors attempts to express religion in creative and transformative ways, beyond the binaries in which we are so often trapped. For Gaiters, the sacred in the memoir of Khan-Cullors is a "tool for freedom."

For Noëlle Vahanian, the constriction of our identity is a sin, and Chapter 13, "Genocide and the Sin of Identity," serves as a personal reflection or memoir about how identities are imagined and constructed in ways that produce genocide. Drawing on her own Armenian ancestry and its connection to the oft-overlooked Armenian Genocide, Vahanian declares that we become an "I" in such a way as to be affirmed and consolidated as a "we." This production is a fabulation, because "identity is a form of self-deception that ontologizes imagined realities at the expense of forgotten or unthinkable identities." We need a secular theology of language to name and expose the traces of these unthinkable and forgotten identities.

In the last chapter, Chapter 14, "Mystic S/*Zong!*," J. Kameron Carter offers an extraordinary interpretation of an uncontainable text, the poem *Zong!* by M. NourbeSe Philip. *Zong* is the name of a British slave ship on which around 150 African slaves were murdered in 1781 when supplies of drinking water ran low, and the crew threw slaves overboard to drown so as to cash in on the insurance money taken out on these slaves. Philip produces her poem, *Zong!*, with words from a 1783 court case, but they are fragmented, disjointed, and shredded by how they are written, in nonlinear fashion, with breaks, cuts, and gaps between and within words. This text recovers the memory of the dead slaves, but does so not as an imagined whole, only through the apparatus of death that rendered their deaths legally justified by colonial jurists.

Carter stages Philip's poem, and reads it as a sacred mystical text that renders Blackness visible through its devastation and deformation by colonial violence in act and word. According to Carter, "*Zong!* subtly engages the political theology, and specifically the ritual, ceremonial, and sacramental logics, that harnessed the sacred to the European project so as to underwrite the oceanic and legal internment of those thrown overboard from the slave ship *Zong* and that more broadly ground (racial) capitalism as a project of Western salvation." Carter's counter-political theology of the Black sacred as glimpsed through Philip opens us up to other practices of the sacred, other forms of what is called political theology, and a mystical otherworldliness without any self-evident or self-contained world. We suggest that such an otherworldliness inhabits what we call our world and limns what we call our political theologies—in all their forms.

Through the breaks and gaps of this very volume's uncontainable conversation, the reader will glimpse a poetics of the sacred. The politics and the theology work at the edges of what political theology has meant. The counter-political is not anti-political; the counter-theological is not anti-theological. Amid these transdisciplinary contestations of its legacy, political theology as such remains in play. But not in power. In place of the destructive force of political exceptionalism, in face of the Anthropocene culpability of theological exceptionalism, we do not land in some final oneness. Not in this volume, not in this saeculum, not in this eschaton. From the perspective of this edge, diversity will not flatten into pale consensus. Might we then mark the radicality of difference not as exception but rather as *inception*?[16] The eschatological novum arises amid our ecosocial planet of entanglement not as final top-down salvation—the model of global exceptionalisms—but as an irrepressible intersectionalism. It may dynamically align us in our differences. In the edginess of our most shareable language, we do not find a unified vocabulary but an enlivening solidarity.

NOTES

1. Carl Schmitt, *Political Theology: Four Chapters on the Concept of Sovereignty*, trans. George Schwab (Chicago: University of Chicago Press, 1985), 1. This book was originally published in German in 1919.
2. See Carl Schmitt, *The Nomos of the Earth: In the International Law of the Jus Publicum Europaeum*, trans. G. L. Ulmen (New York: Telos Press, 2006).
3. See Gary Dorrien, *Social Democracy in the Making: Political and Religious Roots of European Socialism* (New Haven, CT: Yale University Press, 2019).
4. Patricia Hill Collins and Sirma Bilge, *Intersectionality* (Cambridge: Polity Press, 2016), 204.
5. See Catherine Keller, "The Gallop of the Pale Green Horse: Pandemic, Pandaemonium and Panentheism," in *Pandemic, Ecology and Theology: Perspectives on COVID-19*, ed. Alexander J.B. Hampton (London: Routledge, 2021).
6. "Current and Future Global Climate Impacts Resulting from COVID-19," *Nature Climate Change* 10, 913–919, 2020. https://www.nature.com/articles/s41558-020-0883-0.
7. Bruno Latour, *Down to Earth: Politics in the New Climatic Regime*, trans. Catherine Porter (Cambridge: Polity Press, 2018), 1.
8. Ibid., 19 (emphasis in original).
9. Ibid., 33.
10. Ibid., 40 (emphasis in original).
11. Ibid.
12. Ibid., 38.
13. Donna J. Haraway, *Staying with the Trouble: Making Kin in the Chthulucene* (Durham, NC: Duke University Press, 2016), 1.
14. Ibid., 2.
15. See Carol Wayne White, *Black Lives and Sacred Humanity: Toward an African American Religious Naturalism* (New York: Fordham University Press, 2016).
16. See Catherine Keller, *Political Theology of the Earth: Our Planetary Emergency and the Struggle for a New Public* (New York: Columbia University Press, 2018), chap. 1. She counters the sovereign exception of Schmittian political theology with a collective ecosocial inception.

PART I

◦◦ Political Theology
and the Anthropocene

1. The Anthropocene as Planetary Machine

WILLIAM E. CONNOLLY

To inhabit the geological era recently known as the Anthropocene is not to live during a time when—as if flouting millions of years of long, slow change in oceans, species evolution, climate, glaciers, monsoons, and deserts—humanity writ large suddenly became a geological force. Such a statement asserts two mistakes: the assumption of planetary gradualism with which it starts and the charge of generic human responsibility with which it closes. First, geology, paleontology, oceanography, glaciology, and other earth sciences—starting as late as the 1980s—finally exploded the story of planetary gradualism that had informed the nineteenth-century geologist Lyell and the evolutionary theorist Darwin. It is an interesting question: What kind of metaphysical and cosmological assumptions in Christian providentialism and its remainders in secular thought made such sciences take so long? Especially when some predecessors, such as Kropotkin, Cuvier, Mary Shelley, and Nietzsche had already challenged gradualism? And why did the humanities, social scientists, and citizen activists even take longer?

Second assumption: "Humanity" did not become a geological force in the modern era. Rather, state capitalism, socialism, and communism, organized around internally differentiated priorities of fossil extraction, productivism, and consumption abundance, became major geological forces by dint of their institutional demands and spiritual priorities. They imposed new, rapidly accelerating burdens and injuries on racially defined constituencies, the lower classes inside the old capitalist states, and several regions outside those centers. So much, so obvious, though the corrections do require adjustments in geological definitions of the "Anthropocene."

If you interrogated the five great mass extinction events that occurred before these modern systems of political economy triumphed, it would also become clear how capitalism and others are not THE sole geological forces of rapid, deep change today either. These modern political economies, rather, spawn climate *triggers* that can be inflated or dampened by planetary *forcings* and self-organizing *amplifiers*. We thus need concepts of cascading causality to explore multiple, intersecting planetary trajectories populated with varying degrees of agency. Not all planetary forces are agents, in the sense of exuding at least some capacity to strive, feel, and help to bring something new into the world. But blind forces and purposive agents of different sorts do interact in the Anthropocene—as they did during slow and bumpy periods long before it emerged.

Gilles Deleuze and Félix Guattari did not examine the Anthropocene in relation to capitalist and communist practices of productivism. D&G, however, did open a door to such examinations through a series of concepts that underline the ways diverse human cultural practices are profoundly entangled with a host of nonhuman forces and agencies. These concepts together challenge the sufficiency of human exceptionalism, sociocentrism, cultural internalism, and planetary gradualism that had heretofore graced much of Euro-American philosophy, the humanities, and social sciences.

Several D&G concepts are pertinent to the inquiry in question. One pair—smooth and striated space—is exemplary. A few paradigms of smooth space are oceans, deserts, glaciers, mountain ranges, the atmosphere, mist, creative thinking, the stratosphere, steppes, and prairies. Several smooth spaces expand or contract over time, making huge differences to possibilities of life in and around them. Certainly, each is also susceptible to new practices of striation that would organize it more sharply. The introduction of longitude and latitude onto ocean maps is a modest example of striation. So is the division of prairie land into territories marked by moats, river borders, passport controls, county divisions, racial divisions, state bureaucracies, surveillance systems, class hierarchies, highway systems, and/or territorial walls.

The D&G interventions compel social thinkers to address the shifting densities and intensities of drought zones, monsoons, ocean currents, desertification, rates of glacier flow, hurricanes, atmospheric composition, and so forth. D&G thus introduced several categories that cut off sociocentrism at the pass—the latter being the quaint idea still lingering in some quarters that key social processes can be explained almost solely by reference to more basic social processes.

When you think of how various planetary processes themselves slide and bump into shifting mixtures of social life, other D&G concepts present themselves as candidates too. Assemblage, rhizome, multiplicity, body without organs, plane of composition, and abstract machine pop up for consideration.

But I suspect the idea of an abstract machine may do even more work to rethink the bumpy trajectories of the Anthropocene, partly because of its emphasis on fecund processes that both involve and exceed human powers and partly because of its focus on imbrications between elements of diverse types in processes of formation, consolidation, and deconsolidation. A couple of things D&G say are relevant. Abstract machines "are defined by the fourth aspect of assemblages, in other words, the cutting edges of decoding and deterritorialization.... Therefore they make the territorial assemblage open onto something else, assemblages of another type, the molecular, the cosmic: they constitute becomings." And "each abstract machine can be considered a 'plateau' of variation."[1] An abstract machine thus composes and links heterogeneous *temporalities* that are self-organizing to various degrees. The earth itself is an abstract machine: It "asserts its own powers of deterritorialization, its lines of flight, its smooth spaces that live and blaze their way for a new earth."[2] Here the idea of "machine"—with bumpy, evolutionary, self-organizing capacities—challenges both Eurocentric life/nonlife dualities and reductionist philosophies of materialism that sought to overtake them. Both.

An abstract machine, in the sense deployed here, includes moving, morphing *planetary* complexes that exceed the power of the ensemble of forces and agencies that constitute it. A planetary machine is *machinic* (rather than mechanistic, cybernetic, or organic) in that it evolves new speeds and capacities as it draws energy from earthquakes, capitalist emissions, ocean currents, deforestation, volcanoes, methane bursts, microbes, and the sun to cut into prior stabilizations; *planetary* (in this instance) in that it imposes asymmetrical regional, racial, class, and species consequences on the face of the earth; *abstract* in that it is irreducible to an aggregation of the forcings and agencies that compose it, such as, say, capitalism, white evangelicalism, technoscientific formations, imperial patterns of trade and finance, tectonic plates, cultural *ressentiment*, species evolution, viral and bacterial flows, desert advances, ocean currents, acidification, and glacier flows; and it is *complex* (or nonlinear) in that the heterogeneous forces that compose it impinge on each other, periodically *infuse* one another, and respond to these intrusions in ways that exceed the power of the triggers. Doing so will endow the self-organizing machine with evolving shapes, speeds, and trajectories.

CAPITALISM AND THE ANTHROPOCENE

I understand, with D&G, capitalism to be imperfectly contained by a shifting "axiomatic" that exceeds both a determinate mode of production and the rationality of impersonal market processes. The axiomatic, as it morphs, enables some activities, constrains others, and captures yet others. Such an image of capitalism outstrips any mode of economism, partly because it includes shifting spiritualities that infuse the institutions of production, investment, governance, class struggle, and consumption, partly because it secretes atmospheric emissions that change climate, and partly because it faces planetary forces with powers of self-amplification that jostle it in multifarious ways.[3] The bumpy relations between an axiomatic and the outside often compel a regime to search and grope in the dark as new events unfold or erupt.

A capitalist axiomatic of enablement and constraint might consist, for instance, of private ownership and pursuit of profit, a focus on fossil fuel extraction, a commodity form of consumption, labor pushed kicking and screaming toward the commodity form, states organized as servants and/or regulators of the axiomatic, and banks with varying degrees of independence. These axioms can then be augmented or contracted to foster diversities within capitalism writ large. Some variations take the form of *democratic* capitalism in which competing parties shuffle between enthusiastically subordinating themselves to the vicissitudes of the axiomatic and regulating it to protect workers, consumers, public goods, and nonhuman species; *fascist* capitalism in which a dictatorial party mobilizes a few intense factions to guide private capital and to exercise terror, surveillance, and racist control over others; *Keynesian* capitalism in which unions acquire increased institutional power and a social net for workers, the poor, the old, and the infirm is established; and *neoliberal* capitalism in which democracy becomes hollowed out, corporate regulations are stripped, state subsidies for capital flourish, and a myth (or "overcoding") of market rationality is invoked to vindicate those practices.

Under conditions of stress neoliberal capitalism can morph toward fascist capitalism, as occurred after the Great Depression in several states and as a host of new social movements drive to accomplish today in the United States, Poland, Hungary, Austria, Turkey, Brazil, and Italy. The racial dog whistles and thinly denied white triumphalism that marked neoliberalism now become bullhorns. Big Lies, aggressive racial and religious nationalism, voter suppression, corruption of courts, intelligence agencies and judicial policies, harsh policing of territorial borders, market testing of new modes of cruelty, and media intimidation now attain new heights of intensity. The Big Lie Scenario plays an outsize role in such regimes, in which leaders both dramatize false accusations against others to mobilize a base and disclose tells about themselves in doing so.

The key connections between extractive capitalism, the galloping Anthropocene, and new fascist movements in old democratic states today and tomorrow are perhaps these. First, climate warming, drought, stuttering monsoons, glacier melts, wildfires, extreme storms and so on press upon vulnerable and exploited regions outside old capitalist states, increasing pressure to civil wars and forced migrations within the latter. The resulting racialized refugee pressures upon old capitalist states create happy hunting grounds for the purveyors of aspirational fascism in those regimes. Second, as those flames are fanned by aspirational fascists—with Donald Trump leading the way in America—white workers and the lower middle class in deindustrialized zones are told that only by returning to the old days of fossil fuel extraction, steel and automobile production, and white triumphalism can they regain the levels of entitlement acquired precariously in the 1950s and early 1960s. This combination pulls some to embrace climate denialism and support an authoritarian leader; it encourages others (particularly in white upper middle and donor classes) to fund such expressions of public belief to fend off challenges from the Left.[4] White triumphalism and climate denialism thus support each other today, in part because it would indeed take radical reform of dominant practices over a single decade to respond to the perils of the Anthropocene.

"Accelerationism"—in its left-wing expressions—is the contemporary claim that the only way to respond to neoliberal capitalism today is to accelerate its own tendencies to self-destruction and austerity until it collapses from its own contradictions.[5] The frustrations pushing critics into accelerationism are understandable. But I note that left-wing proponents of accelerationism tend to underplay the acceleration of the Anthropocene itself that is well under way. If they did attend to it, it is doubtful that they would be able to pretend that a new, just society would emerge out of wreckage of the old. Accelerationism, indeed, may incite the fascist responses its proponents decry.

That is why I support a series of rapid, positive interim policies and practices to start current capitalist states, first, beyond extractive capitalism and, second, beyond the class organization of acquisitive desires joined to the differential ability of people in different subject positions to fulfill them. Today, given the urgency of time and the resentments of several neglected constituencies, it assumes the character of an improbable necessity, *improbable* because so many powerful forces resist it, *necessary* because it will take a series of rapid changes on multiple fronts to slow down the Anthropocene.

Capitalism—with its endemic pressures to expand growth, exploit nature, workers, and consumers, extend income and wealth hierarchies, generate crises, and deploy fossil fuels—thus plays a crucial role in the advance of the Anthropocene. But other forces also make signal contributions to its trajectory and speed. Indeed, capitalist states vary significantly in the extent to which they continue the extractive course. The United States—the home of a virulent evangelical/neoliberal assemblage that is morphing toward aspirational fascism—pursues a highly destructive path. Indeed, white evangelicalism became an axiom key to US neoliberal capitalism in the 1980s, showing how some axioms of capitalism are not economistic in shape.

Put another way, as the evangelical/neoliberal machine slides or gallops closer to an embrace of fascist capitalism in America, climate denialism and casualism become axioms of that assemblage. The slide of neoliberalism down this incline can be seen in the Republican Party's expansive views of presidential sovereignty, its pursuit of a territorial wall, its retreat from free trade, its refusals to criticize presidential racism, its readiness to embrace huge deficits to gain tax breaks for the rich, its willingness to short-circuit a series of established congressional norms to appoint aggressive judges and overturn congressional oversight, its readiness to participate in cover-ups of Trump's conspiracy with Russia to corrupt a democratic election, and its eager appointment of an attorney general with fascist aspirations. As each week passes, the list grows.

THE LATE ANTIQUE LITTLE ICE MACHINE

We can discern more closely how capitalism is exceeded by a climate dynamic to which it makes a major contribution by attending to other times when climate change was in play before either state capitalism or state communism existed. We need not turn merely to the period 250 million years ago when 90 percent of life was wiped out, or 66 million years ago when 50 percent of life was extinguished, though the previous cascading, nonhuman processes are also pertinent to this current planetary machine. We can look closer at hand to the fall of Rome.

According to Kyle Harper, in *The Fate of Rome,* the Roman Climate Optimum lasted from about 200 BCE to about 150 CE; that period was suitable for lavish crops, population growth, and the take-off of imperial expansion.[6] The "Late Antique Little Ice Age"—an only recently discovered climate machine—started later and coalesced with the devastating plagues induced by the unwitting importation of black rats and fleas from the East through consolidation of new trading routes.[7] These two events further weakened the Empire. Such bacterial, insect, animal, and climate incursions into the Empire, of course, mean that purely hermeneutic or sociocentric approaches to the decline of Rome do not suffice; the participants themselves had little idea of the sources of the plague and no idea of the source of the climate change. Many sought the sources in divine judgments and punishments.

Indeed, the rapid growth of Constantinian Christianity in Rome correlates loosely, first, with the dates of pestilence and, later, with climate change, perhaps in part because that version of Christianity could blame the suffering on the weakness of the pagan gods, the desert of Romans (a Second Coming was promised), and the capacity of an *omnipotent* God to overcome the two phenomena by bestowing a blissful afterlife on deserving believers.

"The natural catastrophes of the sixth century induced one of the greatest mood swings in human history. The occlusion of the sun, the rattling of the earth, and the advent of world-wide plague stoked the fires of eschatological expectation across the Christian world and beyond."[8] We discern here a Christian/imperial complex that underlines recurrent connections between the spiritual ethos of a time, shifting planetary conditions, and the shape of a regime.

How, though, did the Late Antique Little Ice Age, already simmering, acquire new momentum in 536 AD and surge until around 545, creating cold years that outstripped the now better known Little Ice Age that reached its peak in the seventeenth century? Recent geological, ice core, isotope, chronicle, and tree ring evidence suggests that the Late Antique Little Ice Age was intensified by a huge volcano in 536 AD that released massive amounts of sulfur into the stratosphere. This cooling effect bolstered the cyclical "sun dimming" already under way; soon thereafter, it was intensified by another huge tropical volcano that finished it off. The next great plague correlated with these events.

As Harper puts it, "These harsh years quietly added stress to an imperial order already stressed."[9] Harper folds volcanic, sun dimming, climate, plague eruptions, emperor impositions, imported rats, infected fleas, and inflated existential anxieties into yet other forces to explain the fate of Rome.

Planetary/culture shifts of importance are seldom reducible to an ensemble of efficient causes. The elements of a cascading ensemble penetrate each other as they also impinge on one another, enabling heterogeneous entities with varying degrees of porosity and efficacious power to form new compositions.

One thing to note today is how earlier accounts of the rise and fall of Rome did not stress the role of the Climate Optimum or the Late Antique Little Ice Age, though the plagues were noted. Some Roman chroniclers themselves had complained about changes in climate, but modern historians apparently did not emphasize them, perhaps because they had inhaled the fumes of the planetary gradualism that still dominated the earth sciences.

Except for a few minor voices—Kropotkin, Cuvier, and Nietzsche among them—stories of planetary gradualism only began to break in the major earth sciences after the discovery in 1980 by Luis Alvarez of the massive asteroid 66 million years ago that instigated a monstrous, rapid mass extinction. It took another long decade before the new story of periodic planetary volatilities was widely digested in the earth sciences.[10] And, again, longer yet before Euro-American philosophy, the humanities, and the social sciences digested these findings.

One more thing before we depart Rome. As Catherine Keller argues in *Political Theology of the Earth*, it is pertinent to attend to a series of loose historical relays and reverberations between the Roman Church's insistence that God created the world from nothing, the analogy Constantine draws between a sovereign God above time and an Emperor who rules his subjects without question, the unity soon demanded between Empire and that Christian faith by Justinian, the later rise of Calvinism, the quest by the Church of England to ground Christianity in an Anglo-Saxon race, the transfiguration of theologies of divine omnipotence by Carl Schmitt into a secular doctrine in which the state sovereign becomes He who decides, white evangelical demands in America for identity between Constantinian doctrine and a white Christian nation, capitalist firms that demand authoritarian control over workers, and fascist movements demanding sovereign, unquestioned rule over an entire "people."[11]

This is definitely not to say that there is a single, straight line running from the first pattern of insistence to later assertions of ruthless, sovereign entitlement. These are, rather, loose cultural lineages of association, inspiration, and reverberation. Some themes and associations may wane for a while and then assume new intensity under novel conditions of stress. Today—when people worry again about the shaky place of human life in the cosmos—old patterns of insistence floating in several doctrines, spiritualities, and institutions readily find new modes of expression. Such transfigurations can attract larger constituencies under stress, especially if they already find expression in the disciplinary bodily practices of several churches, military discipline, corporate work disciplines, the stressed veterans, state doctrines, action films, frustrated workers, and aspiring leaders.

That is why those who are democrats, pluralists, egalitarians, ecologists, and critics of totalist claims to sovereignty must also draw sustenance today from counter-traditions within and outside Judaism and Christianity. The minor European traditions *within* range from those which read the very Genesis of the world through a God who worked upon bubbling materials already there, to the life of Jesus as a non-sovereign source of inspiration, through the story by the Roman philosopher Lucretius of how the world evolves without divine guidance, to the thought of Spinoza, through earth scientists who detect powers of self-organization in the evolution of the earth and species change, to modern process philosophies, through ecologically attentive notions of the Anthropocene as an abstract machine irreducible to a single sovereign authority.

The danger of fascism now is bound immediately to white resentment in several old capitalist states against people of color at home and growing refugee flows, some of which will accelerate due to the close relation between regional drought and civil wars. A deep, longer range source of danger is lodged in the fact that *the future promises extractive capitalism advances to maintain its legitimacy are based on desperately protected and institutionalized assumptions profoundly at odds with acceleration of the Anthropocene.*

Late modern capitalism, if or when it loses the democratic practices that have often been entangled with it, becomes fascism. That is so in part because drives to keep the capitalist machine going during difficult times among a populace that had heretofore internalized free speech, citizen movements, open elections, and a critical media now require more state repression and intense mobilization of deindustrialized constituencies to keep pluri-egalitarian dissidents under wraps.

We can now perhaps draw these threads together by suggesting why neither the Anthropocene as a unique planetary configuration nor the theme of the Capitalocene may be quite up to perform the functions either is called upon to serve today. The focus now is on the latter.

In an impressive and provocative book Jason Moore calls on us to replace the theme of the Anthropocene with the Capitalocene.[12] The former label is too generic; the new term allows us to concentrate on how a new political economy—capitalism—became a major geological force for the first time in history. The golden spike was driven in 1610. Moore then shows how, to sustain its patterns of growth under unfavorable conditions, advanced capitalist states have been pressed to create "cheap natures" through high-tech inventions to reduce costs of production and maintain profits. So far, so illuminating and pertinent.

Nevertheless, there are limits to that analysis as so far presented. First, spiritual and existential components of the cultural processes are underplayed in this account, as the critical emergence of Constantinianism and, later, the evangelical/neoliberal machine illustrate. Second, it tends to draw attention away from the critical role of large, planetary self-organizing amplifiers today in the gallop of the Anthropocene, almost acting as if planetary change always moved on long, slow time before the advent of the "Capitalocene." Third, its proponents may not acknowledge sufficiently the need to rethink nineteenth-century ideals of extraction, productive growth, consumption abundance, and smooth community embedded in communist ideals.

Those are some reasons that make me hesitate to adopt the term "Capitalocene." That being said, I learn from those who organize their thinking around that idea—particularly with respect to how neoliberal capitalism has been pressed to produce "cheap natures" to sustain itself—and I welcome coalitions and alliances across these differences. During the contemporary era there is no single center, class, or intellectual hegemony around which resistance and critical coalitions must be formed. More of us must become critical, cross-regional, eco-pluralizing activists today.

THE ANTHROPOCENE AS PLANETARY MACHINE

Climate—as an abstract machine periodically evolving and morphing in its dominant components, speeds, and trajectories—is imbricated with a host of planetary and cosmic forces. The example of Rome helps teach that lesson. We can think of the cyclical intensities of sunspot formation, the elliptical pattern of the earth's rotation, the wobble of the earth, and the periodic shift in its tilt. Call these cyclical *forcings*. There are also intermittent asteroid showers, changes in the ratio of oxygen to carbon and nitrogen, volcanic eruptions, earthquakes, hurricanes, wildfires, and tsunamis. These form less cyclical and predictable modes of nonhuman volatility. Call them noncyclical *drivers*. Any conjunction between a forcing and a driver can induce dramatic climate effects as the self-organizing history of ice ages, interglacial periods, mass extinction events, monsoon interruptions, desertification, the ocean conveyor, and sharp turns in species evolution show. And as the rapid organization of the Late Antique Little Ice Age shows again.

The ocean conveyor system, for instance, was consolidated millions of years ago well after the oceans had been formed and before any humans appeared to think of themselves as potential masters of the earth. The conveyor carries warm, surface water from the Gulf of Mexico north toward Greenland where cooling, more saline water dives down in a spinning fashion to flow south along the ocean floor until it reaches the Indian Ocean. There the heating water rises again to the surface to flow north toward the Gulf. It is a self-organizing system formed originally out of dissonant connections between climate, wind currents, gravity, the Coriolis effect, and shifting water densities. It also closed down 12,700 years ago when a new ice age formed and somehow stopped the flow. The Gulf Stream is now at its weakest level in 1,600 years.[13]

The vicissitudes of the ocean conveyor provide merely one manifestation of how differentials of latitude create a highly imperfect index of climate differentials. The first European invaders of Jamestown and St. Augustine in North America encountered huge problems because the invaders had anchored seasonal estimates of temperature and precipitation on an assumed parallel between latitude and climate. In fact, perhaps due to a slowing of the ocean conveyor, the late sixteenth- and early seventeenth-century Euro-invaders encountered a Little Ice Age, a phenomenon magnifying the difference between climate and latitude.[14] The places they so ruthlessly invaded were much colder and inhospitable to their practices of food production than anticipated.

Let's narrow the focus a bit to explore contemporary intersections between less cyclical, nonhuman *amplifiers* and the *triggers* of extractive capitalism to probe the shape and trajectory of the Anthropocenic machine today. Massive capitalist CO_2 emissions, agri-methane releases, and deforestation projects trigger climate warming today, as they did for a couple of centuries before the Great Acceleration in the 1950s.

Here is a short list of self-organizing climate amplifiers, processes that magnify the effects of capitalist triggers through self-organization:

melted ice absorbs much more solar heat than solid ice so as to place a glacier melt rate on a self-promoting spiral; rivers formed on top of melting glaciers dive through cracks and gaps (moulins) in the ice to create flotillas upon which the glacier now floats more rapidly;

freezing water in the moulins following summer melts exploded the Antarctic Larsen B shelf in three days in 2002, when glaciologists had previously thought it might take seventy years or more;

the breakup of the West Antarctic Ice Shelf—the most recent breakoff was the size of Delaware—eliminates old bulwarks against accelerated movement of the continental glacier;

the heating of oceans and tundra from accumulated CO_2 emissions could release frozen methane clathrates in the tundra and ocean crystals, further accelerating warming (as may have happened during the great extinction event 250 million years ago after eruptions of the Siberian flats);

as the Greenland glacier melt accelerates, enlarged pools of water allow algae to cover more of the ice's surface, reducing the albedo effect (reflection rate of sun rays) from 90 percent to under 20 percent, thereby further speeding up the glacier melt;

melting glaciers in Greenland could disrupt or stop the key downward thrust of the ocean conveyor system at its most vulnerable point near Greenland, as the melts pour fresh water onto the ocean surface lighter than the salty water;

the expansion of drought in the Sub-Sahara and African Horn press suffering grazers and farmers to cut down more vegetation or flee, decreasing further the CO_2 absorptive capacities of the land, promoting civil wars, increasing refugee pressure, and fostering fascist temptations in the receiving regimes;

intensification of periodic El Niños through climate warming in the Pacific could interrupt monsoon seasons over India and China, placing huge populations at risk; these results, which have occurred before, could in turn unleash a series of volatile political events, including mass starvation, social violence, and swelling refugee drives;

growing deforestation in Brazil, Colombia, Gulf States, the Congo, and elsewhere—due variously to the needs of subsistence farmers, capital timber projects, and the effects of increasingly intense hurricanes—generate more CO_2 emissions, increasing the rate of forest fires and climate change as they do; the resulting expansion of drought zones again presses many subsistence farmers to clear new forest areas.

These self-organizing amplifiers bump and fold into each other as they form an abstract machine with several cultural spiritualities and capitalist triggers already noted. They accentuate pressure on capitalist states to change their ways rapidly. Or to fend off growing refugee pressures, build territorial walls, and forge fascist responses to an accelerating planetary machine.

The machine itself is forged by movements back and forth between the entrenched priorities of extractive capitalism, the growing lead times between drilling and production during a time of extreme drilling technologies, white *ressentiment* against other regions and peoples of color, neoliberal hubris, race and class exploitation, imperial drives, hungry dispossessed peoples, impositions of selective austerity, growing fossil fuel emissions, agricultural deforestation, refugee pressures, ocean shifts, spiraling glacier melts, expanding drought zones, loss of fisheries, and ocean acidification. In this convoluted system of multi-, interfolding temporalities disparate forces and agencies work within and upon each other to produce a planetary machine in which no single factor, agency, or force is entirely in charge. An abstract, planetary machine, with momentum of its own.

The interacting triggers and amplifiers in motion mean that even a radical reduction in atmospheric emissions (triggers) would not be matched immediately by a parallel reduction in warming, drought expansion, rising seas, extreme storms, forest fires, species losses, hurricane severity, civil wars, refugee migrations, and ocean acidification (the lingering myth of climate parallelism).

But it is possible to slow down its acceleration through an activist assemblage of critical constituencies mobilized across several regions to demand radical reworking of capitalist institutions of investment, production, and consumption, retooling the spiritual ethos that occupies dominant institutions, and enactment of mitigation and reparation payments to regions that have contributed the least and suffer the most from this planetary machine.[15] More participants in such an assemblage also need to cultivate spiritualities prepared to embrace an earth replete with periodic planetary volatilities. The formula is to put internal and external pressure on key states, corporations, churches, universities, localities, banks, and unions at the same time. Such efforts will be extremely difficult to mobilize and sustain, but there is nothing in the very logic of capitalist society that makes them impossible. And the stakes are high.

If and as these modes of cross-regional activism gain traction, critical thinkers also need to rework creatively a series of contending nineteenth-century ideals of material abundance and spiritual hubris, for as several existing regimes incite more and more cynicism, resignation, *ressentiment*, and nihilism—depending on the constituency involved—the most familiar counter-ideals to them fail to excite much confidence either. Fascism can fill the vacuum if, when democratic capitalism founders, familiar noncapitalist ideals do not refurbish themselves. They, too, may require reconstitution during an era of capitalist institutionalization of mastery, asymmetries of regional suffering, and the acceleration of planetary amplifiers.

I hope to join others in pursuing that task in a future study.

NOTES

1. Gilles Deleuze and Félix Guattari, *A Thousand Plateaus*, trans. Brian Massumi (Minneapolis: University of Minnesota Press, 1987), 510, 511.
2. Deleuze and Guattari, *A Thousand Plateaus*, 423.

3. In this essay, I project an attenuated relationship between a *creed* and the *spiritualities* that occupy it. You might, say, support an Augustinian theology infused with receptive love for those who do not embrace your creed, and I might support a Deleuzian creed of immanent naturalism while espousing a spirituality of plurality. This means that, to compose a pluralist assemblage of opposition to fascism and support for programs to curtail climate change, diverse creedal constituencies can participate together by exploring affinities of spirituality between them across creedal differences. This theme is first developed in William E. Connolly, *Capitalism and Christianity, American Style* (Durham, NC: Duke University Press, 2008).

4. For a book that sought to diagnose the Trump movement as it was coming to power see William E. Connolly, *Aspirational Fascism: The Struggle for Multifaceted Democracy under Trumpism* (Minneapolis: University of Minnesota Press, 2017). The last chapter explores how to pursue egalitarian pluralism and responses to the Anthropocene together in ways that might help break up the dangerous assemblage Trump has consolidated. It also begins to reshape some of the contending ideals that have competed for hegemony in the twentieth century.

5. See Alex Williams and Nick Srnicek, "Manifesto for an Accelerationist Politics," in *#Accelerate: The Accelerationist Reader*, ed. Robin Mackay and Armen Avanessian (Cambridge, MA: MIT Press, 2014). Other essays in that volume are also useful. The best critical engagement with accelerationism I have read to date is Steven Shaviro, *No Speed Limit* (Minneapolis: University of Minnesota Press, 2015). Shaviro, drawing on both Marx and Deleuze/Guattari, identifies the nihilism and cynicism that can readily occupy accelerationism; he embraces the acceleration of aesthetic drives that contest the bind of a capitalist mobilization of acquisitive desires and their concurrent frustration in old capitalist states.

6. Kyle Harper, *The Fate of Rome: Climate, Disease, and the End of Empire* (Princeton, NJ: Princeton University Press, 2017).

7. To be more precise, sporadic cooling and droughts started in the fifth century, but the Antique Little Ice Age hit most sharply after 530 CE. "We might consider the period ca AD 450–530 the prelude to the Late Antique Little Ice Age" (Harper, *The Fate of Rome*, 251). Harper also reviews the competing views of Justinian and Cassiodorus during this period about the relation of the Empire to larger planetary forces. Justinian found the processes to be regular and orderly; Cassiodorus found them to be volatile. Though I am not independently versed in the thought of Cassiodorus, it sounds like the first thinker fits the major tradition and the latter slides closer to the minor tradition, as those two multifarious traditions have been presented in this text.

8. Harper, *The Fate of Rome*, 277.

9. Harper, *The Fate of Rome*, 254.
10. This story is well told by Michael Benton, *When Life Nearly Died* (London: Thames, Hudson, 2005).
11. See Catherine Keller, *Political Theology of the Earth: Our Planetary Emergency and the Struggle for a New Public* (New York: Columbia University Press, 2018).
12. Jason Moore, *Capitalism in the Web of Life* (London: Verso, 2015).
13. See Jonathan Watts, "Domino-Effect of Climate Events Could Move Earth into a 'Hothouse' State" (August 2018), https:www.theguardian.come/environment/2018/aug/06/domino-effect.
14. For a thoughtful discussion of early European "settler" misunderstandings of the changing climate on the continent they invaded see Sam White, *A Cold Welcome* (Cambridge, MA: Harvard University Press, 2016). White does not focus much on how various Amerindian peoples themselves coped with the combination of climate pressure and European invasions.
15. I pursue the cross-regional politics of swarming in *Facing the Planetary* (Minneapolis: University of Minnesota Press, 2017), chap. 5. The point now is to see how the danger of fascism grows as delays in promoting such an agenda continue.

2. Anthropocenic Journeys

MICHAEL NORTHCOTT

In the summer of 2016 I visited the Bay Area of Northern California and Sequoia and Yosemite National Parks and Muir Woods National Monument, all for the first time. The trip was in homage to John Muir, whose *My First Summer in the Sierra* remains a classic of environmental history and nature writing, and whose efforts to secure and extend nationally protected lands in the American West earned him the accolade of "founding father" of America's National Park system, which celebrated its one hundredth anniversary in 2016. I visited the home of John Muir north of the city at Martinez, where he worked for twenty years with his father-in-law to improve and extend the orchard business he married into before he took up campaigning for wilderness full time. I camped and hiked with the Sierra Club in Yosemite, which John Muir founded, around June Lake high in the Sierras, and I visited Sequoia National Park and Redwood National and State Parks.

Driving through California's snow-melt-dependent and intensively farmed Central Valley on the way to Yosemite, I stopped to walk among the citrus trees that are grown in huge numbers and are micro-watered through the dry heat of a Central Valley summer with black porous hosepipe invented on a kibbutz in Israel. I drove past vast acreages of similarly irrigated vegetable crops and huge cattle feedlots where animals are corralled in vast numbers for fattening up with corn from the Midwest. And I passed signs on farmers' land saying Trump for President, and Vote Trump to Get Back Our Water. The signs told me that California farmers believe their water problems come not from climate change but from the water conservation efforts of the United States federal government, and the White House, which is its lead agency. The science indicates that water issues in California are primarily related to agricultural overextraction from the Sacramento and San Joaquin River Basins and their underground aquifers, and reduced winter snowpack—the principal source of water in these river systems—from anthropogenic climate change.[1] Central California supplies 8 percent of the US food supply, but this rate of production relies on overintensive agriculture that is mining water unsustainably. Far from addressing these problems, Trump in his presidential campaign promised to get government out of the way of the people, by tearing up environmental protections and energy reforms related to climate change.

Two years later, in the fall of 2018 smoke from fires on the West Coast of North America spread across the whole region and eventually reached Europe, by which time fires had burned millions of square miles of land, destroyed whole towns, and tens of thousands of homes in Oregon and British Columbia as well as Northern California. But far from learning from such events, the Trump administration appointed leaders of the Environmental Protection Agency who commenced unraveling decades of environmental regulation directed at the protection of air, water, endangered species and their habitats, including the National Parks of which Muir was honored as the founder in 2016 on the year of my visit to his home state.

The Trump administration also declared that the United States would pull out of the international climate regime and its efforts to reduce greenhouse gas emissions in response to climate change, and in particular that it would not honor reductions in greenhouse gas emissions, and other commitments, made under the 2015 Paris Accord by the administration of President Obama. Trump also closed down the federal government for a long stretch at the end of 2018, which led to further environmental destruction in California, in particular in its National Parks, of which Joshua Tree suffered the most damage from vandals who destroyed thousands of rare flowering cacti with four-wheel-drive vehicles in the absence of park wardens to protect them. Trump closed the government in protest at the failure of the United States House of Representatives to grant him funds to build a proposed concrete and metal barrier 1,500 miles long on the Mexican border from the Gulf Coast of Texas along the Rio Grande to Tijuana, California. The proposed barrier represents an effort to divide a bioregion that is one region ecologically and culturally, albeit divided by a national border imposed after numerous land grabs by the United States into Mexican territory in the nineteenth century. Trump claimed that Mexicans and Central Americans attempting to migrate to the United States across the border were a "national security threat," although their numbers were fewer than they had been under previous administrations, and there are already barriers in place in the most populous parts of the border. This account also neglects that the climate of Northern Mexico and the Southern United States is warming significantly, rivers are drying up, and traditional agricultural is becoming nonviable. Climate change is therefore the principal cause of northward migration from Central America and Mexico into the United States, and the United States is the leading nation in the causation of climate change with its huge historic emissions of greenhouse gases, which are the legacy of its leadership in fossil fuel extraction, which began in the California oil boom from which Stanford Oil (now Exxon) began.[2]

"There is only one Earth," as Barbara Ward and René Dubos first prophetically argued in a 1972 Penguin book titled *Only One Earth*, which now lies yellowing on my book shelves.[3] Mars is not an option, as Alfred Russel Wallace, the originator, with Darwin, of the modern theory of the evolution of species, stated in a book titled *Man's Place in the Universe*, published in 1903. Space is not the Final Frontier despite the Star Trek series. Humans and species cannot dwell in the black lifeless vacuum of space outside the fragile 15-kilometer life-sustaining envelope known by scientists as the "critical zone." But the United States government, having reached the moon and having sent robotic probes to Mars and Saturn, acts as though it does have plans to exit Earth when it exits international climate and biodiversity treaties designed to prevent global ecological collapse and neglects the sustainability of its own ecosystems: and this despite the indisputable fact that some of its own peoples, and species, are already enduring extreme effects of climate instability and loss of ecological resilience from species decline, habitat destruction, and drought. The Southwest is in extreme drought with the desert cities of Phoenix and Las Vegas experiencing dust storms and becoming infeasibly hot in the summer months; Texas is running out of drinking water; Florida's coastal cities are gradually being inundated by rising seas while summer wildfires on the Pacific Coast, including even in Alaska in the summer of 2020, are devastating forests and rural communities.

The marine biologist Rachel Carson wakened my generation to the ecological crisis in her environmental classic *Silent Spring*.[4] The book combined natural science and romanticism in a powerful narrative that sparked the modern environmental movement in the United States, and which spread to Europe and beyond. Carson was dying of breast cancer when she wrote the book and testified to Congress about the human as well as ecological effects of the widespread spraying of agrochemicals such as DDT, which was then to be found in the milk of breastfeeding mothers in France because they had consumed pesticide residues in food and water. Pesticides and herbicides intervene at the microbial level of enzymes, hormones, and electrical signals between cells, disrupting the electromagnetic forces and signaling systems that give and sustain life. But humans too have bodies and are organisms sustained by those same microbial signaling systems. Hence, when these nervous system and hormone disruptors get into human bodies—in the womb, from mother's milk, or from food and water—they disrupt evolved mechanisms that give life, control organ functioning, and suppress cancers. And hence as agrochemical use increases, not only are fields and woods increasingly silent in spring and summer and autumn, as bird songs are "silenced in the Sedge," as John Keats put it in the metaphor of Carson's title, but humans are experiencing a growing epidemic of cancers, nervous disorders, and of diseases such as SARS 1, H1N1, and SARS-CoV2, which originate in ecologically problematic animal-keeping practices on factory farms, in markets, and in the mingling of human and animal genes in virology laboratories and vaccination manufacture.[5]

Carson's book, and her electrifying testimony before Congress, led the Republican President Nixon to set up the Environmental Protection Agency in 1970, whose protection duties President Trump's appointees were unraveling. Nixon also signed the Clean Water and Clean Air Acts into law, although the US congressional system requires that such acts must be regularly renewed, and here again Trump—and before him G. W. Bush with Dick Cheney—have used necessary renewals as ways to amend and undermine these crucial pieces of legislation.

If the United States has begun to unravel and subvert the efforts of a Carson-influenced generation to protect the environment from pollution and species from extinction, the European Union has not only adopted the US model of regulatory protections of the environment, endangered species and scientifically significant natural habitats and ecosystems, but built on it and ramped it up. The most significant area globally in which Europe leads environmental protection concerns climate change. As I have explained in more detail elsewhere, the EU was the most powerful international actor pursuing efforts to globally restrain greenhouse gas emissions, and although the United States succeeded in reducing the effectiveness of such efforts through its insistence on ineffectual carbon trading initiatives, it remains the case that without European leadership the international effort to reduce greenhouse gas emissions would be much less advanced.[6] For all that, however, the effort is not succeeding in reducing global emissions or stemming climate change. This is principally because counting emissions is like locking the stable door after the horse has bolted.[7] Under what Bruno Latour calls the global Climate Regime, nations are required to count only the greenhouse gas emissions directly attributable to consumption and production activities within their territories and not those emissions embedded in their imports and investments in fossil fuel extraction elsewhere.[8] Hence, although a nation's domestic emissions may appear to decrease in "Nationally Declared Commitments" as required by the Paris Accord of 2015, its net global emissions of its bankers, corporations, householders, and international investments may still increase.

The United Nations' Climate Regime, over twenty-five years since its founding, is not changing the inexorable upward movement of Charles Keeling's measure of carbon dioxide in the atmosphere, which Keeling kept going through threatened funding cuts on the slopes of Mauna Loa in Hawaiʻi for over forty years. Levels of CO_2 in the atmosphere have now reached those last seen on earth 50 million years ago in the Pleistocene when giant reptiles dominated the terrestrial habitat, mammals were still in the process of evolving, there was no terrestrial ice, and the oceans were 30 meters higher than at present. Without reductions in atmospheric CO_2 back to something like 350 parts per million James Hansen estimates that it is only a matter of time before the new atmospheric greenhouse gas state melts polar and mountain ice and rising sea levels inundate all the cities, towns, and villages that are at less than 30 meters above sea level, which is where the majority of human settlements exist.[9]

There has long been an argument that it is possible to "dematerialize" economic growth by investing in "sustainable" technologies such as renewable energy and recycling of materials. But the evidence is increasingly clear that this is not happening. Growth in economic activities continues to produce growth in extractive industries, destruction of nonhuman habitats, consequent declines in species numbers, species extinctions, and growth in pollution of the atmosphere, oceans, rivers, and soils. Not only are fossil fuels still being extracted and burned in record amounts but the ongoing pursuit by every nation and business of economic growth without regard for terrestrial limits on atmospheric pollution and fresh water depletion and the deployment of industrial technologies to extract and harvest ever more animal, mineral, and plant resources from ever more remote regions are systematically reducing the capacity of the Earth and its creatures to resolve the overspill of atmospheric and water pollution that the industrial growth economy is generating.

The oceans until the present have absorbed 70 percent of greenhouse gas emissions since the beginning of the Industrial Revolution, but they are slowing in their capacity to do this for two reasons. First, as they become more acidic and warmer, shellfish, plankton, and coral find it harder to reproduce, and hence fewer of these creatures, which at end of life lock carbon into the sea floor, are being born.[10] The second reason is because industrial fishing is systematically emptying the oceans of life. Ninety percent of numbers of sea creatures have been harvested by huge industrial trawlers in the last fifty years, in the main by the vast, government-subsidized and sonar-equipped fishing fleets of Japan, Spain, Korea, Russia, the United States, and China.[11]

The other vital terrestrial means of greenhouse gas absorption are soils and forests. But despite more than twenty years of global climate negotiations, a 2010 global biodiversity treaty, and a UN-sponsored biodiversity regime, the year 2018 saw the largest area of rain forest ever to be destroyed in one year. Rain forests are the most biodiverse ecosystems on Earth. They are home to myriad endemic species, as well as Indigenous peoples. They are also vast carbon and methane stores since, over millennia, fallen trees and tree litter build up greenhouse gas-rich soils, which, when cleared of moist tropical forest by logging and burning, release long buried greenhouse gases.

The tropical forested island of Papua New Guinea is on the opposite side of the planet to the Western United States but Freeport-McMoRan, a large mining corporation based in Phoenix, Arizona—a city at clear risk from extreme climate change—enjoys the support of the US Department of State, which encouraged the Indonesian takeover of West Papua New Guinea in 1962, as part of its Cold War "anti-communist" strategy in the region.[12] Subsequently the Indonesian government, based almost a thousand miles away in Jakarta, has used the tropical island as an extractive resource site while suppressing Papuan claims to their own land and resources, and imposing Javanese politicians in the local parliament as governors and elected representatives of Papua.[13] The Freeport gold mine in Papua has been operating for fifty years and its operations have been associated with death and violence in West Papua since the original Indonesian annexation in 1962, while the beneficiaries of the mine are not Papuans but Javanese politicians and bureaucrats, and US shareholders.[14]

Mining and industrial agriculture corporations continue to deplete the Earth's remaining tropical forests even though these are not only homes to Indigenous peoples and a huge range of endangered species but also represent regional, and even planetary, "lungs," since they produce vast quantities of oxygen, and act as regional "air conditioners" of tropical lands by drawing moisture from the oceans and turning it into cooling mist and clouds that lower ambient temperatures. Tropical cities without these natural cooling mechanisms are hot and humid places where it is hard for residents to sleep without electric fans or air-conditioning. Tropical forests, in contrast, are surprisingly habitable for humans (and other animals), provided one knows the difference between toxic and nontoxic plants and other creatures. But ever since Europeans and Americans like John Muir and David Livingstone wrote about them, they are imagined in the Western mind as wilderness empty of people. When Muir wrote up his journey to the Amazon, he spoke of a place without people, and yet the Amazon has been inhabited for millennia by peoples who at different times have developed complex infrastructure such as roads and large collections of dwellings and cultural artifacts, which new satellite surveys of the forests are uncovering.[15] If Westerners imagined them first as ancestral homes rather than wilderness, it is likely that more attention would have been paid to their systematic destruction by postcolonial elites and their corporate backers in the last fifty years.

This destruction has in the main not generated economic development for the peoples who inhabit tropical and subtropical lands. On the contrary, former colonizing nations—and most notably the United Kingdom, the United States, France, and the Netherlands—have since the 1960s transformed the remnants of empire, such as islands in the Caribbean and the Atlantic, into quasi-legal "tax havens," where trillions of dollars in cash, and corporate and personally owned assets, are secretively sequestered by politicians, criminals, business corporations, and "High Net Worth Individuals." Many of them are located in postcolonial nations in Africa, Asia, and Latin America. Tax havens put this wealth beyond the reach of the legal assemblies of the nations from which the wealth has been stripped, at grave cost to the habitability of these nations. Hence, tax havens play a definitive and not a marginal role in the advancing ecological and climate crises. They also substantially reduce the capacity of developing (and even developed) nations to construct infrastructure such as covered drains, potable water supplies, climate-proof housing areas, decent public health care, transportation, and educational services. This elite capture of developing country wealth is combined with elite capture of media, which reduces public access to the means by which developing nations are being robbed of biodiverse, resilient, and resource-rich ecosystems. Hence while in almost every nation on earth there is a palpable sense that the environment is becoming, or threatening to become, less favorable to human and nonhuman life, this is not translating into changes in the destructive and extractive model of wealth accumulation and industrial development, nor of the postcolonial capture of the fruits of development by domestic and foreign elites.

The central dilemma is that the climate and extinction crises are driven by a very small number of corporate agencies and individuals—far fewer than the global "one percent" identified by David Graeber and the Occupy movement. These few actors are not only capturing wealth inequitably with the collusion of Western financial services. They are also, through bribery and lobbying, and through corporate control of media, systematically depleting the capacity of the multiple assemblies of human beings in their parliaments, and city, village, and community councils, to respond effectively and urgently to the planetary signs of serious ecological disturbance that are occurring.

The combined effects of the vast colonial and postcolonial pillage of land and ocean ecosystems are now seriously depleting the capacity of the other creatures with whom humans share ecosystem habitats to resolve and repair the damage *Homo industrialis* is doing to the earth, and hence the effects are now Earth-system-wide. James Hutton, the eighteenth-century pioneer of the scientific living Earth theory and the inventor of "deep time," was the first modern scientist to argue that the Earth is a living and continuously co-producing assembly of rocks, plants, insects, fishes, and animals.[16] James Lovelock revisited and updated this idea when he invented the "Gaia theory," in which he showed how rocks and living creatures on the Earth's surface had co-generated a climate suitable for mammalian and thus human life.[17] Hutton's *Theory of the Earth* and Lovelock's Theory of Gaia both indicate that the Earth is composed of a multi-agential, "co-creaturely" assembly of billions of agents, which, since the explosion of complex multicellular life forms in the Cambrian period 541–485 million years ago, have multiply and mutually created a climate and habitat state unique in the known universe capable of supporting ever more complex life forms, and a range of species diversity that has subsequently grown larger after every major speciation shift, culminating in the evolution of Neanderthals, and then *Homo sapiens*, in the last 200,000 years.

Photosynthesis was the key Earth process that made the emergence of human life possible. As plants, both in the oceans and on land, evolved to capture and transform the sun's radiated energy into multicellular organic structures and thereby turn carbon into oxygen, atmospheric carbon and methane were reduced, in turn cooling the early hot earth, and gradually producing a mix of atmospheric gases ideal for the growth of forests and for the evolution of mammalian life within them. This 500-million-year-old process, which transformed the original heavy mix of carbon dioxide, methane, and nitrogen in the early earth atmosphere, buried these gases as biomass—including shellfish, leaves, and branches—into the Earth's crust, where, under the pressures of encroaching and receding oceans and ice, biomass turned into sedimentary rocks and subterranean gases and liquids, which the fossil fuel and mining industries have been extracting and putting back into the atmosphere for the last two hundred years, so putting at risk the geohistoric balance of gases on which much life, including humans, depends.[18] We now know that living organisms inhabit the deep structure of the Earth's surface down to at least 5 kilometers below ground level and in the deepest ocean trenches 3 kilometers below the sea surface and that the atmosphere is also a co-evolving composition of gases that responds to subterranean activity—and especially surface volcanic eruptions and methane bursts in melting ice—and that earthquakes occur in response to changes in surface weight such as large-scale ice melt and large humanly created bodies of water such as that held back by the Yangtze dam. In raising Earth's greenhouse gas levels to those not seen for 50 million years, industrial humans are in effect awakening a "sleeping giant," provoking more seismic activity as well as strengthening storms, increased water vapor and heavier precipitation, and at the same time growing deserts.[19]

The extraction, as fossil energy, of prehistoric "buried sunlight" has fueled the vast increase in human wealth, industry, and consumption of goods and services in the last one hundred years. It has also enabled a huge growth in human numbers and an extension in human longevity thanks principally to better nutrition, potable water, and drains. In consequence *Homo sapiens*, together with the billions of animals they have domesticated, now outweigh the mass by weight of all land-dwelling animals. And fossil fuels, despite significant commitments to renewable energy in the last thirty years, remain the key components in the changed material relationship between humans and Gaia, which is gradually tipping the evolutionary balance so that humans, though so lately entered into geological time, now have the guiding hand in the future shape of life on the planet, and hence the naming of this planetary transformation as the new geological epoch of the "Anthropocene."[20]

The huge scale of human activity on the planet that fossil fuels have made possible has tilted the evolutionary balance toward one species—*Homo sapiens*—who are now responsible for what is now known as the "Sixth Extinction" in geological history, and the first caused by one species. Fossil-fueled mechanical devices are extracting what are known as "natural resources" from every Earth region and discarding wastes from their use in industrial production in rivers, oceans, soils, and the atmosphere. With this planet-wide scale of habitat disturbance wild creatures are losing their homes and their ability to co-generate atmospheric, oceanic, and terrestrial conditions that are favorable to themselves, and to humans, as currently evolved.

English novelist J. G. Ballard was perhaps the first to suggest in *Drowned World* in 1962 that the planetary state brought on by humanly generated global warming will result in the evolution of new creatures, including new reptilian life forms, which will be better adapted to the warm, moist, and stormy conditions of a planet 2–6 degrees centigrade warmer than the epoch of the Holocene.[21] His science fiction world depicts geological time going backward to the Triassic era with tropical jungle taking back European cities.[22] The novel shows humans finding adapting to this world hard indeed as their urban and farming infrastructures are overwhelmed and gradually rendered uninhabitable. Ballard's imaginary depicts future humans surviving in drowned cities on the upper floors of tower blocks, moving around on rubber inflatable boats while at risk of scary encounters with the suddenly evolved reptiles that have taken up residence in the now cavernous underwater floors of the same buildings and swimming in the channels between them.

Leaving aside apocalyptic futures, the most durable and increasingly visible Earth-changing product of fossil fuels and industrial production, about which people are becoming aware (thanks in particular to a notable documentary highlighting the issue by the naturalist documentary maker David Attenborough) is plastic, which was first produced as "bakelite" to replace lacquerware and rubber—made respectively from the bark and sap of tropical trees—in the 1920s. Plastic is now so extensively utilized in consumer products, industrial infrastructure, and human services that it is found as dust in the air, as microfibers in water, as deposits in soil where it fuses with rock, as vast gyres of plastic flotsam in the oceans, and as microscopic particles in the bloodstreams of humans and other animals. Many houses and offices are, like cars, lined roof to floor with plastic in the form of floor and ceiling materials, vinyl paint, or fabric coverings, and they are filled with many plastic items from electrical devices to furnishings to kitchen and bathroom implements. Buildings are also often wrapped in plastic in the form of colored insulation panels, which, when improperly installed, can rapidly turn into an inferno, as residents of London's Grenfell Tower tragically experienced in 2016.[23]

Over time as plastic products erode, or are discarded, they fragment and pass from waste facilities into water catchments and ultimately into the oceans.[24] No one knows the health effects for humans of microplastic in air, food, and water. But plastic is already a major cause of death among sea creatures, including birds, fish, and mammals, which mistake floating plastic as food and even feed it to their progeny. Turtles that ingest plastic ultimately die of starvation as they become too buoyant and are unable to dive for food. Beached whales have been found with huge quantities in their stomachs. Albatross chicks have been found also to have died of starvation having been fed a diet rich in plastic items. On land, the mixing of plastic with soils and water is producing a novel marker of the birth and development of plastic in the sedimentary layer of soil, which is already visible when one digs over an old plot of land to make a garden, or excavates a site for building. Industrial humans have created more artifacts, devices, and technologies than all the predecessor humans combined. And their incredible ingenuity and success in creativity is overwhelming the Original Creation, and this has, albeit unintentionally, given modern humans the guiding hand on the current and future evolution of Earth's habitat and the future of life.

Theologians in the Christian tradition, the tradition I try to inhabit, have over two thousand years gradually built a set of concepts for describing the creation and unfolding of life on Earth around the idea of a divine Creator. These origin stories are strongly influenced by the classical Greek philosopher Aristotle's idea of a divinely originated First Cause at the creation of life and the Earth. The classical idea of a First Cause gives the defining role in the creation and trajectory of life to a single originating set of events performed by one individual being—God—albeit that in the Christian tradition this being is described as Three in One and hence not as a monad. This idea has definitively shaped the origin story of life that Christians, Muslims, and Jews learn in their assemblies and teachings in such a way that all three traditions have lost the idea, present in their scriptures, as well as now in numerous scientific texts, that the Earth on which humans dwell is the composition of the multiple agencies of myriad creatures in space and time over geological epochs stretching back to the pre-Cambrian and continuing into the present and future of life. This idea in the present is most associated with the Gaia theory or to give it its more "respectable" name, Earth System science. I suggest that the idea of the Earth as a multi-agential composition of living beings also needs to be reclaimed by monotheists, and more particularly Christians, as they confront the reality of a changing trajectory of life in which their own species has come, albeit unintentionally, to play an increasingly influential role. Instead of a single universe-generating, earth-originating, and species-creating cascade of events which rapidly brought everything out of nothing—*ex nihilo*—into being, Gaian science suggests that life, creatures and now especially humans, are continuously in the process of making and shaping life's habitat in ways that shape its ongoing trajectory and future.

The theologian who best anticipated the problem for the old doctrine of First Cause that geological and biological discoveries, such as those of James Hutton and Alexander von Humboldt, were already generating in the early nineteenth century was Friedrich Schleiermacher. He argued in his magnum opus *The Christian Faith* that there had entered into Christian theology because of the Greek First Cause concept a distinction between the creation and the preservation (or conservation) of life that is superfluous if one reflects more deeply on the lived experience, and scientific descriptions, of biological life.[25] Instead Schleiermacher suggested that it made more sense to think of the creation of life as a continuous process, or in Latin "creatio continua," a possibility that was first hinted at in Christian theology by Thomas Aquinas in the high Middle Ages. If as humans "we find ourselves always and only in a continuous existence," there is no need to separate the original acts of the divine creation and the divine development of all things into the two doctrines of "creation" and "providence." Instead the world's "absolute dependence" on God as creator means both that the world was created by God and is continuously sustained by God.[26]

The problematic of First Cause thinking is revealed in a number of ways over recent centuries, and in particular in the encounters between Christian theologians and modern science. Take the example of extinction. For centuries First Cause thinkers believed that all species existent on the planet were created at one time by the Creator and hence when geologists and biologists began to uncover unrecognizable fossils, their proposals that they were extinct instances of creatures that lived before the epoch of humans was resisted.[27] Similarly, when James Hutton argued that the evidence he uncovered of igneous volcanic rocks having impacted and pushed up sedimentary strata—as in Glen Tilt and at Siccar Point on Scotland's Southeast Coast—his proposal was resisted as contradicting the Christian belief in an instantaneous creation of the Earth, and species, in their present forms just six thousand years before Hutton lived. Theological resistance to the discoveries of deep time and extinct species helps explain declining recognition in Christian, and post-Christian, cultures of the agential influences of other creatures. Conversely it also helps explain ongoing weak recognition, or even full-blown rejection, of the potential of human influences to affect other creatures and the habitats that have co-evolved with them, which humans have often reengineered to the point of extinguishing other resident species.

Given Earth System and Gaian understandings of the multiple agential roles of other creatures in composing the Earth that humans evolved to enjoy and overspread, there is an urgent need for philosophers and theologians to reimagine and re-narrate the co-creaturely agency of *all* life on Earth in composing and conserving a habitable planet for all creatures, and to find ways to include the agency of "the others" in human assemblies and human development. This is so especially because industrially empowered humans by overpowering the Earth are reducing the capacity of the Earth System or Gaia not just to absorb but to *repair* the threats to the habitats of presently existing species—including the industrial humans with their complex and in some ways quite fragile supply lines—which this overbalancing represents. There is, in other words, a scientifically significant, but also a moral and spiritual, interrelationship between the ongoing scale of human harvesting of nonhuman materials and life forms and the reduced agency of the other beings with whom humans share the Earth to fix things, and so restore the damage humans are wreaking.[28]

Although there are many in the United States and the United Kingdom who have gone along with populist and mass media claims that climate science and species protection are forms of "big government" that oppress "little people," and hence who wish, with Trump or through "Brexit," to sweep away federal government and European Commission environmental protections, a new kind of popular campaigning, and politics, for the Earth is emerging, associated with the English-originated Extinction Rebellion movement, and the Friday school climate strikes begun by the charismatic Swedish teenager Greta Thunberg. Against the loss of agency of creatures and citizens, these new movements are using civil disobedience and symbolic ritual tactics to challenge the debt-fueled, elite-captured, growth-oriented, "business as usual" consensus, which sees children even in the developed world dying from asthma caused by NoX and microscopic particles that emanate principally from diesel-powered vehicles, or deprived of nutritious food by welfare cuts, and political participation closed down by austerity, with one English local authority even refusing to hold elections in 2019 because it is "bankrupt." In response to Trump and Brexit, a number of political theorists and theologians are responding to the dangerous postpolitical drift of the late capitalist state through a revival of anarchist theory, as a new way of composing political agency beyond liberalism—variously conceived as the "nomadic horde" (Gilles Deleuze), the swarm (William E. Connolly), the 99 percent (David Graeber and the Occupy Movement), or the "politics of virtue" (John Milbank and Adrian Pabst). These philosophical and theological moves are accompanied by the eruption of a new kind of politics, which has particular appeal to the young who are less likely than previous generations to identify with traditional political parties whose names and organizational affiliations hark back to the labor/property mode of production of industrial capitalist societies.

My first experience of one such "postpolitical" movement—Extinction Rebellion—was in the old market town of Yeovil in Dorset in Southwest England in December 2018. I was staying as the guest of the Anglican Franciscan Mother House of Hilfield Friary nearby and went on the protest march at the prompting of one of the friars. The plan for the "action" was for a symbolic funeral procession of mourners dressed in black behind two coffins representing the Earth and extinct species. The protesters were called to assemble on the churchyard beside Yeovil's very fine medieval town-center parish church of St. John, and were to process, with the aid of a drum and other instruments, around the principal shopping streets, and open air market, at 11:00 on a Saturday morning when the streets, which are mainly pedestrianized, would be crowded with shoppers from the town and the surrounding rural villages.

The gathering place, St. John's Churchyard, is a grass area free of gravestones or other markers and maintained as grass and pedestrian paths by the local council, which had apparently adopted the area when it laid out a new pedestrianized shopping area some years earlier. The organizers had constructed a gazebo where marchers could sign up for Extinction Rebellion and pick up leaflets, posters, and artifacts connected with related activities in the area, including an anti-fracking campaign and Dorset Wildlife Trust. I walked among and chatted with the other marchers who were of all ages, with a preponderance of young people dressed for the most part in dark velvet, with hats and other accoutrements intended to fit with the funereal theme. As we were preparing to march, I saw that my companion, the friar, was at the church door talking with a small group, which included the rector of the parish and one of the police officers in attendance on the march to oversee public order. I went over to the small group and gathered from the conversation, which was a little animated, that while Extinction Rebellion had, as required, informed both the local council and the police of their intended protest march, they had not thought it was necessary to inform the rector. The rector was pointing out to the friar, who had decided to ring the rector on the previous day to forewarn him, that although the council maintained the churchyard, it was in fact church property. He felt that permission should have been sought in advance from him as rector, and he said that had it been he would have refused it as he did not think it appropriate for the church to be associated with political demonstrations.

The conversation drew to an end, and the formal demonstration began with a requiem address through a loudspeaker by a march leader dressed in English mourning dress of top hat and tails, and then the march proceeded around the town. On one coffin was daubed the words "Our Future," and a second coffin had atop it a large soft toy evidently representing a baby orangutan sitting on a green globe. At the front two large banners were carried declaring "Climate Emergency" and "Stop Extinction." As we walked around the town, I passed the rector, who was running an errand, and exchanged smiles, and he pointed to some horse dung on the pavement, which he amusedly indicated needed clearing up by us demonstrators, though actually we had no horses, and so I said it was not ours! The procession wound round the town, with police in yellow jackets in attendance and shoppers bemusedly looking on, and wound its way back to the churchyard.

The rector was at his church door on our return and had resumed the conversation about permissions and ownership. I said to him that part of the problem was that the space used by the demonstration appeared to be council-run secular space since there were no markers on it indicating it was sacred ground. I suggested he was missing a missional opportunity and that the church could organize a design competition among its young people for engraved stones to be placed on the paths at the four corners to indicate symbolically that it was holy ground. He was a vicar of an evangelical persuasion, and I thought in my suggesting a missional opportunity that he might see the event as opening an opportunity for witness. I then asked his permission to look round the interior of the church, which he cheerfully gave.

St. John's Yeovil is a fine example of late medieval Gothic Perpendicular, which was an architectural style creating exceptionally tall and wide windows, which enabled the classic medieval Gothic-arched east-facing sanctuary window to be replicated at almost the same height along the high (hence "Perpendicular") walls. The result at Yeovil as elsewhere is of a building flooded with light from the heavens refracted by stained glass (some also medieval). These buildings represented significant engineering achievements in an era before pre-stressed steel and concrete enabled buildings to be constructed with solid glass curtain walls. They are also highly symbolic structures representing in stone, glass, and timber the doctrines and ritual practices of Christians accrued over many centuries. They were designed literally to "bring heaven down to earth" by capturing the celestial light of the sun so it floods the place of worship. They also allowed more of the stories of the life of Christ, and of the saints—intermingled with local paying worthies—to be depicted in the larger windows. Medieval churches were designed as microcosms of the macrocosm of the heavens and the earth into which the symbolisms of the incarnate logos and the sacraments were also fully woven. In addition to the tall windows stars were often picked out in yellow or gold leaf on blue ceilings, the sanctuary east end window often depicted the sun rising in stained glass, as well as refracting the sunrise in the early morning and the rose window beloved of Gothic designers, despite its exceptional engineering fragility, depicted, like the foliage atop Gothic capitals, the weaving of the plants that mediate the light of the sun in the form of nutrition that gives life to all other creatures. Unless funds were lacking, the churches were also usually built in a classic cruciform shape, with the crossing forming a space where the "holyrood" or carved wooden screen divided the nave from the choir and sanctuary, echoing the "holy of holies" in Hebrew Temple architecture, which Margaret Barker convincingly shows was also deeply cosmological.

All of these features are present in some form in St. John's Yeovil, and knowing this, I entered it with anticipation from the somewhat frazzled atmosphere outside. My first encounter was the baptismal font, or at least it ought to have been, since from the first church buildings the font was placed to the left of the main south door where it acts as a kind of ancient membership detection device, since in the first centuries only those who had been baptized were permitted to sit in the main body of the nave, and to remain in the liturgy after the reading of the gospel and the sermon for the sacred mystery of the Holy Eucharist. Passing through the waters of baptism sets apart nonmembers and members, and hence the font is by the door like a card reader in a gym or a reception desk in a hotel. But the fine medieval carved font at St. John's Yeovil was hidden beneath a set of moveable exhibition displays that surrounded it, and to see it I asked the ladies who were selling items from the displays if I could have a look, which they were happy to let me do. As I did so, they explained that they no longer used the font for baptisms, instead using a portable bowl that was placed on a stand on the wooden stage that I now saw occupied the crossing between the nave and the sanctuary, and which was accompanied by a large electronic sound and projection system which was also in evidence waiting to be set up for Sunday. I briefly explained the reason the font is where it is and was met with surprised interest, since evidently the church members were not accustomed to reading their church in the way I just have: the evangelical charismatic style of worship they followed did not engage this great microcosmic structure whose main purpose was to act as a physical space to keep the elements off the stage: the instruments and sound system of the worship team as well as the seats of the audience.

As I walked round the building and saw its current state and usage, I had what the former Bishop of Durham, Ian Ramsey, would have called a "penny-dropping" moment. There was a significant symbolic disconnect between a medieval church building designed to "speak" in stone, glass, and timber of the divine glory and ontic power of creatures and the cosmos to priests and worshippers within and the message and media of contemporary evangelical worship practiced in the current building, led by a rector who felt aggrieved that defenders of life on Earth were risking the reputation of his microcosm of a church building with their radical Earth-defending politics and rituals. Far from the demonstration being a missional opportunity, I could now see more clearly how it might be seen as a contradiction, perhaps even a pagan subversion, of the deeply humanocentric gospel preached and performed within a church building, and with whose myriad medieval references to the macrocosm of the Earth, and to the medieval conception of the Great Chain of Beings from God and the Angels to insects and leaves, it is entirely out of synch.[29]

I tell this story to indicate that not everything in the garden is rosy between the followers of the God who first created life in Eden and the radical defenders of creatures and their habitats in the new, and old, environmental protest movements. What that early Extinction Rebellion event revealed is that there is a radical disconnect between the beliefs and practices of many, and especially evangelical, Christians and the climate and extinction emergencies. Historically, and in enduring art and architecture, and in many texts, Christian culture is filled with Earthy and celestial symbolism of both divine creativity in making and upholding the cosmos, of how things can go awry in God's Earth, and of divine restoration as represented in the Christ events, and in the enduring witness of church, word, and sacrament to the cosmological and human context and significance of those events. In this symbolic thought world of the medieval church the co-agency of all creatures including angelic hosts and terrestrial creatures such as palm trees, sheep, fishes, vines, flowers, and leaves all have a part to play in the work of restoration.

Given the visual and textual testimony that is evident in Christian culture to this co-creaturely co-agential imaginary, the question is how did Christianity, at least in its recent guises, grow so apart from, so out of sympathy with, the creatures? How did Christians lose the sense that they are in the midst of a "great cloud of agents" who are earthly as well as heavenly? This is a question to which I have devoted much of my writing and teaching career. In 1996 I coined the phrase "soul salvation" to explain it and argued Augustine, under the influence of Mani and Plato, was significantly responsible for the turn away from a holistic conception of salvation and toward the human soul in Latin Christianity. The best-known answer is that of Lynn White Jr., to which I have responded elsewhere.[30] For now it is enough to note that there are many Christians engaged in British Extinction Rebellion actions and organizing in Scotland and England, and there were two Anglican clergy and an Anglican friar in that Yeovil procession even as the local vicar bemoaned it.[31] And in a timely fashion the head of the world's oldest continuously existing economic corporation—the Vatican—has under the eminence of Pope Francis lately proposed in an encyclical instruction to "all people of good will," including Indigenous people and environmentalists as well as people of the Christian and other faiths, that, after many hundreds of years of exclusion from the story of salvation, Catholic Christianity once again holds, officially, that the other beings with whom humans share a common home are included in the divine plan of salvation, and not only the souls of humans. Creatures, in other words, are on the way to becoming agents again in the Christian imaginary.[32] The urgent politico-theological task is to transform the currently Promethean trajectory of humanity's dominance of the collectivity of beings which composed an Earth filled with life toward a posthumanist balance in which the other beings once again are permitted to express agency alongside humans in the shared and sacred work of repairing and recovering what Lovelock calls the "homeostasis" of Gaia.[33]

NOTES

1. J. S. Famiglietti, M. Lo, and S. L. Ho, "Satellites Measure Recent Rates of Groundwater Depletion in California's Central Valley," *Geophysical Research Letters* 38, no. 3 (2011): L03403.
2. Shuaizhang Fenga, Alan B. Kruegera, and Michael Oppenheimer, "Linkages among Climate Change, Crop Yields and Mexico–US Cross-Border Migration," *PNAS* 107, no. 32 (2010): 14257–62.

3. Barbara Ward and René Dubos, *Only One Earth: The Care and Maintenance of a Small Planet* (New York: Penguin Books, 1972).
4. Rachel Carson, *Silent Spring* (Boston: Houghton Mifflin, 1964).
5. See further Michael S. Northcott, "Covid-19, Human Ecology, and the Ontological Turn to Gaia," in *Pandemic, Ecology and Theology*, ed. Alexander Hampton (London: Routledge, 2020), 90–102.
6. Michael S. Northcott, *A Moral Climate: The Ethics of Global Warming* (Maryknoll, NY: Orbis Books, 2007).
7. See further Michael S. Northcott, *A Political Theology of Climate Change* (Grand Rapids, MI: Wm. B. Eerdmans, 2013).
8. Bruno Latour, *Down to Earth: Politics in the New Climate Regime*, trans. Catherine Porter (Cambridge: Polity Press, 2018).
9. James Hansen, Makiko Sato, Pushker Kharecha, et al., "Target Atmospheric CO_2: Where Should Humanity Aim?" *Atmospheric and Oceanic Physics* 2 (2008): 217–31.
10. Frederic Gazeau, Christophe Quiblier, Jeroen M. Jansen, et al., "Impact of Elevated CO_2 on Shellfish Calcification," *Geophysical Research Letters* 34 (2007): L07603.
11. Vanessa F. Jaiteh, Steve J. Lindfield, Sangeeta Mangubhai, et al., "Higher Abundance of Marine Predators and Changes in Fishers' Behavior Following Spatial Protection within the World's Biggest Shark Fishery," *Frontiers in Marine Science* 3 (2016): 1–15.
12. D. McLean, "American and Australian Cold Wars in Asia," *Australasian Journal of American Studies* 9, no. 2 (1990): 33–46.
13. Bobby Anderson, "Papua's Insecurity State Failure in the Indonesian Periphery," *Policy Studies*, no. 73 (Honolulu, Hawai'i: East-West Center, 2015).
14. Chris Ballard, "The Signature of Terror: Violence, Memory, and Landscape at Freeport," in *Inscribed Landscapes: Marking and Making Place*, ed. Bruno David and Meredith Wilson (Honolulu: University of Hawai'i Press, 2002), 13–26.
15. John Muir, *John Muir's Last Journey: South to the Amazon and East to Africa: Unpublished Journals and Selected Correspondence*, ed. Michael P. Branch (Washington, DC: Island Press, 2004).
16. James Hutton, *Theory of the Earth with Proofs and Illustrations*, vols. 1–3, (Edinburgh: W. Creech, 1795).
17. James Lovelock, *Gaia: A New Look at Life on Earth* (Oxford: Oxford University Press, 1979).
18. Rolf Peter Sieferle, *The Subterranean Forest: Energy Systems and the Industrial Revolution* (Winwick, Cambridgeshire: White Horse Press, 2001).

19. Bill McGuire, *Waking the Giant: How a Changing Climate Triggers Earthquakes, Tsunamis, and Volcanoes* (Oxford: Oxford University Press, 2013).
20. For a fuller discussion of the religious and ethical implications of the Anthropocene see Michael S. Northcott, "On Going Gently into the Anthropocene," in *Religion and the Anthropocene*, ed. Celia Deane-Drummond, Sigurd Bergmann, and Markus Vogt (Eugene, OR: Cascade Books, 2017), 19–34.
21. J. G. Ballard, *The Drowned World* (London: Dent, 1962).
22. David Ian Paddy, *The Empires of J. G. Ballard: An Imagined Geography* (Canterbury, Kent: Gylphi, 2015), 32.
23. G. MacLeod, "The Grenfell Tower Atrocity: Exposing Urban Worlds of Inequality, Injustice, and an Impaired Democracy," *City* 22, no. 4 (2017): 460–89.
24. Jenna R. Jambeck, Roland Geyer, Chris Wilcox, et al., "Plastic Waste Inputs from Land into the Ocean," *Science* 347, no. 6223 (2015): 768–71.
25. Friedrich Schleiermacher, *The Christian Faith*, English trans. 1928, Reprinted with an introduction by Paul T. Nimmo (London: T & T Clark, 2010), 144.
26. Schleiermacher, *Christian Faith*, 142.
27. T. A. Appel, *The Cuvier-Geoffrey Debate: French Biology in the Decades Before Darwin* (Oxford: Oxford University Press, 1987).
28. On the need to better articulate the agency of other beings see Bruno Latour, "How Better to Register the Agency of Things," Tanner Lectures, Yale University, New Haven, 26–27 March 2014, and at http://www.bruno-latour.fr/sites/default/files/137-YALE-TANNER.pdf, accessed 2 July 2020.
29. For a powerful cosmological and ecologically sensitive reading of medieval architecture of the kind evident in St. John's Yeovil see Gordon Strachan, *Chartres: Sacred Geometry and Sacred Space* (Edinburgh: Floris Books, 2003); on the medieval Christian imaginary of the Great Chain of Being see Arthur O. Lovejoy, *The Great Chain of Being: A Study of the History of an Idea* (Cambridge, MA: Harvard University Press, 1976).
30. Michael S. Northcott, "Lynn White Jr. Right and Wrong: The Anti-Ecological Character of Latin Christianity, and the Pro-Ecological Turn of Protestantism," in *Religion and Ecological Crisis: The "Lynn White Thesis" at 50*, ed. Todd le Vasseur and Anna Peterson (New York: Routledge, 2016), 61–74.
31. For an insightful theological commentary on Extinction Rebellion see Stefan Skrimshire, Faith and Action Series: "The Religion of Extinction Rebellion" (23 January 2020) at https://religioninpublic.com/2020/01/23/fa-series-the-religion-of-extinction-rebellion, accessed 2 July 2020.
32. *Encyclical Letter Laudato Si' of the Holy Father Francis; On Care for Our Common Home* (Vatican City: Libreria Editrice Vaticana, 2015).

33. On homeostasis see further James Lovelock and Lynn Margulis, "Atmospheric Homeostasis by and for the Biosphere," *Tellus* 26, no. 1–2 (1974): 2–10. For a discussion of particular ecological projects in which this rebalancing is already under way see Michael S. Northcott, "Hope and Ecology," *Historical and Multidisciplinary Perspectives on Hope*, ed. Steven van den Heuvel (New York: Springer, 2020), https://www.springer.com/gp/book/9783030464882.

3. Resisting Geopower: Political Theologies of the Anthropocene

AUSTIN ROBERTS

What if the doleful doings of the Anthropocene and the unworldings of the Capitalocene are the last gasps of the sky gods, not guarantors of the finished future, game over?
—DONNA HARAWAY, *Staying with the Trouble*

A growing sense of ecological emergency permeates our present. Earth scientists now tell us that atmospheric greenhouse gas concentrations are at their highest levels in three million years; extinction rates are at least as fast as Earth's five mass extinction events; and anthropogenic alterations to the global nitrogen cycle are unlike anything that has occurred in possibly as much as 2.5 billion years.[1] Increasingly frequent news reports of floods, droughts, wildfires, hurricanes, and other extreme weather events around the world make it alarmingly clear that climate disruption already threatens many human communities and strains current sociopolitical structures—a condition unlikely to improve anytime soon. This geohistorically unprecedented situation raises a number of difficult questions about our planetary futures: How might the currently dominant neoliberal political order begin to adapt in response to intensifying ecological crises? Will the logic of climate emergency be used to justify new forms of antidemocratic power and human exceptionalism—or might it instead catalyze an ecopolitical shift toward what Alfred North Whitehead called "a democracy of fellow creatures"?[2] Moreover, what kinds of collective actions and imaginaries might need to be cultivated to effectively resist neoliberal and neofascist expansions of human sovereignty over the Earth, and to support democratic movements for ecosocial justice?

In what follows, I explore possible answers to these questions, first by tracking current debates about the earth sciences and geoengineering theories in order to discern the shifting character of political sovereignty and human supremacy within our "new climatic regime."[3] As we will see, one potential response to anthropogenic environmental challenges is to *intensify* human societal impacts over the planet by attempting to technologically control the operation of the Earth System—in particular, by manipulating the Earth's thermostat, so to speak. Despite its risks for further ecological destabilization, this technofix is evidently attractive to certain politicians, billionaires, and other elites largely because it seems to provide a way to sustain the capitalist status quo. It would also almost certainly empower a relatively small group of technocrats to control the Earth System on behalf of billions of other citizens, yet without any clear path to reverse course once this eco-regime was in place—thereby jeopardizing democratic ideals and norms for years, decades, or even longer. Such a scenario might currently sound like science fiction. Even so, I argue that a technocratic mode of planetary governance that utilizes geoengineering is becoming increasingly likely to materialize in a state of climate emergency.

Under such conditions, political sovereignty would thus become literally *geological* in scope, and human supremacy would become *godlike* in its aspirations for planetary exceptionalism and control. In the later sections of this essay, I look to the work of a number of ecotheorists and political theologians in order to theorize this potentially geological expansion of sovereignty as an exceptionalist *geopower*, and to scrutinize what I see as its underlying *theopolitical* imaginary.[4] Central to my analysis is an engagement with the work of Carl Schmitt, who argues that the idea of sovereignty in Western political thought must be understood as a secularized theological concept—specifically one that is derived from the classical theistic conception of one omnipotent God. Moreover, as we will see, it is precisely this theology that Schmitt himself eventually exploits as a way to *boost* political sovereignty. Based on this critical examination of Schmitt's account of sovereignty, I interpret the political theology of geopower as being rooted in a secularized imaginary of divine omnipotence. Here the Earth remains subordinate to a controlling figure of transcendence: a supernatural Deity then, the technoscientific Anthropos now. Consequently, I argue that effectively resisting geopower will not only require the mobilization of activist movements for climate justice but also the construction of theopolitical *counter*-imaginaries that conceive of humanity and divinity otherwise than as exceptionalist geosovereigns.

To conclude this essay, I consider one important example of such an imaginary in the work of Catherine Keller, who proposes a "political theology of the earth" in response to our escalating ecopolitical crises. Through a creative retrieval of Whitehead's philosophical conception of divinity, Keller unfolds an explicitly "counter-exceptionalist" theology as a critical alternative to Schmitt's theopolitical vision. Whereas for Schmitt, the image of a metaphysically exceptional God of sovereign omnipotence functions to empower an antidemocratic politics, Keller reveals how Whitehead's notion of divinity as a *counter*-sovereign mode of immanent creativity might alternatively serve to energize democratic movements for ecosocial justice. As such, precisely as a counter-imaginary to the secularized theology of omnipotence that subliminally fuels old and new forms of sovereignty, I ultimately suggest that Keller's political theology may prove vital to resisting the emerging geopower—and indeed, for empowering efforts to shift *"catastrophe into catalyst"* for democracy.[5]

NARRATING THE ANTHROPOCENE

Owing to the increasingly disruptive impacts of human societies on the Earth System as a whole, earth scientists have in recent decades started to call our present geological epoch the Anthropocene—"the new age of humans." After being popularized in 2000 by the atmospheric chemist Paul Crutzen and the marine biologist Eugene Stoermer, the Anthropocene has become the subject of a great deal of research and intense debates across multiple disciplines.[6] At the same time, it has become widely accepted within the earth science community as an indispensable term, as evidenced by the news in 2019 that an influential panel of scientists voted to confirm the Anthropocene as an official slice of geologic time.[7] Conceptually, the Anthropocene points to the fact that modern human societies have profoundly altered the functioning of the planet as an integrated system, particularly since the mid-twentieth century when human impacts on the Earth System intensified at an exponential rate.[8] The Anthropocene is not, therefore, a trendy new name for the "environmental crisis" but rather signifies an unprecedented event in human and geologic history. Humans have nearly always impacted local environments—causing extinctions, clearing forests, and so on—but only very recently has a certain subset of our species caused a planetary-scale shift that could soon lead to the collapse of current societal structures, and a sixth mass extinction event in the coming centuries. The Anthropocene thus marks a permanent bifurcation in the trajectory of the Earth System, rendering it more unstable and unpredictable than it was during the 10,000-year Holocene.

Beyond the earth sciences, however, scholars such as Jason Moore and Donna Haraway have criticized the concept of the Anthropocene, contending that it is a misnomer. From their perspective, the new epoch is more accurately named the "Capitalocene," because it was the capitalist world system that mainly caused the geological shift—and not therefore "humanity as an undifferentiated whole" or "Species Man," as some scientists have seemed to suggest.[9] While agreeing that extractive capitalism is largely to blame for the rupture in the Earth System, postcolonial historian Dipesh Chakrabarty nevertheless makes a powerful argument for the conceptual importance of the geological Anthropocene. For him, the concept crucially indicates the "collapse" of human and earth histories.[10] It thus requires thinking beyond the limited histories of modern capitalist societies and fully situating our species within the bumpiness of geohistory and the boundaries of the Earth System. Only by thus relating the smaller histories of capital to the universal history of life on this planet might we become capable of confronting the "shared catastrophe that we have all fallen into," Chakrabarty insists.[11]

Yet another way of narrating the Anthropocene is gaining in popularity, and it sharply contrasts with the views of Moore, Haraway, and Chakrabarty. Not far from where I live in Northern California is the Breakthrough Institute: a neoliberal, technocratic think tank that optimistically promotes the creation of a "good Anthropocene." For these self-described "ecomodernists," the scientific announcement of a new age of humans indicates that our species has gained impressive new capacities for planetary control. Thus, in an article for the *Breakthrough Journal*, Erle Ellis argues that the Anthropocene ought to be celebrated as "a new geological epoch ripe with human-directed opportunity."[12] Ecomodernists such as Ellis thus prefer not to frame the advent of the Anthropocene primarily as a dire threat to human societies, nor as a sign of humanity's short-sightedness, but rather as an "amazing opportunity" for us to accelerate modern civilizational progress, and to realize our full potential as global environmental managers.[13]

To be sure, ecomodernists do not deny that the Anthropocene poses significant challenges for human societies. Nevertheless, they insist that these challenges can ultimately be met through the development of a "vibrant postindustrial capitalism," as the founders of Breakthrough put it.[14] This updated, high-tech, ostensibly "green" version of global capitalism will supposedly enable the absolute "decoupling" of human societies from nature, the continued pursuit of endless GDP growth, and ever-new technological solutions to environmental and societal problems that may arise in the future. As such, ecomodernists argue that we should embrace our role as pilots of Earth by becoming its techno-capitalist managers—thus explicitly defying calls from grassroots environmentalists to end the modern drive to transcend nature and instead radically scale down consumption and acknowledge ecological limits to growth.[15] "Nature no longer runs Earth," writes ecomodernist Mark Lynas. "We do. It is our choice what happens here." We are therefore "the God Species," he claims.[16] As ecomodernist Stewart Brand likewise asserts, "We are as gods and might as well get used to it."[17] Such proclamations of human supremacy arguably exemplify the unfolding imaginary of geopower. Moreover, they serve to ideologically justify the deployment of geoengineering technologies—which may very well become the most extreme manifestations of geopower.

ENGINEERING THE EARTH SYSTEM

In light of ecomodernist calls for humans to "play god," it is no surprise that such thinkers tend to favor geoengineering as a method of counteracting climate change. As the science writer Oliver Morton explains, geoengineering can be defined as "the deliberate modification of the earthsystem on a global scale."[18] One widely advocated geoengineering scheme involves the deployment of direct-air capture technologies in order to scrub CO_2 from the atmosphere. Yet as Morton points out, for the foreseeable future, this method "cannot be implemented on a remotely large enough scale because there is no proven technology for taking carbon dioxide out of the air that is practically or economically up to the job."[19] Currently, the most frequently discussed and technologically plausible geoengineering proposal is a type of solar radiation management known as "stratospheric particle injection," which calls for continuously spraying sulfate aerosols into the upper part of the atmosphere to reflect more sunlight back into space. Unlike direct-air capture techniques, solar engineering is relatively inexpensive and could now be deployed on a large scale (e.g., through high-flying aircraft). This strategy would create a hazy veil of sulfur pollution in the sky that would "mimic the way volcanic eruptions cool the planet," explains climatologist Michael Mann.[20] Thus, at least in theory, solar engineering would allow humans to control the Earth's thermostat while deferring greenhouse gas mitigation efforts and the transformation of carbon capitalism.

However, the cure might be worse than the disease. Numerous studies suggest that this technofix would alter rainfall patterns and temperatures in geographically uneven ways, likely causing droughts in regions of Africa and Asia.[21] Solar engineering also presents a number of temporal challenges, including the so-called termination shock. As Naomi Klein explains the issue, "Once you start spraying . . . it would basically be impossible to stop because if you did, all the warming that you had artificially suppressed . . . would hit the planet's surface in one single tidal wave of heat, with no time for gradual adaptation."[22] And even if scientists did find a way to halt stratospheric spraying without causing a termination shock, geoengineering researchers suggest that the spraying would have to continue for decades, or even a century to lower and stabilize global temperatures. Compounding the potential problem of a termination shock, Klein also points out that "because of the huge variations in global weather patterns from one year to the next . . . as well as the havoc already being wreaked by global warming," accurately evaluating the efficacy of this technofix would probably require at least a decade-long experiment.[23] In short, solar engineering would be a risky and likely dangerous operation, and would provide neither an immediate nor a simple solution to the climate crisis.

Despite these kinds of concerns, however, geoengineering predictably appeals to certain neoliberals and conservatives whose positions of power evidently lead them to ignore—or actively oppose—grassroots environmentalist arguments to fully decarbonize economies and ecologically constrain our political systems. Thus, along with the Breakthrough Institute, large corporations such as ExxonMobil,[24] billionaires such as Bill Gates,[25] popular writers such as Steven Pinker,[26] conservative think tanks such as the American Enterprise Institute (AEI),[27] mainstream economists such as Lawrence Summers,[28] and governments including the Trump administration have all expressed support for geoengineering.[29] Some of these advocates—like AEI—are Promethean enthusiasts about such geotechnologies, whereas others—like Summers—are in varying degrees more cautious. However, each and every one of them is willing to take the risk of manipulating the entire planet for human ends.

If such large-scale technofixes were ever deployed, this might mark the apotheosis of the modern dream to dominate a mechanized nature—as when Descartes expressed his hope for human knowledge to expand to such a point that we could become *"masters and possessors of nature."*[30] And at least apart from some sort of robustly democratic process of implementation (which is difficult, if not impossible to imagine), geoengineering would also very likely mean that *some* humans would have unprecedented control over the planet. Geopower would thereby become a concrete reality.

Considering the fact that climate disruption is largely the result of elite self-interest, corporate greed, and liberal institutional failures, is it even remotely credible to suppose that a small group of technocrats would engineer the Earth in a just and compassionate way? The latter scenario seems highly implausible, for as ethicist Clive Hamilton asks rhetorically, "If a just global warming solution cannot be found, who can believe in a just geoengineering regime?"[31] Furthermore, considering the complex structure and partially unpredictable dynamics of the Earth System—with its multiple subsystems that interact through massive feedback loops, nonlinear processes, and constant energy flows—are humans even actually *capable* of safely engineering the planet?

As Bruno Latour argues, this too seems unlikely. Thus, in his important critique of anthropocentric narratives of the Anthropocene, Latour insists on replacing the modern mechanistic image of "Nature" with the *nonmodern* image of "Gaia," which for him signifies a lively planetary assemblage of more-than-human powers that actively resist total human mastery. "And if Gaia cannot be compared to a machine," Latour contends, then "it cannot be subject to any sort of *re-engineering.*"[32] Biologist Sallie Chisholm likewise maintains that geoengineering theories are in serious tension with current scientific understandings of the Earth as a dynamic system:

> Proponents of research on geoengineering simply keep ignoring the fact that the biosphere is a player (not just a responder) in whatever we do, and its trajectory cannot be predicted. It is a living breathing

collection of organisms (mostly microorganisms) that are evolving every second—a "self-organizing, complex, adaptive system" (the strict term). These types of systems have emergent properties that simply cannot be predicted. We all know this! Yet proponents of geoengineering research leave that out of the discussion.[33]

Such critiques profoundly call into question any possibility of solving the climate crisis through large-scale technofixes. The alternative solution is arguably clear enough: We need a rapid decarbonization of economies through massive expansions of clean and renewable energy, and ultimately, to transition to an ecological civilization that values the common good(s) of people and planet over the endless pursuit of profit.[34]

Concerningly, however, geoengineering remains a live and attractive option in the minds of many today—whether it is framed as a fulfillment of humanity's "manifest destiny" over nature, as some Prometheans seem to suggest; or in more guarded terms, as a last-ditch response to save humanity from future climate chaos. Moreover, as climate disruption continues to intensify in the Anthropocene, a geoengineering scenario becomes increasingly likely to play out. In fact, even the most recent report from the UN's Intergovernmental Panel on Climate Change suggested solar engineering as a possible "remediative measure" for extreme climate breakdown.[35] An earlier NASA report likewise frames the technique as a potentially necessary response to a "climate emergency." Disturbingly, the authors of the latter report go on to suggest that, "*In a crisis*, ideological objections to solar radiation management may be swept aside."[36] Public spaces for serious debates about geoengineering could, in other words, be foreclosed in a state of emergency.

We must now therefore consider the real possibility that an extreme climate emergency may be used to justify bypassing democratic processes so that technocrats can dim the sun to "save the planet." Moreover, as we have seen, because solar engineering would be difficult to stop after being deployed on a large scale and would have to be sustained for many years to take full effect, it would likely become a long-term operation of necessity. A state of climate emergency could therefore give way to what Giorgio Agamben describes as an "unprecedented generalization of the paradigm of security as the normal technique of government."[37] When Agamben wrote this line in 2003, it was in the context of a critical analysis of the shifting character of modern politics, and he was not evidently thinking about the climate crisis. His theoretical gaze was instead focused on issues and events surrounding the "War on Terror." In particular, Agamben was theorizing the national security state's massive expansion of surveillance techniques and policing activities as a permanent normalization of the emergency powers of Western democracies. What I am now suggesting is that, in the Anthropocene, emergency powers may once again be invoked and normalized through an even more radical, indeed *planetary*, generalization of security as the normal technique of government—precisely through the deployment of geoengineering technologies in response to climate chaos.[38]

POLITICAL THEOLOGY OF PLANETARY SOVEREIGNTY

The growing possibility of such a scenario raises urgent political questions. As Hamilton asks, "Who would determine that an emergency exists? Who would authorize the emergency response, and from where would they derive their legitimacy?"[39] From the standpoint of political theology, these questions immediately call for a critical consideration of the nature of sovereignty. In the well-known opening line of *Political Theology* (1921), Carl Schmitt asserts that it is precisely "the sovereign . . . who decides on the exception"—that is, the one who can unilaterally declare the existence of a crisis that requires an exceptional form of response.[40] For Schmitt, sovereignty is therefore founded on the ability to decide on a "state of exception," which occurs in times of "extreme emergency" when the sovereign suspends legal and constitutional norms, and subsequently applies "extraordinary measures" to restore public order. The sovereign accordingly reveals itself to be an essentially "unlimited authority," Schmitt contends, "which means the suspension of the entire existing order."[41]

Political sovereignty is thus defined by Schmitt as the capacity to transcend democratic decision-making and the law in a state of exception—just as the theistic doctrine of omnipotence includes the power to override creaturely decisions and the laws of nature in order to impose the divine will. As I previously indicated, this theopolitical parallel is not lost on Schmitt. Indeed, for him, the image of a metaphysically exceptional God is not only analogous to political sovereignty, but also helps to legitimize his antidemocratic politics through a *"theologization of the political,"* as Adam Kotsko explains.[42] Schmitt thus argues for the need to symbolically transfer a traditional view of theistic transcendence to the sovereign power of the state.[43] In this way, Schmitt's fusion of totalizing conceptions of the political and the theological supports what Clayton Crockett critically describes as "an anti-democratic *machine of domination.*"[44]

However, in a more general and fundamental sense, Schmitt also claims that throughout modernity, the political and the theological have remained tightly interwoven phenomena—so much so that it is impossible to isolate the conceptual terrain of either realm from the other. This brings us to the central postulate of his text:

> All significant concepts of the modern theory of the state are secularized theological concepts not only because of their historical development—in which they were transferred from theology to the theory of the state, whereby, for example, the omnipotent God became the omnipotent lawgiver—but also because of their systematic structure, the recognition of which is necessary for a sociological consideration of these concepts. The exception in jurisprudence is analogous to the miracle in theology.[45]

In other words, Schmitt is here claiming that secular political concepts (e.g., the sovereign, the exception) have not only been *historically substituted* for theological ones (e.g., divine omnipotence, the miracle)—which is the standard secularization thesis—but also remain *inherently interrelated* with theology.[46] As such, a purely secular form of politics does not exist—or as Keller glosses Schmitt's thesis, *"Politics is always already theological."*[47]

Considering Schmitt's theory of political sovereignty as secularized theology, current calls to technologically control the Earth System may now begin to appear as secular incarnations of the totalizing ideal of theistic power. In this increasingly influential political theology of the Anthropocene, the omnipotent God has thus become the technocratic *God-species*—creator, sustainer, and savior of the new geological epoch—while theistic faith in top-down interventions morphs into what Donna Haraway calls "a comic faith in technofixes." Although Haraway distances herself from the discourse of political theology, on my reading of her work on the Anthropocene, she perceptively underscores how a certain kind of theology is implied in technoscientific visions of an engineered planet. For her, the modern faith that "technology will somehow come to the rescue of its naughty but very clever children," is not only dangerously naïve—scientifically, ethically, and politically—but essentially *"amounts to the same thing"* as a religious faith that "God will come to the rescue of his disobedient but ever hopeful children."[48] Both forms of faith thus pin their ultimate hope on what Haraway calls "technoid sky gods."[49]

Similarly, environmental historians Christophe Bonneuil and Jean-Baptiste Fressoz have discerned an underlying theological imaginary within ecomodernist accounts of the Anthropocene. On their reading, such narratives effectively pitch techno-capitalist solutions to current crises as a kind of "anthropocenic gospel," and in turn project modern science as "savior" of the masses.[50] This secularized "gospel" promises universal salvation through a new "eco-technocratic government,"[51] and to transform our fears of planetary catastrophe into the "giddiness of [human] omnipotence."[52] Informed by the writings of Agamben and Schmitt, Bonneuil and Fressoz thus contend that this gospel now provides ideological support to an antidemocratic *"geopower,"* which they theorize as an emerging form of sovereignty that posits the "Earth as a 'system' to know and govern as a totality, in all its components and functions."[53]

In resonance with Bonneuil and Fressoz, political philosophers Joel Wainwright and Geoff Mann (W&M) likewise draw on the works of Agamben and Schmitt to theorize possible Anthropocene futures. From their perspective, climate change is creating the conditions for the emergence of *"planetary sovereignty*, defined by an exception proclaimed in the name of preserving life on Earth." By "planetary," they mean that this new form of sovereignty would exert its power at a transnational scale, and that it would attempt to manage the operation of the entire Earth System through technological means.[54] Although a planetary sovereign might be realized in a number of ways, W&M predict that it would most likely take the form of a technocapitalist "Climate Leviathan." Inspired by the Hobbesian conception of the state as a mortal god that enables an *"escape* from the state of nature,"[55] they theorize Climate Leviathan as a geological expansion of neoliberal governance that "reflects the dream of a sustainable capitalist status quo,"[56] and predict that it would most likely be coordinated by a small group of planetary managers (e.g., scientists, representatives of leading capitalist nations) who would collectively have the power to "determine what measures are necessary and what and who must be sacrificed in the interests of life on Earth."[57] If Leviathan does materialize, W&M argue that it would be constituted through a decision to "seize command, declare an emergency, and bring order to the Earth, all in the name of saving life."[58]

What all of these theorists make clear is that, with the arrival of the Anthropocene, the theopolitical problem of sovereignty has returned with renewed intensity. As exemplified by godlike aspirations to technologically control the feedback loops between the atmosphere and the biosphere, the political sphere is now beginning to stretch beyond nation-states and global capital to encompass the entire Earth System. Climate Leviathan, geopower, sky gods—each of these theopolitical figures of sovereign exceptionalism help conceptualize the planetary-scale "adaptation of the political" that is already beginning to take place.[59] But for the sake of a more democratic becoming of humans with the Earth, how might the embryonic machine of geopower now be resisted—or at least democratically restrained?

BEYOND THE SOVEREIGN EXCEPTION

At the level of concrete praxis, resisting geopower will almost certainly require an intensified mobilization of activists who are committed to working for ecosocial justice on a radically democratic basis. Perhaps this will come about (at least in part) through the continued unfolding of what Klein calls "Blockadia": a globally emergent climate justice movement composed of "increasingly interconnected pockets of resistance" to the extractive capitalist interests that fuel the climate crisis. As Klein further explains, Blockadia is ultimately a grassroots phenomenon that brings together environmentalists, students, farmers, local shop owners, and others who have chosen to bypass "top-down environmentalism" in pursuit of "a deeper form of democracy, one that provides communities with real control over those resources that are most critical to collective survival—the health of the water, air, and soil." With its deployment of multiple eco-activist strategies—including "packing local council meetings, marching in capital cities, being hauled off in police vans, even putting their bodies between the earth-movers and earth"[60]—Blockadia thus demonstrates the promise and possibility for what William Connolly has called a "politics of swarming." Taking inspiration from the cooperative activities of honeybees, Connolly envisions an ecopolitical swarm for climate justice that would hold together diversities of knowledge, strategy, identity, and creed—even as it might ultimately cohere into a planetary activist assemblage by strategically coordinating its "disparate energies and creative insights until a citizen movement becomes possible across world regions."⁶¹ In addition to Klein's account of Blockadia, incipient political swarming might also now be glimpsed in the efforts of such activist groups as Extinction Rebellion and the Sunrise Movement, and in the work of such environmental organizations as the Indigenous Environmental Network, 350.org, and the EcoCiv Institute—all of which diversely challenge extractive capitalist forces, and aim to secure just and sustainable futures.

Resisting geopower, however, must also arguably take place at the level of human imaginaries—which brings us back to political theology. As I have tried to show through my analyses of Schmitt's theologization of the political and geopower's underlying imaginary, the work of political theology involves critically investigating the conceptual transfers between modern politics and theology. But for many of its contemporary practitioners, including myself, political theology also includes an explicitly *constructive* task. Why is this the case?

Insofar as modern politics always already includes a more or less hidden theological dimension that shapes a public's understanding of power, informs its practices, and provides it with a vision of the way the world ought to be, then resisting any political status quo will arguably require *counter-theological* interventions into a collective's social imaginary.⁶² The de/constructive work of political theology can therefore be understood as the public dissemination of alternative symbols of meaning and ultimacy as critical replacements for those that help legitimize dominant power structures—such as the imaginary of sovereign exceptionalism that now fuels the emerging geopower. As Keller importantly clarifies in her work on the subject, this is not to say that political theology attempts to "exercise control over another's unconscious mind," but rather that it seeks to initiate a "radical change of practice" through the "subliminal insertion" of alternative theologies into politics.⁶³

Based on this understanding of political theology, Keller argues compellingly in her *Political Theology of the Earth* for a theological imaginary in which the classical theistic doctrine of "omnipotence gives way to a *depth of creative indeterminacy*"—which consequently calls into question the Schmittian theopolitics of sovereignty.⁶⁴ Indeed, it is precisely this countertheology of divine indeterminacy that Keller hopes may then begin to subliminally infuse modern politics as a democratizing lure toward ecosocial justice. As she explains the driving motivation for her project, "It is the chance of an *ecosocial inception*, the emergence of a new public and a new earth, that a political theology of the earth nurtures."[65] On my reading of her work, Keller's radically democratic political theology may also then provide a strategic antidote to the theopolitical exceptionalism that now drives the incipient geopower, while simultaneously serving to energize an ecopolitics of swarming through its alternative metaphors of ultimacy.[66] Although Keller unfolds her larger project in conversation with a wide variety of scholarly discourses, here I want to conclude by showing how Whitehead's thought provides a particularly important source of inspiration for her theopolitical counter-imaginary.

Although Whitehead never engaged Schmitt's work, Keller reads his philosophy as effectively challenging Schmittian theopolitics, in part because Whitehead was sharply critical of the ways in which theology and totalizing forms of politics often become intertwined.[67] While looking back over the history of Western theocratic politics, Whitehead argues that traditional forms of theism are partly rooted in a power-craving confusion of theological concepts with imperialistic ideals. On his analysis, when orthodox Christianity accepted an image of God on the model of sovereign power, "the Church gave unto God the attributes which belonged exclusively to Caesar." God was thereby conceived as an all-powerful ruler who unilaterally imposes "his" will upon the world. Yet for Whitehead, this divinization of sovereign power was ultimately an idolatrous betrayal of "the Galilean origin of Christianity," which was rooted in a theological "vision of humility" and non-imperialist "love."[68] It is precisely in the context of this critique of Christian theism, I suggest, that Whitehead's thought can be seen to intersect with Schmitt's political theology—even as the two philosophers arrived at diametrically opposed theopolitical conclusions. Thus, whereas Schmitt called for a theologization of the political on the model of divine sovereignty, Whitehead resists this theopolitical (con)fusion—albeit, from the other direction, as a dangerous *politicization of the theological* on the model of imperial rule.

However, Whitehead does not then halt his philosophical project with a theopolitical critique of theism. Indeed, after rejecting images of God as "the ruling Caesar, or the ruthless moralist, or the unmoved mover," Whitehead draws theological inspiration from the Galilean vision of humility and love to reimagine divinity as the noncoercive "poet of the world." For Whitehead, God thus becomes the immanent source of radical novelty for creaturely becoming and a cosmic lure toward the divine "vision of truth, beauty, and goodness."⁶⁹ Crucially, Whitehead develops this theopoetic perspective in opposition to the notion of a metaphysically exceptional deity of absolute power, "at whose fiat the world came into being"—which is, of course, precisely the form of theism that Schmitt exploits to boost the politics of sovereignty.⁷⁰

In an unintentional rebuttal to Schmitt's theopolitical notion of the sovereign exception, Whitehead thus insists that "God is not to be treated as an *exception* to all metaphysical principles," but rather as "their chief *exemplification*."⁷¹ In Whitehead's philosophy, what God thus exemplifies, explains Keller, is the indeterminate cosmic process of relational creativity, whereby everything actual "exists only as an interdependent activity of becoming."⁷² As Keller suggests, divinity is not therefore excepted from the cosmos as the "Sovereign Decider providentially choosing on His own, then imitated by other sovereign and separate subjects." Rather, this immanental theos only ever acts in the world relationally—and so, *"nonexceptionally,"* as a co-creative lure to novel possibility and wider solidarities amid a democracy of fellow creatures.⁷³ It is then precisely this theopoetic imaginary of a nonexceptional deity that Keller creatively retrieves and deploys to effect a *counter*-theologization of the political. In resistance to the Schmittian "power of the sovereign exception," Keller thus offers a democratizing theology for the Anthropocene—one which is not based on the exceptionalist theo-logic of omnipotence that now informs geopower, but which imagines divinity otherwise in order to affirm "the potentiality of an ecosocial inception."⁷⁴

Whether or not a planetary form of sovereignty is ever fully realized in the Anthropocene, it is now clear that it presently exists *in potentia*—and thus already requires critical confrontation. As Wainwright and Mann argue, "Insofar as its possible emergence already organizes expectations of the future, [planetary sovereignty] indelibly shapes the present."⁷⁵ What will become of the political in the Anthropocene? How will it adapt to a destabilized Earth? We cannot be certain, but it is unlikely to remain the same. Perhaps a top-down geosovereign will soon consolidate in response to climatic emergency. Or perhaps, if the now merely possible becomes actual, a swarm of democratizing energies will irrupt from below to co-create a common good of people and planet. Emergency might then "not serve the sovereign state of exception," writes Keller, but "trigger instead the inception, the emergence of a new collective."[76] It seems to me that we must now hope for and work toward such a future.

NOTES

The epigraph is from Donna J. Haraway, *Staying with the Trouble: Making Kin in the Chthulucene* (Durham, NC: Duke University Press, 2016), 57.

1. Simon L. Lewis and Mark A. Maslin, *The Human Planet: How We Created the Anthropocene* (London: Penguin, 2018), 75, 243, 248.
2. Alfred North Whitehead, *Process and Reality*, ed. David Ray Griffin and Donald W. Sherburne, corrected edition (New York: Free Press, 1978), 50.
3. I am borrowing this expression from Latour, who uses it to "summarize the present situation, in which the physical framework that Moderns had taken for granted, the ground on which their history had always played out, has become unstable." Bruno Latour, *Facing Gaia: Eight Lectures on the New Climatic Regime* (Cambridge: Polity Press, 2017), 3.
4. The term "geopower" is variously defined in the environmental humanities. For Elizabeth Grosz, geopower names the inhuman powers *of* "the earth itself: forces which we as technical humans have tried to organize, render consistent and predictable, but which we can never fully accomplish insofar as the earth remains the literal ground and condition for every human, and non-human, action." Although I appreciate Grosz's conception of geopower, my use of the term is inspired by Christophe Bonneuil and Jean-Baptiste Fressoz (as indicated in this essay), for whom geopower signifies a technocratic form of human power *over* the Earth. See Elizabeth Grosz, Kathryn Yusoff, and Nigel Clark, "An Interview with Elizabeth Grosz: Geopower, Inhumanism and the Biopolitical," *Theory, Culture & Society* 34, no. 2–3 (2017): 135.
5. Catherine Keller, *Intercarnations: Exercises in Theological Possibility* (New York: Fordham University Press, 2017), 190.
6. Paul Crutzen and Eugene F. Stoermer, "The 'Anthropocene,'" *IGBP Newsletter* 41 (May 2000): 17–18.
7. Meera Subramanian, "Anthropocene Now: Influential Panel Votes to Recognize Earth's New Epoch," *Nature*, May 21, 2019, http://www.nature.com/articles/d41586-019-01641-5.
8. This post-1945 period is known as the "Great Acceleration," and it is now the leading candidate for the Anthropocene's start date. See Will Steffen et al., "The Trajectory of the Anthropocene: The Great Acceleration," *Anthropocene Review* 2, no. 1 (2015): 81–98.

9. Jason W. Moore, ed., *Anthropocene or Capitalocene? Nature, History, and the Crisis of Capitalism* (Oakland, CA: PM Press, 2016), 81, 51.
10. Dipesh Chakrabarty, "The Climate of History: Four Theses," *Critical Inquiry* 35, no. 2 (2009): 207.
11. Chakrabarty, 218.
12. Erle C. Ellis, "The Planet of No Return: Human Resilience on an Artificial Earth," *Breakthrough Journal* 2 (Fall 2011): 43.
13. Erle C. Ellis, "Neither Good Nor Bad," *New York Times*, May 23, 2011, https://www.nytimes.com/roomfordebate/2011/05/19/the-age-of-anthropocene-should-we-worry/neither-good-nor-bad.
14. Michael Shellenberger and Ted Nordhaus, *Break Through: From the Death of Environmentalism to the Politics of Possibility* (New York: Houghton Mifflin Harcourt, 2007), 249.
15. For an overview of Breakthrough's "post-environmentalist" platform, see John Asafu-Adjaye et al., *An Ecomodernist Manifesto*, 2015, https://doi.org/10.13140/RG.2.1.1974.0646.
16. Mark Lynas, *The God Species: Saving the Planet in the Age of Humans* (Washington, DC: National Geographic, 2011), 8.
17. Cited in Ronald Bailey, "Better to Be Potent Than Not," *New York Times*, May 23, 2011, https://www.nytimes.com/roomfordebate/2011/05/19/the-age-of-anthropocene-should-we-worry/better-to-be-potent-than-not.
18. Oliver Morton, *The Planet Remade: How Geoengineering Could Change the World* (Princeton, NJ: Princeton University Press, 2017), 23.
19. Morton, 26.
20. Michael E. Mann and Tom Toles, *The Madhouse Effect: How Climate Change Denial Is Threatening Our Planet, Destroying Our Politics, and Driving Us Crazy* (New York: Columbia University Press, 2016), loc. 1863, Kindle.
21. For a recent scientific study that warns of various ways in which solar engineering could backfire, see John T. Fasullo et al., "Persistent Polar Ocean Warming in a Strategically Geoengineered Climate," *Nature Geoscience* 11, no. 12 (2018): 910. For a list of 27 risks of solar engineering, see Table 1 of Alan Robock, "Albedo Enhancement by Stratospheric Sulfur Injections: More Research Needed," *Earth's Future* 4, no. 12 (2016): 644–48.
22. Naomi Klein, *This Changes Everything: Capitalism vs. The Climate* (New York: Simon & Schuster, 2014), 260.
23. Klein, 269.
24. As Hamilton notes, "The oil company . . . funded a report . . . concluding that sulphate aerosol spraying would be a much cheaper response to global warming

than phasing out fossil fuels. Its CEO, Rex Tillerson, has also described climate change as an 'engineering problem' with 'engineering solutions.'" Clive Hamilton, *Earthmasters: The Dawn of the Age of Climate Engineering* (New Haven, CT: Yale University Press, 2014), 78.

25. According to Hamilton, Gates is "the world's leading financial supporter of geoengineering research." Hamilton, 74. Oliver Morton similarly describes Gates as "the field's sugar daddy." Morton, *The Planet Remade*, 156.

26. Pinker is an ecomodernist who cautiously advocates for geoengineering, arguing that it might be a necessary response to worst-case future scenarios. Steven Pinker, *Enlightenment Now: The Case for Reason, Science, Humanism, and Progress* (New York: Viking, 2018), 152–54.

27. Klein reports that AEI has supported geoengineering since 2008, running conferences, publishing reports, and testifying to Congress about the issue, "all with the consistent message that geoengineering isn't a Plan B should emission cuts fail, but rather a Plan A." Klein, *This Changes Everything*, 282–83.

28. In Summers's own words, "If climate change does prove disastrous in any near-term scenario, geoengineering will be our only hope." Lawrence H. Summers and Richard J. Zeckhauser, "Policymaking for Posterity" (National Bureau of Economic Research, September 2008), 33, https://www.nber.org/papers/w14359.pdf.

29. James Temple, "The US Government Has Approved Funds for Geoengineering Research," *MIT Technology Review*, December 20, 2019, https://www.technologyreview.com/2019/12/20/131449/the-us-government-will-begin-to-fund-geoengineering-research/.

30. René Descartes, *Discourse on Method and Meditations on First Philosophy*, trans. Donald A. Cress, 4th ed. (Indianapolis, IN: Hackett, 1999), 35. Emphasis added.

31. Hamilton, *Earthmasters*, 182.

32. Latour is inspired by scientist James Lovelock's Gaia theory, which recognizes the Earth as a whole as actively maintaining conditions for life to continue. Latour, *Facing Gaia*, 96.

33. Cited in Klein, *This Changes Everything*, 267.

34. The term "ecological civilization" comes from China's Communist Party, but it has also been taken up in the United States by such scholars as John B. Cobb Jr. and Eileen Crist, and by the Indian eco-activist Vandana Shiva. For a radically democratic, eco-socialist theory of ecological civilization, see Philip Clayton and Justin Heinzekehr, *Organic Marxism: An Alternative to Capitalism and Ecological Catastrophe* (Claremont, CA: Process Century Press, 2014).

35. Heleen de Coninck and Aromar Revi, "Chapter 4: Strengthening and Implementing the Global Response" (IPCC SR1.5, June 4, 2018), 10, https://report.ipcc.ch/sr15/pdf/sr15_chapter4.pdf.
36. Lee Lane et al., "Workshop Report on Managing Solar Radiation" (NASA, April 2007), 20, https://ntrs.nasa.gov/archive/nasa/casi.ntrs.nasa.gov/20070031204.pdf. Emphasis added.
37. Giorgio Agamben, *State of Exception*, trans. Kevin Attell (Chicago: University of Chicago Press, 2005), 14.
38. Here I am trying to further develop the important reading of Agamben's quote that is briefly suggested in Joel Wainwright and Geoff Mann, *Climate Leviathan: A Political Theory of Our Planetary Future* (London: Verso, 2018), 4, 31.
39. Hamilton, *Earthmasters*, 156.
40. Carl Schmitt, *Political Theology: Four Chapters on the Concept of Sovereignty*, trans. George Schwab (Chicago: University of Chicago Press, 2006), 5.
41. Schmitt, 12.
42. Adam Kotsko, *Neoliberalism's Demons: On the Political Theology of Late Capital* (Stanford, CA: Stanford University Press, 2018), 28. Emphasis added.
43. Schmitt, *Political Theology*, 37. See also Melanie Johnson-DeBaufre, Catherine Keller, and Elias Ortega-Aponte, eds., *Common Goods: Economy, Ecology, and Political Theology* (New York: Fordham University Press, 2015), 8.
44. Clayton Crockett, *Derrida after the End of Writing: Political Theology and New Materialism* (New York: Fordham University Press, 2017), 45.
45. Schmitt, *Political Theology*, 36.
46. Here I am indebted to Crockett's postsecularist reading of this particular passage in Clayton Crockett, *Radical Political Theology: Religion and Politics after Liberalism* (New York: Columbia University Press, 2013), 79, 91.
47. Catherine Keller, *Political Theology of the Earth: Our Planetary Emergency and the Struggle for a New Public* (New York: Columbia University Press, 2018), 8.
48. Haraway, *Staying with the Trouble*, 3. Emphasis added.
49. Haraway, 186n57.
50. Christophe Bonneuil and Jean-Baptiste Fressoz, *The Shock of the Anthropocene: The Earth, History and Us* (London: Verso, 2016), 73, 84.
51. Bonneuil and Fressoz, 93, 95.
52. Bonneuil and Fressoz, 85.
53. Bonneuil and Fressoz, 87–88.
54. Wainwright and Mann, *Climate Leviathan*, 29.
55. Wainwright and Mann, 4.
56. Wainwright and Mann, 30.

57. Wainwright and Mann, 15.
58. Wainwright and Mann, 31.
59. On the "adaptation of the political," see Wainwright and Mann, 79.
60. Klein, *This Changes Everything*, 253–54.
61. William E. Connolly, *Facing the Planetary: Entangled Humanism and the Politics of Swarming* (Durham, NC: Duke University Press, 2017), 125.
62. On the concept of "social imaginaries," see Charles Taylor, *A Secular Age* (Cambridge, MA: Harvard University Press, 2007), 159–211.
63. Keller, *Political Theology of the Earth*, 44.
64. Keller, 18. Emphasis added.
65. Keller, 179. Emphasis added.
66. Like Connolly, Keller suggests "a new public strategy of 'swarming,'" which is based on the "cooperative rhythms of the bees that we are now exterminating." Keller, 38.
67. Although Whitehead was writing around the same time as Schmitt, Keller notes that he "was unaware of 'political theology' as such." Keller, 137.
68. Whitehead, *Process and Reality*, 342–43.
69. Whitehead, 343, 346.
70. Whitehead, 342. In *Political Theology* Schmitt implicitly links his conception of sovereignty to the classical theistic doctrine of creation "out of nothingness" (66).
71. Whitehead, *Process and Reality*, 343. Emphases added.
72. Keller, *Political Theology of the Earth*, 138.
73. Keller, 140.
74. Keller, 160.
75. Wainwright and Mann, *Climate Leviathan*, 18.
76. Keller, *Political Theology of the Earth*, 62.

PART II

◆ Destruction and Suicide

❧ 4. The Tradition of Destruction (Kafka's Law)

GIL ANIDJAR

I do not know whether it is possible to date a definite expansion of two lexicons, two linguistic fields of sorts, which have surely taken hold of academic prose by now, and that will occupy me here to a preliminary and limited extent with reference to law (note that I do not say: political theology).[1] The first of these lexicons has to do with *violence*. It is of course well recognized that there are innumerable forms (and instances) of violence, and many of them have generated a justifiably massive scholarly and journalistic interest. It is, however, remarkable that this particular discursive expansion is perhaps matched only by the ostensible paucity of terms with which we designate these actions and events that we call *violent*, in their individual and collective forms or dimensions, as well as in their effects. Beginning with the two forms I just mentioned (individual, collective), these actions and events insistently offer themselves as qualified iterations, episodic narrations of a selfsame violence, an otherwise inchoate force registered by different instruments and factions, each calibrated and authorized to argue for a differential recognition of an adjectival nature: physical or psychic violence, sexual and racial, political and economic, ethnic and religious violence, and more. And there is, indeed, much more. There is, for instance, the violence of words, injurious speech acts, that align themselves or clash with the efficacy of legal (if not only legal) pronouncements. And there is the violence done to the environment, the violence of worlds ending, what Catherine Keller calls "our planetary emergency."[2]

The second lexicon I am struggling with is, I think, equally broad and comparably inchoate. It is related to the previous one, though by no means identical with it. I speak this time of the language of "labor, work, and action" (to invoke Hannah Arendt's typology), of the powers of making that have been celebrated at the very least since Giambattista Vico announced the convertibility of truth and, precisely, making (the *verum factum* principle). I refer as well to the general concern with production or with construction, with constitution and with performance. Whether one invokes Vico and Marx on the history we presumably make, John Austin (the jurist) or John Langshaw Austin (the philosopher) on commands and other performatives, Nietzsche or Foucault (and the vagaries of a power that, repressive or oppressive no longer, would be persistently enabling and productive); whether one traces the felicities and infelicities of scientific discoveries, the rhetoric of self- and collective making, or the current spike in the popularity of activism, we generally appear to be seized within an active and agentive moment or momentum, one that has lately left only a minute opening to dogged contrarians strangely invested in passivity (Levinas, Agamben). One could do worse than go Heideggerian here and contend with a metaphysical tradition that, between being and nothingness (or, in Reiner Schürmann's powerful reformulation, being and acting), and ontotheological to its core (think: *creatio ex nihilo*), remains insistently structured by the oppositions of praxis and poiesis, doing and making, action and passion, and, once again, much more.

What I try to argue, with a little help from Kafka, is that this dual ubiquity of violence and of construction ("Im Anfang war die Tat," in Goethe's glorious phrasing) has left us somehow impoverished in confronting a different "motion" (that is Aristotle's word) than the felicitous, or violent, emergence of deed or doer, something else than the making of world and of history, or the social construction of everything. I shall speak, therefore, neither of passivity nor of becoming, but rather of becoming nothing, of destruction, of the tradition of destruction.

But first, and by way of background, back to the classics, and to the uncanny proximity of two early iterations of suicide bombing, of what would come to be called "suicide bombers." It is the proximity of these two figures that has prompted me to reckon with the tradition of destruction. This proximity signaled a different heading than the celebrated "Athens and Jerusalem," which prides itself on its democratic achievements and on its celebration of the individual and individual rights. For it was, was it not, King Leonidas of Sparta, who avowedly led his fellow citizens on a suicide mission that would take down with them as many Persians as martially possible. Elsewhere on the eastern Mediterranean coast, and not so distant in time, another famous hero was growing his hair, a Hebrew judge of all people, to bring down a crowded temple upon thousands of Philistine souls—and upon his own. It is all too often forgotten that Samson died in Gaza, but the lesson should have gotten through. For the tradition I speak of, which has long been known under the heading "Athens and Jerusalem," is constituted—or de-constituted—by a more covert, and broken, trajectory which deserves another, if not necessarily better, moniker. *Sparta and Gaza*: The tradition of destruction.[3]

What does that have to do with law? I am not sure I should be attempting to answer this question, but I shall venture to address it nonetheless. I begin with the uncontroversial assertion, I think, that law, as we know and fail to know it, essentially testifies to the metaphysics of action and of construction I have been recalling. However we define law and its "creatures," that is, law is and concerns itself with conduct and action, with acts, deeds, and behavior, and with innumerable practices.[4] Immanuel Kant on the moral law might serve here as a convenient authority on this and on the authority of law too, claiming as he famously does that "we do accept the moral law as an authoritative standard of conduct that provides sufficient and overriding reasons for action and we are motivated to act by our judgments of what it requires."[5] Hans Kelsen puts it equally clearly, who writes that "the norm which confers upon an act the meaning of legality or illegality is itself created by an act, which, in turn, receives its legal character from yet another norm."[6] Whether or not it *makes* sense, Ronald Dworkin avers in his turn, the law "makes us what we are. . . . We are subjects of law's empire, liegemen to its methods and ideals, bound in spirit while we debate what we must therefore do."[7] I could go on by way of William Blackstone ("Law . . . signifies a rule of action; and is applied indiscriminately to all kinds of action, whether animate or inanimate, rational or irrational")[8] or Karl Llewellyn ("What . . . officials do about disputes is, to my mind, the law itself"),[9] and all the way to Bruno Latour's *fabrique*, the making of law.[10] But I shall end my list of examples with Robert Cover, whose work predictably provided much of the impetus that guides this paper. "Law is a force," Cover strikingly writes, it is a force, "like gravity, through which our worlds exercise an influence upon one another, a force that affects the course of these worlds through normative space. And law is that which holds our reality apart from our visions and rescues us from the eschatology that is the collision in this material social world of the constructions of our minds."[11]

I cite Cover for a number of reasons, but mainly because his formulations on "violence and the word" have fostered a rich body of scholarship, which, enduring and discerning in its preoccupation with violence and with action, has, as it were, gravitated toward the unthematized distinction that concerns me here, namely, the distinction between violence and destruction, and indeed, between action and destruction. If violence too has come to be perceived in its constructive and constitutive dimension ("Violence thus constitutes law in three senses: it provides the occasion and method for founding legal orders, it gives law [as the regulator of force and coercion] a reason for being, and it provides a means through which the law acts," write Austin Sarat and Thomas Kearns),[12] it leaves unthought the possibility that destruction might belong to a different register, a different order (and disorder) altogether. Neither repressive nor productive, destruction might well be a power, a form of power, yet it is one that brings form and perhaps force itself to an end. Strictly speaking, destruction brings *nothing* about, it brings about nothing, and it might therefore have to be thought otherwise than according to paradigms of action and creation, of production, construction or constitution, command and performance. Destruction, moreover, does its un-work, it can do its nonwork, without violence at all (think of the destruction—means and ends—that is plastic). What I want to propose is therefore to revisit the all too symmetrical opposition established by Aristotle long ago between generation and destruction, between coming to be and coming to nothing.[13]

Now, nothing—the nothing, if you prefer, which comes about—is a well-known preoccupation of Franz Kafka. Like Aristotle, Kafka proposed an entire, and largely untapped, lexicon of destruction and termination, of disintegration and of corruption, of desolation and demolition, of ruination and putrefaction, consumption and consumation (to be distinguished, to some extent, from consummation), of devastation and of annihilation. One could surely adduce more than ample evidence to that effect from *The Trial* alone, but I shall restrict myself here to one notorious extract, a few sentences really, namely, the last sentences of chapter 9 of that book and the conclusion of those "exegetico-Talmudic" waves, as Derrida calls them, waves that follow and overtake Kafka's famous story, the story or parable known as "Before the Law."[14] In these last sentences, as he is about to leave the Cathedral, K. finally approaches the realization that I too will seek. He realizes that he is nothing, that he has become nothing. Without force or compulsion, K. begins to understand that nothing is what the law wants, even if, perhaps especially if, it is not quite an act, if nothing is not quite what the law *does*. Nothing is not, in other words, the *product* of the law, nor perhaps is it its effect or consequence either. It is not what the law *makes*, even if the law wills it. Nothing is rather what comes to be in the vicinity of the law.

> "Don't you want anything more from me?" asked K. "No," said the priest. "You were so friendly to me for a time," said K., "and explained so much to me, and now you let me go as if you cared nothing about me, *jetzt aber entläßt du mich, als läge dir nichts an mir.*" "But you have to leave now," said the priest. "Well, yes," said K., "you must see that I can't help it." "You must first see who I am," said the priest. "You are the prison chaplain," said K., groping his way nearer to the priest again; his immediate return to the Bank was not so necessary as he had made out, he could quite well stay longer. "That means I belong to the Court," said the priest. "So why should I want anything from you? The Court wants nothing from you, *Das Gericht will nichts von dir*. It receives you when you come and it dismisses you, *es entläßt dich*, when you go."[15]

Does the law have force? Is force—the capacity to act and the instrument of action—what the law is about here? Is the law a matter of making and doing or is it a letting be, even better, a letting go? Law receives you and lets you go and you are—nothing. The law itself reveals nothing and may be understood as nothing. In its relation to nothing, with nothing as its mode of relation, what if law could be thought as the tradition of destruction?

I shall begin by recalling that Jacques Derrida ends his own reading of Kafka's parable by quoting the very lines lines I just read, citing them without further comment. It would be wrong, however, to consider that Derrida has left them unread. Let me be more precise. Throughout his essay, Derrida repeatedly attends to the nothing, *rien*, that "presents itself," as it were, in Kafka's text.[16] Just as with Freud, whom he also reads, Derrida refers to an event—not an act, not a production—an event which is also "a sort of non-event, an event of nothing [*un événement de rien*] or a quasi-event which both calls for and annuls a narrative account."[17] Kafka's story, which is the story of an interrupted story, a story interrupted by the law, is also "the story of the law," which is said by Derrida to trace and mark "the looming dominance or difference in height," a difference that increasingly distinguishes between the doorkeeper and the man from the country (207). The height, the difference, grows, it "gradually alters itself to the man's disadvantage and [it] seems to measure the time of the story" (208). This difference—which is also a *différance*—marks the delay and the deferral of the law; it is what the law is and says, "a nothing that incessantly defers access to itself" (ibid.). Again and again, Derrida refers to the narrative and to the event as "an event which arrives *at* not arriving, which manages not to happen" (210). The law, in this narrative, is like the text of the law, the door of the law, which the doorkeeper famously closes. And "as he closes the object," writes Derrida, "he closes the text. Which, however, closes on nothing [*Qui pourtant ne ferme sur rien*]" (210). We find ourselves therefore before the law, "*before* this text that, saying nothing definite and presenting no identifiable content beyond the story itself, except for an endless *différance*, till death" (211). Like K., like us perhaps, the man of the country is slowly but surely brought down to his knees. He is brought to his final and definitive end.

Having alluded to the lethal—literally, annihilating—dimension of the law, Derrida does not go on to elaborate further on the death penalty, on the force of law and the violence of the law, as he would over the course of later years in books and seminars that have now been published. Here Derrida attends to the guarding and protective dimension of the law. And the gatekeeper does stand guard after all, though there are other guardians, other keepers, each more powerful than the other. Indeed, if the law, for Derrida reading Kafka, is "the nothing that forbids itself" (209), if the law is forbidden, *interdite*, it is also because the law is guarded and safeguarded (200), because it is protected (212, 214). The law enjoys "institutional protection" (214), and one could therefore surmise that the law is *différance*, yes, differed and deferred, but also *défendue*, forbidden and defended. In a formulation that anticipates what he will later have to say about autoimmunity ("L'un se garde de l'autre," is the way Derrida puts it in *Archive Fever* and in *Politics of Friendship*), Derrida explains that the law "*guards itself*, it guards itself without doing so, guarded by a doorkeeper who guards nothing, the door remaining open—and open onto nothing" (206). One might feel authorized to invoke a famous image from the Jewish tradition and suggest that the law is therefore a fence, nothing but a fence. And as we are ourselves contemplating destruction and means of destruction, guards, gates, and weapons, means and modes of execution, now may also be the moment for us to reflect on the difference—if there is one—between defense and offense, between fence and fencing, between a security fence and an offensive wall. Kafka knew something about law, and he knew something about walls and fences. He also knew something about the tradition of destruction.

Let me return, then, to destruction, and to the nothing that the law wants. Giorgio Agamben is another thinker of the law who reads the law and Kafka with and against Derrida (and Cacciari and others). Agamben is also quite explicit about joining a host of mostly Christian readers who identify the man from the country as a messianic figure. Agamben ambivalently endorses this view and insists that that messiah is a resistance fighter, that his behavior is not to be understood as the mere despairing effect of the potent delay and deferral that constitute the workings of the law. Rather, "the entire behavior of the man from the country is nothing other than a complicated and patient strategy to have the door closed in order to interrupt the law's being in force."[18]

I must admit to not being entirely convinced, but that is less important than the fact that, as he upholds the "forcelessness" of the law, Agamben himself argues for the duality (or "bi-unitary") dimension of the messianic event. He thus refers to the "true sense of the division of the single Messiah (like the single law) into two distinct figures" (174). One of these figures, Agamben also makes clear, "is a disconsolate figure who redeems nothing and whose destruction coincides with the destruction of history" (173). The reason why my agreeing or disagreeing with Agamben seemed nonetheless important to mention is that Agamben himself mentions this disconsolate figure bound for destruction in order to disagree with the role he is said to play. Still, the two figures of that Messiah which is not one do include "one which is consumed in the consummation of history, *una che si consuma con la consumazione della storia*, and the other which happens, so to speak, only the day after his arrival" (174). Consumation or consummation? This would in any case be why, against Derrida's reading, "Before the Law" would not be narrating the advent of nothing. Kafka would rather testify to the law being without force, that is, to the coming of the Messiah, the other.

It was, of course, Walter Benjamin, who, well aware that, "in every case it is a question of how life and works are organized in human society," first registered the fact that "Kafka tears open the sky behind every gesture."[19]

After Benjamin, I have been concerned with the consuming or consummating gesture, the devastating drama, whereby the man from the country comes undone at the gates, albeit not quite at the hands, of the law; the way in which he is, more precisely, destroyed, brought to the gates, to the threshold of oblivion and nothingness, annihilated by the force without force of the law, the nothing of and willed by the law. For Kafka, Benjamin also pointed out, "hammering is real hammering and at the same time nothing" (137). This may begin to account for the disagreement between Agamben and Derrida, but it also reminds us that, for Kafka, the citizen is "at the mercy of a vast machinery of officialdom."[20] Some of the "devastating processes" involved, the reality of modernity and the force of law, and "the technology of modern warfare" (hammering and nothing), were experienced by Kafka in a way that, Benjamin suggests, exceeds the capacity of any single individual (142).

> What I mean to say, explains Benjamin, is that this reality can virtually no longer be experienced by an *individual*, and that Kafka's world, frequently of such playfulness and interlaced with angels, is the exact complement of his era which is preparing to do away with the inhabitants of this planet on a considerable scale. The experience which corresponds to that of Kafka, the private individual, will probably not become accessible to the masses until such time as they are being done away with. (143)

Kafka, according to Benjamin, attends to the tradition of destruction, a tradition that can hardly be said to be simply available (it might only be so after they—we—are done away with). As the man of the country well realized, the tradition—the law—does not present itself but awaits its consumation or consummation. Or else it is the nothing that it is, which unfolds and awaits so. Understandably, then, Kafka's "gestures of terror are given scope by the marvelous *field for play, der herrliche Spielraum*, which the catastrophe will not entail."[21] I do not believe one would need much force to read this field of play along the lines of what Derrida called *différance*. But be that as it may, it too brings us back to the law and to the catastrophe, to the tradition of destruction, to which Kafka (and Benjamin too) undoubtedly attended. It has been years, centuries in the making, that is, in the unmaking. And just like K., just like the man from the country, we are thus confronted with something to which law is hardly reducible, but of which it is nevertheless an essential iteration. This law—and perhaps it is every law, but that remains to be seen—is, after all, meant only for us. And this law wants, from us, nothing more than nothing.

> Over the many years, the man observes the doorkeeper almost incessantly. He forgets the other doorkeepers and this first one seems to him the only obstacle to his admittance to the Law. He curses his unhappy fate, loudly during the first years, later, as he grows older, merely grumbling to himself. He turns childish, and since he has come to know even the fleas in the doorkeeper's collar over his years of study, he asks the fleas too to help him change the doorkeeper's mind. Finally his eyes grow dim and he no longer knows whether it's really getting darker around him or if his eyes are merely deceiving him. And yet in the darkness he now sees a radiance that streams forth inextinguishably from the door of the Law. He doesn't have much longer to live now. Before he dies, everything he has experienced over the years coalesces in his mind into a single question he has never asked the doorkeeper.[22]

At the end of his life, the man from the country is still asking after the law, asking for "the institution of life," so aptly described by Pierre Legendre. He does not realize that the law, which undoubtedly institutes and constitutes, acts and makes and regulates, the law has, by a different logic altogether, turned him to nothing. "Now his life is drawing to a close." It's not personal, even if it was always meant for him, only for him. Like many of us, he has been waiting. He has waited for nothing and it has caught up with him. The man from the country redeems nothing, and his destruction coincides with the destruction of history, its consumption or consummation. The tradition of destruction. It is as if nothing had happened, as if nothing had come to pass.

NOTES

1. Let this be the place to express my gratitude for the TTC invitation that threw us to the edge of political theology—to Catherine Keller, Andrea White, and Clayton Crockett. By suspending the term here, I by no means intend to renege on a commitment—the proliferation of words—I have honored (and for my

part, no doubt, dishonored) together with others on a number of occasions, here as well. On the edge, however, I find myself increasingly uncertain about the discursive and institutional space the phrase "political theology" has come to occupy, the conceptual and geographical realms it has been made to designate. After all, the enriching conversations I have learned from and partaken of may or may not gain from that particular heading. Toward an expansion of our imagination, and a different rhetoric, I single out, at the Drew conference, Beatrice Marovich, who generously responded and reminded me of the powers of death, and of "decreation" of the creature (on which more below); Wren Hills and his meticulous attention to catachresis; Jay Kameron Carter and his powerful reading of NourbeSe Philip's "poethics," and Catherine Keller who explained "perpetual perishing" to me, writing elsewhere that "'undoing' as ontological may mark the gentlest pulse of time, or it may mark time as crisis" (Catherine Keller, *Cloud of the Impossible: Negative Theology and Planetary Entanglement* [New York: Columbia University Press, 2015], 225). I am also grateful for questions, comments, and papers by Mary Keller, Prabhsharanbir Singh, Balbinder Bhogal, and Karen Bray.

2. Catherine Keller, *Political Theology of the Earth: Our Planetary Emergency and the Struggle for a New Public* (New York: Columbia University Press, 2018), and see Michael S. Northcott, *A Political Theology of Climate Change* (Grand Rapids, MI: William B. Eerdmans, 2013).

3. I elaborate on "Sparta and Gaza" in a lecture I gave at the Center for Middle Eastern Studies, UC Berkeley in February 2016 (www.youtube.com/watch?v=oQ_xD7YVzUg), and see lareviewofbooks.org/article/histories-of-violence-anatomy-of-destruction. To be clear though, I am obviously not arguing that we are lacking *accounts* of destruction, or that destruction has escaped our attention altogether (at TTC, Winfield Goodwin, Kelly Brown Douglas, Jay Carter, and Andrea White brilliantly demonstrated such attention). I am, however, wondering whether and how destruction has become an object of thought rather than of narration, a concept and a distinct form of power rather than an event or a destination like, say, the apocalypse (on which, see Catherine Keller's remarkable *Apocalypse Now and Then: A Feminist Guide to the End of the World* [Minneapolis: Fortress Press, 1996]).

4. The phrase "creatures of law" appears in H. L. A. Hart, *The Concept of Law* (Oxford: Oxford University Press, 1994), 5; in her response to this paper, Beatrice Marovich underscored the creaturely, and pointed me toward Simone Weil and her thought of decreation. Marovich shows the number of ways in which "destruction is genealogically bound to political theology," arguing that the law, as I describe it here, may for instance be thought along the lines of Weil's divinity. Indeed, if the divine gesture is withdrawal, absence, void, if "decreation

is the act of 'unmaking the creature in us'" (as Marovich explains elsewhere, quoting Weil), then "we become nothing *but* a creature—undone into our bare creatureliness" (Beatrice Marovich, "Simone Weil," in *Agamben's Philosophical Lineage*, ed. Adam Kotsko and Carlo Salzani [Edinburgh: Edinburgh University Press, 2017], 295; and see Beatrice Marovich, "Recreating the Creature: Weil, Agamben, Animality and the Unsaveable," in *Simone Weil and Continental Philosophy*, ed. A. Rebecca Rozelle-Stone [London: Rowman & Littlefield, 2017], 164–202). I hope to return to these suggestive arguments elsewhere.
5. Immanuel Kant, *Critique of Practical Reason*, trans. Mary Gregor (Cambridge: Cambridge University Press, 2015), ix.
6. Hans Kelsen, *The Pure Theory of Law*, trans. Max Knight (Clark, NJ: Lawbook Exchange, 2005), 4.
7. Ronald Dworkin, *Law's Empire* (Cambridge, MA: Belknap Press of Harvard University Press, 1986), vii.
8. *The Sovereignty of the Law: Selections from Blackstone's* Commentaries on the Laws of England, ed. Gareth Jones (London: Palgrave Macmillan, 1973), 27.
9. Karl N. Llewellyn, *The Bramble Bush: The Classic Lectures on the Law and Law School* (Oxford: Oxford University Press, 2008), 5.
10. Bruno Latour, *The Making of Law: An Ethnography of the Conseil d'État*, trans. Marina Brilman and Alain Pottage (Cambridge: Polity Press, 2010).
11. Robert Cover, "Foreword: *Nomos* and Narrative," *Harvard Law Review* 97, no. 4 (1983): 10.
12. Austin Sarat and Thomas R. Kearns, Introduction to *Law's Violence*, ed. Sarat and Kearns (Ann Arbor: University of Michigan Press, 1993), 3–4.
13. See Aristotle, *Categories* 15a–15b; *Topics* 114b, 124a; *On the Heavens*, 282a; and see my "Becoming Nothing" at the *Immanent Frame* (https://tif.ssrc.org/2017/11/15/becoming-nothing/).
14. Jacques Derrida, "Before the Law," trans. Avital Ronell, in *Acts of Literature*, ed. Derek Attridge (New York: Routledge, 1992), 219.
15. Franz Kafka, *The Trial* (New York: Schocken, 1974), 221–22.
16. Derrida, "Before the Law," 191.
17. Derrida, "Before the Law," 198; and further: "The law is silent, and of it nothing is said to us. Nothing . . . [*et d'elle il ne nous est rien dit. Rien . . .*]" (208); "the same madness defers the law as the nothing that forbids itself [*comme le rien qui s'interdit*]," (209); Kafka's narration thus "leads us past a portal that it comports, in internal boundary opening onto nothing, before nothing [*une limite interne n'ouvrant sur rien, devant rien*], the object of no possible experience" (212); ultimately, it is "as if nothing had happened," Derrida reiterates, "as if nothing had come to pass [*comme si rien ne se passait*]" (212).

18. Giorgio Agamben, "The Messiah and the Sovereign: The Problem of Law in Walter Benjamin," trans. Daniel Heller-Roazen, in Agamben, *Potentialities: Collected Essays in Philosophy* (Stanford, CA: Stanford University Press, 1999), 174.
19. Walter Benjamin, "Franz Kafka," trans. Harry Zohn, in Benjamin, *Illuminations*, ed. Hannah Arendt (New York: Schocken, 1968), 121–22.
20. Walter Benjamin, "Some Reflections on Kafka," trans. Harry Zohn, in Benjamin, *Illuminations*, ed. Hannah Arendt (New York: Schocken, 1968), 141; this text is extracted from a letter Benjamin wrote to Scholem in June 1938.
21. I quote this sentence from a different translation of the same letter by Manfred R. Jacobson and Evelyn M. Jacobson in *The Correspondence of Walter Benjamin*, ed. Gershom Scholem and Theodor Adorno (Chicago: University of Chicago Press, 1994), 564.
22. Kafka, *The Trial*, 214.

❦ 5. Suicide Notes
(In Remembrance of David Buckel)

WINFIELD GOODWIN

This essay offers nothing.[1] (And nothing but it, so help me God.) Despite constructive intentions, the following unfolds in the wake of a peculiar destructiveness. A species of self-destruction, to be sure—but one that is not entirely my own. And one that I, for one, cannot manage to wrestle toward meaning or some other end. Because the truth is that the kind of destructiveness I have in mind ends only in death. It sort of starts there too.

In other words, this essay takes shape as an unfinished series of suicide notes: notes on self-destruction and its politics, on the practice of suicidal protest and the literature of political theology. More restrictively, what follows is an inconclusive report on a recent protest suicide that reads political theology—the theologico-political critique of violence in particular—as a suicidal form of reflection, a thinking of self-destruction.

"I APOLOGIZE FOR THE MESS"

Just after dawn on April 14, 2018, David Buckel departed from his home in Brooklyn with a small metal shopping cart in tow and wound the way up the sloping streets of his neighborhood toward nearby Prospect Park. On a nondescript patch of grass nestled between the forested pathways, open fields, and other green spaces that form the heart of the park, Buckel stationed his cart and emptied out its principal contents: a bag filled with soil composted from biodegradable waste, two plastic jugs of gasoline. Seated on top of the small circle of soil he had spread over the surrounding ground, Buckel doused his body with the gas and set himself on fire. By the time passersby, park rangers, and emergency personnel arrived at the scene, shortly after 6 a.m., all that remained there was Buckel's charred corpse, his abandoned shopping cart, a few personal effects, and a note he had addressed to first responders.

Buckel emailed copies of this note to major news-media outlets in the moments before he set his body ablaze. "I am David Buckel and I just killed myself by fire as a protest suicide," the letter opens.[2] It continues:

> Pollution ravages our planet, oozing un-inhabitability via air, soil, water, and weather. Our present grows more desperate, our future needs more than what we've been doing. Most humans on the planet now breathe air made unhealthy by fossil fuels, and many die early deaths as a result. . . . My early death by fossil fuel reflects what we are doing to ourselves.[3]

> Privilege usually comes in some way from others' pain, whether intended or, more often, not. The pain may be from exploitation, as is often true in the making of clothes and food crops, and our choice to buy such clothing or food supports the harm to exploited humans, animals, or the Earth. That harm can live on through so many other choices we make, not just with what we wear and what we eat.[4]

> A lifetime of service may best be preserved by giving a life.[5]

> Honorable purpose in life invites honorable purchase in death.[6]

> I hope it is an honorable death that might serve others.[7]

> This is not new, as many have chosen to give a life based on the view that no other action can most meaningfully address the harm they see. . . . Here is a hope that giving a life might bring some attention to the need for expanded actions, and help others give a voice to our home, and Earth is heard.[8]

> I apologize for the mess.[9]

In life, Buckel made headlines (and history, so to speak) as a civil rights attorney and LGBTQ advocate at Lambda Legal during the 1990s and early

2000s. Recognized especially for his role in the *Brandon v. County of Richardson, Nebraska* case, Buckel was an instrumental figure in the fight to establish protections for queer persons under the law, as well as in the campaign for marriage equality. All this before he turned fifty, in 2008, and retired from legal work altogether to dedicate his time and energy to environmental organizing. (In the final years of his life, Buckel served in leadership at the NYC Compost Project at Red Hook Community Farm, the largest site in the United States that recovers and processes waste using exclusively renewable resources.)[10] In the perspective of his intimacy with the law, his vocation of institutional reform, and his legacy of activist engagement more widely, Buckel's fatal, final act appears all the more shocking, baffling even. In the end, that is, in death, Buckel made news once again but for quite different reasons than before—this time in mourning of the moving and shaking and history-making that he left undone.

By committing suicide as an act of protest, and especially by choosing fire as the element of his end, Buckel cites an extensive archive of events of "political self-destruction" from the past century, inscribing his name among the striking number of "self-immolations" that have taken place in the wake of the Vietnam War.[11] (From Saigon to Sichuan, to Sidi Bouzid and now Brooklyn, New York: *This is not new,* Buckel knew.) There is much more that should be noted about this particular form of suicide as a special type of protest, about the purported roots of the practice in "religious" rites of "sacrifice," and about the imperative to distinguish this sort of destructiveness from, say, a "suicide bombing."[12] For the time being, however, I will postpone these otherwise pressing concerns in order to dwell on the details of Buckel's deliberate self-destruction.

What is novel, distinctive, or singular about David Buckel's death appears to pertain to the purpose with and position from which he performed this act of undoing. Purpose, because Buckel's self-burning is allegedly the first act of auto-annihilation to be staged as a protest of the planet's anthropogenic destruction, the only suicidal protest to date to state (his word was *reflect*) the injustice of ecocide. And position, because Buckel is not the kind of subject that normally figures in accounts of self-burning or the politics of suicide.[13] An exceptionally capable, seemingly well, relatively wealthy, super-responsibilized, and highly accomplished whitecisgaymarriedfamilymanandallaroundgoodsamaritan—this was not "your average American." As one report puts it, Buckel was "a healthy man with a satisfying career and a loving family—a man who lived an almost saintlike life of helping others—[and who] died in a painful way in a public park . . . abruptly reducing a unique living system into ash."[14]

I walk in Prospect Park often and have taken to stopping by the site of Buckel's death, a patchy stretch of grass neighbors have since transformed into a kind of shrine. While there, I can't help but wonder what it was like for him to walk along his way that day. What it might have been like to accompany him as he spread the soil and set the fire. Whether he sat in stillness the whole time he burned, what happens to flesh and bone in flames, how long exactly such a death takes. . . . I wonder about this wondering, the strange combination of shock and awe, horror and admiration I feel for this person, his gifts, his death (and whether thinking like this makes me a monster).[15] And I wonder how one is meant to think and write from this place, whether there is any way to translate wordlessness before Buckel's "incandescent act of speech," his "terrible act of reason," into a faithful payment of respect.[16]

TOX/ECOLOGY: THE ENVIRONMENT OF SLOW DEATH

In her introduction to *The Right to Maim,* Jasbir Puar analyzes the pop-cultural rhetoric surrounding a series of "queer youth suicides" that took place during the fall of 2010.[17] Troubled by the effort of this rhetoric to repackage the lives-lost as content for a media campaign, that is, to resurrect or "recapacitate" the dead with the promise that "It Gets Better," Puar interrogates the cruel optimism on which the campaign is premised. "What kinds of slow deaths have been ongoing that a suicide might represent an escape from?" she asks alternatively.[18] Bearing in mind the specific case of Buckel's (queer) suicide, what I would like to ask after Puar is whether the language of "escape" accurately captures the line of flight enacted in the event of a suicidal protest. Could it be that Buckel's death gestures toward more than merely escape? If so, could his self-destructive protest be read instead as an engagement with the slow-goings-on that don't get better? That is, as a mode of critical encounter with the very conditions of ongoingness, survival, and endurance?

Puar borrows the phrase "slow death" from Lauren Berlant, for whom it refers to the "phenomenon of collective physical and psychic attrition from the effects of global/national regimes of capitalist structural subordination and governmentality."[19] A name for the protracted "wearing out" of persons and communities consumed with the "reproduction of predictable life," the precarious labor of living-on under conditions of neoliberalized capital, slow death describes the contemporary coincidence of "life-building" activity with the "attenuation" of livelihood itself.[20] Slow death therefore encodes the reconfiguration of matters of life and death within the historical present, their rearrangement in time and space. Temporally, the slowness of slow death defines for Berlant the becoming "durational" of death within regimes of governmentality—the fact that fatality comes to appear in the logic of biopolitics as an immanent "risk" to be managed, as an "endemic" feature of survival rather than the discrete event of life's transgression or absolute end.[21] Slow death thus consists spatially in the scale of time Berlant calls "crisis ordinariness"; it coalesces as the "temporally labile atmosphere" or "environment" of our precarious endurance.[22]

Berlant's notion of slow death captures a central element of the broader phenomenon of injury and exclusion that Puar thematizes in terms of "debility."[23] Debilitation—the production of disability, obstruction of mobility, and relative reduction "capacity"—is not a by-product, inadvertent side effect, or collaterally damaging consequence of biopower. Rather, debility is a "supplementary," and so prosthetically pivotal, aspect of sovereignty's present constitution, an attendant end or strategy of the powers of life/over death today.[24] Expressive of the mutation of sovereign prerogative from the "right to kill" into a "right to maim," debilitation (shooting to "stunt" or otherwise targeting to disable) is in fact the covert precondition of biopolitical productivity.[25] Tracking toward neither the optimal flourishing of life nor the definitive finality of death, debility occurs instead as a profoundly productive destruction in and of the living. A mode of "value extraction" from "populations that would otherwise be disposed of," debilitation proceeds through the tactical construction of certain collectives as chronically injured or incapacitated, foreclosed from resources of recognition and recovery, and thereby forcibly kept alive as-maimed.[26]

This technology of vitalizing violation ("machine of capacitation" or "ableist mechanism that debilitates") is grounded in what Puar identifies as the "geopolitics of racial ontology." [27] Debility is in other words oriented by the "racialization of bodies expected to endure pain, suffering, and injury." While the right to maim takes aim primarily at the bodies of human persons and communities, it also proceeds by violating the very place or territory a given population inhabits. In its destruction of determinate lands and infrastructures, the geopolitics of racial ontology delineates for Puar a geography of "spacio-cide," a "necropolitics of place."[28] Put otherwise, the "actuarial" techniques of biopolitics—which prop up a global network of "capital-ability" by subjecting dysselected bodies and spaces to deliberate debilitation—materialize in, as, and through "environmental racism."[29] Of course, the eco-systemic racism of "disposability" is already well documented.[30] Figured as "disposable bodies" and "rubbish peoples," racially subordinated collectives have been forcibly displaced to the front lines of anthropogenic environmental destruction, abandoned to dangerous levels of toxicity, pollution, risk, and exposure.[31] But the destructiveness of environmental racism exceeds biopolitical disposal. Rather, the racialized distribution of environmental destruction constitutes an economy, ecology, or geography of debility, an infrastructure of destructive extraction—as in the neocolonial enclosure of Black, Brown, and Indigenous collectives within Western modernity's red- and green-lined "death-worlds."

In a word, the "environment of slow death" is racist. The "atmosphere" of debility reveals itself in the effects of environmental racism. In its insidiousness—its asymmetrical though largely imperceptible sedimentation of pollution throughout space, its deferred dispersal of toxic effects in time—the "slow violence" of environmental destruction happens according to the debilitating rhythm of slow death.[32] Degrading basic infrastructures and deteriorating resources requisite to ordinary living; gradually disabling the conditions for, and contexts of, any and all potential capacity in the first place; wearing down and choking out collectives anthropic and otherwise-earthly alike, "bio-sovereign" power has shorted the planetary future and is trading on "in/human" debility in the time that remains.[33]

SLOW SUICIDE

Toward the end of their reflection on the subject of attenuated survivance, Berlant explains that

> impassivity and other politically depressed relations of alienation, coolness, detachment, or distraction, especially in subordinated populations, can be read as affective forms of engagement with the environment of slow death, much as the violence of battered women has had to be re-understood as *a kind of destruction toward survival*.[34]

They have in mind most immediately the forms of "interruptive," "lateral," or "negative" agency—the "small pleasures" of "self-abeyance" or "counter-dissipation" within the context of slow death—that are legible in activities like eating, overeating, hoarding, and otherwise holding fast to the attachments that barely keep things together anymore.[35] How might the practice of protest suicide be situated in relation to the "politically depressed relations" of impassivity, alienation, coolness, detachment, or distraction? Is it possible to read suicidal protest as an "affective form of engagement with the environment of slow death"? Or as a kind of political agency, however "lateral" or "negative"? Can Buckel's suicide be translated as a *"kind of destruction toward survival"*? And if not, could it be that his deliberate self-destruction articulates a critique of the very conditions of survival instead?

Buckel intended for his death to be without witness, the sight of his scorched flesh kept under the cover of early morning's dim light. A remarkable feature of this design is the fact that it shifts the scene of encounter with his suicide from the traumatic frame of the act itself to the traces of destructiveness left in its aftermath, away from immediate exposure to his burning body and toward things called to mind in remembrance of his remains. To encounter Buckel's self-destruction on its own terms—that is, to read it as an explicit act of protest—is to insist on the potential for suicide to encompass a kind of political engagement. To read Buckel's suicidal engagement for its politics is therefore to attend to debris, to what remains within or is released in the afterlife of his protest. What appears at stake politically in the wake of Buckel's self-destruction—in the fate of his body, of course, but also in the text of his last letter/suicide note, which situates this happening within its historical present—is expressly the environment of slow death. Slow death *as* an environment or atmosphere; the slow death of *the* environment. (*Most humans on the planet now breathe air made unhealthy by fossil fuels, and many die early deaths as a result. . . . My early death by fossil fuel reflects what we are doing to ourselves.*) Moreover, Buckel stages a spectacular, albeit short-lived, subversion of these debilitating geopolitical conditions precisely in and through the form or style of his suicide.[36]

As a form of fatality, fire gives death stubbornly and takes life slowly. In fact, it is almost always impossible to determine postmortem when and in exactly what way the dying had come to pass in flames, whether it was eventual asphyxiation or instantaneous shock to a bodily system that dealt the final blow. Whatever the case may be, it is this essential, excruciating slowness that makes self-immolation so politically potent or spectacular as a practice of protest. In an instant, self-burning draws death near at the very same time that it draws the dying out. This is thus a destructiveness that *takes time*—a death that disfigures the human body while disorienting the ordinary life of time in the process. Call it slow suicide.

To remember Buckel's slow suicide is therefore to reckon with its deformation of forms at the threshold of life and death—the figure of the body, on one hand, and, on the other, the frame of time itself. In the slowness of his self-burning, Buckel somatically speeds up the peculiarly protracted form of violence that *is* ecocide. Saturated in fossil fuel, his burning body amplifies or accelerates the slow death of the planetary ecosystem, revving the rhythms of extraction, emission, and ongoing extinction that have catalyzed catastrophic changes to Earth's climate. This temporal acceleration enacts, at the same time, a drastic reduction of space: an intensive contraction of pollution's planetary extensiveness; a sudden "consum(m)ation" or lethal condensation of environmental destruction in Buckel's flesh and bone.[37] By way of this truly monstrous "abridgement," however—this conversion of the climate of crisis ordinariness into an extraordinary instant of incineration—Buckel's protest suicide gestures toward something more complex than the onrushing destruction of Earth "alone."[38] Rather, his performance of self-destruction also signals the forms of debility and "early death" that are being dealt to marginalized communities and the places they call home slowly in the meantime.

As a suicidal engagement with the atmosphere of slow death, Buckel's self-destruction may thus be read as an embodied critique of the administration of life/apparatus of lethality that occupies this environment and capitalizes on its exhaustion—the government of environmental racism, the bio-sovereign assemblage that affords the relative privilege of capacity and exacts injury, suffering, and chronic debility according to the geopolitics of racial ontology. (Affords *by* exacting: extracts.) In other words, Buckel's suicide stages a scandalous "counter-spectacle" to the distinctively unspectacular violence of debilitation—the power that "will not let die," the force of destruction that is often occluded or normalized outright.[39] Scandalous, because Buckel's self-burning surfaces and seizes on the slow violence of debility that biopower reserves strictly for its own right. That is, through the maiming and eventual annihilation to which he subjects his own eminently capacitated body, Buckel disorients and diverts ("sabotages," perhaps) the productive-destructive forces of debility and slow death that are ordinarily mined and weaponized in relation to bodies that have been racially marked for disposal in advance.[40] The incandescent speech of Buckel's self-burning may therefore be interpreted as a final refusal to be worn out by the demands of biopolitically capacitated "life" and as a fatal divestment from this racialized economy or toxic ecology of slow death.

THEOLOGICO-POLITICAL POSTSCRIPT

Granted the variety of disciplines and dispositions that seem to gather under the heading of political theology, one thing that seems integral to this genre of thinking is an extensive critique of *Gewalt*. (Sometimes I wonder whether the literature could even be framed as an extended response to Walter Benjamin's "Zur Kritik der Gewalt.")[41] That last word is translated as violence typically, but it conveys something also of force, power, and authority, of sovereignty and governance.[42]

According to this Benjaminian trajectory, political theology has articulated a critique of state or legal *Gewalt*: the violence that is constitutive of and operative within the apparatuses of the state; the force that imposes legal order as authoritative and preserves the law as sovereign power over life. Along these lines, political theology advances a critical analysis of the powers ruled legitimate under exceptional (and increasingly normalized) circumstances, the forces justified as means toward the end of law, order, and "security." "Impure" because instrumentalized; corrosive because coercive; fateful and guilt-inducing—this is a violence understood to derive ultimately from the order of "myth."[43]

As such and at the same time, political theology has also pursued the *Gewalt* of critique itself: the "hostile" force or "counter-violence" that critical praxis should convey; the power that would "impart" itself as truly radical or revolutionary, "pure," "divine."[44] Analogous to the "proletarian general strike," this divine *Gewalt* "consummates" an "upheaval" without causing or constructing a thing; it upends attempts at justification and is itself instead the striking "manifestation" of justice in an instant—a moment of "unbinding" and "expiation" from law's mythic one-two-step of imposition and preservation, an irruption of "anarchic" freedom, the condition of a strange sort of "happiness" even.[45] "Bloodless," we are led to believe; potentially "nonviolent" but at best paradoxically so, this power or force that would be divine is a kind of violence nonetheless.[46] It offers no "way" out of, no way other than, the "medium" of destruction.[47]

Divine destructiveness is discerning though—annihilating, but "relatively" rather than absolutely so.[48] (Almost like the US military's unmanned drones, this form of violence is said to set sights on restricted zones.) As divine, it strikes first of all definitively against the *Gewalt* of myth: "deposing" the force of law and "abolishing" the power with which the state is welded together, the violence it wields for the sake of its sovereignty.[49] But this critical counter-violence appears to take aim also at a specific species of legally constituted, captured, and abandoned life in the world.[50] It destroys "mere life" for the sake of the "soul of the living," in one translation.[51] In another, it deposes the "biopolitical body of bare life" in order to elaborate the "impotentiality" of an otherwise "form-of-life," before which law would become "deactivated," over which power would be "inoperative," for which "force" would be "destituent" and "use" "profaned."[52] In the name of the divine, the critique of *Gewalt* has therefore called forth the destruction of a certain kind of subject or the negation of a certain sort of self—the death, that is, of a genre and a government of the (barely) living.[53] It signals, in so many words, that critical violence has self-destructive tendencies, that there is something to be divined in the way, in the wake, of a political suicide. (Pardon the proverbial death sentence.)

If the "destructive character" is, for Benjamin, animated by "the feeling, not that life is worth living, but that suicide is not worth the trouble," I would like to risk a bit more trouble by suggesting that suicide is indeed worth a thought.[54] (The late Benjamin may have done so too.)[55] To affirm that self-destruction reveals something about the critique of *Gewalt* is not to adjudicate on suicidal protest in general, nor is it to advocate auto-annihilation as a proper political "program."[56] (Such pursuits would be undertaken in vain, I worry. Worse, they seem to manifest a failure to do justice to this strange form of force from the start—mistaking it for means instrumental to some or another end, sacrificing its destructiveness to a higher creative purpose.) In the particular instance of David Buckel's protest suicide, self-destruction enacts political critique as a recalibration of the respective rates and rhythms of living and dying, as a shift in the scale of a destructiveness that is personal and planetary at once, a scrambling of the speed of earthly downfall in its enormity and its intimacy. Buckel's protest unto death therefore compels theoretical attention, but not to be monumentalized, martyred, or redeemed by some narrative convention or other. What demands recognition in the event of Buckel's self-burning is the manner in which suicidal protest "contravenes" the flow of time instantaneously, the way his death sabotages the normal procedures of politics- and business-as-usual.[57] After all, the critique of *Gewalt* is inseparable from a seismic or "explosive" practice of historical "remembrance." This method of remembrance "seizes" on the memories of suffering and histories of oppression that "flash up" and "flit by" within a "moment of danger" in order to "arrest" history's incessant forward march and blast open its homogeneity in the time of "real emergency" that is, or could be, "now."[58]

Here, now, in this moment of danger, I end with an echo of Buckel's parting wish: *Here is a hope that Earth is heard.*

NOTES

1. Thank you to my teachers—for everything, really, and especially for all of the patience with my nothingness.
2. J. Oliver Conroy, "A Lawyer Set Himself on Fire to Protest Climate Change. Did Anyone Care?" *Guardian*, 15 April 2019, https://www.theguardian.com/environment/2019/apr/15/david-buckel-lawyer-climate-change-protest.
3. Edward Helmore, "David Buckel: Friends Mourn LGBT Lawyer Who Self-Immolated," *Guardian*, 20 April 2018, https://www.theguardian.com/us-news/2018/apr/20/david-buckel-lgbt-lawyer-self-immolation-new-york.
4. Victoria Scrimer, "The Self-Immolation of David Buckel: Towards a Postdramatic Activism," *Critical Stages/Scènes Critiques*, no. 23 (2021), https://www.critical-stages.org/23/the-self-immolation-of-david-buckel-towards-a-postdramatic-activism/#back1.
5. Jesse Barron, "The Lives They Lived: David Buckel," *New York Times*, 27 December 2018, https://www.nytimes.com/interactive/2018/12/27/magazine/lives-they-lived-david-buckel.html.
6. Jeffrey C. Mays, "Prominent Lawyer in Fight for Gay Rights Dies after Setting Himself on Fire in Prospect Park," 14 April 2018, https://www.nytimes.com/2018/04/14/nyregion/david-buckel-dead-fire.html.
7. Maryam Zafar, "Cornell Law Alumnus Self-Immolates to Protest Destruction of the Planet," *Cornell Daily Sun*, 17 April 2018, https://cornellsun.com/2018/04/17/cornell-law-alumnus-self-immolates-to-protest-destruction-of-planet/.

8. Cleve R. Wootson Jr., "He Fought For Same-Sex Marriage for Years—And Set Himself on Fire to Protest Global Pollution," *Washington Post*, 15 April 2018, https://www.washingtonpost.com/news/post-nation/wp/2018/04/15/he-fought-for-same-sex-marriage-for-years-and-set-himself-on-fire-to-protest-global-pollution/.

9. Chris Wiley, "The Site of an Environmentalist's Deadly Act of Protest," *New Yorker*, 30 August 2019, https://www.newyorker.com/culture/photo-booth/the-site-of-an-environmentalists-deadly-act-of-protest.

10. "Compost Operation," Red Hook Farms, 17 August 2021, http://www.added-value.org/compost. "Red Hook Community Farm Compost Operation," *Brooklyn Botanical Garden*, 17 August 2021, https://www.bbg.org/gardening/red_hook_community_farm_compost_operation.

11. I place the word "self-immolation" in scare quotes here to signal hesitation about this familiar turn of phrase, specifically concerning the act of translation it already presupposes implicitly. Etymologically, immolation refers in the Latin of *immolare* to the act of "sprinkling with sacrificial meal," and later more simply to "sacrifice." In light of the intimacy asserted between sacrificial violence and the force of law, however—given, in a word, the sacrificial economy through which sovereign violence is understood to subsist in law—self-immolation seems to me an infelicitous figure of speech for reflecting faithfully on the strange form of self-destructiveness embodied in an event of suicidal protest. Therefore, in the effort to think through Buckel's death outside the terms of sacrifice and redemption, or otherwise than as a martyrology or hagiography, I have opted consequently for the more literal, more graphic, grammar of self-burning and self-destruction as consistently as possible in the following pages. (See, along these lines, Nicholas Michelsen, *Politics and Suicide: The Philosophy of Political Self-Destruction* [New York: Routledge, 2016], 57–98.) Popularly speaking, self-immolation is, of course, a common cultural translation for performances of protest suicide, and it has been so especially since 1963—when those now-infamous images of the Mahayana Buddhist monk Thích Quảng Đức's spectacular death by fire on the war-torn streets of Saigon first circulated in Western media networks. In the afterlife of Đức's auto-annihilation, a few of the most widely reported acts of political self-burning, i.e., of self-immolation as a practice of protest, have been the deaths of Jan Palach (Prague, 1968), Tapey (Sichuan/Tibet, 2009), and Mohammed Bouazizi (Sidi Bouzid, 2011). During the era of the Vietnam War, a series of self-burnings performed in protest of American militarization also occurred within the United States domestically. See note 13 for further details.

12. In addition to Michelsen, *Politics and Suicide*, see also Banu Bargu, *Starve and Immolate: The Politics of Human Weapons* (New York: Columbia University Press, 2014); Banu Bargu, "Why Did Bouazizi Burn Himself? The Politics of Fate and Fatal Politics," *Constellations* 23, no. 1 (2016): 27–36; and Talal Asad, *On Suicide Bombing* (New York: Columbia University Press, 2007).
13. Bargu's and Michelsen's respective analyses of hunger-striking and self-burning focus on "necroresistance" in non-Western/Euro-American regions, namely in Turkey, Tunisia, the former Czechoslovakia, and elsewhere in Eastern Europe, North Africa, and the Middle East. For his part, Asad's text characteristically flips the script to reveal the Christian and post-Christian West's constitutive fixation with suicidal violence, as incarnate crucially in the case of Jesus of Nazareth. (See Asad, *On Suicide Bombing*, 65–92.) Noteworthy among the relatively short list of "self-immolations" that have taken place within the United States are especially a few that took place during the course of the Vietnam War—namely, Norman Morrison (Washington, DC, 1965), Alice Herz (Detroit, 1965), and Roger LaPorte (New York City, 1965).
14. Barron, "The Lives They Lived 2018: David Buckel."
15. On the phenomenology of wonder, see Mary-Jane Rubenstein, *Strange Wonder: The Closure of Metaphysics and the Opening of Awe* (New York: Columbia University Press, 2008). On the metaphysics of monstrosity, see Mary-Jane Rubenstein, *Pantheologies: Gods, Worlds, Monsters* (New York: Columbia University Press, 2018).
16. Barron, "The Lives They Lived 2018: David Buckel"; and James Verini, "A Terrible Act of Reason: When Did Self-Immolation Become the Paramount Form of Protest?" *New Yorker*, 16 May 2012, https://www.newyorker.com/culture/culture-desk/a-terrible-act-of-reason-when-did-self-immolation-become-the-paramount-form-of-protest.
17. Jasbir Puar, *The Right to Maim: Debility, Capacity, Disability* (Durham, NC: Duke University Press, 2017), 11–16.
18. Puar, *The Right to Maim*, 11.
19. Lauren Berlant, *Cruel Optimism* (Durham, NC: Duke University Press, 2011), 95.
20. Berlant, *Cruel Optimism*, 96.
21. Puar, *The Right to Maim*, 11–12. See also Michelsen, *Politics and Suicide*, 126–62.
22. Berlant, *Cruel Optimism*, 100–101.
23. Puar, *The Right to Maim*, x, 128, 141–47.
24. Puar, *The Right to Maim*, xvii, 24, 136.
25. Puar, *The Right to Maim*, x, 143.
26. Puar, *The Right to Maim*, xviii, 136–39, 144.

27. Puar, *The Right to Maim*, xiv, xviii, 50–61.
28. Puar, *The Right to Maim*, 133–36; and Thom Davies, "Toxic Space and Time: Slow Violence, Necropolitics, and Petrochemical Pollution," *Annals of the American Association of Geographers* 108, no. 6 (2018): 1537–53. See also Elizabeth Povinelli, *Geontologies: A Requiem to Late Liberalism* (Durham, NC: Duke University Press, 2016).
29. Puar, *The Right to Maim*, xx, xv, 134. See also Ghassan Hage, *Is Racism an Environmental Threat?* (Malden, MA: Polity Press, 2017).
30. Henry Giroux, "Violence, Katrina, and the Biopolitics of Disposability," *Theory, Culture & Society* 24, nos. 7–8 (2007): 305–9.
31. "It is the 'rubbish people'—literally described as objects of disposability—whose exclusion from the imaginaries and practices of biopolitical incorporation are necessary, whose debilitation upholds the terms of cultural rehabilitation" (Puar, *The Right to Maim*, 82, quoting Raewyn Connell, "Southern Bodies and Disability: Re-thinking Concepts," *Third World Quarterly* 32, no. 8 [2011]: 1376).
32. Rob Nixon, *Slow Violence and the Environmentalism of the Poor* (Cambridge, MA: Harvard University Press, 2011).
33. On the cooperative interplay of historically distinctive apparatuses of power in contemporary "biosovereign assemblages" see Bargu, *Starve and Immolate*, 43–54, 70–77. For a conceptualization of the "inhuman" in connection explicitly with the biopolitics of debilitation see Puar, *The Right to Maim*, 146–49. On the inhuman as a crucial term of racial and geological grammars, see also Kathryn Yusoff, *A Billion Black Anthropocenes or None* (Minneapolis: University of Minnesota Press, 2018).
34. Berlant, *Cruel Optimism*, 117.
35. Berlant, *Cruel Optimism*, 100, 114–17, 285n66.
36. "The weaponization of life, understood as a form of expression, also invites us to complicate our understanding of violence by restoring an independent role to *form* as having distinctive qualities, certain political and ethical effects of its own. I find Benjamin's interpretation of violence illuminating in order to conceive of the weaponization of life as a particular form of violence whose technique of self-destruction renders it not only expressive of a content but also with specific implications of its own. . . . Following his thought, we may think of the weaponization of life not only as the political expression of passions (such as rage) but also as articulating, in its very form, a similar aporia: the desire and call for justice and, at the same time, the recognition of the impossibility of its realization under the political conditions in which these violent performances take place" (Bargu, *Starve and Immolate*, 17–18).

37. "Our hyperactive vocabulary leaves little room to dwell on destruction and termination, on disintegration or corruption, desolation and demolition, ruination and putrefaction, consumption and consumation (with one 'm,' though consummation is implied), devastation or annihilation" (Anidjar, "Becoming Nothing").
38. Walter Benjamin, "Theses on the Philosophy of History," in *Illuminations: Essays and Reflections*, trans. Harry Zohn, ed. Hannah Arendt (New York: Schocken Books, 2007), 263; Giorgio Agamben, *The Time That Remains: A Commentary on the Letter to the Romans*, trans. Patricia Dailey (Stanford, CA: Stanford University Press, 2005), 142–45; Keller, *Political Theology of the Earth*, 133; and Berlant, *Cruel Optimism*, 10, 117, 169.
39. Bargu, *Starve and Immolate*, 349–50.
40. "Sabotage" is a term with an interesting history, which I learned from Mitchell, *Carbon Democracy*, 21–27. The word was initially coined in a 1909 publication by Émile Pouget to describe the methods of striking used by Scottish dockworkers, French railwaymen, and German coal miners in their demand for livable labor conditions within the increasingly industrialized—and carbonized—Europe of the turn of the twentieth century. These methods consisted in "the slow-down, the work-to-rule and other means of interrupting the normal functioning of a critical process" through "foot-dragging" and otherwise frustrating the processes of coal extraction, refinery, and distribution. The premise of these methods was for the laborers to "work as slowly and clumsily as the unskilled men brought in to replace them," and—withholding their skill and expertise, their *capacities*, in and as a refusal of productive expectation—to thereby exert demands on states and markets in the interest of democratic and egalitarian political and economic arrangements. Over the course of the intervening century, "sabotage" has been co-opted for use as a term to describe strategies of statecraft and warfare. Nevertheless, its original connection with carbon-based industries, labor organizing, and practices of protest centered on *slowing things down* strikes me as peculiarly pertinent to this reflection on Buckel's slow suicide. I am mindful here not only of Walter Benjamin's conceptualization of divine violence as analogous to the "proletarian general strike" but also of Lauren Berlant's attention to forms of "slow living" as modes of resistance to the forces of "slow death." In a footnote referencing the slow-food movement as an example of such nonsovereign counter-living, Berlant writes, "Along with its critique of neoliberal agricultural policies, [this movement] translates *the impulsive improvisation around recalibrating the pacing of the day into a collective program for deliberative being in the world in a way opposed to the immediatist productive one of anxious*

capital" (Berlant, *Cruel Optimism*, 285n64). See also Berlant's extended discussion of related practices in collective and anarchist forms of "ambient citizenship" and "juxtapolitical engagement" in "On the Desire for the Political," chap. 7 of *Cruel Optimism*.

41. Walter Benjamin, "Critique of Violence," in *Reflections: Essays, Aphorisms, Autobiographical Writings*, trans. Edmund Jephcott, ed. Peter Demetz (New York: Schocken Books, 2007), 277–300. For a few crucial instances of commentary on Benjamin's cryptic critique see Jacques Derrida, "Force of Law: The 'Mystical Foundation of Authority'" (1991), in *Acts of Religion*, ed. Gil Anidjar (New York: Routledge, 2002), 228–98; Giorgio Agamben, "On the Limits of Violence" (1970), in *Towards the Critique of Violence: Walter Benjamin and Giorgio Agamben*, ed. Brendan Moran and Carlo Salzani (New York: Bloomsbury, 2015), 231–38; Giorgio Agamben, "Threshold," in *Homo Sacer: Sovereign Power and Bare Life*, trans. Daniel Heller-Roazen (Stanford, CA: Stanford University Press, 1995), 63–70; Judith Butler, "Walter Benjamin and the Critique of Violence," in *Parting Ways: Jewishness and the Critique of Zionism* (New York: Columbia University Press, 2012), 69–98; and Werner Hamacher, "Afformative, Strike," trans. Dana Hollander, *Cardozo Law Review* 13 (1991–92): 1133–57. I am aware that in this formulation of "political theology" I have failed to address what is perhaps its foremost point of reference: the work of Carl Schmitt. However, I privilege Benjamin's critique of *Gewalt* here for the sake of focusing discussion on modes of destructiveness that manifest a resistance to the violent force of law and to the supposedly sacrosanct status of a life captured in sovereignty's legal ban.

42. Gil Anidjar, "Becoming Nothing," *The Immanent Frame: Secularism, Religion, and the Public Sphere*, 15 November 2017, https://tif.ssrc.org/2017/11/15/becoming-nothing/. See also "Histories of Violence: Anatomy of Destruction—Brad Evans Interviews Gil Anidjar," *Los Angeles Review of Books*, 17 September 2018, https://lareviewofbooks.org/article/histories-of-violence-anatomy-of-destruction/#!; Anidjar, "Weapons (Inscription, Destruction, Deconstruction)," *Political Theology* 19, no. 2 (2018): 95–104; and Anidjar, "On the Political History of Destruction," *ReOrient* 4, no. 2 (2019): 144–65.

43. Benjamin, "Critique of Violence," 290, 294–97.

44. Benjamin, "Critique of Violence," 300; Agamben, "Threshold," 63; Butler, "Walter Benjamin and the Critique of Violence," 85.

45. Benjamin, "Critique of Violence," 281–82, 291–93, 297; Butler, "Walter Benjamin and the Critique of Violence," 73, 84, 88–89, 90–92.

46. Benjamin, "Critique of Violence," 291, 297; Butler, "Walter Benjamin and the Critique of Violence," 77–80. Or is it exactly? What distinguishes destruction

from violence? And how might such a distinction complicate consideration of divine *Gewalt*?
47. Anidjar, "Becoming Nothing."
48. Benjamin, "Critique of Violence," 297–98.
49. Benjamin, "Critique of Violence," 291, 300; Agamben, "Threshold," 63–65; Butler, "Walter Benjamin and the Critique of Violence," 79, 85.
50. Benjamin, "Critique of Violence," 297–99.
51. Butler, "Walter Benjamin and the Critique of Violence," 83–91. The "living soul" is, in Butler's rendering of Benjamin's "Critique," composed only of a "sacred transience," an eternally recurrent rhythm of "downfall."
52. Agamben, "On the Limits of Violence," 236–37; and Agamben, *Homo Sacer*, 187–88. On "deactivation" see Giorgio Agamben, *State of Exception*, trans. Kevin Attell (Stanford, CA: Stanford University Press, 2005), 64. On "inoperativity" see Agamben, *Homo Sacer*, 60–62. On "destituency" see Giorgio Agamben, "For a Theory of Destituent Power," public lecture in Athens, 16 November 2013, *Chronos* 10 (2014): http://www.chronosmag.eu/index.php/g-agamben-for-a-theory-of-destituent-power.html. On "profanation" see Giorgio Agamben, *Profanations*, trans. Jeff Fort (New York: Zone Books of the MIT Press, 2007). See also studies of the "forms-of-life" manifest historically in monastic and messianic communities: Agamben, *The Time That Remains*; Giorgio Agamben, *The Highest Poverty: Monastic Rules and Form-of-Life*, trans. Adam Kotsko (Stanford, CA: Stanford University Press, 2013); Giorgio Agamben, *The Use of Bodies*, trans. Adam Kotsko (Stanford, CA: Stanford University Press, 2014).
53. On Agamben's interest in a particularly Pauline "death of the self," placed in dialogue with Foucault's later writings on the technology of dispossession immanent within Christian practices of asceticism see Colby Dickinson, "With Which Political Theology Are We Dealing? Reassessing the Genealogy of Political Theology and Looking Toward Its Future," *Praktyka teoretyczna* 3, no. 17 (2015): 123–42.
54. Walter Benjamin, "The Destructive Character," *Punkto* 2011, https://www.revistapunkto.com/2011/12/destructive-character-walter-benjamin.html.
55. Michael Taussig, *Walter Benjamin's Grave* (Chicago: University of Chicago Press, 2006).
56. On the aporetic coincidence of an instrumentalization *and* abolishment of instrumental rationality in the violence of suicidal resistance see Bargu, *Starve and Immolate*, 16–17; and, "Why Did Bouazizi Burn Himself?" 33–34.
57. Butler, "Walter Benjamin and the Critique of Violence," 91–92.

58. Benjamin, "Theses on the Philosophy of History," 255. See also Judith Butler, "Flashing Up," in *Parting Ways: Jewishness and the Critique of Zionism* (New York: Columbia University Press, 2012), 102, 104, 105, 111, 113. Reflecting on Benjamin's historical practice, Butler writes, "Remembrance attends to the way that history acts now as well as to what opens up within that reiterated history to reclaim the history of the oppressed. The measure of a life is the way that history continues to act in the present, which means, of course, that the presence of those contingent moments accumulate, chances or wagers, flash upon flash, a struggle for the past which is the only way to transform the present. . . . Somebody's memory is interrupting someone else's march forward, and perhaps this happens precisely because something of that suffering over there resonates with the one over here, and everything stops. Remembrance may be nothing more than struggling against amnesia in order to find those forms of coexistence opened up by convergent and resonant histories. Perhaps for this we still do not have the precise name" (Butler, "Flashing Up," 113).

6. Catachresis in the Margins: Notes on Theologico-Political Method

LAWRENCE E. HILLIS

What then is truth? A mobile army of metaphors, metonymies, anthropomorphisms: in short, a sum of human relations which became poetically and rhetorically intensified, metamorphosed, adorned, and after long usage, seem to a nation fixed, canonic, and binding; truths are illusions of which one has forgotten that they are illusions; worn-out metaphors which have become powerless to affect the senses, coins which have their obverse effaced and now are no longer of account as coins but merely as metal.
—FRIEDRICH NIETZSCHE, "On Truth and Falsity in Their Ultramoral Sense"

In the opening remarks of a waylaid lecture, Giorgio Agamben is said to have illuminated the impulse for the persistent primacy of law and theology throughout his colossal *Homo Sacer* project. "A first answer," he confessed, "which is obviously a joke—but every joke has a serious core—would be because these are the only two fields in which Michel Foucault did not work."[1] If one is to take the anecdote seriously, for Agamben, and those inclined to trace the postmodern emergence and amplification of political theology through him, the paradigm of the discourse's contemporary iteration can be presented, in part, as an extension of Foucault's genealogical critique of power into these domains. This is not to suggest that Foucault was oblivious to the raw *Gewalt* of the state—as some in the Marxist tradition would perhaps accuse him—but, rather, that his nascent methodology required a tactical suspension of the theologico-political for the sake of developing an alternative, "strategical model, rather than the model based on law."² Though the State certainly exerts a significant "prohibitionary force" on "a whole series of power networks that invest the body, sexuality, the family, kinship, knowledge, technology and so forth," Foucault deemed such an alternative analysis necessary since the meta-power of the State cannot adequately account for the dynamic and indeterminate network of power relations that are the "necessary basis for the great negative forms of power"; and in which the fullness of State violence is ultimately realized.³

Less an omission than an elision, Foucault's *performative silence* along these lines consists in a decentering of the macropolitical in favor of the peripheral and the capillary—those sanguine edges where the field of force relations is simultaneously most brutal and most exposed. "In this way," Foucault posited, "we will escape from the system of Law-and-Sovereign which has captivated political thought for such a long time."⁴ Nevertheless, one would be hard-pressed to describe the advent of the twenty-first century as the culmination of this expected epistemic emancipation. Something is rotten in the State of Democracy, and it becomes increasingly difficult to tell if the Prince's madness is feigned: The social (de)marginalization of racism, antisemitism, and Islamophobia; the structural reinvigoration of misogyny, homophobia, and misopedia; the reappearance of fascism and the compounding global climate crisis; the growing glut and gluttony of autocrats and oligarchs—all constellations point to the ongoing captivity of political thought in the West.

As a (de)constructive response to the eschatological failure of the Hegelian "end of history," political theology in the Continental style constitutes a *critical return* to the analysis of arterial power. Unfortunately, however, continuity with the insights of Foucault and his contemporaries has not always been maintained in the commendable alacrity to address pressing political issues. As Vincent Lloyd has observed, at times "the novelty of 'political theology' allows it to be deployed without worrying about the genealogical criticisms that have been leveled against the categories of religion and politics."⁵ However, in its more robust texts, the discourse offers the promise of an alternative hermeneutic: a mode of genealogical analysis that seeks to unveil and deconstruct the preconceptual inheritance of religion and politics through an investigation of their entangled theoretical practices—theology and law.⁶ This hereditary relationship becomes discernible not only in the resonances that emerge across their imbricated *praxis* and *liturgia* but also, and perhaps more perniciously, through the discursive-epistemic horizons which "they" selectively yet anonymously instate, displace, safeguard, and exploit to divide and circumscribe the power-knowledge assemblages available to the body politic. Supplemented by Jacques Derrida's reflections on violence and semiotics, it would seem that one cannot truly address, or be addressed by, the *avenir* of justice until this preconceptual inheritance is accounted for.[7]

Accordingly, multiple essayists who have addressed the fragmentary theologico-political problem in recent years have begun to implement a *way of seeing* that performs not only a critique of modernity and secularism but paradoxically, "secular criticism, attentive to text and context, ever vigilant of ideologically inflected concepts, the friction between text and ideology exposing both—that is, making both vulnerable."[8] In doing so, they have begun to identify and articulate how particular icons and figures, long lodged in the archives of history and discourse, *function* to generate the distinctions and divisions through which law and theology manifest the conceptual and affective worlds in which the West lives, moves, kills, and has its being.[9] This chapter seeks to identify, elucidate, and elaborate this method by tracing its polyphonic crystallization across the work of multiple influential scholars within the discourse. It remains to be seen if, by expounding this innovative process, we might divine new ways to disrupt and deactivate the system of Law-and-Sovereign that continues to hold our collective political imagination captive.[10]

THEOLOGICO-POLITICAL SIGNATURES

> One stands back in relation to this manifest set of concepts; and one tries to determine according to what schemata (of series, simultaneous groupings, linear or reciprocal modification) the statements may be linked to one another in a type of discourse; one tries in this way to discover how the recurrent elements of statements can reappear, dissociate, recompose, gain in extension or determination, be taken up into new logical structures, acquire, on the other hand, new semantic contents, and constitute partial organizations among themselves. . . . Such an analysis, then, concerns, at a kind of preconceptual level, the field in which concepts can coexist and the rules to which this field is subjected.
>
> —MICHEL FOUCAULT, *The Archaeology of Knowledge*, 60

To present political theology as a genealogical critique of power in the discourses of law and theology is to foreground and scrutinize the synchronic and diachronic displacement of the significant concepts each utilizes in the apprehension and distribution of *auctoritas*, *potestas*, and ultimately, *violencia*. Identifying his method as *philosophical archaeology*, Agamben has employed a Foucauldian historiography to show how specific figures, perceptible from antiquity to the present moment, reveal the presence-absence of a hidden yet ubiquitous paradigm. His most well-known text traces the tortured figure of *homo sacer*—the "sacred man" who may be killed but not sacrificed—in order to show how the distinction between bare life and political life (*bios/zoē*) undergirds the biopolitical. In doing so, he sought to reveal the "sovereign exception" to be the structuring principle of law (and, presumably, theology) through which "the camp," and thereby both the Holocaust and the subsequent proliferation of refugee camps, might be rendered intelligible as the paradigm of modernity.[11] Subsequent works within that series have followed a similar trajectory by silhouetting various other icons that sleep in the archive, significantly advancing the argument in the incisive text *The Kingdom and the Glory* wherein Agamben attempts to demonstrate the historical and liturgical centrality of economy (*oikonomia*) and glory (*kabhod*). Announcing the necessity of developing an "economic theology," that manuscript asserts that by "bringing these questions back to their theological dimension" in the Trinitarian doctrine, one might be able to "catch a glimpse of something like the ultimate structure of the governmental machine of the West."[12]

That enigmatic paradigm, which Agamben attributes to the reciprocal oscillation of the ontic and ontological contours of the Trinity in orthodox Christian doctrine, becomes discernible as *glory*: "the place where theology attempts to think the difficult conciliation between immanent trinity and economic trinity, *theologia* and *oikonomia*, being and praxis, God in himself and God for us."[13] For both religious and political collectives, glory performatively obscures the cohesion of transcendental values with an immanent ordering of the world by negotiating and authorizing the terms (both constitutional and linguistic) through which those seemingly irreconcilable spheres coincide. Incidentally, though Agamben does not explicitly note the connection, this line of argumentation was prefigured by Carl Schmitt as "the problem of sovereignty" in the often overlooked second chapter of *Political Theology*, where he declared:

Every legal thought brings a legal idea, which in its purity can never become reality, into another aggregate condition and adds an element that cannot be derived either from the content of the legal idea or from the content of a general positive legal norm that is to be applied. . . . Looked at normatively, the decision emanates from nothingness.[14]

Which is to say, as Walter Benjamin riposted in his *Critique of Violence*, in its constitution and preservation Law includes a covert metaphysical-mythical operation at its core.[15] This never-neutral mediation of the relationship between living beings and the *logos*, especially as it takes its form in the politicization of bare life in the biopolitics of modernity, is, as Agamben argues early on in *Homo Sacer*, "the metaphysical task *par excellence.*"[16]

However, both *Homo Sacer* and *The Kingdom and the Glory* take Schmitt's formulations a step further by insisting that the resulting "theo-doxological machine" is not merely a regrettable remnant of individual legal decisions. Instead, Agamben argues, the entirety of Western ontology revolves or resonates around a fundamental lacuna traceable at least as far back as Aristotle's *Categories*—though, in good Derridean fashion he would not suggest that it originated there.[17] Tracing this genealogy of sovereign power, Agamben suggests that glory functions as "the secret point of contact through which theology and politics continuously communicate and exchange parts with one another."[18] However, the exact nature of this exchange remains intractably opaque and thereby troubles the clear definitions and distinctions that Schmitt made use of in his proto-structuralist analysis of secularization.

Following an insight of Thomas Mann, Agamben ultimately concludes that these complex translations between politics and theology are only possible because "underneath the garments there are no body and no substance." "Theology and politics," he goes on, "are, in this sense, what results from the exchange and from the movement of something like an absolute garment that, as such, has decisive juridical-political implications."[19] Consequently, despite its critical importance to the operation of imperial power, glory remains "nothing but the splendor that emanates from this emptiness, the inexhaustible *kabhod* that at once reveals and veils the central vacuity of the machine."[20] Glory is nothing: no-thing. Not truly a concept proper, but a *signature*, which, in the course of designating secularization as such, Agamben describes as:

Something that in a sign or concept marks and exceeds such a sign or concept referring it back to a determinate interpretation or field, without for this reason leaving the semiotic to constitute a new meaning or a new concept. Signatures move and displace concepts and signs from one field to another without redefining them semantically.[21]

Nevertheless, despite its lack of formal content or stable signification, glory is not devoid of material significance. More than an abstract linguistic phenomenon, glory (and, as we will soon see, blood) is a "signature [*segnatura*] that marks bodies and substances politically and theologically, that orientates and displaces them according to an economy that we are only now beginning to glimpse."[22] Though the discursive figures under interrogation have been erased and effaced by time and circulation, it seems that their hidden vestige—in collusion with the *arcanum imperii*—continues to classify and manipulate bodies, both corporeal and political. Signatures participate, one might say, in an *affective economy* that is central to the operation of the biopolitical, and, one must assume, the biotheological.[23]

Gil Anidjar has also brought considerable resources to bear on this discursive-affective economy with his monograph, *Blood: A Critique of Christianity*. Considering an extensive array of historical and literary sources, Anidjar investigates how blood emerges as "a mark, a citation, and a repetition" that Christianity—signifying the historical operations of Western European Christendom and its modern incarnations as secularism, globalization, and Orientalism (among others)—has left on the world.[24] A constitutive facet of modernity's historical inheritance, it seems that wherever one turns, blood suffuses the conceptual frameworks of the West, making/marking meaning and delimiting the relation and duration of the syntagms that operate within these semiotic networks. However, this crimson trace should not be mistaken for the physiological substance itself (though sometimes it *is* that, but always also more). Anidjar outlines what blood is *not* in his prefatory remarks,

> Blood is not found here as an object, nor is it a subject. It is neither a thing nor an idea. And blood is not a concept. It is not an operator, neither actor nor agent. Blood mobilizes and condenses, it singles out and constitutes, a shifting *perspective* (ebbing and flowing, later circulating) like one of those images and forms—elements, again, or complexes of culture—that fills the material imagination.[25]

In this sense, like glory, and by his own admission, blood functions as a signature that, without having specific content or clearly delimited contours *itself*, persists and permeates by marking, classifying, and categorizing other(ed) bodies. Without seeking to suggest that they are the same, we might draw these analyses into extreme proximity by counterfeiting a plagiarization of Agamben in order to present blood as "nothing but the [sanguinity] that [flows] from this emptiness, the inexhaustible [*Blutgewalt*] that at once reveals and veils the central vacuity of the machine."[26]

The impressionistic portrait that these theologico-political genealogies confront us with is far more complex and lively than the still lifes typical of "religion and politics"—an association between two artificially sequestered fields which have been quarantined, presumably for the health of both, in compliance with the secular principle. However, the common intention that runs through the works of Anidjar and Agamben is not reducible to a simplistic denunciation of this sort of secularism, though its apparition is certainly a common target of reproach.[27] Instead, leaning on Foucault's *Archaeology of Knowledge*, it would seem that both of these critical inquiries are principally concerned with mapping the *preconceptual level*, which, in itself, can never be represented coherently as a set of stable concepts. Instead, it might be best intuited through an apophatic-archaeological method as something like a negative field that, "instead of outlining a horizon that rises from the depths of history and maintains itself through history," can be described "at the most 'superficial' level (at the level of discourse), [as] the group of rules that in fact operate within it."[28]

To carry the impressionist metaphor through, the pursuit of the signature would be less concerned with, say, the autograph on *"Impression, soleil levant,"* than with the complex ways in which Claude Monet's hazy brushstrokes serve as a paradigm for the aesthetic intuitions of his time. Marks that serve as a cipher for the subtle ways in which radically contingent conceptual frameworks mediated the artist's apprehension of the natural world—itself a construction of what is, in fact, considered "natural." In this sense, signatures materialize as the disparate and dispersed elements of discourse that reveal the schemata of the preconceptual field from which emerges, according to Foucault,

> discursive regularities and constraints that have made possible the heterogeneous multiplicity of concepts, and, beyond these the

profusion of the themes, beliefs, and representations with which one usually deals when one is writing the history of ideas.[29]

Consequently, both Agamben and Anidjar are less preoccupied with defining the content of these empty signatures—blood and glory—but instead proceed by showing how these liminal figures *function* to generate the very distinctions by which other conceptual assemblages, and thereby networks of power-knowledge, become intelligible and corporeally operative. If we could properly name these texts as representative of a broader methodological style or animating interest within the discourse of political theology, without thereby negating the generative fragmentation of the discourse as a whole, then we might provisionally call it *preconceptual critique*.[30]

CHRESIS AND CATACHRESIS

Whereas at the genesis of Anidjar's remarkable text, blood had been presented as a signature utilizing Agamben's lexicon, by its final revelation a vital transformation has occurred in which blood is transubstantiated into Derridean terminology as a *catachrestic concept*. The languid ink of the penultimate page trickles over and bleeds out at last:

> There is nothing natural about blood, and the confusion as to its literal or figurative status (a key site of difference "between bloods"), its physiologic or theological existence, is crucial to understand Christianity, to consider and reflect upon it. . . . Blood is not quite an object, not a thing either. It is neither old nor new; although it is also that and more. Nor is blood a discourse that would regiment, precisely, the course of blood through the realms of human and inhuman existence. . . . As a "metaphor" that does not relate to a literal term, whose referent is anything but granted, blood is, it should be treated as, *catachrestic*.[31]

Despite the monstrous abridgment incurred by skipping directly from the preface to the final page, this act of translation cannot be overlooked (in part because Anidjar himself has designated translation as his method) as the apposition of *signature* and *catachresis* calls the relationship between these two highly technical terms into question. Are they equivalent? Perhaps a new set of nonsynonymous substitutions? Do they gesture toward an identical, unnameable, referent? In what way do they leave their mark on discourse? In what manner do they order and displace bodies—and bodies of meaning? That is to say, how is it that these indistinct terms bridge the breach between the linguistic and the nonlinguistic, the philological and the affective?

The conventional etymology of catachresis traces it to the ancient Greek *katakhresis* [κατάχρησις] (to misuse), which is a combination of *kata-* meaning "down"—which carries a strong sense of "perversion"—and *kresthai* "to use," which also carries valences of "to need."[32] The resulting tension between "rhetorical abuse" and "necessary use" inflected into the very heart of the term prefigures the oppositional, yet commonly self-contradictory, linguistic traditions that name catachresis as either the progenitor of all language or its most notorious vagabond.[33] A member of the former category, Marcus Fabius Quintilian, whose *Institutio Oratoria* (95 CE) had a profound impact on Augustine of Hippo, Martin Luther, Erasmus, and Jacques Derrida, defined catachresis (*abusio* in Latin) as "the practice of adapting the nearest available term to describe something for which no actual [i.e., proper] term exists."[34] However, even in this concise definition, the aporetic necessity that initially distinguishes catachresis from metaphor [*translatio*] breaks down almost immediately as Quintilian proceeds: "As for poets, they indulge in the abuse of words even in cases where proper terms do exist, and substitute words of somewhat similar meaning."[35] This cognitive drift and the rhetorical enigma it reveals have subsisted throughout the history of linguistics, with various philosophers assigning a different role and import to the rhetorical device.

In contemporary usage, catachresis is defined most succinctly within Gayatri Chakravorty Spivak's postcolonial apparatus as "a concept-metaphor without adequate referent," and names a particular form of semiotic violence that functions as a core element of colonialism: the production of subalternity through the forcible imposition of the imperial grammatological framework. According to her account, however, breaking open the catachrestic nature of these idiomatic concepts gives rise to a new mode of parodic resistance in a "process by which the colonized take and reinscribe something that exists traditionally as a feature of imperial culture."[36] In these entangled modes, Spivak typically applies the term to such concepts as "nationhood, constitutionality, citizenship, and democracy, all of which are coded within the legacy of imperialism, and hence lack adequate referents in a non-Western context."[37] From this perspective, the Derridean morphology at work in the identification of catachrestic imperial concept-metaphors seems to coincide with Agamben's investigation of the "empty machine" that lies dormant within Western theo-ontology, and the economy of violence it sustains.[38] Common to both trajectories, it seems that only an interrogation of discursive misuse can point the way to one of the central problems of political theology: the identification of the effaced means by which a tradition or culture generates, names, and utilizes its reserve of significant theologico-political concepts in the discourses of power.[39] After all, within Derrida's analysis of the *Phaedrus*, the Schmittian "monopoly to decide" that distinguishes the "essence of the state's sovereignty" would seem to first appear through the codification of *logos* itself through the suppression of *tokos*.[40]

The collision of these two distinct methods manifests most clearly in the ninth, and final, volume of the *Homo Sacer* series, *The Use of Bodies*. There, in a serendipitous coincidence, Agamben dedicates a short chapter to a philological analysis of *chresis/chresthai* that troubles the conventional translation of the term offered above as "to use" or "utilization." Following the work of one of Émile Benveniste's students, Georges Redard, he argues that in classical Hellenistic culture and philosophy chresis belonged to a class of "oracular words" and "does not seem to have a proper meaning but acquires ever different meanings according to the context."[41] In this mode, chresis functioned in the "middle voice" (*mesotes*) to denote a "zone of indetermination between subject and object" wherein "the agent is in some way also object and place of action" and thereby also reciprocally affected by the relationship.[42] It is in this way that *chresthai theoi* can mean "to consult an oracle" (as opposed to "to make use of the gods") and *chresthai te polei* can mean "to participate in political life" (as opposed to "to make use of the city").[43] Reflecting on the anachronistic reduction of the concept at work in contemporary translations, Agamben hypothesizes that the modern conception of "use" is itself a "fundamental political category" that emerges from the juridico-religious sphere.[44] Such an insight is helpful in elucidating Derrida's poststructural development of catachresis, as it no longer, *pace* Quintilian, indicates the simple application of an improper term. Rather, catachresis implicitly calls into question the metaphysics operative within Western philosophy that authorizes the "proper use" of language (and of bodies), through the capture and suppression through inclusive-exclusion (ex-ceptio) of the inexhaustible polysemy of language.

The connection between chresis, catachresis, and imperial power is immediately apparent from the outset of Agamben's political philosophy, as he consistently traces the paradigm of the "state of exception" back to the experience of language itself. Developing the connection early on in *Homo Sacer*, he writes:

> Language is the sovereign who, in a permanent state of exception, *declares* that there is nothing outside language and that language is always beyond itself. The particular structure of law has its foundation in this presuppositional structure of human language. It expresses the bond of inclusive exclusion to which a thing is subject because of the fact of being in language, of being named. To speak [*dire*] is, in this sense, always to "speak the law," *ius dicere*.[45]

Even here, though, the sovereignty of language and law cannot be separated from the domains of religion and theology. As Agamben notes later on in *The Use of Bodies*, the "epochal change in the ontology of the West" that produced modern subjecthood and the retroactive erasure of "oracular" chresis crystallized during the codification of Trinitarian theology and the emergence of the theory of hypostases used in the theo-ontological deification of Christ.[46] From there, this new orientation toward being, use, and action proliferated beyond the enclaves of the erudite through sacramental theology and the celebration of the mass, which "presents us with something that is inseparable from the sign yet irreducible to it, a character or signature that by persisting in a sign makes it efficacious and capable of action."[47] Returning to Anidjar thus equipped, we can see how the theo-ontological apparatus that rendered the blood of Christ of *use* for salvation is precisely what later enabled the juridical-ontic production of "a newfound distinction between bloods."[48]

CATACHRESTIC VIOLENCE

All the exemplary figures of the violence of law are singular metonymies, namely, figures without limit, unfettered possibilities of transposition and figures without figures.
—JACQUES DERRIDA, "Force of Law: The Mystical Foundation of Authority"

In a prescient paper presented to the European Graduate School in August of 2016, Judith Butler embarked on an extensive exegesis of the linguistic distinction between violence and nonviolence. Inspired by a series of tragic incidents that had recently shocked the West (the Gezi Park massacre being iconic in this regard), Butler struggled even to begin her ruminations as the nature of the skirmishes exposed a fundamental problem encountered when "approaching violence":

> One seeks to grab hold of the definition only to find that one has been seized instead by a framework which makes possible the stabilization of the definition itself. Indeed, it is not only that one form of violence shapeshifts into another, but the very distinction between violence and nonviolence can invert, calling into question the stability of the distinction.[49]

By her account, this enigmatic instability appears to be an elemental characteristic of the relationship between violence and law. Nonviolence names the force sanctioned by law, yet, when the law itself is that which has been declared violent—principally through an indictment of its incarnations (such as the police)—then the legitimacy of the law is called into question. However, it is a question that never seems to reach a just verdict; a phenomenon materially manifested in the perennial incapacity of courts to find officers of the law guilty of the wrongful use of force—even in documented cases in which a disavowal of homicide appears inarguable.[50]

The resiliency of this inversion, Derrida seemed to suggest in his essay "Force of Law: The Mystical Foundation of Authority," is animated by the *performative tautology* of legitimacy and law, which "structures any foundation of the law upon which one performatively produces the conventions that guarantee the validity of the performative thanks to which one gives oneself the means to decide between legal and illegal violence."[51] The law is legitimate because "legitimacy" signifies a state of normative standing before the law. Such standing before the law is normative only as a condition of the original legitimacy of the law. The legitimacy of the law is the law of legitimacy—the allusion to supposedly antiquated codes of inheritance proving meaningful wherein nonviolence plays the bastard child, legally unrecognized by the "father" and thus with no standing before the law.

In this sense, it would seem that the performative tautology constitutes a structural naming practice that extends the authority to sanction violence indefinitely, while simultaneously effacing how, as the Nietzschean epigraph presented the issue, such a relationship came to be "poetically and rhetorically intensified." By Walter Benjamin's account, the result is characteristic of constabulary force: a suspension of the distinction between law-constituting and law-preserving violence in which it is no longer possible to distinguish between the breaking and making of law.[52] Similar to Agamben's elucidation of the sovereign exception, one is accosted by a maddening Möbius strip whose singular face and sharpened edge loop infinitely in and out of discursive intelligibility. Consequently, nearing the close of her remarks, the inexorable oscillation between these epistemological grammars forced Butler to throw up her hands in resignation and opine that we had entered into the domain of "a sort of catachresis," wherein, "it would seem that we've passed into another language where names, or the sound of the name, no longer refers in one way."[53]

Taken together, these complex investigations of the role of language in the production and legitimization of violence provide multiple approaches to the *triton genos* that seized Derrida's attention in the third essay of *Sauf le Nom*, "Khōra." There, in exploring the playful abuse of words in Plato's creation narrative, he observed,

> Almost all the interpreters of the *Timaeus* gamble here on the resources of rhetoric without ever wondering about them. They speak tranquilly about metaphors, images, similes. They ask themselves no questions about this tradition of rhetoric which places at their disposal a reserve of concepts which are very useful but which are all built upon this distinction between the sensible and the intelligible, which is precisely what the thought of the *khōra* can no longer get along with.[54]

According to Derrida, it seems that in his inability to provide an intelligible name for that which he was attempting to describe, Plato whimsically substituted a term that, while not precisely a functional metaphor, constitutes something like a generative *linguistic gesture*. Only in this negative capacity does *khōra* function as the "receptacle, imprint-bearer, mother, or nurse" of the divide between *mythos* and *logos*—and yet, *khōra* is not *properly* any of these things at all.[55] As such, *khōra* comes to perform for Plato, and now represents for Derrida, those "figures without figures" that Western philosophy relies on from its inception and yet, rendered invisible by entry into normative language, can no longer be recognized for what they are: catachreses.[56]

It is in this sense that Derrida "reads catachresis at the origin," as Spivak notes in passing at the close of her classic essay "Can the Subaltern Speak?"[57] This "origin" is not precisely diachronic, however, or at least not simply diachronic, for what distinguishes *khōra*—functioning here as a metonym for catachresis—from the rest of the conceptual framework is that, as "the possibility of naming" this problem of rhetoric is "more situating than situated"; it is that which gives the concept of placement its very sensibility. Consequently, *khōra*, like blood and glory, does not hold any positive content that can properly be traced back to a fully identifiable referent, and therefore one can only, as Derrida noted about such figures, "receive it, if not to comprehend it, to conceive it."[58] However, the conception of these "singular metonymies" is not simply of a historical or abstract nature, nor does their reception and utilization seem synchronically coherent. Instead, despite their opaqueness, they are reproduced over and over again as a performative iteration in each moment that a catachrestic figure, or its subsidiary concept-metaphors, are spoken into being in the pursuit of a political project.[59]

The question remains, however, what role the identification of catachrestic figures and performative tautologies has in the construction and implementation of a counter-imperial political theology. Having alerted her audience to the manifold forms of violence produced by the State's weaponization of catachresis, Butler ventured a creative answer in the conclusion of her lecture through a distinctive reading of Walter Benjamin's *Critique of Violence* that explored an alternative potential for this category of rhetorical abuse. Catachresis, she hypothesized, appears to be—as the impossibility of translation—precisely what allows Walter Benjamin to reconfigure "nonviolence" as "divine violence," an act of parodic sabotage strategically designed to disrupt the performative tautology of legitimacy and law:

> He is showing, enacting, how that name [violence] can be redeployed in the instances where it would seem to be most intuitively foreign. ... Not just situating that naming practice critically within political frameworks and their self-justificatory schemes, but acting, renaming, destroying the one instance of the word by using it now to name its opposite.[60]

In this sense, it would seem that the ongoing struggle to apprehend the meaning of Benjamin's notorious text is not simply a consequence of his obtuse insistence on an incomprehensible use of terminology: this "divine violence" which drives one mad. Instead, as a counter-imperial catachrestic figure, "divine violence" presents the Western theologico-political tradition with an inverted mirror of its torqued structural naming practices. In doing so, the reader is invited to consider *why* such incomprehensible language is *required* to perform an effective critique of power, authority, and violence.

This is precisely the concern of Derrida's extraordinary text *White Mythology*, in which, attempting to account for Western philosophy's reliance on metaphor, he concludes that the fundamental instability of language represented by catachresis has been repeatedly recognized but persistently bracketed in an attempt to divert the potent effects of its epistemological destabilization of metaphysical systems.[61] Derrida writes there, in remarkable parallel to Agamben's definition of signature, "catachresis does not go outside the language, does not create new signs, does not enrich the code; yet it transforms its functioning: it produces, with the same material, new rules of exchange, new meanings."[62] Philosophical language, he goes on, is "a system of catachreses with a capital resource of 'forced metaphor,'" which—presupposing that the act of naming "goes to meet a concept that is already present"—continually mistakes its own conceptual artifacts as "real" and as "natural" despite their lack, as Spivak's postcolonial theory has shown, of an adequate referent.[63] Derrida concluded the chapter with a scathing indictment of the convention,

> It is just so that philosophy has traditionally interpreted its powerful catachresis: a torque turning back to a sense already present, a production (of signs, or rather of meanings), but this as revelation, unveiling, bringing to light, truth.[64]

In this spirit, we might hypothesize that one of the distinctive features of theopoetics and constructive theology—as exemplified by the deconstruction of truth, light, and revelation in Catherine Keller's *Face of the Deep*—can be observed in how they implicitly destabilize the operation of catachrestic concepts within theological discourse.[65]

More broadly, it seems that the heart of Derrida's broader intellectual project persistently returns to the identification of the catachrestic contours of any transcendental signifier operative within a metaphysical binary. It is precisely for this reason that his work has been so generative in the destabilization of many of the idiomatic structures of the West that, subjected to intense scrutiny, are revealed not to have an adequate referent: gender, race, sexuality, humanity, adolescence, citizenship, criminality, and so on.[66] To make the claim more directly, although Spivak's postcolonialism has shown us that the core concepts of empire can be catachrestic in the province (colony), the possibility of a similarly radical critique emerges through the recognition that imperial concepts are always already catachrestic in the Capital (metropole).[67] In this way, Derrida's principal rhetorical insight coincides with Foucault's prevailing intuition about the nature of power/knowledge, which Stephen Moore has described as "showing how discourses of knowledge, which are also discourses of truth, covertly conspire to produce that which they purport to describe."[68]

Far more than simple misuse, catachrestic figures function as limit concepts: linguistic-affective gestures that exist simultaneously inside and outside of language. Reorienting or displacing meaning according to hidden rules of exchange and translation, they execute the role of the sovereign exception in discourse by producing a zone of indistinction between the preconceptual and the concrete. Capturing thought itself, these signatures function to transfer a theo-ontological imprint into the material world in each performative iteration of naming through the "insoluble interweaving of words and facts, of reality and meaning . . . a linguistic utterance that is also, in itself, immediately a real fact, insofar as its meaning coincides with a reality that it produces."[69] It is in this way that the ongoing weaponization of the Western philosophical tradition generates and sustains linguistic-affective resonance machines that produce dominant concepts whose catachrestic contours have been occluded and effaced. Now taken as natural, these torqued concept-metaphors assemble political life according to the strictures of a negative field that generates and deploys power/knowledge formations in ways that continue to elude sustained recognition or even cognitive coherency. In terms of theologico-political method, both deconstruction and "the science of signatures" can be understood as techniques of denaturalization through which the foundation of a conceptual edifice is progressively revealed, traced, mapped "back" to its catachrestic "origin"—figures such as blood, glory, *khōra*, and divine violence that emerge at the preconceptual horizon.[70] In this sense, we might come to theorize that, to plagiarize Anidjar's plagiarization of Carl Schmitt as a partial summary of this chapter:

All significant concepts of the history of the modern world are *catachrestic* concepts. This is so not only because of their genealogical generativity, but also because of their rhetorical instability, the recognition of which is necessary for a theologico-political consideration of these concepts.[71]

CONCLUSION

When foregrounding these genealogical critiques, and the rhetoric made vulnerable by them, it would seem that Carl Schmitt's paradigmatic thesis becomes suspect, or at least subject to an alternative reading. For what exactly does it mean to claim that "all significant concepts of the modern theory of the state are secularized theological concepts" if, in some ethereal yet all too real sense, Christianity—as Anidjar has argued—*is* secularism, *is* orientalism, *is* religion—whatever that is anyway—*is* theology, *is* the state, and *is* modernity for that matter?[72] This is not quite to say that the conjunction "political theology" is reducible to an ultimately meaningless tautology—performative or parodic, imperial or emancipatory. For what Agamben and Anidjar have attempted to demonstrate is that the religious and the secular, the theological and the political, are not fixed categories, and cannot be neatly exchangeable. Instead, we might think of them as non-synonymous signatures that do not simply serve as masks for each other, but "function together as covers, strategic devices and mechanisms of obfuscation and self-blinding, doing so in such a way that it remains difficult, if not impossible, to extricate them from each other—or us from either of them—as if by fiat."[73] In the final analysis, it seems that the impulse to trace the displacement and translation of these theologico-political concept-metaphors across disciplines, discourse, cultures, and geographical areas, is an attempt to discern the complex coordination of the preconceptual field that governs the production of the normative frames utilized in the justification of violence.[74]

Presented in this way, we might begin to perceive how the ongoing captivity of political thought in the West is conditioned and authorized by the deployment of not-quite-fictive concepts, signified through not-quite-stable terms and icons, materially enfleshed in highly dynamic corporate institutions, and historicized through the production of a constrained cultural memory.[75] This state of capture is the province of white mythology, a historical artifice of the metaphysicians, and a theologico-political discourse circumscribed by a set of torqued terms: radically contingent yet far from arbitrary, more than merely accidental—occidental.[76] Consequently, political theology at its best participates in the identification, denaturalization, and destabilization of the preconceptual-metaphysical assemblage that produces the everyday distinctions that we commonly take for granted: secular-religious, political-economic, and philosophical-scientific, among many more.[77] In mapping the use (*chresis*) of catachrestic figures, political theology seeks to elucidate, as Agamben put it, a "topological zone of indistinction, which had to remain hidden from the eyes of justice," and from which emerges the most confounding theologico-political paradoxes: equality that is not equal, freedom that is not free, and violence that is not violent.[78]

NOTES

The epigraph is from Friedrich Nietzsche, "On Truth and Falsity in their Ultra-moral Sense," in *The Complete Works of Friedrich Nietzsche*, vol. 2: *Early Greek Philosophy and Other Essays*, ed. Oscar Levy, trans. Maximilian A. Mügge (New York: Macmillan, 1911), 180.

1. Quoted in, Gladden J. Pappin, "Explaining Agamben," review of *The Kingdom and the Glory: For a Theological Genealogy of Economy and Government*, by Giorgio Agamben, trans. Lorenzo Ghiesa with Matteo Mandarini; *The Highest Poverty: Monastic Rules and Form of Life*, by Giorgio Agamben, trans. Adam Kotsko; and *The Church and the Kingdom*, by Giorgio Agamben, trans. Leland de la Durantaye, *First Things* (January 2014): 57–59.
2. Michel Foucault, *The History of Sexuality:* vol. 2: *An Introduction* (New York: Vintage Books, 1990), 102.
3. Michel Foucault, *Power/Knowledge: Selected Interviews & Other Writings 1972–1977* (New York: Vintage Books, 1980), 122. See also Judith Butler, *Frames of War: When Is Life Grievable?* (New York: Verso Books, 2016), 149–50. "In this case, an alliance would need to stay focused on methods of state coercion (ranging from immigration tests to explicit torture) and on the invocations (and reductions) of the *subject, nature, culture, and religion* that produce the ontological horizon within which state coercion appears necessary and justified. The operation of state power takes place within an ontological horizon saturated by power that precedes and exceeds state power. As a result, we cannot take account of power if we always place the state at the center of its operation. . . . Further—and this is not particularly new—the state both produces and presupposes certain operations of power that work primarily through establishing a set of 'ontological givens.'"

4. Foucault, *The History of Sexuality*, 97.
5. Vincent W. Lloyd, Introduction to *Race and Political Theology*, ed. Vincent W. Lloyd (Stanford, CA: Stanford University Press, 2012), 16.
6. In her recent monograph, *Political Theology of the Earth* (New York: Columbia University Press, 2018), Catherine Keller presents theology as a religion's theoretical practice: "If religion has never been apolitical, still even as *political*, it is never simply identical with politics—that is, with the structures of the state, and so with institutions that religious practice may shape, sanctify, question or protest. *Theology* names a religion's theoretical practice (that theo does double work). So then theology is not politics, but it is always already political" (8). It seems, though, that a reciprocal definition might be similarly helpful. In a statement analogous to Keller's: If politics has never been areligious, still even as *religious*, it is never simply identical with religion—that is with the structures of the Church, and so with institutions that political practice may demarcate, authorize, marginalize, or acclaim. *Law* names the theoretical practice of the political. So then law is not religion, but it is always already religious
7. Jacques Derrida, "Force of Law: The 'Mystical Foundation of Authority,'" in *Deconstruction and the Possibility of Justice*, ed. Drucilla Cornell, Michel Rosenfeld, and David Gray Carlson (New York: Routledge, 1992), 20. "One must be *juste* with justice, and the first way to do it justice is to hear, read, interpret it, to try to understand where it comes from, what it wants of us, knowing that it does so through singular idioms . . . and also knowing that this justice always addresses itself to singularity, to the singularity of the other, despite or even because it pretends to universality. Consequently, never to yield on this point, constantly to maintain an interrogation of the origin, grounds and limits of our conceptual, theoretical or normative apparatus surrounding justice is on deconstruction's part anything but a neutralization of interest in justice, an insensitivity towards justice. On the contrary, it hyperbolically raises the stakes of exacting justice; it is sensitivity to a sort of essential disproportion that must inscribe excess and inadequation in itself and that strives to denounce not only theoretical limits but also concrete injustices, with the most palpable effects, in the good conscience that dogmatically stops before any inherited determination of justice."
8. Lloyd, Introduction to *Race and Political Theology*, 17.
9. Derrida, "Force of Law," 13. "The basis for a modern critical philosophy, indeed for a critique of juridical ideology, a desedimentation of the superstructures of law that both hide and reflect the economic and political interests of the dominant forces of society. . . . The very emergence of justice and law, the founding and justifying moment that institutes law implies a performative force, which is always an interpretive force: this time not in the sense of law in the service

of force, its docile instrument, servile and thus exterior to the dominant power, but rather in the sense of law that would maintain a more internal, more complex relation with what one calls force, power or violence."

10. It should be noted that, while not one of this chapter's primary interlocutors, Dorothee Sölle uses the strategy of approaching political theology as a hermeneutic in her counter-Schmittian text *Political Theology* (New York: Fortress Press, 1974). There she distinguished political theology from "theology of politics," "political interpretation," or even "social gospel" writing: "Political theology is rather a theological hermeneutic, which, in distinction from a theology that interprets reality from an ontological or existentialist point of view, holds open a horizon of interpretation in which politics is understood as the comprehensive and decisive sphere in which Christian truth should become praxis" (59). As a result, Sölle posits, observing that the ways that theological concepts and doctrines manifest into political reality reveal how certain "preunderstandings" circumscribe theological reflection and, thereby, made vulnerable to ideological critique, political theology can function as an "instrument of self-criticism for theology" that will allow "the gospel [to] become free once again from its illusory, destructive, systematic fixations" (63).

11. Giorgio Agamben, *Homo Sacer: Sovereign Power and Bare Life*, trans. Daniel Heller-Roazen (Stanford, CA: Stanford University Press, 1998), 8–12.

12. Giorgio Agamben, *The Kingdom and the Glory: For a Theological Genealogy of Economy and Government,* trans. Lorenzo Ghiesa with Matteo Mandarini (Stanford, CA: Stanford University Press, 2011), xii.

13. Ibid., 208.

14. Carl Schmitt, *Political Theology: Four Chapters on the Concept of Sovereignty*, trans. George Schwab (Chicago: University of Chicago Press, 2005), 30–32.

15. Walter Benjamin, "Critique of Violence," in *Reflections: Essays, Aphorisms, Autobiographical Writings*, trans. Edmund Jephcott, ed. Peter Demetz (New York: Schocken Books, 1986), 293–96.

16. Agamben, *Homo Sacer*, 8. See also, Agamben, *The Kingdom and the Glory*, 82: "Power—every power, both human and divine—must hold these two poles together, that is, it must be, at the same time, kingdom and government, transcendent norm and immanent order."

17. Giorgio Agamben, *The Use of Bodies*, trans. Adam Kotsko (Stanford, CA: Stanford University Press, 2015), 115.

18. Agamben, *The Kingdom and the Glory*, 194.

19. Ibid.

20. Ibid., 211.

21. Giorgio Agamben, *The Signature of All Things: On Method*, trans. Luca D'Isanto with Kevin Attell (New York: Zone Books, 2009), 37.
22. Agamben, *The Kingdom and the Glory*, 193–94.
23. Agamben, *The Signature of All Things*, 40–41. "A signature does not merely express a semiotic relation between a *signans* and a *signatum*; rather, it is what—persisting in this relation without coinciding with it—displaces and moves it into another domain, thus positioning it in a new network of pragmatic and hermeneutic relations. In this sense, the yellow patch on a Jew's coat and the colored mark of the bailiff or of the courier are not merely neutral signifiers referring to the signified "Jew," "bailiff," or "courier." By shifting this relation into the pragmatic and political sphere, they express instead how one must comport oneself before Jews, bailiffs, or couriers (as well as the behavior that is expected from them)."
24. Gil Anidjar, *Blood: A Critique of Christianity* (New York: Columbia University Press, 2014), ix.
25. Ibid., xii.
26. Ibid., 12–13. "This tradition of violence, finally, is a 'philosophy of history' . . . the legal tradition Benjamin describes, that is ruled by the intention to preserve itself—and God knows it has. Today still; today especially. It is a tradition that, Benjamin makes clear, is defined or distinguished by blood, that rests on blood (and recall that its critique should no longer call our attention to 'what the deed does to the victim,' that is, to the latter's blood, but rather to 'what it does to God and the doer'). . . . Now, as many have underscored, Benjamin refers to that very tradition under the heading of 'mythical violence.' What seems to have escaped the attention of translators and interpreters, however, is that he gives it another, much more telling name. It is one simple word or perhaps indeed a proper name that gathers, with utmost conciseness and clarity, everything that 'divine violence' (and Benjamin himself) opposes, the tradition of violence and power that we are still confronted with: *Blutgewalt*."
27. See Gil Anidjar, "Secularism," *Critical Inquiry* 33, no. 1 (2006): 52–77.
28. Michel Foucault, *The Archaeology of Knowledge* (New York: Vintage Books, 2010), 62.
29. Ibid., 63.
30. As a method in philosophy of history, conceptual history can be traced to Carl Schmitt through its founders, Reinhart Koselleck and Otto Brunner, who were strongly influenced by Schmitt and his commitment to a "sociology of concepts." Schmitt's nascent method focused on the synchronic and diachronic analysis of the concrete contexts in which ideas emerge and change. See Timo Pankakoski, "Conflict, Context, Concreteness: Koselleck and Schmitt on Concepts,"

Political Theory 38, no. 6 (2010): 749–79. In solidarity with the approach of conceptual history, yet distinct from it, preconceptual critique would trace a different trajectory by recognizing that the conceptual assemblages that Schmitt addressed in *Political Theology* were, in fact, preconceptual concepts which cannot be accounted for in quite the same manner. Much like, as Agamben notes, what "Gernet used to call, using an infelicitous term, *prelaw*, in which terms that we customarily consider juridical appear to act in a magic-religious manner. More than a chronologically earlier stage, we must here think of something like a threshold of indistinction that is always operative, where the juridical and the religious become truly indistinguishable." Agamben, *The Kingdom and the Glory*, 188 (emphasis added).

31. Anidjar, *Blood*, 257–58.
32. S. Hawthorne and A. Klinken, "Catachresis: Religion, Gender, and Postcoloniality," *Religion & Gender* 3, no. 2 (2013): 160.
33. See Patricia Parker, "Metaphor and Catachresis," in *The Ends of Rhetoric: History, Theory, Practice*, ed. John Bender and David E. Wellbery (Stanford, CA: Stanford University Press, 1990), 60–73.
34. Ibid., 60. Citing Quintilian, *Institutio Oratoria*, trans. H. Rackham (Cambridge, MA: Harvard University Press, 1935), 8.6.35–36.
35. Ibid., 61.
36. Bill Ashcroft, Gareth Griffiths, and Helen Tiffin, eds., *Postcolonial Studies: The Key Concepts*, 3rd ed. (New York: Routledge, 2013), 41.
37. Hans Leander, *Discourses of Empire: The Gospel of Mark from a Postcolonial Perspective* (Atlanta, GA: Society for Biblical Literature, 2013), 40.
38. Agamben, *The Kingdom and the Glory*, 211.
39. Jacques Derrida, "Khōra," in *On the Name*, trans. John P. Leavey, ed. Thomas Dutoit (Stanford, CA: Stanford University Press, 1995), 126. "Philosophy cannot speak directly, whether in the mode of vigilance or of truth (true or probably) about what these figures approach. The dream is between the two, neither one nor the other. Philosophy cannot speak philosophically of that which looks like its 'mother,' its 'nurse,' its 'receptacle,' or its 'imprint-bearer.' As such, it speaks only of the father and the son, as if the father engendered it all on his own."
40. Schmitt, *Political Theology*, 13. Jacques Derrida, "Plato's Pharmacy," in *Dissemination*, trans. Barbara Johnson (London: Athlone Press, 1981), 82–83.
41. Agamben, *The Use of Bodies*, 24.
42. Ibid., 28.
43. Ibid., 24.
44. Ibid., 23.
45. Agamben, *Homo Sacer*, 21 (emphasis added).

46. Agamben, *The Use of Bodies*, 135.
47. Agamben, *The Signature of All Things*, 50.
48. Anidjar, *Blood*, 133.
49. Judith Butler, "Distinctions on Violence and Nonviolence" (public open lecture for the students of the Division of Philosophy, Art & Critical Thought at the European Graduate School EGS, Saas-Fee/Switzerland, August 12, 2016).
50. The first iteration of this article was written between 2018 and 2019, and the connections that I have attempted to draw between catachresis, the use of bodies, and police violence have been haunted by the emergence of the Black Lives Matter movement following the deaths of Trayvon Martin, Eric Garner, Michael Brown, Walter Scott, Freddie Gray, Meagan Hockaday, Deborah Danner, Alton Sterling, Philando Castile, Grechario Mack, Kenneth Ross Jr., and Isaiah Lewis. At that time, none of the charges brought against the officers involved in these incidents of state violence had resulted in conviction. In the intervening time during which this chapter was revised and finalized, public outcry against the killings of George Floyd and Breonna Taylor have inspired global protests against ongoing police violence and structural inequalities that disproportionately target people of color. There is hope that this nonviolent struggle will secure critical reforms in the coming years, such as the annulment of qualified immunity and the defunding of police departments in favor of integrated social services. However, to date, despite numerous important victories, prior to the April 2021 verdict against Derek Chauvin for the murder of George Floyd, no police officers had been convicted of the wrongful use of force, manslaughter, or murder. These are incredibly important matters that deserve sustained scholarly attention, but I have felt it best to defer my own voice in favor of redirecting attention to the work of my colleagues and mentors of color whose experience, expertise, and incisive scholarship appear within this volume: J. Kameron Carter, Kelly Brown Douglas, and Seth Gaiters.
51. Derrida, "Force of Law," 33.
52. Benjamin, "Critique of Violence," 286–87.
53. Butler, "Distinctions on Violence and Nonviolence": "To halt a violent regime is very often called 'violent,' even if it is not halted through physically violent means. And so it may be that our naming practice has to undergo a translation from one epistemic framework to another and that we ourselves have to become translators between these frameworks in order to begin the process of understanding why violence and nonviolence are constantly subjected to these oscillating frames. If we call the cessation of legal violence, 'violent,' then we've committed a catachresis of a sort, using the name in a way that seems rather

improper. It would seem that we've passed into another language where names, or the sound of the name, no longer refers in one way. And to call this cessation of legal violence divine seems to recall what Benjamin claimed in 1916 . . . namely, that the divine name marks the problem of translation, which is of course, another problem of passage. Not just the question of how to translate this or that passage, but the very possibility of a passage from one language, one framework, into another. . . . Not just situating that naming practice critically within political frameworks and their self-justificatory schemes, but acting, renaming, destroying the one instance of the word by using it now to name its opposite."

54. Derrida, "Khōra," 92.

55. Ibid. "This problem of rhetoric—particularly of the possibility of naming—is, here, no mere side issue. . . . We shall be content for the moment with indicating it, and situating it, but it is already clear that, just like the khōra and with just as much necessity, it cannot easily be situated, assigned to a residence: it is more situating than situated, an opposition which must in its turn be shielded from some grammatical or ontological alternative between the active and the passive. We shall not speak of metaphor, but not in order to hear, for example, that the khōra is *properly* a mother, a nurse, a receptacle, a bearer of imprints or gold. It is perhaps because its scope goes beyond or falls short of the polarity of metaphorical sense versus proper sense that the thought of the khōra exceeds the polarity, no doubt analogous, of the *mythos* and the *logos*."

56. Jacques Derrida, "White Mythology: Metaphor in the Text of Philosophy," trans. F. C. T. Moore, *New Literary History* 6, no. 1 (1974): 44. "There being no longer any properly named reference in such a metaphor, the figure of speech sets out on a voyage into a long and hidden sentence, a secret recitative, with no assurance that we shall be led back to the proper name. The metaphorization of metaphor, its bottomless overdeterminability, seems to be written into the structure of metaphor, though as its negative side."

57. Gayatri Chakravorty Spivak, "Can the Subaltern Speak?" in *Colonial Discourse and Post-Colonial Theory: A Reader*, ed. Patrick Williams and Laura Chrisman (New York: Columbia University Press, 1994), 104.

58. Derrida, "Khōra," 96.

59. See, for example, Talal Asad on the concept of "modernity," in Talal Asad, *Formations of the Secular: Christianity, Islam, Modernity* (Stanford, CA: Stanford University Press, 2003), 12–13. "Many critics have taken the position that 'modernity' (in which secularism is centrally located) is not a verifiable object. They argue that contemporary societies are heterogeneous and overlapping, that they contain disparate, even discordant, circumstances, origins, valences,

and so forth. My response is that in a sense these critics are right . . . but that what we have here is not a simple cognitive error. Assumptions about the integrated character of 'modernity' are themselves part of practical and political reality. They direct the way in which people committed to it act in critical situations. These people *aim* at 'modernity,' and expect others (especially in the 'non-West') to do so too. This fact doesn't disappear when we simply point out that 'the West' isn't an integrated totality. . . . The important question, therefore, is not to determine why the idea of 'modernity' (of 'the West') is a misdescription, but why it has become hegemonic *as a political goal*, what practical consequences follow from that hegemony, and what social conditions maintain it."

60. Butler, "Distinctions on Violence and Nonviolence."
61. Derrida, "Khōra," 92. "The consequence which we envisage would be the following: with the two polarities, the thought of the *khōra* would trouble the very order of polarity, of polarity in general, whether dialectical or not. Giving place to oppositions, it would itself not submit to any reversal. And this, which is another consequence, would not be because it would inalterably be *itself* beyond its name but because in carrying beyond the polarity of sense (metaphorical or proper), it would no longer belong to the horizon of sense, nor to that of meaning as the meaning of being."
62. Derrida, "White Mythology," 59.
63. Gayatri Chakravorty Spivak, *A Critique of Postcolonial Reason: Toward a History of the Vanishing Present* (Cambridge, MA: Harvard University Press, 1999), 331: "Far from being an 'effacement' of the past, [postmodern architectural 'historicism'] can be read as a questioning of the identification of continuist narratives of history with History as such, perhaps even a reminder to the necessarily class-mixed users of public space that at the limit, History, rather than being a transcendental signifier for the weight of authority (or the authoritative explanation) is a catachresis, a metaphor that has no literal referent." See also Gayatri Chakravorty Spivak, *Outside in the Teaching Machine* (New York: Routledge, 2008), 127. "[Catachresis is] a metaphor without a literal referent standing in for a concept that is the condition of conceptuality."
64. Derrida, "White Mythology," 60.
65. See Catherine Keller, *Face of the Deep: A Theology of Becoming* (London: Routledge, 2003).
66. In this, Derrida's linguistic analysis of catachresis runs parallel to Alfred North Whitehead's mathematical exposition on "the fallacy of misplaced concreteness." See Alfred North Whitehead, *Science and the Modern World* (New York: Free Press, 1925), 58.

67. In a congenial manner, and similarly influenced by Derridean thought, the Gramscian/post-Marxist political philosophers Ernesto Laclau and Chantal Mouffe have utilized catachresis in their materialist account of rhetoric to describe the way in which empty signifiers function in the "articulatory logic of hegemony" to blur the distinction between particular discursive formations—such as *the social* or *the people*—and the field of discursivity itself. See Ernesto Laclau and Chantal Mouffe, *Hegemony and Socialist Strategy: Towards a Radical Democratic Politics* (1985; New York: Verso Books, 2014), 96–101, 120–31. See also Ernesto Laclau, *On Populist Reason* (New York: Verso Books, 2005), 71–72, wherein he suggests that "catachresis is more than a particular figure: it is the common denominator of rhetoricity as such. This is the point where I can link this argument with my earlier remarks on hegemony and empty signifiers: if the empty signifier arises from the need to name an object which is both impossible and necessary, from that zero point of signification which is nevertheless the precondition for any signifying process, the hegemonic operation will be catachrestical through and through. As we shall see, the political construction of 'the people' is, for that reason, essentially catachrestical."

68. Stephen Moore, *Poststructuralism and the New Testament: Derrida and Foucault at the Foot of the Cross* (Minneapolis: Fortress Press, 1994), 87.

69. Agamben, *The Kingdom and the Glory*, 181. "Quintilian, who in his *Institutiones oratoriae* minutely describes the linguistic gesture in all it variants, writes, in relation to its unquestionable efficacy, that it is the hands themselves that speak ("ipsae loquuntur": II, 3, 85). It would be impossible to define more precisely the power of a linguistic gesture that is irreducible to a scansion or to a mere emphasizing of the discourse: there where the gestures become words, the words become facts. We find ourselves in the presence of a phenomenon that corresponds, even if apparently through an inverse process, to the insoluble interweaving of words and facts, of reality and meaning that defines the sphere of language that linguists call performative . . . a linguistic utterance that is also, in itself, immediately a real fact, insofar as its meaning coincides with a reality that it produces. . . . This means, in all truth, that the performative utterance is not a sign but a signature [segnatura], one that marks the dictum in order to suspend its value and displace it into a new nondenotative sphere that takes the place of the former. This is the way we should understand the gestures and signs of power with which we are occupied here."

70. Derrida, "Force of Law," 7–8: "Besides, it was normal, foreseeable, desirable that studies of deconstructive style would culminate in the problematic of law (droit), of law and justice. Such would even be the most proper place for them,

if such a thing existed. A deconstructive interrogation that starts, as was the case here, by destabilizing or complicating the opposition between nomos and physis, between thésis and physis—that is to say, the opposition between law, convention, the institution on the one hand, and nature on the other, with all the oppositions that they condition; for example, and this is only an example, that between positive law and natural law (the différance is the displacement of this oppositional logic), a deconstructive interrogation that starts, as this one did, by destabilizing, complicating, or bringing out the paradoxes of values like those of the proper and of property in all their registers, of the subject, and so of the responsible subject, of the subject of law (droit) and the subject of morality, of the juridical or moral person, of intentionality, etc., and of all that follows from these, such a deconstructive line of questioning is through and through a problematization of law and justice. A problematization of the foundations of law, morality and politics."

71. Anidjar, *Blood*, viii.
72. Anidjar, "Secularism," 52–77.
73. Ibid., 62.
74. See Judith Butler on "normative frames" in Judith Butler, *Frames of War: When Is Life Grievable?* (New York: Verso Books, 2016), 147–48. Consequently, political theology is provided with an opportunity for reflection and potential intervention wherever a catachrestic figure is shown to be operative in a given culture: For example, the "child" and the "synthomosexual" in Lee Edelman, *No Future: Queer Theory and the Death Drive* (Durham, NC: Duke University Press, 2004), or the "free black" in Calvin L. Warren, *Ontological Terror: Blackness, Nihilism, and Emancipation* (Durham, NC: Duke University Press, 2018).
75. Anidjar, "Secularism," 63. "More generally, in its secularized form, Christianity invented (or fashioned or produced or enforced or yet definitively institutionalized by way of knowledge and law—whichever of these you think is better to describe the massive power of hegemony and its operations) Judaism and Islam—the Jew, the Arab, or, to be perfectly historical about it, the Semites—as religions, and more precisely, as being at once *the least and the most religious of religions. And of races.* . . . In doing so, Orientalism—that is to say, secularism—became one of the essential means by which Christianity failed to criticize itself, the means by which Christianity *forgot and forgave* itself."
76. Jacques Derrida, "White Mythology," 11. "What is metaphysics? A white mythology which assembles and reflects Western culture: the white man takes his own mythology, his *logos*—that is, the *mythos* of his idiom, for the universal form of that which it is still his inescapable desire to call Reason. . . . What is white

mythology? It is metaphysics which has effaced in itself that fabulous scene which brought it into being, and which yet remains, active and stirring, inscribed in white ink, an invisible drawing covered over in the palimpsest."

77. Anidjar, "Secularism," 60.
78. Agamben, *Homo Sacer*, 37.

PART III

◦→ Affective and Axiomatic Interventions

7. Doing Theology When Whiteness Stands Its Ground

KELLY BROWN DOUGLAS

When I was about seven years old, I was riding with my parents through the inner city of my hometown of Dayton, Ohio. It was a rainy evening. I looked out the window of the car and noticed a little girl and boy crossing the street. They were about my age, and Black like me. I presumed them to be sister and brother. They were a bit disheveled and not properly dressed for the cold rainy weather. From my seven-year-old perspective they looked poor and hungry. Tears filled my eyes as I imagined for them a life of struggle. In the midst of my tears I made a silent vow that one day I would come back and rescue those two children from the blight of Dayton's inner city.

Initially, I fantasized that I would grow up, while they remained young; perhaps I would become a teacher and somehow change their life options. As I got older, the thought of those children never left me. They created within me a deep sense of accountability to the poor and marginalized people of our society. I was determined to find a vocation that would make a difference in their lives. But aside from the thought of those children there was something else that motivated me: my love for Jesus.

I grew up in St. Margaret's Episcopal Church, the only Black Episcopal church in Dayton. Every Sunday I would awaken my parents, asking them to take me to church. On most Sundays I attended both the 8:00 a.m. and 11:00 a.m. services with Sunday school in between.

One of the reasons I liked going to church was because I loved hearing stories about Jesus. One of the most compelling, yet saddest, stories I heard was about his manger birth. As a little girl, I simply could not understand how people could allow a baby to be born in a cold barn, in a manger. I cried every time we sang, "Away in a manger, no crib for a bed, / The little Lord Jesus lay down his sweet head." Every time I heard that hymn I was reminded of the little girl and boy I had seen on that rainy evening. Somehow, I instinctively knew that there was a connection between Jesus's manger birth and their inner-city life. As time went on, I would try to figure out that connection, but not before passing through a period of profound doubt.

I entered college with a deep pride in my Blackness, along with an intense understanding of what W. E. B. Du Bois meant when he said, "The problem of the Twentieth Century [in America] is the problem of the color-line."[1] My own experiences of growing up in a segregated city had schooled me in the violence of whiteness. I had witnessed Dayton's race riots and knew what it felt like to be called the "N" word. These experiences and more had made me very wary of white people.

As a six-year-old I heard the whispers of the adults around me talking about how awful it was that the church was bombed and how those four little girls were killed. I can remember hearing someone say that "the white man" who did it would probably never be caught, and if he were to be caught, nothing was likely to happen to him. I now know they were talking about the 1963 Birmingham Church bombing. Around that same time, I remember seeing pictures on the news of white policemen with dogs attacking Black children. I didn't know just what I was watching, but those images were seared into my mind. I also remember eavesdropping as my parents talked about a man in Mississippi, Medgar Evers, who was killed in his driveway in front of his family, and what a shame it was—and again how nothing would probably happen to whoever did it, if they ever found him.

It was no doubt these whispered conversations and violent images that prompted me one day to ask my father why white people didn't like us. (In my mind, I was sure there must be something we had done to warrant such treatment.) Although I don't remember his answer, I do remember thinking that if only I could figure it out, then maybe we could do something about it and then white people would stop treating us so badly.

I let the subject drop for a while, but I didn't stop thinking about it. A few weeks passed. I remember I was standing on the porch with my father when I resumed our conversation, as if it had never stopped. "Daddy," I said, "I figured out the answer to my question." He looked at me quizzically. "What question was that?" he asked. I responded: "The answer to what we did that made white people not like us and treat us so badly." "Oh," he said. "What did you figure out?" I answered: "We didn't do anything. They just treat us like this because they want to, it could be anybody, it just happens to be us."

That's how I resolved the problem in my child's mind. Little did I know at the time that it wasn't just us, and that it was more than simply a question of whether or not white people liked us; that wider understanding would have to follow in time. What was important for me then was the discovery that there was nothing wrong with Black people; rather, there was something wrong with white people. This was my first understanding of whiteness and the problem with white people as enforcers of the color line.

As my wariness of white people grew, I became increasingly impatient with the color line that set perimeters around Black life. Moreover, I recognized that as long as the color line existed, far too many Black children would be born into life-negating inner-city circumstances. My accountability to children like those I had encountered in my childhood became a passionate commitment to dismantle the white racist color line. Ironically, as that commitment grew, my belief in Jesus waned.

By my junior year of college, my childhood love for Jesus was slowly giving way to a deep skepticism. I wanted to know if the Jesus I loved unconditionally as a child unconditionally loved me back. After all, the Jesus of my Sunday school lessons was always pictured as white. This alone made me skeptical of His love for me, even as it led me to question the appropriateness of my love for Him.

How could a white Jesus ever care about me, not to speak of caring for poor Black children? And how could I, a Black person, ever have faith in a white Jesus? I didn't want to abandon the church, or Jesus, but I needed answers to these questions. I was experiencing an agonizing crisis of faith.

Recognizing my angst, the college chaplain, David Woodyard, introduced me to James Cone's book *A Black Theology of Liberation*. He said that it might help me answer some of my questions. I was doubtful; Woodyard was white. But I decided to read the book anyway.

When I opened the book, I could not believe what I was reading. Cone pronounced, "Jesus is the black Christ!" As he further explained, "The definition of Christ as black means that he represents the complete opposite of the values of white culture . . . (and) leads the warfare against the white assault on blackness."[2] After reading these words my questions were answered. If Jesus was Black like me, that meant I could be Black with a love for Jesus without contradiction. And most significantly, as Cone made clear, because Jesus "was born in a stable and cradled in a manger (the equivalent of a beer case in a ghetto alley)," He was one with Black children trapped behind the life-draining color line of inner city realities.[3] Essentially, Cone's declaration of Jesus's Blackness opened up for me a whole new appreciation of my faith, and hence, a renewed love for Jesus. My angst turned to excitement. This discovery marked the beginning of my purposeful theological journey. I share this early part of my theological journey for two important reasons.

First, inasmuch as my theological journey was about me seeking to understand my faith (*fides quaerens intellectum*, Anselm), then from the very beginning my theology has been framed by the violent reality of the color line that is whiteness. Second, therefore, while I have certainly never described myself as a political theologian, especially as that has been understood through the Eurocentric lineage of Carl Schmitt,[4] for me the theological has always been political. Indeed, the core of Christian faith itself means that Christian theology is intrinsically a political theology. In this chapter, therefore, I explore the meaning of whiteness and its theological/political implications and challenges, especially in these times, in these current political times.

THE COLOR LINE: A MATTER OF WHITE SUPREMACY

Some fifty years after asking my father why white people treated Black people so badly I found myself asking that question again. And once again, it would be images of Black children in the street that were haunting me. They were the faces of Trayvon, Jordan, Renisha, and Jonathan. These were young black men and women being murdered at the hands of white people—for no apparent reason other than being Black. Worse yet, the white people who killed them were getting away with it. The memory of my father's words, "Nothing will happen to the white man who did it," were echoing in my mind. History was repeating itself, and I needed to know why. And now, for me, there was more at stake for me than the reassurance that Black people did nothing to deserve such treatment. Our children's lives were at stake. My son's life was at stake. I needed answers.

Those answers began with the recognition that is about a lethal culture of white supremacy that is undergirded by two narratives—anti-Blackness and Anglo-Saxon exceptionalism. Because I speak of both of these more fully in other places, I address them only briefly here as they bear on my understanding of Christian theology as political theology.

The narrative of anti-Blackness became most conspicuous with Europeans' earliest incursions into the African continent. These Europeans were immediately struck by the African's dark skin. As the historian Winthrop Jordan says, when describing the English incursion on the African continent, "One of the fairest-skinned nations suddenly came face to face with one of the darkest peoples on the earth."[5] Beyond the difference in skin color, Europeans also noted the fullness of the African's lips, the broadness of their noses, and the texture of their hair in comparison with their own. In the European imagination, the Africans' physiognomy signaled a genetic difference. When coupled with the dissimilarity of dress and customs, not to speak of religions, the European interlopers on the African continent became convinced that the "Blackness" of the Africans was more than skin deep. They believed it penetrated through to the very character and soul (which some Europeans claimed Africans did not possess) of the people, thereby signaling a people who were so thoroughly uncivilized that they were more beastly than human.

The nature of the anti-Black narrative itself now becomes clear. It is about more than a chauvinistic repulsion to skin color and cultural differences. It is a narrative that negates the very humanity of a people and in so doing considers that people as dangerously uncivilized. In this regard, Europeans and eventually white Americans regarded Black people as those who needed to be controlled and patrolled in order to protect civilized humanity, most notably white people.

This brings us to the second narrative which undergirds the culture of white supremacy: Anglo-Saxon exceptionalism.

When America's Pilgrim and Puritan forebears fled England in search of freedom, they believed themselves descendants of an ancient Anglo-Saxon people, "free from the taint of intermarriages," who uniquely possessed high moral values and an "instinctive love for freedom." Fueled by this myth Americans crossed the Atlantic with a vision to build a nation that was politically, culturally—if not demographically—true to their "exceptional" Anglo-Saxon heritage. As such, America was envisioned as a testament to the sacredness of Anglo-Saxon character and values, if not people. American exceptionalism *was* Anglo-Saxon exceptionalism. In this regard, to be an Anglo-Saxon was the measure of what it meant to be an American. American identity was equated with Anglo-Saxon identity. In order to safeguard America's mythic Anglo-Saxon vision and sense of self a pervasive culture of whiteness was born. The point was this: Whiteness became the perfect way to mask the fact that America was actually a nation of immigrants, most of whom—even those from Europe—were not actually Anglo-Saxon.

Invariably, therefore, whiteness forged an impregnable wall between America's myth of Anglo-Saxon exceptionalism and those who might compromise it: specifically, all those persons on the other side of whiteness. Hence white culture, with an anti-Black narrative as its defining feature, was born. There was nothing that opposed whiteness more than Blackness—not only in color but also in what Blackness presumably signified about a people. To reiterate, Blackness signified an uncivilized and beastly people, while whiteness signaled a moral and virtuous people. With this opposition between whiteness and Blackness a white supremacist culture was born.

White supremacist culture in its various manifestations is that which perpetuates the idea of white superiority and—especially through its legal and extralegal expressions—helps whiteness to "stand its ground" against any corrupting or threatening intrusions into the white Anglo-Saxon space—namely, the intrusion of Black bodies.

With this recognition of white supremacist culture two things become clear to me. First, perhaps stating the obvious, the very notion of white supremacy depends on the narrative of anti-Blackness since the notion of white superiority rests on the idea of Black inferiority. Second, whiteness itself must be regarded as a violent identity construct inasmuch as it is defined in dehumanizing opposition to that which is non-white, notably Blackness. This is so because any system of thought or culture that objectifies or dehumanizes another human being must be understood as violent. Furthermore, such systemic and cultural violence initiates a cycle of violence in which the objectified being, in this instance Black bodies, become entrapped.

And so, this brings me full circle. For in this search for answers some fifty years after my question to my father, not only was I affirmed in my childhood understanding that there was nothing wrong with Black people that warranted deadly treatment from white people, but I also came to understand that that the problem was about more than what white people thought about Black people.

White supremacy is about safeguarding the illusion of America's sense of exceptionalism—in other words, protecting whiteness—hence the white space. It does not matter whether or not white people recognize themselves as racist. What matters is that this country's very identity is inextricably connected to an Anglo-Saxon exceptionalist myth that must be protected at all cost.

Indeed, this is what the "Make America Great Again" politics of "protectionism" unleashed during the Trump presidency is all about. It is the twenty-first-century version of the color line. Put simply, the promise to "Make America Great Again" is an effort to carry forth the legacy of the Anglo-Saxon myth and the culture of whiteness that sustains it. In this regard, the color line is about more than simply a white/Black binary. It reflects a line of defense against any people who are deemed a threat to the notion of Anglo-Saxon superiority.

This means that we must understand whiteness not only as that which stands in opposition to Blackness, but also as a symbol of the oppressive webs of power that oppress and demean the humanity of any people seen as a threat to the very systems and structures that white supremacist narratives and culture have birthed and serve to uphold. These systems and structures are inexorably oppressively, evangelically, patriarchal, heteronormative and bi-gendered. For the point of the matter is that white supremacy is based on a notion of Anglo-Saxon exceptionalism that valorizes Protestant puritanical white-hetero-patriarchy. And so to speak of white supremacy is also to speak of xenophobic, misogynistic, LGBTQ phobic, Christo-centric oppressing realities.

So now, what does all of this mean for those of us who claim to be Christians—that is, followers of a God made incarnate in one who was crucified?

The crucifixion signifies at least two things: the height of human evil and Jesus's utter solidarity with crucified classes of people. Let us first look at what it means for it be the height of human evil. That Jesus was crucified reflects the human No to the justice that is God and hence what God promises for God's earth.

To reinforce that which we know, that Jesus was God incarnate means that Jesus was the perfect embodiment of God's movement in human history. This is a movement toward God's just future. Hence, Jesus could proclaim that the "kingdom of God is at hand," because it in fact was at hand in the very ways that Jesus lived and moved and had his being in the world.

Because of the way in which Jesus revealed God's just future, He was not simply an immediate threat to those powers that were the guardians of an unjust sociopolitical status quo. Rather, he was a threat to the very order of things. This was a human order that opposed God's just future. It is in this way that Jesus's crucifixion was a result of ecclesial and political powers colluding to put an end to that which Jesus so perfectly embodied—the future that was God's just earth. In so doing they said NO to God and God's just future. This No reflects the height of human evil.

But then there is more. For, the crucifixion tells us something not simply about human opposition to God, but it also tells us something about God's solidarity with humans.

In Jesus's first-century world, crucifixion was the brutal tool of sociopolitical power. It was reserved for slaves, enemy soldiers, and those held in the highest contempt and lowest regard in society. To be crucified was, for the most part, an indication of how worthless and devalued an individual was in the eyes of established power. At the same time, it was reserved for those who threatened the "peace" of the day—as pointed out above.

To understand the meaning of crucifixion in Jesus's time helps us to recognize that Jesus's crucifixion affirms his absolute identification with the Trayvons, the Jordans, the Renishas, the Sandras, and all the other victims of white supremacist violence. For just as Jesus was seen as a threat to the forces of power in his day, Black people are seen as a threat to the forces of Anglo-Saxon power and superiority in twenty-first-century America. Moreover, by refusing to save himself from crucifixion as he was mocked by the crowds, Jesus "let go" of anything that would compromise his utter solidarity with those among the crucified class—in this instance, nonwhite persons. As the Salvadoran theologian Jon Sobrino puts it, "The cross, for its part, tells of God's affinity with victims."[6] It is, therefore, in light of the cross that I now understand the meaning of Christ's Blackness.

Furthermore, inasmuch as the cross reflects the crucifying realities of a white supremacist culture, the Blackness of Christ is about more than a white/Black color line. Rather it is about the color line of white supremacy. In this regard, Christ's Blackness indicates His deep and personal identification with people of color and others as they suffer the pain, heartache, and death exacted upon them by the insidiousness of white supremacist culture. And so, we might paraphrase the Gospel question for today: "But Lord, where did we see you dying and on the cross?" And Jesus would answer: "On a Florida sidewalk with Trayvon, or at the US/Mexican border with an immigrant refused asylum, or in a detention center with a brown child separated from his or her parents, or in a juvenile court with the Black child trapped in the poverty-to-prison pipeline, or with the trans-child whose very existence is negated. As you did to one of the least of these, you did it to me."

When I was a young girl, it was Jesus's manger birth that held the most meaning for me. That He was born in the starkness of a manger allowed me to feel connected to Him as a child, but more importantly to see His connection to that Black girl and boy that had made such an imprint upon my childhood imagination. His manger birth convinced me that he understood the struggles, if not the hopes and dreams, of Black children who were trapped in "manger-like" conditions of living. Jesus's manger birth continues to have theological significance for me as it indicates His intrinsic bond with those on the outside, that is, on the wrong side of the color line. Nevertheless, as my youthful images of Black children crossing the street became overtaken with images of Black children dying in the street, it was Jesus's crucifying death that came to the forefront of my faith.

And so now the theological journey that began with doubt about my love for Jesus and Jesus's love for Black children trapped in the vulgarities of inner-city life continues with appreciation for the inherently political nature of Christian theological reflection and for the fact that such reflection must begin with forthrightly naming white supremacy as a crucifying reality that stands in opposition to the very love of the Jesus I came to know as a child.

NOTES

1. W. E. B. Du Bois, *The Souls of Black Folk* (Original Classic Edition, Kindle Edition, G&D Media, 2019), 1.
2. James H. Cone, *A Black Theology of Liberation*, 40th anniv. ed. (Maryknoll, NY: Orbis Books, 2010; Kindle Edition), 127, 128.
3. Ibid., 120.
4. Reference to the publication of Carl Schmitt's *Political Theology* in 1922. See Carl Schmitt, *Political Theology: Four Chapters on the Concept of Sovereignty*, trans. George Schwab (Chicago: University of Chicago Press, 2006).

5. Winthrop D. Jordan, *White Over Black: American Attitudes toward the Negro, 1550–1812* (Chapel Hill, NC: Published by the Omohundro Institute of Early American History and Culture and North Carolina University Press, 2012; Kindle Edition), 6.
6. Jon Sobrino, *Christ the Liberator: A View from the Victims* (Maryknoll, NY: Orbis Books, 2001), 88.

8. Paul between Protagoras and Rancière: "On the basis of equality, . . . that there may be equality"

LARRY L. WELBORN

Beneath the xenophobia and racism that poison social relations today yawns the abyss of inequality. Economists bring the distressing news that inequality has now reached historic levels not seen since before the Great Depression: The richest 1 percent of the world's households now hold more than half of global wealth; indeed, the richest sixty-two persons on earth now possess more wealth than the rest of humanity combined.[1] As inequality approaches the maximum that is politically sustainable, a number of social scientists have begun to ask whether capitalism has reached its end.[2] Immanuel Wallerstein judges that the current crisis of capitalism is "structural" and cannot be countered by tactical adjustments.[3] Wallerstein does not venture to predict what kind of system will replace capitalism but clearly regards the current cycle of rising costs and global disorder as a death spiral, which will make the restoration of a stable capitalist system impossible.[4] Wolfgang Streeck diagnoses the condition of contemporary capitalism as one of "multi-morbidity" resulting from the "destruction of collective agency in the course of capitalist development."[5] Therefore, what will come after capitalism, in the final crisis that is now underway, Streeck suggests, is not socialism or some other well-defined system, but an "interregnum"—that is, "a period of social entropy, or disorder,"[6] characterized by economic stagnation, oligarchic redistribution, plundering of the public domain, and global anarchy. For those who must live through the period when capitalism hangs in limbo, social scientists foresee a precarious existence. Individuals will have to adapt to constant disruptions in a social matrix from which collective institutions have been eroded. Streeck summarizes the survival skills needed by users of post-capitalism's entropic social networks: "coping, hoping, doping, and shopping."[7]

In my view, the philosopher Alain Badiou has offered the most accurate diagnosis of what is happening at this moment in history. Rather than forecasting the end of capitalism, or hailing the arrival of an entropic "interregnum," Badiou identifies what we are now experiencing as "an unprecedented regression" to an older form of political economy in which an "imperial oligarchy" has "unlimited power" over the world.[8] Strikingly, the conclusion of the philosopher converges with the findings of political scientist Jeffrey Winters that a regressive distribution of wealth and power is now underway.[9] According to Winters, the difference in "material power" between the top 100 households and the bottom 90 percent now approximates the difference between a senator and a slave in the early Roman Empire.[10] Nor is Badiou reluctant to name the group responsible for this "retrograde consummation of the essence of capitalism," in terms that evoke the Roman emperor and his cartel in their exploitation of the Mediterranean: "It is a regime of gangsters."[11] Badiou asks: "How can we accept the law of the world being laid down by the ruthless interests of a camarilla of inheritors and parvenus?"[12]

An unrecognized resource of political will and spiritual fortitude in the struggle against the retrograde consummation of capitalism is the appeal of the apostle Paul to the principle of "equality" in his second epistle to the Corinthians. How many persons, indeed how many Christians, know that Paul spoke of "equality" and stipulated, moreover, that "equality" is both the ground and the goal of relations between Christ believers—between those who enjoy "abundance" and those who suffer "lack"? Not many, I suspect, since I have never heard a sermon on this text from a pulpit in capitalist America! But is it not astonishing that, through two thousand years, and with only a few exceptions,[13] Paul's word about "equality" has been, so to speak, an oracle of silence? It is testimony to the power of the Eusebian image of Paul as the guarantor of a divinely willed hierarchy that Paul's exhortation to "equality" has been effectively silenced.[14] If the first, faint echoes of Paul's invocation of "equality" are now to be heard in the essays of a few philosophers,[15] it is because these thinkers are acutely aware of the danger that hangs over the present: that structural inequality, like that which once characterized the Roman Empire, may now crush the human spirit. It is the wager of this essay that the philosophers' sense of Paul as a contemporary to a perilous moment for humanity may finally give Paul's word of "equality" a degree of audibility.[16]

The hermeneutic that governs this essay is that which Walter Benjamin gave to historical materialists in "On the Concept of History" and in some notes to his unfinished *Arcades Project*. In contrast to the method of historicism, which seeks, by forgetting the subsequent course of history, to lay hold of the eternal meaning of a work, and in contrast to the liberal assumption that a work is susceptible of a variety of legitimate interpretations, depending on the interpreter's perspective, Benjamin proposed that a work contains a temporal index that connects it to a specific epoch, and that it comes forth to full legibility only for a person who is singled out by history at a moment of danger, a perilous moment like the one in which the work was composed.

This essay proposes to extract Paul's appeal to "equality" from the history of Christian interpretation and to relocate Paul's oracle within a stream of egalitarian thought that reaches from Protagoras, the celebrated sophist of the fifth century BCE, to Jacques Rancière, the most rigorous and challenging thinker of equality in this generation. But before undertaking this transposition, we should identify the obstacles to a retrieval of Paul's thought within Christian tradition. First, and most important, the church has lost its messianic vocation[17] and has become, at least since the fourth century CE, a hierarchical institution with little trace of the "pneumatic democracy" that characterized the epoch of Jesus and Paul.[18] Even if there are isolated and heartening exceptions, it is a sad fact that the Christian church in general remains divided along lines of class and race, and that, as Martin Luther King Jr. observed, "Eleven o'clock on Sunday morning is the most segregated hour of the week in America."[19] And despite the courageous apostolic exhortation of Pope Francis to say, "No to an economy of exclusion. . . . No to the inequality which spawns violence,"[20] the leaders of Christian denominations have remained largely silent in the face of the oligarchic restructuring of society that is now underway. It may be that the church will only recover its messianic vocation, when the edifice of institutional Christianity has been entirely demolished, as Dietrich Bonhoeffer insisted, when the church has given away its property, when pastors take no salary, but earn their living in secular vocations, "participating in the worldly tasks of life in the community—not dominating but helping and serving."[21] If the church does not grasp the historic crisis and awaken to its messianic calling, then, Giorgio

Agamben warns, the danger is clear enough: "The church will be swept away by the disaster menacing every government and every institution on earth."²²

I hope it will not be regarded as a symptom of *acedia*, an indolence of the heart, that I despair of the possibility that a scholar of early Christianity can do anything to assist the church in the recovery of its messianic vocation. But as a historian and philologist, I can at least identify and seek to demolish the principal exegetical obstacle to an awareness and understanding of Paul's appeal to "equality"—which is, first of all, the equivocal translation of the word ἰσότης as "a fair balance" in the influential New Revised Standard Version of the Bible.²³ In a recent discussion of "the gospel and the economy" with Walter Brueggemann at a large church in southwest Ohio, I observed that Paul appealed to "equality" as the principle of economic relations between Christ believers in 2 Corinthians 8:13–15; the renowned Old Testament theologian retorted: "Don't you mean 'a fair balance'?"²⁴ This translation, which has little lexical support,²⁵ may fairly be characterized as pusillanimous. Ἰσότης means "fairness" only when it is used in combination with other virtues, such as "justice," as in Colossians 4:1, which advises masters to "show justice and fairness" (τὸ δίκαιον καὶ τὴν ἰσότητα παρέχεσθε) in their treatment of slaves.²⁶ But in a number of cases in which ἰσότης appears in combination with other terms, consultation of the context reveals that "equality" supplies the content of the term.²⁷ So, for example, in Polybius's account of why the inhabitants of the Peloponnese adopted the constitution of the Achaeans, the historian asserts that the object was to secure the advantages of "equality and fraternity" (ἰσότης καὶ φιλανθρωπία).²⁸ When this text is adduced, alongside Colossians 4:1, as an example of ἰσότης with the meaning "fairness" or "fair dealing," as it is in the lexica,²⁹ insufficient attention is paid to the context, where Polybius gives his opinion that "nowhere could one find a political system more truly and deliberately devoted to equal right of speech (ἰσηγορία) and freedom of speech (παρρησία), and so entirely democratic (καὶ καθόλου δημοκρατία) than among the Achaeans."³⁰ In virtually every instance in which ἰσότης stands alone,³¹ the meaning is "equality,"³² especially "political equality,"³³ in keeping with a long tradition of thought in which "equality" (ἰσότης, τὸ ἴσον), alongside "freedom" (ἐλευθερία), was the fundamental principle of Greek democracy.³⁴ Cognizant of this tradition, the authors of the major historical-critical commentaries on 2 Corinthians consistently translate ἰσότης in 2 Corinthians 8:13–14 as "equality" or "Gleichheit," rather than "a fair balance."[35]

Whether such lexical observations will carry any weight against the capitalist interpretation of Paul, which has been and still is the mainstream of Pauline scholarship,[36] is very doubtful. In what remains, then, the task is to relocate Paul within a subversive stream of egalitarian thought that has its origin in the Greek world, so that a new group of philosophically minded readers, most of them Marxists, some of them irreligious, may come to understand the potency of the concept that Paul invokes by appealing to ἰσότης and may take Paul as a comrade in the struggle for equality.

We begin with Protagoras whose theory of the equality of all human beings contributed to the development of democracy at Athens.[37] In the *Protagoras*, Plato puts into the mouth of the famous sophist a "myth" of the origins of human society.[38] When human beings first attempted to "come together" in communities, they "did wrong" to one another through lack of "the political art" (ἡ πολιτικὴ τέχνη).[39] Zeus, fearing that the human race would destroy itself, sent Hermes to give "respect" (Αἰδώς) and "right" (Δίκη) to human beings so that they might come together in friendship and regulate the affairs of cities.[40] Hermes asked Zeus whether the civic virtues should be distributed in the same way as the arts and crafts, with different skills given to different individuals, or whether "respect" and "right" should be implanted in all.[41] "To all" (ἐπὶ πάντας), Zeus replied, "and let all have their share [καὶ πάντες μετεχόντων]; for cities cannot be formed if only a few have a share of these as of other arts [οὐ γὰρ ἂν γένοιντο πόλεις, εἰ ὀλίγοι αὐτῶν μετέχοιεν ὥσπερ ἄλλων τεχνῶν]."[42] Zeus further decreed that anyone who cannot partake of "respect" and "right" should be put to death, as being a plague to the city.[43] Protagoras then draws the conclusion: "Hence it comes about that people in cities, and especially in Athens, when they meet for deliberation on a political matter, in which it is necessary to be wholly guided by justice and good sense, reasonably allow advice from every man [εἰκότως ἅπαντος ἀνδρὸς ἀνέχονται], since it is held that everyone partakes of this excellence [ὡς παντὶ προσῆκον ταύτης γε μετέχειν τῆς ἀρετῆς], or else cities could not exist."[44]

Protagoras's point is that all people possess the art of political judgment, and in this respect may be said to be equals. Thus, the Athenians were justified in extending the right of free speech (ἰσηγορία) to all citizens. To be sure, Protagoras does not claim that all people have the same proficiency in the political art. Yet the verdict of G. B. Kerferd seems justified: "The importance of this doctrine of Protagoras in the history of political thought can hardly be exaggerated. For Protagoras has produced for the first time in human history a theoretical basis for participatory democracy."[45]

A papyrus fragment of a text by the sophist Antiphon appears to argue for the equality of all peoples.[46] Unfortunately, the papyrus is so lacunose that it is impossible to be certain about the referent of the article (τούς) in the first sentence of the text,[47] so that scholars are reduced to speculation on the precise nature of the contrast being drawn—whether between classes, or laws, or gods.[48] Nevertheless, the text of the crucial phrase is not in doubt: "for by nature, at any rate, we are all sprung up to be alike in all respects, whether barbarians or Greeks" (ἐπεὶ φύσει γε πάντα πάντες ὁμοίως πεφύκαμεν καὶ βάρβαροι καὶ Ἕλληνες εἶναι).[49] Thus, a number of scholars credit Antiphon with the view that all peoples are equal by nature, though not by custom.[50]

In his discussion of ideal constitutions in the *Politics*, Aristotle attempts to counter the arguments of the fifth-century political theorist Phaleas of Chalcedon, who proposed the extension of the principle of "equality" into the socioeconomic sphere.[51] According to Aristotle, "Phaleas considers it necessary for states to have equality in two things, property and education" (ὁ Φαλέας οἴεται γὰρ δυοῖν τούτοιν ἰσότητα δεῖν ὑπάρχειν ταῖς πόλεσιν, κτήσεως καὶ παιδείας).[52] Aristotle makes Phaleas the "first to introduce the idea" (τοῦτ᾽ εἰσήνεγκε πρῶτος) that "the estates of citizens must be equal" (δεῖν ἴσας εἶναι τὰς κτήσεις τῶν πολιτῶν),[53] and later claims that the measure for "the equalization of possessions" (ἡ τῶν οὐσιῶν ἀνομάλωσις) was "unique" (ἴδιον) to Phaleas.[54] Phaleas realistically acknowledged that equality of property would be easier to introduce in new colonies at the time of their foundation but hoped that a leveling of the classes might also be achieved progressively in established cities through a system of marriage dowries in which land would be transferred from rich to poor, but not in the reverse direction.[55] Scholars debate whether Phaleas's idea for equalizing property was purely theoretical or was proposed as a law at Chalcedon, or in one of its colonies; the decision turns on how Aristotle's term εἰσφέρειν (in the quotation above) is to be understood.[56] Not surprisingly, Aristotle, no admirer of democracy, is sharply critical of Phaleas's program of radical equality but concedes that Phaleas's proposal for equality of property was directed at the prevention of civil strife, στάσις.[57]

When Paul's appeal for partnership in the collection for the poor is situated in this subterranean tradition of egalitarian thought, one notices something overlooked by the commentators: The word "equality" is used *twice* in 2 Corinthians 8:13–15—first in the prepositional phrase ἐξ ἰσότητος, and then in the purpose clause ὅπως γένηται ἰσότης. In the first instance, Paul refers to the *ground* of the collection; in the second, to its *goal*. I translate as follows: "For the purpose [of the collection] is not that there [should be] relief for others and affliction for you, but rather [it should be] on the basis of equality [ἐξ ἰσότητος]. At the present time, your abundance should supply their lack, in order that their abundance may supply your lack, so that there may be equality [ὅπως γένηται ἰσότης]. As it is written: 'The one who had much did not have more, and the one who had little did not have less.'" The commentators elide Paul's reference to the equality of persons by translating ἐξ ἰσότητος abstractly: "according to the measure (or norm) of equality."[58] But in the first two clauses of verse 13, Paul speaks of "others" (ἄλλοι)—that is, the Jerusalem saints—for whom the collection will be a "relief," and of "you" (ὑμεῖς)—that is, the Corinthian believers—for whom the collection may represent a "hardship." That the reference to "equality" is introduced in this way implies that the "equality" of which Paul speaks as the ground of the collection is *an equality between persons*, in the radical democratic sense posited by Protagoras and Antiphon. Paul then uses ἰσότης in the purpose clause of verse 14 to designate the goal of the collection: "At the present time, your abundance [should be] for their lack, in order that their abundance may also be for your lack, so that there may be equality." Paul formulates an antithesis between abundance and lack that can be resolved only through an equitable distribution of resources. In the relationship that Paul seeks to establish between Christ believers of different social classes, "equality" is *the goal of redistributive action*, as in the program of Phaleas of Calcedon.

We are assisted in grasping the magnitude of Paul's argument by Jacques Rancière, who was trained in the Greek and Latin classics before turning to philosophy.[59] Rancière seeks to emancipate himself from the circular logic of inequality in which sociologists, like many philosophers, are trapped by the decision to presuppose equality, and then to verify the presupposition—namely, that "intelligence is the same in all its operations and belongs to everybody."[60] Thus, Rancière asserts that "equality is not a fiction, . . . the fanciful dream of fools and tender souls, . . . but a reality."[61] Rancière argues that every transaction between a superior and an inferior, a master and a slave, "presupposes the equality of the one who commands and the one who is commanded."[62] "There is no service that is carried out, no knowledge that is imparted, no authority that is established without the master having, however little, to speak 'equal to equal' with the one he commands or instructs. Inegalitarian society can only function thanks to a multitude of egalitarian relations."[63] Rancière concludes: "It is this intrication of equality in inequality that the democratic scandal makes manifest."[64]

Rancière is not content merely to invoke equality as the principle of rupture in the oppressive regime of global capitalism, but seeks, in his own way, to be an agent of emancipation in the class struggle. Consistent with his presupposition of the equality of all intelligences, Rancière does not put himself forward as the teacher of a capacity or the master of a discipline in relation to those involved in the class struggle. Rancière holds that the reality of equality can be enacted by anyone—in any situation, from any starting point, in a multiplicity of ways.[65] All that is necessary is a prior decision to participate in an intelligence that belongs to everybody. "Emancipation designates that prior decision to enact the capacity of anybody and to verify it."[66] This decision always takes the form of a "dissensus," since the new belief dissociates a person from the capacities which are assumed to be his and disrupts the distribution of times and places to which he is assigned.[67] Rancière adduces Rosa Parks as an example: "The young black woman of Montgomery, Alabama, who, one day in December 1955, decided to remain in her seat on the bus, which was not hers, in this way decided that she had, as a citizen of the United States, the equal rights she did not have as an inhabitant of a State that banned the use of such seats to individuals with one-sixteenth or more parts of 'non-Caucasian' blood."[68] As an ally of such self-emancipated persons, Rancière confesses to the desire "to tip the balance of equality and inequality that is at work in every situation," in the confidence that "every situation can be cracked open on the inside and reconfigured in a different regime of perception and signification."[69]

In asserting that "equality" is the basis of the relationship between Christ believers, it seems likely that Paul was invoking the experience of Christ believers in their baptism: in 1 Corinthians 12, Paul reminds his readers, "For in one Spirit we were all baptized into one body, whether Jews or Greeks, whether slaves or free"—a formula of inclusion that not only affirms unity and diversity, but also posits equality between believers in Christ.[70] For the source of Paul's extension of the principle of "equality" into the sphere of economic relations between Christ believers, we must look to the inner logic of Paul's theology—to Paul's belief in a God who had voluntarily impoverished himself: "For you know the generous act of our Lord Jesus Christ, that on account of you he became poor, so that by his poverty you might become rich" (2 Cor. 8:9).

In conclusion, we may note that Paul's most egalitarian pronouncements in his Corinthian correspondence are connected with the arrival of reports from Corinth, and that Paul's informants evidently represented lower-class members of the Christian community. In 1 Corinthians 1:11 Paul states that it has been "made known" (ἐδηλώθη) to him "by Chloe's people" (ὑπὸ τῶν Χλόης) that there are "dissensions" (ἔριδες) among the Corinthians. The expression οἱ Χλόης (literally, "those of Chloe") denotes her slaves or freedmen, or both.[71] The information that they bring had evidently been omitted from the official correspondence of the *ekklēsia* (cf. 1 Cor. 7:1; 8:1; 12:1; 16:1; 16:12).[72] Further, the news that divisions (σχίσματα) had erupted when the Corinthians came together ἐν ἐκκλησίᾳ to eat the Lord's Supper is described by Paul as an oral report (ἀκούω), whose bearers he discreetly shields with anonymity (1 Cor. 11:18).[73] That anyone other than lower-class Christians would have reported to Paul on the hunger and humiliation of "the have-nots" at the communal meal is hardly credible. Finally, the report about women who were praying and prophesying in the assembly in 1 Corinthians 11:2–16 is likewise anonymous.[74] Thus, Paul's extension of the principle of "equality" into the sphere of economic relations between Christ believers builds on and develops egalitarian and democratic impulses that were already at work in the earliest Christian communities,[75] empowering the voices of the poor, slaves, and women in the discourse of the assemblies.[76]

NOTES

I wish to express my gratitude to Melanie Johnson-Debaufre, the respondent to this paper; her impact on my conclusions is reflected in the final paragraph of this essay.

1. Joseph Stiglitz, *The Price of Inequality: How Today's Divided Society Endangers Our Future* (New York: W. W. Norton, 2012), 1–2, 7–8; Thomas Piketty, *Capital in the Twenty-First Century* (Cambridge, MA: Harvard University Press, 2014); Ricardo Fuentes-Nieva and Nick Galasso, "Working for the Few: Political Capture and

Inequality," *Oxfam Briefing Paper* 178 (2014): 2; Branko Milanovic, *Global Inequality: A New Approach for the Age of Globalization* (Cambridge, MA: Harvard University Press, 2016); Deborah Hardoon, Ricardo Fuentes-Nieva, and Sophia Ayele, "An Economy for the 1%: How Privilege and Power in the Economy Drive Extreme Inequality and How This Can Be Stopped," *Oxfam Briefing Paper* 210 (2016): 2.

2. Branko Milanovic, "A Note on 'Maximum' US Inequality," *globalinequality* (December 2015), http://glineq.blogspot.com/2015/12/a-note-on-maximum-us-inequality.html?m=1. See also the Appendix "The Limits of Inequality" in Walter Scheidel, *The Great Leveler: Violence and the History of Inequality from the Stone Age to the Twenty-First Century* (Princeton, NJ: Princeton University Press, 2017), 445–56; Immanuel Wallerstein, Randall Collins, Michael Mann, Georgi Drerluguian, and Craig Calhoun, *Does Capitalism Have a Future?* (Oxford: Oxford University Press, 2013); Wolfgang Streeck, *How Will Capitalism End? Essays on a Failing System* (London: Verso, 2016).

3. Immanuel Wallerstein, "Structural Crisis, or Why Capitalists May No Longer Find Capitalism Rewarding," in *Does Capitalism Have a Future?* 21.

4. Wallerstein, "Structural Crisis," 32, 36.

5. Streeck, *How Will Capitalism End?* 12–13.

6. Streeck, *How Will Capitalism End?* 28–34.

7. Streeck, *How Will Capitalism End?* 41–45, drawing on the work of Sabine Donauer, *Faktor Freude: Wie die Wirtschaft Arbeitsgefühle erzeugt* (Hamburg: Edition Körber, 2015).

8. Alain Badiou, *The Rebirth of History: Times of Riots and Uprisings* (London: Verso, 2012), 4–5, 14.

9. Jeffrey A. Winters, *Oligarchy* (Cambridge: Cambridge University Press, 2011).

10. Jeffrey A. Winters, "Oligarchy and Democracy," *American Interest* 7, no. 2 (2011), https://www.the-american-interest.com/2011/09/28/oligarchy-and-democracy/.

11. Badiou, *The Rebirth of History*, 12.

12. Badiou, *The Rebirth of History*, 12.

13. E.g., the commentary of Cornelius a Lapide (1614), trans. and ed. W. Cobb, *The Great Commentary of Cornelius a Lapide, II Corinthians and Galatians* (London: Hodges, 1897), 117, recounting stories told by Patristic writers about Paulinus of Nola and St. Paula, as examples. In the twentieth century see Petros Vassiliadis, "Equality and Justice in Classical Antiquity and in Paul: The Social Implications of the Pauline Collection," *St. Vladimir's Theological Quarterly* 36 (1992): 51–59; idem, "The Collection Revisited," *Deltion Biblikon Meleton* 11 (1992): 42–48; David G. Horrell, "Paul's Collection: Resources for a Materialist Theology," *Epworth Review* 22, no. 2 (1995): 74–83; Steven J. Friesen, "Paul and Economics:

The Jerusalem Collection as an Alternative to Patronage," in *Paul Unbound: Other Perspectives on the Apostle*, ed. Mark D. Given (Peabody, MA: Hendrickson, 2010), 27–54; Julien M. Ogereau, "The Jerusalem Collection as κοινωνία: Paul's Global Politics of Socio-Economic Equality and Solidarity," *New Testament Studies* 58, no. 3 (2012): 360–78; L. L. Welborn, "'That There May Be Equality': The Contexts and Consequences of a Pauline Ideal," *New Testament Studies* 59 (2013): 73–90.

14. Paul's emphasis on equality has been largely silenced, particularly in the Pastoral Epistles; see, e.g., M. F. Wiles, "The Domesticated Apostle," in *The Writings of St. Paul*, ed. Wayne A. Meeks (New York: Norton, 1972), 207–19. See also the image of Paul in Eusebius, *Hist. eccl.* 1.1.2, 1.12, 2.1, 2.3, 2.22, 3.4, with the commentary of Ward Blanton, *A Materialism for the Masses: Saint Paul and the Philosophy of Undying Life* (New York: Columbia University Press, 2014), 6–7, 184–87.

15. E.g., Jacob Taubes, *The Political Theology of Paul*, ed. Aleida Assmann (Stanford, CA: Stanford University Press, 2004); Alain Badiou, *Saint Paul: The Foundation of Universalism* (Stanford, CA: Stanford University Press, 2003); Giorgio Agamben, *The Kingdom and the Glory: For a Theological Genealogy of Economy and Government* (Stanford, CA: Stanford University Press, 2011). On the shift from "political theology" to "economic theology," see now Ward Blanton, "A New Horizon for Paul and the Philosophers: Shifting from Comparative "Political Theology" to "Economic Theology," in *Paul and Economics: A Handbook*, ed. Thomas R. Blanton IV (Minneapolis: Fortress Press, 2017), 397–423.

16. On the hermeneutic implied in this judgment, see the preface to L. L. Welborn, *Paul's Summons to Messianic Life: Political Theology and the Coming Awakening* (New York: Columbia University Press, 2015), xi–xvii.

17. See esp. Giorgio Agamben, *The Church and the Kingdom* (London: Seagull Books, 2012), 41, in a discourse delivered in Notre Dame Cathedral in the presence of the Bishop of Paris and other high-ranking clerics.

18. The expression "pneumatic democracy" in reference to the "paleontological" period of the early Jesus movement is taken from Adolf von Harnack, *Einführung in die Alte Kirchengeschichte: Das Schreiben der römischen Kirche an die korinthische aus der Zeit Domitians (I. Clemensbrief) übersetzt und den Studierenden erklärt* (Leipzig: Hinrichs, 1929); repr. in *Encounters with Hellenism: Studies on the First Letter of Clement*, ed. Cilliers Breytenbach and L. L. Welborn (Leiden: Brill, 2004), 1–2, 74.

19. Martin Luther King Jr., sermon at the National Cathedral in Washington, DC, on March 31, 1968.

20. Pope Francis, *Evangelii Gaudium: The Joy of the Gospel* (New York: Crown, 2014), esp. chap. 2, "Amid the Crisis of Communal Commitment."

21. From Bonhoeffer's prison letters, cited in Charles Marsh, *Strange Glory: A Life of Dietrich Bonhoeffer* (New York: Alfred A. Knopf, 2014), 379.
22. Agamben, *The Church and the Kingdom*, 41.
23. *The New Oxford Annotated Bible with Apocrypha: New Revised Standard Version*, ed. Michael D. Coogan (Oxford: Oxford University Press, 2010), 2033.
24. Walter Brueggemann, "Follow the Money: Gospel Hopes for the Economy," a lecture delivered on Saturday, September 16, 2017, at Westminster Presbyterian Church, Dayton, Ohio.
25. BDAG 481 *s.v.* ἰσότης 1 "*equality*, ἐξ ἰσότητος *as a matter of equality* 2 Cor. 8:13; also ὅπως γένηται ἰσότης *that there may be equality* vs. 14": *A Greek-English Lexicon* (hereafter LSJ), compiled by Henry George Liddell and Robert Scott, revised by Henry Stuart Jones (Oxford: Clarendon Press, 1996), 840 *s.v.* ἰσότης 1 "*equality*."
26. Eduard Lohse, *Colossians and Philemon: A Commentary on the Epistle to the Colossians and to Philemon* (Philadelphia: Fortress Press, 1971), 162; BDAG 481 *s.v.* ἰσότης 2, referencing Diogenes Laertius 7.126 and Philo, *Spec. Leg.* 4.231, in addition to Col. 4:1, under the meaning "fairness." But in Philo, ἰσότης means "equality," rather than "fairness," and is translated thus by F. H. Colson, *Philo VIII: On the Special Laws, Book 4* (Cambridge, MA: Harvard University Press, 1939), 151: ἔστι γὰρ ἰσότης μήτηρ δικαιοσύνη ("for the mother of justice is equality"); in the Diogenes Laertius, Zeno's teaching on the proper sphere of each virtue includes the observation, τῇ δὲ δικαιοσύνῃ ἰσότης καὶ εὐγνωμοσύνη ("to justice, equality and fair-mindedness [are subordinate]").
27. E.g., Diodorus Siculus 5.71.2: "He [Zeus] visited practically the entire inhabited earth, putting to death robbers and impious men, and introducing equality and democracy" (τὴν δ' ἰσότητα καὶ τὴν δημοκρατίαν εἰσηγούμενον)—a text which is adduced under the meaning "fairness" in BDAG 481 *s.v.* ἰσότης 2.
28. Polybius 2.38.8.
29. BDAG 481 *s.v.* ἰσότης 2; LSJ 840 *s.v.* ἰσότης II.
30. Polybius 2.38.6.
31. An exception would seem to be Pseudo-Phocylides 137: μοίρας πᾶσι νέμειν, ἰσότης δ' ἐν πᾶσιν ἄριστον ("Render to all their due, impartiality is best in every way"; translation and commentary by P. W. van der Horst, *The Sentences of Pseudo-Phocylides* (Leiden: E. J. Brill, 1978), 205.
32. Aristotle, *Metaph.* 1054b3; Plato, *Grg.* 508a; etc.; perhaps also Menander, *Monostichoi* 259: ἰσότητα τίμα, μὴ πλεονέκτει μηδένα ("Honor equality, do not defraud anyone"), a text which is adduced under the meaning "fairness" in LSJ 840 *s.v.* ἰσότης II and BDAG 481 *s.v.* ἰσότης 2.
33. E.g., Euripides, *Ph.* 536; Plato, *Lg.* 757a; Aristotle, *Pol.* 4.4.2; Polybius 6.8.4.

34. The foundational study is that of Rudolf Hirzel, *Themis, Dike und Verwandtes: Ein Beitrag zur Geschichte der Rechtsidee bei den Griechen* (Leipzig: Teubner, 1907), 228–320, 421–23, esp. 239–68; see further Gustav Stählin, "ἴσος, ἰσότης, κτλ..," *Theological Dictionary of the New Testament* 3 (1963): 343–55; Klaus Thraede, "Augustin-Texte aus dem Themenkreis 'Frau,' 'Gesellschaft' und 'Gleichheit' I: 70/97," *JbAC* 22 (1979): 122–64.
35. E.g., Hans Windisch, *Der zweite Korintherbrief* (Göttingen: Vandenhoeck & Ruprecht, 1924; repr. 1970), 257–58; C. K. Barrett, *The Second Epistle to the Corinthians* (New York: Harper & Row, 1973), 216–17, 226; Victor Paul Furnish, *II Corinthians: Translated with Introduction, Notes and Commentary* (Garden City, NY: Doubleday, 1984) 399, 407–8; Hans Dieter Betz, *2 Corinthians 8 and 9: A Commentary on Two Administrative Letters of the Apostle Paul* (Philadelphia: Fortress Press, 1985), 37, 67–69; Margaret E. Thrall, *A Critical and Exegetical Commentary on the Second Epistle to the Corinthians*, Vol. 2: *2 Corinthians 8-13* (London: T & T Clark, 2004), 520, 539–40; Thomas Schmeller, *Der zweite Brief an die Korinther. Teilband 2: 2 Kor 7,5–13,13* (Neukirchen-Vluyn: Neukirchener Theologie Patmos Verlag, 2015), 42, 64–65.
36. Steven J. Friesen, "The Blessings of Hegemony," in *The Bible in the Public Square: Reading the Signs of the Times*, ed. Cynthia Briggs Kittredge (Minneapolis: Fortress Press, 2008), 117–28.
37. G. B. Kerferd, *The Sophistic Movement* (Cambridge: Cambridge University Press, 1981), 139–47; Cynthia Farrar, *The Origins of Democratic Thinking: The Invention of Politics in Classical Athens* (Cambridge: Cambridge University Press, 1988), 44–98, esp. 77–98.
38. Plato, *Prot.* 320c–323a. On whether Plato accurately reports Protagoras's ideas, see W. C. K. Guthrie, *A History of Greek Philosophy*, Vol. 3: *The Fifth Century Enlightenment* (Cambridge: Cambridge University Press, 1969), 64, 265–66.
39. Plato, *Prot.* 322b.
40. Plato, *Prot.* 322c.
41. Plato, *Prot.* 322c.
42. Plato, *Prot.* 322d.
43. Plato, *Prot.* 322d.
44. Plato, *Prot.* 322d.
45. Kerferd, *Sophistic Movement*, 144; similarly, M. I. Finley, *Democracy Ancient and Modern* (New Brunswick, NJ: Rutgers University Press, 1985), 28–29.
46. Antiphon Fr. 44(b), *P.Oxy.* 1364 + *P.Oxy.* 3647; Hermann Diels and Walther Kranz, *Die Fragmenta der Vorsokratiker*, vol. 2 (Berlin: Weidmann, 1960), 352–53; Gerard J. Pendrick, *Antiphon the Sophist. The Fragments* (Cambridge: Cambridge University Press, 2002), 180–81.

47. Pendrick, *Antiphon the Sophist*, 351.
48. Arguing for a critique of class distinctions, S. Luria, "Antiphon the Sophist," *Eos* 53 (1963): 63–67. Referring the contrast to laws, M. S. Funghi, "*P.Oxy.* 3647," in *The Oxyrhynchus Papyri*, Vol. 52, ed. Helen M. Cockle (London: Egypt Exploration Society, 1984), 4. Suggesting a reference to different gods, Decleva Caizzi, "Il nuovo papiro di Antifonte," in *Protagora, Antifonte, Posidonio, Aristoteles: Saggi su frammenti inediti a nuove testimonianze da papiri*, ed. Francesco Adorno (Florence: Leo S. Olschki Editore, 1986), 62–63.
49. For the text see Pendrick, *Antiphon the Sophist*, 180, with commentary and observations on the translation choices, 359–60.
50. Hermann Diels, "Ein antikes System des Naturrechts," *Internationale Monatsschrift* 11 (1917): 96–98; Ernest Barker, *Greek Political Theory: Plato and His Predecessors* (London: Methuen, 1918), 85; Wilhelm Nestle, *Vom Mythos zum Logos: Die Selbstentfaltung des Griechischen Denkens von Homer bis auf die Sophistik und Sokrates* (Stuttgart: Alfred Kroner, 1942), 377, 380–81; Mario Untersteiner, *The Sophists* (Oxford: Blackwell, 1954), 251–52; Eric A. Havelock, *The Liberal Temper in Greek Politics* (New Haven, CT: Yale University Press, 1957), 256–58; Guthrie, *History of Greek Philosophy III*, 152–53; David J. Furley, "Antiphon's Case against Justice," in *The Sophists and Their Legacy*, ed. G. B. Kerferd (Wiesbaden: Franz Steiner, 1981), 90; Martin Ostwald, "*Nomos* and *Phusis* in Antiphon's Περὶ Ἀληθείας," in *Cabinet of the Muses*, ed. M. Griffith and D. J. Mastronarde (Atlanta: Scholars Press, 1990), 293–306; Michael Gagarin, *Antiphon the Athenian: Oratory, Law, and Justice in the Age of the Sophists* (Austin: University of Texas Press, 2002), 66–67, 71–72, 86.
51. Aristotle, *Pol.* 1266a39–1267b21, 1274b9. For what is known about Phaleas of Chalcedon, see E. Schütrumpf, *Aristoteles: Politik*, vol. 2 (Berlin: Akademie-Verlag, 1991), 238–41; Trevor J. Saunders, *Aristotle, Politics: Books I and II* (Oxford: Clarendon Press, 1995), 135–40. On Phaleas's theory of equality, see Claude Mossé, *La fin de la démocratie athénienne* (Paris: Presses Universitaires de France, 1962), 234–46; Gabriel Zuchtriegel, *Colonization and Subalternity in Classical Greece: Experience of the Nonelite Population* (Cambridge: Cambridge University Press, 2018), 220–23.
52. Aristotle, *Pol.* 1266b32–35.
53. Aristotle, *Pol.* 1266a39–41.
54. Aristotle, *Pol.* 1274a8–9.
55. Aristotle, *Pol.* 1266b1–6.
56. Zuchtriegel, *Colonization and Subalternity*, 220–21.
57. Aristotle, *Pol.* 1266a39–41.

58. Hans Lietzmann, *An die Korinther I/II* (Tübingen: Mohr Siebeck, 1949), 137; Windisch, *Der zweite Korintherbrief*, 258n.1; Furnish, *II Corinthians*, 399, 407; Betz, *2 Corinthians 8 and 9*, 37, 67.
59. See Jacques Rancière's account of his childhood, youth, and education, along with his involvement in the *Gauche Prolétarienne*, in *The Method of Equality: Interviews with Laurent Jeanpierre and Dork Zabunyan* (Cambridge: Polity Press, 2016), 1–8, 12–20.
60. Jacques Rancière, "The Method of Equality," in *Recognition or Disagreement: A Critical Encounter on the Politics of Freedom, Equality, and Identity*, ed. Katia Genel and Jean-Philippe Deranty (New York: Columbia University Press, 2016), 139–40.
61. Jacques Rancière, *Hatred of Democracy* (London: Verso, 2014), 48.
62. Rancière, *Hatred of Democracy*, 48.
63. Rancière, *Hatred of Democracy*, 48.
64. Rancière, *Hatred of Democracy*, 48.
65. Rancière, "The Method of Equality," in *Recognition or Disagreement*, 139.
66. Rancière, "The Method of Equality," in *Recognition or Disagreement*, 140.
67. Rancière, "The Method of Equality," in *Recognition or Disagreement*, 141.
68. Rancière, *Hatred of Democracy*, 61.
69. Rancière, "The Method of Equality," in *Recognition or Disagreement*, 147.
70. On 1 Cor. 12:13 as an allusion to the baptismal formula, see Lars Hartman, *"Into the Name of the Lord Jesus": Baptism in the Early Church* (Edinburgh: T & T Clark, 1997), 66–67, 87–88. For the egalitarian implications, see Wayne A. Meeks, *The First Urban Christians: The Social World of the Apostle Paul* (New Haven, CT: Yale University Press, 1983), 88.
71. Gerd Theissen, *The Social Setting of Pauline Christianity: Essays on Corinth* (Philadelphia: Fortress Press, 1982), 93; Wayne A. Meeks, *The First Urban Christians: The Social World of the Apostle Paul* (New Haven, CT: Yale University Press, 1983), 59.
72. John C. Hurd, *The Origin of 1 Corinthians* (Macon, GA: Mercer University Press, 1983), 43, 48–49.
73. Hurd, *Origin of 1 Corinthians*, 78–82.
74. Antoinette Wire, *The Corinthian Women Prophets: A Reconstruction through Paul's Rhetoric* (Philadelphia: Fortress Press, 1990); more recently, Jill E. Marshall, *Women Praying and Prophesying in Corinth: Gender and Inspired Speech in First Corinthians* (Tübingen: Mohr Siebeck, 2017).
75. See esp. Cynthia Kittredge, "Rethinking Authorship in the Letters of Paul: Elisabeth Schüssler Fiorenza's Model of Pauline Theology," in *Walk in the Ways of Wisdom: Essays in Honor of Elisabeth Schüssler Fiorenza*, ed. Shelly Matthews,

Cynthia Briggs Kittredge, and Melanie Johnson-DeBaufre (Harrisburg, PA: Trinity Press International, 2003), 318–33.

76. Anna C. Miller, *Corinthian Democracy: Democratic Discourse in 1 Corinthians* (Eugene, OR: Pickwick, 2015), who emphasizes the importance of the democratic discourse of the *ekklēsia* in the Greek cities of the Roman East as an inspiration for early Christian assemblies and for Paul.

⌘ 9. Listening for the Power of the People: A Political Theology of Affect

LISA GASSON-GARDNER

Truth isn't truth.
—RUDY GIULIANI, *Meet the Press*, August 2018

Halo around you, don't have to face it on your own.
—JANELLE MONÁE, "Americans"

Political discourse in the United States is experiencing a crisis of truth. Truth seems to either have no grounding in fact or to be limited to fact alone—and facts alone, arguably, lack the power to unite people to work for justice. Despite ongoing declarations that American society is "post-truth," political theologians and activists who seek to facilitate a coalition of people who share a set of powerful, motivating claims that respond to climate crisis, to white nationalism's (most recent) rise, to fascism, and more must not allow truth to fall into meaninglessness. Truth ought to matter—to be materially connected to the lives of people, specifically the people who are most oppressed by the US system of governance and power.

First, this chapter analyzes the contemporary deployment of reason as the definition of truth, arguing that this version of truth is limited and focused mainly on fact-checking. Stephen Pinker's *Enlightenment Now* serves as a representative example of the elevation of fact-checking as the pinnacle of truth-making. Pinker advocates for a form of supposedly secular (free from religious bias) reason that has no first principles—nothing to "believe in." In doing so, Pinker obfuscates the human element of truth-making, the fallibility and the admixture of beliefs, acknowledged or not. As a result,

Pinker obscures the power, a kind of sovereignty, to set the norms for truth. This essay attempts to free reason from this sovereignty by recognizing the fallibility and unacknowledged beliefs working in current political truth-making.[1] Pinker extends his neutral version of reason into ethical decision-making, which has life-and-death consequences for human beings, creatures, and even the earth. Further, the supposed neutrality of Pinker's reason obfuscates his dependence on a version of the autonomous sovereign subject—the modern liberal subject—who has the ability to exert reason over the other faculties, including feeling. Following J. Kameron Carter, this essay argues that the sovereign subject is a white, heterosexual, cisgendered, able-bodied man and therefore excludes many (most) people not only from decisions about truth, but even from citizenship in the United States.

Depending on the modern liberal sovereign subject, who has the ability to exert reason over feeling, misses the power of affect as it is deployed on the right. This essay argues that the exceptional truth-claims made on the right break the repetitive monotony of life and therefore become a site of excitement, of passion, in truth-making—and that this kind of truth is powerful. The affective dimension of truth is key to understanding the current status of truth in US political discourse. Continually fact-checking those on the right, while important, obfuscates the movement of power—of affective power. The left and the right find themselves at an impasse of fact versus feeling, which leaves progressive causes powerless when faced with claims that are factually inaccurate but affectively powerful. White supremacy/nationalism's latest rise cannot be countered with facts alone; it requires the paradigm-breaking power of affect. And at the same time, affective intensity is a source of power that can be abused, like any form of sovereignty. This essay seeks to articulate an affective truth that is fed by facts, therefore growing materially out of oppressed communities that seek change.

Given these observations, this essay proposes that political theologians seeking to advance progressive justice should listen to music—specifically, this essay argues, to popular music. The multitude already moves as a diffuse, decentered body of power with the potential to challenge sovereignty.[2] The multitude requires a political project—and this essay proposes that in the US context, the people already have a project. If political theologians listen, listen with all their senses, perhaps they will hear the movement of the people, of the multitude.

Pop music does more than confront political theology with the voices of oppressed peoples; it demonstrates how truth-making must operate across the supposed bifurcation of feeling and facts. Listening is not only an act of comprehension of the mind; listening involves the whole body and all the senses. Music can be described with words, but it cannot be reduced to concepts. This essay suggests that by listening to popular music, political theology will be moved, will be shaped by the political project of the oppressed and disenfranchised multitude. Listening is not without the critical skills of reason; political theology must recognize the most recent reassertion of white dominance and listen for the music, the movement that counters it. Music, heard with critical ears, can open political theologians to the prophetic movement of the multitude, which not only speaks truth to power, but performs it. Prophecy exhorts, challenging the failings of leadership in society, while also imagining a different future.

In this essay, the black queer musician Janelle Monáe is one prophetic voice of the multitude. Her song, "Americans," conceives of a different America, one that empowers, even divinizes, Black women, while also physically, materially moving listeners with its infectious pop beat. In "Americans" Janelle Monáe performs truth. In performance, truth is both conceptually presented and affectively felt, opening up the iterative possibility within each moment: The possibility to move differently in each is the possibility of a different world. Performed truth, enacted truth, is, hopefully, change.

THE STATUS OF TRUTH IN THE UNITED STATES

The election of known liar Donald Trump as president of the United States shocked much of the country's progressive left. Communication expert Dana Cloud argues that the left's surprise was a product of how they (we) were listening. The left was busy fact-checking Trump's various lies, while the right was listening to something else. Cloud explains that magnetic appeal of Trump's claims is not in their "truth," if truth is defined as factual correspondence with reality, but rather in their "persuasiveness."[3] The left missed this, because they are limited by their "commitments to rationalism and too-simple understandings of truth."[4] This essay proposes that political theologians, too, are limited by their understanding of truth—and in turn, their ability to communicate truth.

Political theology has thoroughly documented the movement of sovereign power from a transcendent God into the State. At the same time, truth was brought down to earth, becoming the purview of human knowing. This is succinctly captured in Descartes's infamous "I think, therefore I am." Building on this claim of Descartes's, rationalists argued that what is real (and therefore true) is what human beings conceive in their mind. Following this, empiricists claimed that what is real is what can be measured with the human senses. Although Immanuel Kant offered a philosophical theory that unites the noumenal with the phenomenal, popular political understandings of truth are still unsure how to bring together reason and the concrete data presented to the human senses—a binary that doesn't even consider feeling and affect, which are increasingly a source of truth in contemporary politics. This lack of clarity then gets exacerbated in the resonance machine that is US politics, and what results are "alternative facts" on the right and a complicated fact-checking apparatus on the left. The definition of truth therefore matters, because it is one source of the widening ideological divide in political discourse. At the same time, this debate, these constant arguments about what claims are "fake news," serves as white noise drowning out other, more insidious drumbeats, like white supremacy, sexism, and xenophobia.

Truth-claims for extremist groups, like white nationalists and supremacists, are dependent on affective power and cannot be challenged on the basis of facts alone. After the murder of fifty Muslim people in Christchurch, New Zealand, in 2019, articles appeared about the rhetorical strategies of white nationalist manifestos, including the strategy of "shitposting," where an author throws out inflammatory statements, hoping to draw the reader deeper into a radicalized corner of the internet.[5] The claims of white nationalism are not "true," if truth is defined as the correspondence of reality to facts: There is no "white genocide." Yet for an alarming number of people these claims are "true" as affective, effective organizing tools.

What does it sound like to speak truth to this power? Again, the first impulse of progressive communities is to counter hateful claims with facts, with the data that prove the claims are inaccurate. A recent, representative example can be found in Pinker's book *Enlightenment Now*, which undertakes his project on a wide scale, attempting to prove that the world is currently better than it has ever been. For example, he statistically demonstrates that undernourishment has been on the decline since 1970. The first two-thirds of the book are dedicated to these kinds of statistics, attempting to address every imaginable problem, from inequality to climate change.

Pinker does not argue that these problems are nonexistent; rather, he argues that human beings, especially "intellectuals," are suffering from "progressophobia," a fear of recognizing that the world is now better than it has ever been. Pinker claims this fear is brought on by a variety of cognitive biases, like the availability bias that is stoked by a steady diet of negative news stories. "The answer," Pinker declares, "is to *count*," to turn to data—or, as Cloud predicts, to the facts.[6] However, Pinker is aware that facts must—in some way—be evaluated and scaffolded by theories that interpret the data.

Reason is the human faculty that verifies facts, applies logic, and, hopefully, justifies beliefs. For Stephen Pinker, and the Enlightenment thinkers he venerates, human reason is the tool par excellence for evaluating and organizing data. Reason, according to Pinker, is "prior to everything else," but cannot be justified with "first principles"—because we don't "believe in reason."[7] Yet reason is a human faculty—if there are no first principles to anchor and stabilize the operation of reason, then it constantly requires testing and confirmation (which Pinker endorses). Pinker's unfailing confidence in reason disguises the element of human fallibility worked into the constant evaluation of facts. For example, Pinker vehemently argues that science cannot be blamed for "genocide or war."[8] Indeed, if the science is abstracted from human actions, then it is certainly not to blame. However, the operation of science cannot be abstracted from human beings practicing science, human beings whose beliefs might be racist. Science practiced by people who are racist has led to horrific practices on minority groups—for example, the legalized practice of eugenics in the United States that led to the forced sterilization of people of color and people with intellectual disabilities. The results of racist science have been used to shore up racist beliefs. Facts are not a panacea. Facts alone cannot neutralize complex social/cultural problems such as racism, at least not without wading into the messy knot of beliefs and—this essay argues—affect that shores up racist beliefs.

If reason is a valid source of knowledge—and Pinker lists revelation, dogma, authority, charisma, conventional wisdom, and a variety of other forms of knowledge in a list of "generators of error"—then reason is the only tool for making decisions, thereby becoming central to ethics.[9] Here, an unacknowledged dynamic appears in Pinker's argument: His trust in reason obfuscates the operation of power, a kind of sovereignty, in truth-making. If reason requires constant testing and evaluating, even in the arena of ethics, then there is someone or something making decisions that define—and even end—the lives of people. Consider, for example, what happened at the southern US border under the Trump regime, where policy decisions dictated that migrant children were to be cruelly detained in facilities unprepared to house them. Jailed in facilities designed for adults, infants were forced to drink from dirty bottles, toddlers wore dirty clothing, and children were held for months. Trump and government officials claimed their actions were necessary and—even reasonable—given the large number of people who attempt to cross the US border every day. Yet under the Obama administration, children were released from custody and allowed to stay with family while they waited for their immigration hearing. The Trump administration's decision to force children to wait in camps was motivated by white supremacy, which does not recognize immigrants of color as human.

Political theology in the lineage of Nazi Carl Schmitt recognizes the power in decision-making—and the sublimated operation of decision-making power within the modern state. Schmitt infamously claimed, "Sovereign is he who decides on the exception."[10] In his *Political Theology*, the exception is the sovereign power—"the highest, legally independent, underived power"—that cannot be removed from the operation of a state, only abstracted into a possible emergency, into a contingency plan.[11] Despite an entire legal system designed to regulate power—even, in a liberal democracy, designed to place it in the hands of the people—there is always some concrete situation that is not decided by the law, and requires someone or something to decide the exception. Sovereign power, according to Schmitt, is inherited from a traditional version of the Christian God; the sovereign exception, therefore, represents the continued influence of Christian theology in the supposedly secular state.

There is a connection, a parallel, between the transcendent, absolute sovereignty of the Christian God and the sovereign modern liberal subject: the (white, male, cis, able) person who claimed the power to name truth or to say "I am" during the Enlightenment. Again, at the same time divine power was sublimated into the state, the power to define knowledge, or to make truth, was assigned to the sovereign subject. The sovereign self, as described by Mayra Rivera, "was assumed to be the master of his agency; he knew himself and was in control of his emotions and desires."[12] This must be the subject imagined by Pinker, if it is possible to separate the operation of the scientific method from the racist beliefs of the people performing scientific experiments. Importantly, critiquing the sovereign subject is not meant to deny the effectiveness of reason or science, but rather to challenge the absolute decision-making power that is associated with sovereignty. Political theology requires truth that is enriched with reason and empirical data *and* is attentive to the movement of power.

Indeed, the modern liberal subject, seemingly neutral, removed from the messy knots of societal beliefs and debates, has been used to maintain a particular kind of subject—a white, male, cisgendered, able-bodied citizen. J. Kameron Carter argues that, in the United States, political subjects—or citizens—are formed by a national myth, binding together people as an ethnos. Carter contends that the myth of the "White Savior," an echo of the colonialist narrative, mediates citizenship in the West.[13] People who do not conform to the image of the "Global White Masculine" are not recognized as subjects and are thus deprived of political agency and citizenship.[14] Pinker's congruent elevation of the thinking subject is a move that has a long racist and sexist history. Women and people of color (along with many other nonconforming groups) are associated with feeling and desire, which should be subjected to the superior force of reason that is manifest in white men.

In addition, Pinker's insistence that reason is the only valid form of knowledge leaves his encounter with white nationalists claiming "white genocide" bereft of any recourse other than the presentation of data and a demonstration of their flawed reasoning. Arguably, this keeps the conversation at the level of prime-time news punditry, with both the left and right yelling about "fake news." Pinker's level of discourse cannot touch beliefs, because beliefs are grounded in more than simple reason. Yet Pinker's deference to reason requires that human beings deny other forms of engagement with the world—the passionate, affective ones. For Pinker, just because human beings are susceptible to emotions, passions, and desires does not mean that these drives should be slaked, because "a vulnerability is not the same as a need"; nor should affective drives have any part in the ethical, or arguably political, decision-making process.[15] Again, these forms of knowledge are "generators of error." Yet without the ability to address beliefs, which are affectively charged, Pinker will make no headway in counteracting the claims of white nationalists.

It should not be a surprise, then, that the sovereign exception's power is both conceptual and affective. Carl Schmitt argues, "In the exception the power of real life breaks through the crust of a mechanism that has become torpid by repetition."[16] In other words, the norm-breaking (and creating) exception is exciting. The exception is a site of novelty, of newness, which jolts human beings into a moment of attention. A moment of exception is therefore novel, but also the place where humankind can most clearly see the systems of norms and general principles that govern their social and political systems. Schmitt quotes Søren Kierkegaard's assertion that "the exception . . . thinks the general with intense passion."[17] The exception plays not only to reason but also to desires—and to affect. This essay argues that the exception's affective power drives the kind of fact-defying rhetoric that continually emerged from the Trump administration—rhetoric that picked up and amplified the drumbeat of white supremacy. Listening to Trump's exceptional truth-claims made clear that white nationalism and supremacy drove his administration; at the same time, Trump's communication was not only conceptual; it was also affective, rallying crowds with passion. Truth defined according to modern secular reason, therefore, obfuscates multiple forms of power: the power to define subjectivity and citizenship, and the power of passion, desire, and affect. This essay attempts to articulate truth that strips reason of its link to white male sovereignty, while channeling the affective, paradigm-breaking power of the exceptional.

In response to the limitations of truth as conceptualized by secular reason, which tends to be preferred by the left, Dana Cloud proposes that truth must include "embodiment, emotion, narrative, myth, and spectacle."[18] For her, it is by engaging multiple forms of human knowing—not only facts—that progressive causes can embed their political claims in the public imagination. Dana Cloud exhorts the left to do more than "speak truth to power," if truth is limited to facts. In this vein this essay suggests that political theology might look to biblical traditions of prophecy, which are often touted as the model of speaking truth to power. One example is the failed prophecy of Elisha, which demonstrates not only how to speak truth to power, but also the power that comes from listening to music.

THE POWER OF MUSIC TO PROPHESY

In 2nd Kings, the armies of Judah, Israel, and Edom find themselves stuck in the wilds of Edom without any food or water. They had set out to attack the kingdom of Moab, whose king had recently recanted a promise to provide Israel with livestock. Now trapped, the leaders of the armies call to Elisha and ask for help. In this story, Elisha is a prophet in both senses of the word: first, he exhorts the three gathered kings because, of the three, only Jehoshaphat of Judah exclusively follows Elisha's God, and then, second, Elisha predicts the future of what will happen in battle. Importantly, for this reading, before he speaks of the future, Elisha says, "get me a musician," and it is as the musician plays that "the power of the Lord" comes on Elisha. It is this movement of power, the power that comes with music, that is the interest of this essay.

Music, argues political theorist Jeremy Gilbert, "has physical effects which can be identified, described and discussed but which are not the same thing as it having meanings."[19] Music is a part of the human experience that can be expressed in language, but its meaning cannot be reduced to language. This, Gilbert argues, is the affective dimension of music. Gilbert draws on the work of affect theorist Brian Massumi, for whom it is this pre-discursive layer of human experience that constitutes hope or belief in the potential for political and social change. Massumi argues that being present in the moment more intensely opens a "margin of maneuverability" and allows for experimentation with different ways of being.[20] Gilbert argues that the felt experience of music is an example of the intensity Massumi describes. Affect theory draws a distinction between affect as pre-discursive and "feeling" or the culturally constructed forms given to affect. Yet, for Massumi, affect is "transversal," working across both the mind and the body.[21] Therefore, there is no way to tap into "pure" pre-discursive affect, because it is always manifest in space and time. Massumi defines hope as the abstract potential to be different in the world. Music touches more than just the conceptual. It moves the body differently, thereby not only conceiving a different world, but also performing, enacting a different possible world.

Covered with the power of the Lord, a power that comes with listening to music, the prophet Elisha predicts that water will come and fill the valley at sunrise, and it does. In coming at that time, the water catches and reflects the red light of the sunrise. The red water confuses the Moabites, and they attack, thinking the three kings in the valley are fighting among themselves. The armies of the three kings are therefore able to advance, defeating the Moabites. Yet despite this moment of seeming fulfillment, Elisha's musically driven prophecy is one whose truth is widely debated, both historically and narratively.[22] In the next passage, the story pivots and, despite their immediate victory, the three kings are badly defeated by Moab, proving Elisha's promise that "the Lord will hand Moab over to you" inaccurate.

Bracketing debates about this specific prophecy, it is important to recognize the possible—and, at times, desirable—failure of prophecy. From a contemporary ethical viewpoint, perhaps the failure in this story is a relief, because the impulse to control and colonize another nation corresponds to the white supremacy this essay seeks to reproach. There is music in Trump's rhetoric of white supremacy and nationalism. What was often coded at the beginning, woven into a populist economic message, rose to a crescendo of explicit racism. Consider President Trump's racist remarks in which he told four congresswomen of color to "go back" to their country, a statement which fanned the raw fervor of white supremacy.[23] Yet this essay suggests that the prophetic power of music can be engaged without reinscribing white male sovereignty and without falling into a parody of postmodernism in which there are no facts. Critical listening that allows the whole person—mind, body, and more—to be affected can listen for the prophetic political movement of oppressed peoples or of "the multitude," which this essay argues challenges sovereignty.

Since the 1930s, continental philosophers linked metaphors of sight with the Enlightenment's sovereign subject. Famously, Descartes's thinking subject turns "a steadfast mental gaze" on the world and thereby knows it.[24] The subject who sees and knows the world, knows by categorizing, by generating a subject/object divide. The division of the world into subject and object arguably fuels strategies of othering and dehumanization. As demonstrated by J. Kameron Carter earlier in this essay, the ideal subject—the sovereign subject—is a white (cis, het, able) man. Other people—Black people, gender nonconforming people, women, and more—are seen as objects, and therefore as unhuman.

In contrast to the seeing sovereign subject, the listening subject perceives more than concepts. For example, Adrienne Janus listens for the three "resonances of sense" in Jean-Luc Nancy's book *Listening*: first, sense as meaning or conceptual; but also sense as sensual, as touching the senses, touch, taste, smell, and sight; and sense "as movement, sense of direction, and impulse."[25] Listening, this essay proposes, opens up forms of encounter that break through the facts-or-feelings impasse of truth in contemporary political discourse. Listening opens the subject/object form of knowing, which reinforces dominance and othering, into a multiplicity of forms of knowing. Listening is attentive to affect—not only by touching existing forms of feeling, like white supremacy, but also by practicing receptivity to alternative possibilities, different ways of being in the world. Listening critically, this essay proposes, makes it possible to hear the political movements of oppressed peoples and, therefore, to challenge the reinscription of sovereign power in politics.

Listening critically can hear power differently and therefore teach listeners to move differently in the world. Jeffrey Robbins's *Radical Democracy* attempts to lay out a model of political power that channels the diffuse power of the people in order to challenge the perpetual reinscription of sovereign power. Like Pinker, Robbins seeks to challenge the first principles that have limited progress in society; unlike Pinker, Robbins does not turn to a re-elevation of the modern liberal subject. Robbins, engaging the work of Michael Hardt and Antonio Negri, describes "an immanent political theology predicated on the constituent power of the multitude."[26] The multitude is the diffuse power of the people which can move in opposition to the dominating, oppressive power of sovereignty. The multitude has appeared in Black Lives Matter, Occupy Wall Street, and the Women's March. Although Robbins argues that the multitude "needs to be formed into a political body," this essay suggests that political theologians must listen for the movements that are already emerging.[27]

Listening to people traditionally excluded from the conversation requires political theologians to take seriously the forms of communication that are not traditionally used as theological or philosophical texts—for example, popular music. Again, it's not enough to conceptually comprehend the lyrics, which represent the argument—the listener has to be touched, affected, by the music. Political theology that is affected will not only speak truth to power, it will be moved, shaped by the power of the multitude. By making music—affective arguments—political theology becomes able to partner with oppressed communities as they claim their truth. And performed truth, enacted truth, is change.

AN AMERICAN PROPHECY

Take, for example, Monáe's "Americans" from her 2018 album *Dirty Computer*.[28] For a political theologian attempting to listen, the lyrics are both theological and political, attempting to present a vision of America that is worth pledging allegiance to. Overt reference to current issues such as "equal pay for equal work" and the fear Black people experience of "being shot in the head" in an encounter with the police are coupled with an exhortation to work together, to "find a way to heaven." However, this salvation is not in White American Christianity or in what Monáe calls "Jim Crow Jesus rose again." Instead, Monáe invites the listener to "play God" with her—a Black woman. A renewed America is in the divinization, the empowerment, of Black people. By listening to popular music, political theology hears the experience—the material reality—of people who are excepted from citizenship when it is defined by the modern liberal—read: white heterosexual cisgendered able-bodied male subject.

However, to only study the lyrics, which are affectively charged, misses what makes Monáe a wildly successful artist—the music. Remember that music cannot be reduced to concepts. Political theologians who listen must learn to be affected—Monáe's music therefore models a bridge across the supposed bifurcation of feeling and fact in contemporary political truth-making. "Americans" is the last song on her album *Dirty Computer*. It opens with a gospel-inspired choir, giving the listener the sense of soaring above the issues of identity and belonging described earlier in the album. Suddenly, the song breaks out in an upbeat 2/4 tempo, a pop sound reminiscent of the 1950s but inflected with both 1980s synthesizers and the tight beat-making of the present. The effect—affect—is a feeling of hope, though not a hope without caution. And while this hope is informed by the lyrics and the historical context of the musical genres, it arguably arises because the song touches something else—a part of humankind that can't be expressed in language. The experience of music—vibrations touching the body, moving from body to body—points to the material power of affect. Affects shape individual subjects—and aid in the formation of collectives. However, this musically moved power is not abstract or pure—it emerges from Monáe's community.

The affective charge of the music in Monáe's "Americans" explodes through her definition of hope, which is the collective empowerment of oppressed minorities to seek specific, concrete change. She sings, "Halo around you, don't have to face it on your own," thereby inviting a community, a community of divinized Black people, to join her in creating America. In other words, while affective intensity, which might be called a moment of exception, represents the possibility of change, "pure" affect is not political. The political project emerges at the discursive level, where specific communities claim the concrete changes they need.

Indeed, Monáe sings a rich prophecy over America, which predicts a future that has learned from the past and can address present injustices. The affective intensity of her song is framed by the lyric argumentation: The juxtaposition of her identity as American and her identity as Black tempers the hopefulness of the song with a wry humor, an ironic acknowledgment of the impossibility of being Black and American. In this way, the throwback tempo of the music is augmented by a civil rights–style voice. However, the Martin Luther King Jr.–style voice-over does not repeat a famous speech. Instead, Reverend Dr. Sean McMillan speaks to the present, imagining a different future, saying, in part:[29]

> Until same-gender loving people can be who they are
> This is not my America
> Until Black people can come home from a police stop without being shot in the head
> This is not my America, huh!

And later:

> Until Latinos and Latinas don't have to run from walls
> This is not my America

The past-present-future power of these proclamations not only works concretely from the experiences of Black Americans but also works intersectionally across communities of oppressed peoples. In other words, Monáe speaks factually about her experience as a Black queer person while also listening for and amplifying other voices—other queer people, Latinx people, and more. Monáe models listening for the multitude; and then, in turn, performing a moment of the multitude. Her power is not a repetition of white sovereignty, rather it is the unmaking, the dissolution of white supremacy.

White supremacy feeds white nationalism. Facts alone cannot combat the ideology of white nationalism, but perhaps a coalition of affectively empowered people can begin to perform a truth that challenges the stronghold of white nationalism. Monáe speaks a truth that is factually accurate, but also imagines new possibilities and animates them with music, music that affects humans. Monáe therefore demonstrates the performance of a truth that educates and motivates people—and that has a wide reach (her album reached number 6 on the Billboard Charts). By performing truth, political theologians can facilitate community that is affectively bound together in its hope for change—that is bound together in the political project of the multitude. As Monáe sings, "Halo around you, don't have to face it on your own."

NOTES

1. This essay makes use of Carl Schmitt's "sovereign exception," which he describes in his *Political Theology* as the power held by a person, or intuition, to make decisions that fall outside the jurisdiction of the law. This essay attempts to separate sovereignty in its contemporary white male, cisgendered, heterosexual, able-bodied form as it is deployed in modern reason from the affective intensity of exceptional truth-claims, which are used to such great effect by politicians on the right. It is worth noting that Schmitt was highly critical of secularity in his time and leaned into an authoritative model of power. This essay works against Schmitt by criticizing sovereignty; but by finding sovereignty in "secular" depictions of modern reason, the essay agrees with Schmitt's assertion that secularized concepts of the State hide their theological roots. Later the essay will attempt to rejoin affective power with reason, but reason that is stripped of its connection to white male, cis, het, able-bodied sovereignty.
2. The concept of "the multitude" as an alternative to sovereignty is drawn from Jeffrey Robbins's engagement of Michael Hardt and Antoni Negri in *Radical Democracy and Political Theology* (New York: Columbia University Press, 2011).
3. Dana Cloud, *Reality Bites: Rhetoric and the Circulation of Truth Claims in U.S. Political Culture* (Columbus: Ohio University Press, 2018), 20.
4. Cloud, 20.
5. For example, Jane Coaston, "The New Zealand Shooter's Manifesto Shows How White Nationalist Rhetoric Spreads," *Vox*, March 19, 2019, https://www.vox.com/identities/2019/3/15/18267163/new-zealand-shooting-christchurch-white-nationalism-racism-language.
6. Stephen Pinker, *Enlightenment Now: The Case for Reason, Science, Humanism, and Progress* (New York: Penguin Books, 2018), 43.
7. Pinker, 352.
8. Pinker, 389.
9. Pinker, 393.
10. Carl Schmitt. *Political Theology: Four Chapters on the Concept of Sovereignty* (Chicago: University of Chicago Press, 2006), 5.
11. Schmitt, 17.

12. Mayra Rivera, *The Touch of Transcendence: A Postcolonial Theology of God* (Louisville, KY: Westminster John Knox Press, 2007), Loc. 1496.
13. J. Kameron Carter, "Between W. E. B. Du Bois and Karl Barth: The Problem of Modern Political Theology," in *Race and Political Theology*, ed. Vincent Lloyd (Stanford, CA: Stanford University Press, 2012), 85.
14. Carter, 85.
15. Pinker, *Enlightenment Now*, 431.
16. Schmitt, *Political Theology*, 15.
17. Schmitt, 15.
18. Cloud, *Reality Bites*, 2.
19. Jeremy Gilbert, "Signifying Nothing: 'Culture,' 'Discourse' and the Sociality of Affect," *Culture Machine* 6 (2004), https://www.culturemachine.net/index.php/cm/rt/printerFriendly/8/7
20. Brian Massumi, ed., *The Politics of Affect* (Malden, MA: Polity Press, 2015), 7.
21. Massumi, x.
22. See, for example, Jesse C. Long, Jr., "Elisha's Deceptive Prophecy in 2 Kings 3: A Response to Raymond Westbrook," *Journal of Biblical Literature* 126, no. 1 (2007): 168–71.
23. See "Trump Tells Congresswomen to 'Go Back' to the Countries They Came From," *New York Times*, July 14, 2019, https://www.nytimes.com/2019/07/14/us/politics/trump-twitter-squad-congress.html.
24. It was a turn ironically inaugurated by another Nazi, Martin Heidegger.
25. Adrienne Janus, "Jean-Luc Nancy and the 'Anti-Ocular' Turn in Continental Philosophy and Critical Theory," *Comparative Literature* 63, no. 2 (2011): 183.
26. Jeffrey W. Robbins, *Radical Democracy and Political Theology* (New York: Columbia University Press, 2011), 84.
27. Robbins, 121.
28. Janelle Monáe, "Americans," *Dirty Computer* (Los Angeles: Atlantic Records, 2018).
29. Rev. Dr. Sean McMillan is pastor at St. Mark Baptist Church in Long Beach, CA.

PART IV

∾ Global Political Theologies

10. Undressing Political Theology for an Animal-Saint Redress

BALBINDER SINGH BHOGAL

As long as he considers one an enemy and another a friend,
his mind will not come to rest.
—GURU GRANTH SAHIB, *Gauri*, Guru Arjan, *Sukhmani*

First, I renounced ego and self-love.
Second, I renounced the ways of the world.
Renouncing the three compulsions of nature (goodness, desire, sloth),
I look alike upon friend and enemy.
The fourth [nondual, ahuman] quality is revealed by meeting the Saints.
—GURU GRANTH SAHIB, *Aasaa*, Guru Arjan

> Beyond Modernity's Thinkable to What Is Perceivable:
> De-ontologizing Thinking

A range of thinkers has argued for a different frame, positionality, and relation to the notion of religion, beyond its construction as a problematic object that could be "solved, inherited, or abandoned," for "no textualizing, anthropologizing, historicizing approach—however, *critical* it may be—can avoid the trap of humanism."[1] Abeysekara further notes that religion as an unavoidable aporia "has never been thought as a question . . . inseparable from the question of the political."[2] Noting these two insights and building on a previous essay,[3] I employ the grammars of "the animal" and "the saint" that haunt the margins of modernity to speak about alternative epistemologies that humanism desublimates.

Of course, it is hard if not disingenuous to speak out against the sacred methodological cow of "critical thinking" and its normative style of a "hermeneutics of suspicion." And I may well be accused of multiple forms of hypocrisy, but what if we acknowledge that thinking itself may be the problem? "Critical *thinking*," "*thinking* differently," "radical *thinking*," "*thinking* the unthought," "mystical *thinking*"—all assume the stability of the "I" and are thereby circumscribed by the illusory or recently invented frame of secular humanism. What if thinking can only articulate (its inability to transcend) apologias and aporias?

I want to suggest not the *radicalization* but the very transcendence of thought and thereby unsettle, perhaps even reverse, modernity's method and epistemological cul-de-sac, opening to hidden perceptual modalities of sensation and intuition as the ground of being. Alternatively stated: How might a non-Western "death of God" tradition, initiated by the Buddha two and half millennia ago, change the debate?[4] François Laruelle's argument against philosophy is relevant here. Buddhism and Sikhism are more akin to Laruelle's non-philosophy in that no prior decision is made to objectify the world *from* oneself as the projecting subject such that the world becomes a philosophical object *for* the self.[5] No such humanistic "decisional structure" was assumed or enacted by the Buddha or Guru Nanak, as both deconstructed the notion of the "thinking-self" (*aatman, haumai*) in terms of no-self (*an-aatman*) and self-loss (*aap-gavaiai*) respectively. For them, decentering the "thinking-self" was essential to liberation (from compulsions) returning to "liveliness" before thought.

Thus, not only is Western philosophy constitutively blind to its prior dualistic decision, but so too is colonial modernity, including political theology, which similarly assumed *intellectual thinking* as the primary ground for action and reflection. This was surely compounded by the colonial West's political refusal to see the other's episteme as equally legitimate. The Christian West, through policies of containment, demotion, and in some cases demolition of others, continues to suffer from a long-term multi-spatial arrogance, underpinned by the colonial project of epistemicide.[6]

The de-ontologizing of thinking therefore demands both its de-centering and de-colonization. De-ontologizing here means de-subjectifying, given the stranglehold of the thinking-ego in the Western tradition. Although both Guru Nanak and the Buddha acknowledge the importance of rational thinking, neither of them makes it the unmovable Archimedean polestar that it became for the West. In Buddhism and Sikhism a more nuanced, complex, and ultimately ineffable process de-centers the rational subject as the true "sovereign": By losing the ego (*haumai*) as well as its dualistic thinking (*dubidhaa*) a transformative non-egoic subjective register surfaces. Simply put, the "foolish mind" (*man muuraa*) "attached to the love of the other" (*man laagaa duujai bhaai*) is transformed into the "Pure" and "Beloved Mind" (*man-nirmal, man-piaare*)—a mind that "sees no other nor second" (*avara naa duujaa*), revolutionizing subject-object duality.[7] In short, we cannot only *think* about affects, but must *feel* thoughts arising at various unconscious "depths" and superconscious "heights," and this is a matter of attention, maturation, and self-awareness. Indeed, even Laruelle argues that this decisional structure can be grasped only non-philosophically; for example, in meditation the subject as a "captain of consciousness" and thought itself are seriously challenged if not displaced.[8] Although decisional splitting is basic to thinking, absorptive practices (e.g., meditation, chanting, and music), may cultivate an *affective* mind beyond egoic-thought, revealing that there are ways to escape the imprisonment of I-mind (*haumai*). Such an affective orientation allows for the evolution of the psyche to a super-conscious nondual state ("saint"), while not forgoing the already existent subconscious register of the body ("animal").[9] What both saint and animal share is embodied egolessness, spontaneity, and unselfconscious attention.[10]

The sovereign or sublime "self" is therefore not modeled on the vertical structure of domination (self *over* other) but the horizontal reality of interdependence (self *as* other), realigning sovereignty to a *subjectivity beyond egoic thinking*. Such absorptive practices then are not analytic but synthetic; the self exists within the circle of integration and not standing in judgment above or outside it. Indeed, Buddhism denies even the possibility of an unchanging center (i.e., an autonomous subject) that remains itself in a sea of interdependent ceaselessly changing relations (*pratitya-samutpada*).[11] Similarly, Sikhs see an ineffable transcendent-immanent dynamism (*ik-oankaar, nirgun-sargun*), where God and creation are not two (things).[12] One cannot simply think this dynamism, nor think from it, without fundamentally upsetting the protective self-logic of the I-mind (*haumai*). Just as the unconscious cannot simply be read by the conscious mind, nor dreams by the waking state, so this "aliveness" of *radical immanent becoming* confounds the logic of egoic thinking.

In sum, having shifted from the decisional structure of philosophy to the radical immanence of non-philosophy, the notion of the ego-subject is unrecognizably changed. The hierarchy of cognition (*symbolic*) over perception (*semiotic*) is overturned, and feeling/affect restated as the foundation of thinking.[13] Given the authorless aliveness of radical immanence, occurring before the ego, through the ego, and beyond the ego, thoughts come "without a thinker"—hence the metaphors of the animal and saint.

If each body is part and parcel of a "radical immanent becoming" that cannot be thought, then no ideological anchor such as theism, humanism, or secularism can ground thinking. Indeed, the saintly Gurmukh/Bodhisattva presents the possibility of transcending both humanism and its anthropocentrism (via evolved epistemological modes).[14] This alternative epistemology allows for a critical reappraisal of colonial modernity's focus on thought and the thinkable (*intelligibilia*) at the expense of animal instincts (*sensibilia*) and saintly intuitions (*transcendilia*).[15] Hence, I argue that there is a corollary need to identify a temporality prior to secular humanism's historicism given the latter's fictive transition from living sacred time to representational secular time via rational thinking alone. A prior temporality freed of the modern myth of progress has no need, unlike secular humanism, to repress the animal and saintly realms of affect—they are what constitute its aliveness.

Living Ahuman Temporality before *Human Chronologies*

Must not this place of the Other be ahuman?
—JACQUES DERRIDA, *The Animal That Therefore I Am*

While acknowledging the anthropocentric if not humanist projection of secular temporal power, let us refer to this prior temporality that is not tied to human chronology as *ahuman temporality*. As radical immanence, *ahuman temporality* cannot be reduced to productions in measurable time and hence must be distinguished from the particular formations of "secular" time and "secularism" that the West employs to suggest temporal "overcomings" of religion and religious time.[16] By arguing that ahuman temporality is not driven by secularism, I seek to foreground reflections about temporality beyond European Christendom. This is primarily because Sikh "non-philosophy" equates the temporal (*sargun*) with the transcendental (*nirguna*), denying any division between "Creator," "Creation," and "Will," expressed via the "Word," "Name," and "True Guru."[17] *Ahuman temporality* is not therefore a logic that is captured by rationality; it is an incalculable constellation and movement of forces only intimated by animal instincts and gut feelings as well as prophetic intuitions and dreams.[18] As Derrida himself calls the ahuman, "divinanimality"—"the quasi-transcendental referent, the excluded, foreclosed, disavowed, tamed, and sacrificed foundation of what founds, namely, the symbolic order, the human order, law and justice."[19] I figure it as *humanidevality,* which comprises both "secularization" (animal *sensibilia*) and "sacralization" (saintly *transcendilia*) *as a singular process* that human *intelligibilia* necessarily negotiates.

As Dussel notes, the revolution figured by Copernicus "lay not so much in having dethroned the earth from its central position *as in having denied that the universe had a center."*[20] Guru Nanak's non-philosophy similarly decenters all traditions, exemplified by its refusal to place any one language, culture, ethnicity, or group at the center of its singularity. His inherently comparative and "pluriversal"[21] outlook integrates these ahuman (animal-saint) temporal affects via multiple grammars of the Guru Granth Sahib.[22] Guru Nanak himself sings of this ahuman temporality as "God," the "One Being-Becoming," which is "ever-fresh and ever-new,"[23] as is "His love"[24] and "true teaching."[25]

> My Master is forever new; He is the Giver, forever and ever.
> Night and day, I serve my Master; He shall save me in the end.
> Listening and listening (*suni suni*), O my dear sister, I have crossed over [to nirvana].
> —GURU GRANTH SAHIB, 660, *Dhanaasarii,* Guru Nanak

These "ever-fresh" and inherently existential ahuman temporal affects (beyond human law and order) are translated into thought *but are not themselves thinkable.* Thinking is merely one among several modes of perceiving and addressing these forces. Indeed, the Guru's Word is not merely cognitive (knowledge) but affective (poetic and musical), and thus combines literature with aesthetics, philosophy with poetry and song.[26] During the Guru period (1469–1708), Sikh traditions never switched to prose to consolidate and represent their poetry into a *thinking* system—resisting the move to form a political theology with an ideological stance. The point was not to have a knowledge systematized into a belief an ego could hold, but to feel the songs and be transported into a revealed speechless-speech (*akath-kathaa*) beyond egoic capture. Yet the Sikh Gurus were pragmatic enough to build cities, develop commercial economies, invest in architecture, educational, and artistic projects—and thereby found a heterogenous community and "way" beyond the boundaries of language, caste, and "religion."

The Gur-Sikh case therefore reveals a different epistemology at work, one that is beyond thinking and humanism that nevertheless still demonstrates many of the values purported by today's liberal secular model as freedoms. By shifting the focus of secular/religion from being a *"problem"* to the question of *"aporia"*—which is not thinkable—Abeysekara sets in place a series of important readings. We shall return to his work presently. He argues that "if we are to think 'the question of Buddhism,' we must radically rethink the very category of history itself" beyond "the Foucauldian art (or fad?) of (genealogical) historicization," given that it "fails to offer us any new insights into the concepts of history, memory, and time, let alone on the question of the political."[27]

Abeysekara builds his argument having engaged with Qadri Ismail's novel *Abiding by Sri Lanka*, in which Ismail foregrounds "postempiricism" and literature as possible ways forward. These, Ismail suggests, as alternatives to empirical knowledge production of historical anthropology have not served or resolved but merely managed the continued conflict in Sri Lanka. Ismail argues that literature "allows one to learn from the problems it stages: at its strongest, most articulate, most imaginative, it presents problems, and not answers."[28] The shift suggested then is from interpretation to *intervention*, from activism to the *intellectual imagination*, where the problem of the political cannot be (merely) about knowledge production.[29] Even anthropology after the "interpretive turn" that "claims to work (or coauthor) with the native" fails, as its knowledge is still produced in dependence on "the binary of insider/outsider that is fundamental to the history of imperialism itself."[30]

However, Abeysekara argues that Ismail's desire "to resolve/dis-solve the problem of Sri Lanka" ultimately fails. This failure according to Abeysekara is due to Ismail's framing the issue as a "problem" rather than as an aporia— "that which cannot be rethought so as to resolve or transform it, without passage,"[31] for "any attempt to rethink the problem always returns to the problem of resolving/retaining itself, with no guarantee when it will need further resolutions. This is the law of the problem."[32] Abeysekara's answer, following Derrida, is that we have to *think* differently, aporetically. That if we think of religion and its heritage as an aporia, then it "is not something we can move *beyond*. . . . It cannot be replaced or *supplemented*."[33]

To the extent that Abeysekara aporetic thinking halts the thinking self's chatter to ponder the linguistic traps it gets caught by, I am with him. However, as noted above, I am deeply suspicious of yet another form of *thinking* that does not challenge the thinking-self *at root*. Indeed Abeysekara, having been a practicing Buddhist monk, may have had meditation or some such practice in mind, that aporia must call for. If we do not *think* religion, but engage and embody it as a temporal *affective-aporetic* form expressing the changing forces of ahuman temporality, then its dynamic remains "ever-fresh" and "new" *in accordance* with our own *transforming subjectivity* (which, of course, is the difficult part as we become addicted to our ego-story). Merged wholly within that ahuman temporality, and unmoored from egoic-thinking, saints "receive/perceive" new un-centered thoughts from the intelligence that underwrites creation.[34] Ahuman temporalization lived is mysticism—where animal listening and saintly intuitions (to the extent one is able to listen and cultivate these) may form human feelings and thoughts differently, beyond the logic of self, or group interest.

Is not (1) *rational thinking* (philosophy) as it displaces poetry, music, and song, (2) *interpretation* (hermeneutics) as it displaces translation, (3) *representation* (stereotype) as it displaces encounter and indigenous enunciation, the three modes of Western "humanistic" domination? And might not aporetic *thinking* merely suspend the subject in perpetual hesitation and doubt? How to transform the compulsive mind and not merely invent new ways for it to think? To avoid the traps of humanism, historicism, and empiricism, the focus on aporia, postempiricism, and literature (or poetry, music, and song) must be taken further to the realm of affective epistemologies of embodied praxes.

Rather than shift from thinking to perception as argued for here, one might persist and argue that a different form of aporetic thinking is required—one that engages this affective register of aliveness. Simon Critchley seems to argue for precisely this, maintaining that (Greek) tragedy presents such an alternative to Western rational philosophy, for it creates a certain "aliveness" that outstrips thought, and allows us to learn from our precarity, doubts, ambiguity, and conflicts. Seeing a certain hubris in philosophy's "practice of rational affect regulation,"[35] by which the crises of competing truth claims and the unavoidable ambiguity of inscrutable life events are either "tamed" or "explained away," Critchley argues (echoing Buddhism) that tragedy reminds philosophy that "crisis is life and has to be lived as such":[36]

> Tragedy presents a conflictually constituted world defined by ambiguity, duplicity, uncertainty, and unknowability, a world that cannot be rendered rationally fully intelligible through some metaphysical first principle or set of principles, axioms, tables of categories, or whatever. Tragedy is the experience of transcendental opacity.[37]

But, again, this transcendental opacity is viewed only from the angle of egoic-thinking (rational or not), leading him to conclude (following the fifth-century BCE rhetorician Gorgias) "that tragedy is a deception that leaves the deceived wiser than the nondeceived."[38] Further, and more predictably, tragedy leads to a "life of skepticism, where the latter is the index for a certain moral orientation in the world, an orientation that seems to emerge from the disorientation of not knowing what to do."[39] From there it is a short Nietzschean step to stake out the necessity of art (tragedy) such that we do not die of the truth (philosophy): "The vast question that Gorgias's fragment raises is that of the necessity and indeed moral and political productivity of deception, of fiction, of fraud, of illusion."[40]

Rather than question how another form of *thinking* (even when figured as "thinking in action")[41] merely pushes the wall of thought onto another territory via an untidy tragic affect (*catharsis*), Critchley shores up the position of the thinking ego and fails to entertain that that "transcendental opacity" may lead to different orders of perception and intuitive knowledge. Critchley forgets to elaborate the clue of "aliveness" beyond that which the actor Isabelle Huppert gave him, that is toward a mode of non-egoic perceiving that Eastern traditions have exemplified in various forms of breathing and meditation. The Buddha, so it is claimed, "overcame" that transcendental opacity through mindfulness and the praxis of the middle way.

In a similar vein, Zeynep Talay-Turner argues—again following Nietzsche but also the writers Robert Musil and Oğuz Atay—that we are to be "the poets of our life"[42] rather than philosophers, because life is "lived as literature."[43] Reviewing this work, King-Ho Leung summarizes the position succinctly, "If 'writing' is what turns life into literature, we might say that 'reading' is what turns literature into life,"[44] thus transforming philosophy (thinking) into an art of living and writing.

Both Talay-Turner and Critchley turn away from philosophy toward literature (like Ismail above), from a metaphysical abstraction of being to the praxis of becoming and "aliveness"; both argue against the trajectory of Western philosophy, from Plato onward, emphasizing the "unfinishability" (of literature) and the "ambiguity" (of Greek tragedies) respectively. Yet both seem to return to thinking, as though life's challenges and tragic theater only temporarily halt if not elevate the ego. The notion of dissolving "the thinker" of thoughts and transcending the ego on a more permanent basis is not entertained as it is in Eastern traditions: like the "dropping off of body and mind" (Dogen) or "self-loss" in Sikhism.

How not to reduce life to egoic thought, that desublimates its complexity into an egoic projection embedded in a particular worldview? How not to sacrifice *gnosis* (saintly insights) for knowledge assumed to deliver certainty?[45] I argue that literature and tragedy are only answers in part, necessary but too often embedded in the same colonial modernity's "knowledgeable" subject.

The dynamic, pre-egoic nature of what I've been calling ahuman temporality is captured well by King-Ho Leung. Leung (like Laruelle above) provides a way forward by drawing modern subjectivity back to an organic protosubjectivity. He argues we must first acknowledge that Descartes's linking of thinking to being crucially omits life—what I've been calling the aliveness of a radical immanent becoming before "I." That is, we have to shift from Descartes's duality of being and thinking back to an Augustinian tripartite structure of being (*esse*), living (*vivere*), and thinking/understanding (*intelligere*):

> As opposed to Augustine's formulation of the *living* proto-*cogito* that is formally bound up with a theological conception of God as "Life" itself, Descartes' "lifeless" *cogito* is a picture of "thinking without life" that formally opens up a model of "thinking without God"—indeed a *secular* picture of "Godless" thinking. . . . For whereas one can produce or "create" one's own thoughts, the same cannot be said of one's own life. . . . One's life is always given from a source of life other than the thinking self—life is something which *transcends* the realm of thought.[46]

Derrida agrees: The Cartesian "'I am' does not depend on being-in-life but on thinking," which forgets the foundational nature of "respiration, breath, or life."[47] But neither Derrida nor Leung acknowledges that *meditative* breath can act as the bridge between abstract thought and the affective body, thus enabling cognition to reconnect to *living ahuman* perception—as understood by many forms of ancient and medieval yoga. The Gur-Sikh one-many, formless-form, unmanifest-manifest being-becoming is one precisely to be lived, perceived, and merged into, for it is the livingness of life itself.[48] Losing the ego allows the absorption and merger into the Essenceless Primal state of life itself, which is a fearless, hateless, self-ordering intelligence.[49] Then "with my eyes, I perceive the One, embodiment of bliss, to be everywhere."[50]

Under *and* Over *Modernity: Perceiving* Living *Animal-Saintly Affects*

Derrida sees a similarity in the "sovereign" and the "beast," in that both share the transcendence of the symbolic law, being above and beneath it.[51] Similarly, I figure these temporal forces as composed of animal–somatic drives (beast) and divine–prophetic guides (sovereign), but I argue beyond the duality of *humanimality–divinanimality* to propose an engagement with these semiotic and symbolic forces such that the possibility of "becoming-saint" (*deva*) arises—hence my tripartite *humanidevality*.[52]

The evolved state of the saint is possible when the human mind is enlightened: when the "nine doors of the body" reveal the "Tenth Door" of Tantric liberation (*dasam duaar*); when the "three dualistic states of waking, dreaming and deep sleep" dissolve into the nondual "Fourth State" of superconsciousness (*chautaa-pad*), when the "foolish mind" (*man muurai*) is transformed into the "Pure Mind" (*man-nirmal*). But humans live in symbolic abstractions, forming identities, prime among them the "thinking self" of "I am"—that represses the animal body and leaves uncultivated the saintly mind. This linguistic mode of identification has to shift from the ego's intellect (*intelligibilia*) opening to the "natural intelligence of life itself" (*transcendilia*) expressed by the term *hukam* (the impersonal law of ahuman temporality): One has to sacrifice one's egoic thinking to align with *hukam*: "Everyone is subject to *hukam*; none are outside it. O Nanak, one who embodies *hukam* (consciously), has no ego to speak of."[53]

What I've been calling ahuman temporality and humanidevality is expressed in Sikh teachings as the One (*ek*) becoming the many (*anek*), the formless (*nirgun*) becoming formed (*sargun*), as one dynamic process. This process "communicates" to the ego-self through all life (elemental, vegetal, animal) "speaking," automatically, constantly, and endlessly. Through the animal sensorium below (as a body among bodies and a body within bodies), and saintly intuitions above (spoken from anywhere through everything), human feelings and thoughts (within and across bodies) may be radically transformed. Listening to the animal body and being open to the saintly mind would instigate a shift from thinking to sensing, feeling, and intuiting, such that thought is informed by subconscious and superconscious affects that arise as the thinking ego subsides, unveiling a fearless (*nirbaau*), hateless (*nirvair*), spontaneous (*sahaj*), unauthored intelligence (*naam*) that is always already at play. Insights arising from experiencing this alignment with ahuman temporal intelligences cannot be commanded by the thinking self as they arrive independent of any logic, technique, or method. "Opening-up" to aporetic-affective animal-saint intelligences are, to say the least, full of mercurial wonder (*vismaad*), making alignment with *hukam* a "very fortunate" (*vad-bhaagi*) occurrence. The Sikh orientation is captured well by Walt Whitman as he distinguishes between intelligence and intellect: "A bean in its pod confounds the learning of all times. . . . I hear and behold God in every object, yet understand God not in the least."[54]

The problem is that the ego has formed into a stubborn (sociolinguistic) "wall" (*paal*) that muffles out the elemental-phenomenal "voice of the Guru" (written into the fabric of existence). The ego-self suffers a form of temporal amnesic dyslexia remembering only its own delusional cognitive stories while constantly ignoring its own bodily affects and intuitions. It is only through the latter that phenomenal ahuman temporality directly "speaks" (through pain, aging, and disease as well insight and bliss), disrupting thinking's defensive wall. Animal-saint affects are a sea of forces forming a changing territory to the ego's outdated map, like waves of the sea that murmur and then crash against the brick wall of the ego. *Ahuman temporality, humanidevality, hukam, the Guru's songs*—different names for that unnameable sea of psychic and material forces—may become, for a lucky few, an affective "*axe for the frozen sea within us*,"[55] instigating a revolution in perception against the ego-boat's titanic thinking.

The argument here (i.e., the disruption and recontextualization of cognition within affective perception) assumes that modernity's epistemic erasures suppress immanent temporal forces to form modern secular subjectivity in "human *metaphysical* time." This argument represents a counter to the hegemony of the "linguistic turn" where the "linguistic fallacy misunderstands religion as merely a byproduct of language, and misses the economies of affect ... that are the animal substance of religion and other forms of power."[56] That is to say, being converted to modern consciousness costs not only the direct visceral connection to our animal-body, but also the opportunity to "cultivate" the *saintly* mind. We sacrificed our *sensibilia* and *transcendilia* to make human *intelligibilia* "autonomous"; the excision of the animal (*under*-modernity) and the abandonment of the saint (*over*-modernity) at the hands of humanism's thinking self has left us alienated from both "body" and "soul." Worse still, this atrophy traps us in violent projections of the other as irrational animals while we assume superiority as rational humans, thus externalizing our repression through the oppression of others.[57]

Once we recognize that thinking (humanistic or techno-scientific) cannot erase the persistence of the unknown (unpredictable, immeasurable, incalculable, mysterious, incomprehensible), then this itself ensures not only the incomplete nature of our knowledge and thinking but also institutes a permanent structural lack and endemic myopia within any systematized thought.[58] We are forever in need of epistemic and affective modes beyond logical thinking to live and begin approaching life's symbiotic complexity. Despite the conceptual shift into secular rationality, we still retain terms and ideas that reflect the *animal* and *saintly* grammars (from gut feelings to the serendipitous). We are beings that outstrip the contradictions in and of thought, that not only contain spiritual multitudes à la Whitman, but also microbial multitudes à la Yong.[59] The Guru Granth Sahib transposes elite esoteric vocabularies (of the Nath Yogis, Siddhas, Buddhists) into the realm of everyday speech, integrating the "revelations" of Bhagat and Sufi saints through the vernaculars of quotidian experience. Bodily instincts (*kaaiaa, trai-gun*) and saintly insights (*gur-shabad, sadh-sangat*) are thus integrated by the human intellect (*mati*) rather than dismissed. Indeed, "the body is the horse, upon which one rides to the Lord"[60] as well as "an incomparable chamber of jewels [insights]."[61] Whereas the human transcends the limits of the animal body through the ability to delay gratification, the saint transcends the human mind's projections by de-centering its assumed power or will (*aap-gavai*) and aligning it with *hukam*—the ahuman temporal intelligence (*hukam rajaai calanaa*) all subsist within.

The integration of animal and saintly grammars within the human, requires more than thinking: It requires engagement with latent epistemic modes of listening and accepting "voices," affects, intimations beyond conscious thinking. Such an integration (to connect "feeling" with "thinking") has of course been argued for by others.[62] However, most resist the evolutionary transmutation from human to saint, and remain locked within a secular rationality of the limited ego that *merely talks and thinks* of the "impossibility" of resolving these "two" modalities. For example, Nick Mansfield argues that "sovereignty is an unconditionality that gives rise to [conditional] ipseity as an 'inversion' of itself.... Sovereignty and individuality require one another but only in a relationship of mutual *threat*.... The individual will *always fail* to live the subjectivity that sovereignty seems to make available."[63] Why should this be the case? Why absolutize the impossible, failure, and threat when there is a long list of mystics across traditions, time and place that seem to indicate otherwise? Yes, all may fail in *representing* it, but do all fail in *living* it? Certainly, within the Sikh tradition, the Guru and Gurmukh are precisely figures that integrate the sovereignty of unconditional subjectivity already embedded within ahuman temporality with their own particular "individuality"—this is the point of awakening and liberation, to shift from *Manmukh* (egoic I-mind) to *Gurmukh* (ego-less Beloved Mind). Those effecting this subjective evolution (into the saint) are known as the true sovereigns (*sacha-patishah*), pluralizing and democratizing sovereignty; the Sikh evolved ideal thus combines the enlightenment of the saint with the just war of the warrior as a single process. The Sikh "political theology" is then focused on freedom through the double register of objective liberty and subjective liberation—neither assume the friend-enemy distinction as absolute, and both are only possible at the expense of the thinking ego.[64] That one *can* access those ahuman forces phenomenologically—again by psychologically, meditatively, entering the psychosomatic reservoir of one's being—seems essential to this debate.[65]

Epistemologies Otherwise and the Double-Sovereignty of Humanidevality
If the "machinic" (calculable and predictable) repetitions of everyday life are intersected every now and then with the "evental irruption of the unforeseeable" and "miraculous,"[66] is it possible to contact and "steer" that irruption into a disciplined transformation? Against Lauren Berlant's *cruel optimistic* attachments and Donovan Schaefer's affective *compulsions*, Indic

traditions argue that we can erase, or at least overcome, such deep habituations (*samskaaras, vaasanas, trai-gun*) within our own subjectivity. We are not left to only *think* about this irruption of the miraculous within the machinic retrospectively.[67] That is to say, by ignoring "unwholesome" tendencies (to use Buddhist vocabulary), there are "wholesome" or "saintly" aporetic-affective tendencies that, if cultivated, eventually tame the tempest of the mind into a calm unperturbability. Those wholesome tendencies can act as the proverbial Philosopher's Stone: transmuting the base metal of egoic thinking into the gold of selfless flow (*sahaj*), and then "the filthy become pure."[68] In the Guru Granth Sahib that stone (*paaras*) is God/aliveness, found within the community of saints as well as within one's own body.[69]

What I am intimating is moving beyond egoic thinking about how to solve an existential problem we think we already know, toward the "cultivating" of saintliness via the integration of the excised animal and divine grammars through an existential praxis. This involves, as Steven Moore notes, "a knowing with rather than a knowing about."[70] This affective reorientation has the potential to radically reconnect with Whitman's and Yong's *multitudes*. The key distinction is not conceptual (between capital or labor, good or bad, sacred or profane), but affective and existential: that is, the ability to psychically journey *within* to connect with the unauthored intelligences of phenomenal existence beyond thought, and journey *without*, coming back into thought and symbolization such that one is spoken through: "As the Word of the forgiving Lord comes to me, so is it expressed through insight [*giaan/transcendilia*]."[71] How does returning to the unthinkable—Augustine's "God as life," that symbiotic being of beings, the microbial and the multitudes—transform our understanding of Sovereignty?

Sovereignty of Co-Dependent Origination

> The first person who, having fenced off a plot of ground, took it into his head to say this is mine and found people simple enough to believe him, was the true founder of civil society.[72]
> —ROUSSEAU, *Discourse on the Origin and the Foundations of Inequality among Men* (1755)

Therefore, surely, O monks, whatever form [feeling, perception, mental formations, consciousness], past, future or present, internal or external, coarse or fine, low or lofty, far or near, all that form [et al.] must be regarded with proper wisdom, according to reality, thus: "This is not mine, this I am not, this is not my self."[73]
—THE BUDDHA, *Anatta-lakkhana Sutta* (Fifth Century BCE)

Before Laruelle, over two and half millennia ago many Indic traditions understood the illusory (*maaiaa*) language of egoic desire and fear (*trsna*). Objectification does not happen only externally as in Rousseau's claim of land as property, but *first and foremost* it occurs internally, subjectively, by reducing one's whole lived experience into a mere conceptual representation of "I-mind," or the culturally embedded idea of "This I am, this is mine, this is myself" (à la Descartes). The resistance to own, objectify, and reduce the immanent or temporal self to a sociolinguistic abstract "I am" is shared by many Asian traditions—whose beginning is rather "I am not." It is not surprising that the Yoga Sutras, the Guru Granth Sahib, and the Tao Te Ching all begin with the denunciation of egoic thinking.[74]

In recognizing the limits of thinking, we necessarily address the limits of subjectivity. The shift from thinking to affective knowing is matched by a shift from an external Sovereign whose power is universalized over all to the *pluriversal* sovereignty within all beings. Within the Sikh tradition both occur together forming a sovereignty that is doubled. This shift from, or conflation of the Independent Sovereign with an internal co-dependent sovereignty, is one that moves from a vertical domain of domination to a horizontal realm of co-creation. This necessarily implies an ethical shift as false sovereignty over land or over subjectivity does not only occur when the "land" or form of one's body-image becomes the property of the thinking self, but also occurs when the actual land and bodies of *Blacks or Dalits* are stolen as the property of the *White or Brahmin* thinking mind.[75]

Like Michael Naas and Derrida, I want to think democracy and divinity without sovereignty, or more specifically without *Western* notions of sovereignty—to acknowledge the violent and violating imperial projects of Europe's colonizations that formed the "modern/colonial capitalist world system."[76] But rather than ditch the notion of sovereignty (as does John Caputo in his "weak theology")—as though only the West can think sovereignty and consequently only it can dispense with it—we may envisage a sovereignty not limited by its verticality. Caputo argues, "If sovereignty goes to the heart of the modern idea of the nation, that would mean that one way to disturb the sovereign rule of sovereignty and of sovereign nations would be to return to theology and reimagine God." This leads Caputo to conclude that one has to "imagine God without power," though "not without authority," namely, to think of God as a "weak force" or "at most as a kind of 'power of the powerless.'"[77]

The metaphysical (I-mind) relates to the existential (body), much as the universal relates to the particular—such that historically, the (Euro-American) master dominated the (colonized) slave within the context of empire's "I am" sovereignty. This involves the subjugation not only externally (Indigenous peoples) but internally (autochthonous populations). In other words, a *transcendental mechanism* rules over an existential immanence (according to Hardt and Negri)—making the real implications of an animal-saint redress political and profound.[78]

This verticality that dominates the horizontal plane formulates into what Hardt and Negri call "the sovereignty machine," by which European men dominate over non-Europeans, and in which the "civilized first world" defines the "barbaric third world." They also argue that the transitional crisis in authority from (ahuman) revelation to (human) reason (culminating in the European "Enlightenment") is not overcome but merely *deferred*: that the medieval God (*theos*) who stands over nature is *replaced*, not displaced, by modern Man (*anthropos*). Thus, modernity replaced the *transcendence* of divine command with the *transcendence* promised by human thinking, unveiling "a strict continuity between the *religious* thought that accords a power above nature to God and the modern *'secular'* thought that accords a power above nature to Man."[79]

That is to say, despite switching authority, power remained transcendental, hierarchical, and conceptual, whether the shift occurred from God to King, State, Nation, People, or Demos. The unresolved crisis of modernity is the contradictory co-presence of the *immanent lived experience of the multitude* and a transcendent *thinking* power that wants to reduce it to the rule of One Sovereign.[80] That transcendental apparatus fixed the sovereignty of Descartes's *thinking*, Kant's *reasoning*, and Hegel's *historically developing* autonomous subject at the center of authoritative enunciation creating Europe's cognitive empire. Thus, the philosophies of all three aided the counterrevolutionary "transcendent Europe" to define self-other relations in terms of a master-slave dialectic that dismantled Southern epistemologies and economies in the process. That is to say, social contract theory does not merely involve Europeans, it also incorporates a discussion about Europe's new and growing colonies and how to control them.

> Modern sovereignty emerged, then, as the European reaction and domination both within and outside its borders. They are two coextensive and complementary faces of one development: rule within Europe and European rule over the world.[81]

Through empire, imperialism, and colonization the West became the metaphysical head of the world's, that is, the multitude's, affective body. European ideas and their philosophers sit above all other ideas and philosophers. The tension drawn by Hardt and Negri is *not*, however, between East and West, but between two Europes, or two modernities. And I argue that there is a great resonance between the *immanent* form of European modernity and various *immanent* forms of the East, given the coerced humbling of selfhood within the two populations, that are, nevertheless challenged and defeated by a *transcendental* form of modernity that opposes them both.

Both "immanent Europe" and "immanent East" were controlled and their challenge negated by the imposition of a transcendental apparatus or metaphysical ideology, be it Western Enlightenment or modern mimetic Hindu Brahmanism, aimed at vertically splitting apart god from nature, self from other, human from animal, history from myth, or upper-caste (*brahmin*) from lower-caste (*shudra*), orthodoxy (*aastika*) from heterodoxy (*naastika*), thus aligning sovereignty vertically. According to Hardt and Negri this splitting was achieved by the assumption of *mediation* through *thought*.[82] Thus, the rise of the sovereign European subject, through the authority of the Enlightenment's rational, metaphysical, and historical individual, was simultaneously matched by the rise of a new form of mediation, the Sovereign Nation-State—a transcendent political apparatus "used to impose order on the multitude (both within Europe and without in the colonies) and prevent it from organizing itself spontaneously and expressing its creativity autonomously."[83] What might an understanding of sovereignty beyond domination and ideological mediation look like? How might the sovereignty of the pluriversal be intuited?[84]

One way is to shift to the horizontal. To orient ourselves toward animal *sensibilia* and saintly *transcendilia* is to open our human *intelligibilia* to the multiplicity of species-specific intelligences all around us. That is to say, rather than being "a collection of [hierarchically organized] objects," the world, following Thomas Berry, is refigured as a "communion of subjects." Mary Evelyn Tucker argues that the "shift from an anthropo-centric sense of domination to an anthropo-cosmic sense of communion with all life forms" requires us to acknowledge that we "live amidst a multiplicity of intelligences, among them hunting and foraging," "courting and mating," "flying and swimming," "migrating and molting," "communicating and playing intelligences."[85] To "dwell in [such] intimate immensities," Tucker argues, reveals that "animals have been guides and teachers embodying patterned knowledge that draws us out of our self-enclosed human egos."[86] To this list, I would simply add a reminder not to overlook the saint who communicates our kinship with these animal intelligences in a way that is uniquely revealing. From Francis Assisi's to Guru Har Krishan's communion with animals, from Jain and Buddhists practicing *ahimsa* (non-harming) to Zhang Zai's sage who "forms one body with the universe"—all embody not only an intimate pluriversal phenomenology but one, that in the Sikh case, is irreducibly political.

Pluriversal Political Phenomenology beyond the Limits of Thinking Alone
In contrast to the West's transcendental and ideological conceptions of freedom imposed from above onto the reality below, Neil Roberts ties freedom to slavery and its escape, that is to marronage, and as such provides a view that moves from below.[87] If freedom emerges in the slave's escape from and active negation of slavery, then this freedom is tied to the freedom of the animal and its instincts to escape and maintain the sovereignty of its mode of existence. But another freedom exists not only tied to the animal's grammar: the saints' freeing themselves from inner enslavement to the delusion of dualistic consciousness and its vices. This relates to the Indic sense of liberation where philosophy begins not in ideals but in bondage of *maaiaa*, of delusion, of ignorance and vice, of karmically conditioned behavior. If the goal is to regain a freedom one always already has (i.e., it was never given by anyone but lies inherent in nature), then sovereignty is very differently conceived, being intimately tied to one's pure being-becoming as a witnessing consciousness. Both animal and saintly marronage

need to be reconciled, both inner and outer freedoms need to be connected, to approach the double sovereignty the Sikh Gurus proposed and lived.

Extending Roberts's important project of "creolizing political theory," I too desire to ground not only Black, Dalit, or other minorities' historical experience within contexts of escaping *physical* imprisonment as actual slaves, but argue in addition that we need to anchor our analysis on the ground of our own psyches, via affective methods of "escape" from *mental* imprisonment as well—not only to "decolonize the mind" but to "awaken" it. Although *some* have survived the tempest of the middle passage only to become enslaved on a foreign island, *all* have been psychically marooned on the foreign Island of a sociolinguistic ego-consciousness. Paying close attention to how minorities rewrite political theory is not enough: We need also to examine how to regain our animal-saint sovereign consciousness. That is to say, the physicality of the slave body made *animal* as it seeks freedom is as much a resource as the mystic *deva*-mind as it attempts to dissolve mental shackles.

An Yountae connects the theo-philosophical "mystical abyss" to the sociopolitical traumatic abyss submerging the colonial subject.[88] Through this double register of the abyss, he seeks a cosmopolitan "poetics" in the "ruins" of the latter where resistance and survival emerge (just as Roberts seeks freedom in marronage escaping slavery). Yet Yountae's theo-philosophical *thinking about* the abyss (which derives from Neoplatonic mysticism, German idealism, and Afro-Caribbean philosophy) clearly begins to formulate a working *conceptualization* where the abyss operates "dialectically" and in which "the self's dispossession" during the colonial encounter or enslavement is followed by its rediscovery or "reconstruction." In this way Yountae seeks to *politicize* the mystical while *theologizing* the decolonial—a project this chapter resonates with. But, again, a now familiar problem arises: No amount of theory can necessarily discern let alone capture the body's instincts and the mind's intuitions into systematic or dialectical thought. What is clear is those undergoing oppressive violence need much more than rational thinking to survive.

Sikh history lends us an example of what the sovereignty of the pluriversal might look like. What the Sikh revolution offers is a "political phenomenology" that encourages epistemic diversity and requires cultural interdependence, rather than a monolingual "political theology" that promotes epistemic homogeneity, conversion, and dominance. As such, *sikhi* (the Way of Un/learning) engages the voices not only of the privileged and powerful

(Brahmins and Kshatriyas), but more importantly of the marginalized, oppressed, and powerless (lower castes). Sikh notions of sovereignty allowed for the recognition not only of the truth within the saints of most traditions but also the extent to which that truth was not allowed to manifest in society. Sikh notions of "sovereignty" present a new comparative, aporetic-affective epistemic structure of value and action. A salient exemplar may be seen in how within *sikhī* the monological political theology of "friend-enemy" is displaced by the political phenomenology of "friend-friend," as told through the story of Bhai Kanhaiyaa who served water to those thirsty on opposed sides in the midst of battle,[89]

> If the One Lord is my Friend, then all are my friends;
> If the One Lord is my enemy, then all fight with me.
> High and low, bad and good—the comforting canopy of the sky stretches evenly over all.
> It knows nothing of friend and enemy; all beings are alike to it.
> —GURU GRANTH SAHIB, 957

Whereas the "plural" is expressed *conceptually* through a single grammar, and operates as a transcendental thinking that orders the multitude into peoples, the "pluriversal" is expressed through multiple grammars via the immanent ground of the heterogeneous multitude. If the only phenomenological distinction that matters is of psychic depth (within/without), the real battle is not among peoples but within oneself: "If I forget You, then everyone becomes my enemy. When You come to mind, then they serve me."[90] And, "Without the Name, even one's own body is an enemy."[91] The political difference between groups is therefore misleading without acknowledging the difference that lies within at the level of phenomenal consciousness—which is in a process of degeneration, stagnation, or transformation.

Schmitt's thesis is grounded in a pessimism that assumes, as a fundamental axiom (in the West), the enmity between man and man based on the fear of death.[92] Guru Nanak's subjectivity is wholly transformed beyond pessimism and optimism toward an *ahuman temporality*: "I have no anxiety about dying and no hope for living."[93] Such an experiential state assumes not enmity at root of being-becoming (*nirgun-sargun*), but quite the opposite: fearlessness (*nirbhau*) and hatelessness (*nirvair*) as inherent universals in ahuman temporality. Contra Hobbes, this locates the corrupting and divisive influence within the ego's dualistic intellect and language, rather than in its animal instincts and appetites.

The Sikh Gurus rejected sovereignty based on "I am" (i.e., granted through a transcendental political apparatus) and affirmed the sovereignty based on the "I am not" (that no one can bestow, as each individual has to cultivate it in their own immanent lived experience). The Guru Granth Sahib is concerned with integrating the self with the other, the ego with ego-loss, such that a sovereign non-egoic voice arises. It is not a voice that can be owned exclusively by any identity because it arises precisely when that sociopolitical identity is humbled. Recall Guru Nanak's first sentence after such a *sovereign* experience: "There is no Hindu and there is no Musalmaan." In other words *no one can own and represent the voice of the multitude* as it can arise only out of a lived personal and pluriversal experience of self-loss and negation, involving the humility of "I am not" and "I don't know." Ahuman temporality is expressed through the *pluriversal* differences of *humanidevality* and authors an authorless speech of the Saint that in turn reinvests language and thought with ahuman affect:

> Tell me: who can we call good or bad?
> Behold the One (*brahm*); the truth is revealed in the Saint (*gurmukhi*).
> Perceiving (*viicaar*) the Guru's Teaching, I speak the Unspoken Speech (*akath-kathau*).
> —GURU GRANTH SAHIB, 353

Revolution in Perception: Humanidevality and Its Affective Praxes
Moving away from a self-interested thinking toward an existential and affective praxis requires the cultivation and deepening of the self's private relation to itself and others across the public sphere. Though none can direct the wind (*hukam*), some do manage to adjust their sails to attune to that immeasurable power. This humbling causes a temporary de-identification (others are not only for "I") *as* a re-identification ("I" is only for others), allowing a shift in identity politics to differential relations from friend-enemy to friend-friend. Here, conceptual mediation is rejected for experiential merger, and the notion of an open existential Way replaces that of a fixed metaphysical view; conceptualized truth is demoted by the higher value of truthful living.[94] Through socialization we transition in to language, from an "untamed" body to a "cultured" mind, but we need not be trapped by

that transition. For there is the possibility of reintegrating the protosubjectivity of the animal by overcoming the egoic I-mind and its psychic projections, and thus regain our spontaneous and effortless alignment with the temporality of humanidevality (*hukam*)—as we once had in the womb. In the womb we experienced time without I, and were merged within ahuman temporality's being and becoming—"meditating upon Him in unbroken adoration."[95] The existential recollection of that mode of being and becoming is what is meant by the principal Sikh devotional praxis of "remembering the One" (*naam-simaran*).

The *recollection* and integration of the neglected and repressed epistemologies of animal *sensibilia* with saintly *transcendilia*, triggers a transformation in human *intelligibilia*, such that the sinful ego-mind evolves into the saint's beloved mind to regain a dormant but expansive sovereignty that cannot be owned by the ego. Now one's sail is adjusted in harmony with the direction of the ever-changing Wind. Delinking thought from the "I am" thinker in remembrance of the One (*simaran*) and in service (*sevaa*) to others, one begins to sing and fight as a warrior-saint:

> Hari (God) abides in each and every heart; the Saints claim this as true. . . .
> One who is not touched by pleasure or pain, greed, attachment and egotistical pride
> —says Nanak, listen, mind: he is the very image of God ||13||. . . .
> One who does not frighten anyone [saint], and who is not afraid of anyone [soldier]
> —says Nanak, listen, mind: call him spiritually wise (*giaanii*) ||16||.
> —GURU GRANTH SAHIB, 1427

NOTES

Acknowledgments: Thanks to Sophie Hawkins, Puninder Singh Jaitla, Prabhsharanbir Singh, and the anonymous reviewer for their helpful comments.

1. Ananda Abeysekara, "Thinking the 'Question' of Religion: The Aporia of Buddhism and Its Democratic Heritage in Sri Lanka," *Religion* 38, no. 2 (2008): 1.
2. Abeysekara, 1.
3. Balbinder Singh Bhogal, "The Animal Sublime: Rethinking the Sikh Mystical Body," *Journal of the American Academy of Religion* 80, no. 4 (2012): 856–908.

4. The Buddha did not announce the death of god but his absence. Indeed, many gods exist in Buddhist cosmology, but there is no One God behind all thirty-one dimensions of *samsaric* existence; gods lack the *nirvanic* knowledge the Buddha realizes—of how to escape *samsaric* compulsions.
5. François Laruelle, *Philosophy and Non-Philosophy*, trans. Taylor Adkins (Minneapolis: Univocal, 2013). Laruelle argues that various forms of (Western) philosophical thinking are framed by a prior decision that they are all constitutively blind to. This framing decision splits the world into an object such that a subject can grasp it—classically, Descartes's *"cogito ergo sum"* but also Kant's *phenomena/noumena*, Heidegger's ontic/ontological, and even Derrida's *différence/presence*.
6. See Boaventura de Sousa Santos, *Epistemologies of the South: Justice against Epistemicide* (Boulder, CO: Paradigm, 2014), and his *The End of the Cognitive Empire: The Coming of Age of Epistemologies of the South* (Durham, NC: Duke University Press, 2018).
7. This dualistic ego mind (*haumai*) is purified of the compulsions of lust, anger, greed, attachment, and pride. *Haumai*, however, cannot be completely eradicated, nor is this the goal, as it also reflects the principle of *individuation*. *Haumai* is therefore cosmogonic not merely human. The point is not to achieve "no-mind/self" but to transform the mind-self (beyond the compulsions) and tame it to spontaneously flow in tune with *hukam* (the impersonal, intelligent ahuman temporality of existence)—which is ultimately beyond human constructions of vice and virtue, good and evil.
8. Thinking also goes beyond individual thought to its collective programming via the "Conversion to Modernity" through the "Globalization of Christianity." See Peter van der Veer, *Conversion to Modernities: The Globalization of Christianity* (London: Routledge, 1996); and Ewen Stuart, *Captains of Consciousness: Advertising and the Social Roots of the Consumer Culture*, 25th anniv. ed. (New York: Basic Books, 2001).
9. See Donovan Schaefer, *Religious Affects: Animality, Evolution, and Power* (Durham, NC: Duke University Press, 2015). I follow Schaefer's combination of the two streams of Deleuzian and phenomenological affect theories: "Affects are better understood as semi-stable, complex formations of embodied sensation that have coalesced through the advance of ancient evolutionary processes operating in deep time" (Schaefer, 58)—though his animal (biological) emphasis contrasts with the notion of the saint's mystical consciousness developed here.
10. According to Laruelle three "fundamental human types" emerge from non-philosophy: the psychoanalyst, the political militant (Marxist), and the mystic or "spiritual type." Unlike Buddhism, Sikhism combines the latter two making

a political spirituality that combines love with justice in the saint-soldier (*sant-sipaahi*) ideal.

11. No-self is not literal, as it is composed of five changing elements: form, feelings, perceptions, karmic/mental-formations, and consciousnesses. Sikhism similarly incorporates an existential focus.

12. Buddha-nature (*tathagataa-garba*) could be compared to the Sikh notion of Beloved Mind (*man-piaare*), not least because Sikh "scripture," the Guru Granth Sahib (GGS), employs the terms *sunn* (*sunya*; empty) and *nirbaan* (nirvana) to describe the one being-becoming.

13. See Antonio R. Damasio, *Descartes' Error: Emotion, Reason, and the Human Brain* (New York: Avon Books, 1994), and his *The Feeling of What Happens: Body, Emotion, and the Making of Consciousness* (New York: Harcourt Brace, 1999). See also Sara Ahmed, *The Cultural Politics of Emotion*, 2nd ed. (Edinburgh: Edinburgh University Press, 2014).

14. See Bhogal, *Animal Sublime*, for an elaboration of what I mean by the term "mystic/saint." Gurmukhs (lit. 'Gur-facing'), are beings like Bodhisattvas that cultivate an affective orientation to the other as themselves, transcending egoic-subjectivity (self-over-others, or Manmukhs—self-facing).

15. Some Sikh terms for these three are: *sensibilia* (*log, bhog, acet*); *intelligibilia* (*vicaar, buji, cet*); *transcendilia* (*alog, jog, cautaa*). When all three co-inhere, then the "discerning and making of the Guru's Word" results (*gur-shabad-vicaar/kamai*), and the "mind becomes one-pointed" (*ik-man-hoi-ik-chit*).

16. The "secular" is a central modern epistemic category whose "theologico-philosophical, legal-political, and cultural-anthropological" modes reconstruct and organize experience by differentiating it from the "religious" realm. See José Casanova, "Secular, Secularizations, Secularisms," *Social Research* 76, no. 4 (2009): 1049–66. The non-ending-ness of this desire to overcome the religious forces produces a defensive formulation of the secular as an ideology of "secularism"—that pretends to be a techno-scientific worldview, replete with "philosophies of history," and "normative-ideological state projects," where "modern statecraft" and its "epistemic knowledge regime" differentiate science from theology, and morality from religion (Casanova, 1051), history from myth, rationality from emotion, science from culture—evidencing an increasingly dogmatic division. See Vincent Pecora, "Secularism, Secularization, and Why the Difference Matters—The Immanent Frame" (https://tif.ssrc.org/2010/06/18/why-the-difference-matters/), accessed June 20, 2019. Therefore, Casanova and Pecora read *secularization* as a form of temporality beyond *secularism*: Casanova (1050) argues for "a less Eurocentric comparative analysis of patterns of differentiation and secularization in other civilizations and world religions," and

Pecora's notion of a "purposive rationality" that "refuses dogmatic thinking" witnessed *across* cultures.

17. "He is Attributeless (*nirgun*) and All-Attributes (*sargun*); those who *perceive* this reality are the true scholars" (GGS, 128); "You Yourself are the Manifest and Unmanifest" (GGS, 102); "Through His Will, He effortlessly created the Universe" (GGS, 1043); "You alone are the Doer, Cause of Causes. You are the Support of all beings. . . . You are *nirgun*, You are *sargun*" (GGS, 211); "He Himself is Formless and Form; the One is *nirgun* and *sargun*. . . . He is One and Many (*ek-anek*)" (GGS, 250).

18. *Ahuman temporality* and *humanidevality* (defined below) are used interchangeably.

19. See Jacques Derrida, *The Animal That Therefore I Am*, ed. Marie-Louise Mallet, trans. David Mills (New York: Fordham University Press, 2008), 132.

20. Enrique Dussel, *Beyond Philosophy: Ethics, History, Marxism, and Liberation Theology* (Lanham, MD: Rowman & Littlefield, 2003), 192.

21. See Walter Mignolo, "Delinking: The Rhetoric of Modernity, the Logic of Coloniality and the Grammar of De-coloniality," *Cultural Studies* 21, nos. 2–3 (2007): 449–514.

22. See *Shabdarath Sri Guru Granth Sahibji*, vols. 1–4 (1930; Delhi: Delhi Sikh Gurduara Prabandhak Committee, 1992). Compiled in 1604, the Guru Granth Sahib (GGS) contains songs of the Sikh Gurus as well as non-Sikhs (Sufis and Bhagats) as *revelations*; thus, its sacred hymns house multiple voices, languages, castes and traditions—disclosing difference and heterogeneity, not identity, as fundamental to Sikh conceptualizations of the One-Many (*ek-anek*) Being-Becoming, that is "ever-fresh and ever-new" (*neet-naavaa*).

23. GGS, 660.

24. Ibid., 407.

25. Ibid., 242.

26. However, something that is affective, poetic, and musical can remain so only within its originary language. *Gurbani* translated into English cannot be sung without losing its specific affective repertoire. English renditions produce different affects. How different these affects are, is a complex issue that the assumed universalism of New Age "spiritual" music ignores. Thanks to Prabhsharanbir Singh for raising this observation.

27. Abeysekara, 175.

28. Ibid., 176.

29. Ibid., 175.

30. Ibid., 176.

31. Ibid., 178.

32. Ibid., 180.
33. Ibid.
34. Hence the creative dynamism of the Guru Period (1469–1708) where key concepts and traditions were revolutionized and expanded to include a more overtly political form: from the ten *human* Gurus to the one *textual* Guru (GGS), from saints (*sant*) to saint-soldiers (*sant-sipahi*), from devoted "servant" (*das, Nanak-panthis*) to political "lions" (*Singh, Khalsa Panth*), from spiritual center of Harimandir Sahib to political center of Akal Takht.
35. Simon Critchley, *Tragedy, the Greeks, and Us* (New York: Pantheon Books, 2019), 39.
36. Ibid., 95.
37. Ibid., 242.
38. Ibid., 48.
39. Ibid., 24.
40. Ibid., 53–54.
41. Ibid., 21.
42. Zeynep Talay-Turner, *Philosophy, Literature, and the Dissolution of the Subject: Nietzsche, Musil, Atay* (Frankfurt am Main: Peter Lang, 2014), 79.
43. Ibid., 152.
44. King-Ho Leung, "Philosophy as an Art of Living/Writing," *Journal of Political Power* 8, no. 2 (2015): 281–88, esp. 285.
45. "The Cartesian change . . . was not the triumph of the prideful individual subject freed from scholastic shackles so much as the triumph of the quest for certainty over the quest for wisdom. . . . Science rather than living became philosophy's subject, and epistemology its center" (Richard Rorty, *Philosophy and the Mirror of Nature* [Princeton, NJ: Princeton University Press, 1979], 61, cited in King-Ho Leung, "The Picture of Artificial Intelligence and the Secularization of Thought," *Political Theology* 20, no. 6 [2019]: 467n57).
46. Ibid., 462.
47. Derrida, *The Animal That Therefore I Am*, 86–87.
48. GGS, 290.
49. Ibid., 1–8.
50. Ibid., 387.
51. Jacques Derrida, *The Beast and Sovereign*, vol. 1, ed. Michel Lisse, Marie-Louise Mallet, and Ginette Michaud; trans. Geoffrey Bennington (Chicago: University of Chicago Press, 2009).
52. *Humanidevality* combines the human, animal, and *deva*—Sanskrit for "heavenly, divine"; "a deity, god" [from Cologne Digital Sanskrit Lexicon, https://www.sanskrit-lexicon.uni-koeln.de/cgi-bin/tamil/recherche]—which I summarize

as the saintly. This represents not a thinking, but an experiential transformed nondual epistemic mode of being and becoming beyond the ego I-mind, that is creative (*kartaa*), effortless, spontaneous (*sahaj*), fearless (*nirbhau*), hateless (*nirvair*), unborn (*ajuni*), and self-intelligent (*saibang*), and contains the inherent intelligence of the True Name (*satinam*), Word (*shabad*), and Cosmic Sound (*Ik-Oankar*). (From Sikh root *mantra*, which opens the GGS.)

53. GGS, 1.
54. Walt Whitman, *Song of Myself*, 48, in *Leaves of Grass* (1892), 76, from Walt Whitman Archive: https://whitmanarchive.org/published/LG/1891/index.html.
55. Franz Kafka, *Letters to Friends, Family and Editors* (January 27, 1904), trans. Richard Winston and Clara Winston (New York: Schocken Books, 1977), 16.
56. Schaefer, 9–10.
57. The violence resulting from egoic thinking depicted here, relates in part to Gil Anidjar's notion of *destruction* in this volume. The opening line of Rousseau's *Social Contract* (1762), where "Man is born free," but because of the master-slave dialectic, "everywhere is in chains," is also relevant. See Jean-Jacques Rousseau, *Discourse on the Origin and the Foundations of Inequality among Men*, trans. Maurice Cranston (1755; New York: Penguin Classics, 1984).
58. "Thinking about the true One/Way cannot be thought, though one thinks countless times" (GGS, 1); "If anyone says he knows (the true Way), he will be known as the greatest fool amongst fools" (GGS, 6).
59. "Do I contradict myself? / Very well then I contradict myself, / (I am large, I contain multitudes.)"— *Song of Myself*. And "All zoology is really ecology. We cannot fully understand the lives of animals without understanding our microbes and our symbioses with them. . . . We need to zoom out to the entire animal kingdom, while zooming in to see the hidden ecosystems that exist in every creature. When we look at beetles and elephants, sea urchins and earthworms, parents and friends, we see individuals, working their way through life as a bunch of cells in a single body, driven by a single brain, and operating with a single genome. This is a pleasant fiction. In fact, we are legion, each and every one of us. Always 'we' and never 'me.' Forget Orson Welles, and heed Walt Whitman 'I am large, I contain multitudes.'" Ed Yong, *I Contain Multitudes: The Microbes within Us and a Grander View of Life* (New York: HarperCollins, 2016), 5.
60. GGS, 576.
61. Ibid., 821.
62. Whether it involves the balancing of the *restricted economy of the law* with the *general economy of excess*, or balancing the *intimate order* (of existential animal immanence) with the *order of things* (human symbolic abstraction), where the

aim is to be *"human without being a thing"* but simultaneously escape *"the limits of things without returning to animal slumber"* (Georges Bataille, *The Accursed Share: An Essay on General Economy*, vol. 1, trans. Robert Hurley [1967; New York: Zone Books, 1991] and his *Theory of Religion*, trans. Robert Hurley [1973; New York: Zone Books, 1992]), or it's the integration of the semiotic body with the symbolic mind, the genotext with the phenotext (Julia Kristeva, *Revolution in Poetic Language* [New York: Columbia University Press, 1984]), or various ruminations on ipseity (the logic of self-same identity) and a deconstructive unconditionality (of the gift, of justice) (Jacques Derrida, *Rogues: Two Essays on Reason*, trans. Pascale-Anne Brault and Michael Naas [Stanford, CA: Stanford University Press, 2005]), or the Fast and Slow thinking of System 1 and System 2 (Daniel Kahneman, *Fast and Slow Thinking* [New York: Farrar, Straus and Giroux, 2011]), or balancing the right and left hemispheres (Iain McGilchrist, *The Master and His Emissary: The Divided Brain and the Making of the Western World*, new exp. ed. [New Haven, CT: Yale University Press, 2010])—all reveal telling parallels with what is being proposed here.

63. Nick Mansfield, *The God Who Deconstructs Himself: Sovereignty and Subjectivity between Freud, Bataille, and Derrida* (New York: Fordham University Press, 2010), 3–5.

64. GGS, 1100, 1299. The political, in the Western tradition since Schmitt, is constructed as a thinking framed by friend-enemy polemics. *Theological* politics would need to transcend the limits of that thinking, yet current works still reflect that Schmittian bias.

65. Key Gur-Sikh aporetic-affective modes are meditative remembrance (*naam-simaran, naam-japo*), devotional singing (*kirtan*), selfless service (*sevaa*), honest work (*kirat-karo*), sharing one's earnings (*vand-chakko*), and uprooting injustice (*sac-kamai, niau*). There is an overlap here with some work on animism. See Tim Ingold, "Rethinking the Animate, Re-Animating Thought," *Ethnos* 71, no. 1 (2006): 9–20, DOI: 10.1080/00141840600603111. There is the option of "re-wilding" the Earth, but this only occurs when humans step off the stage, as Michael Northcott argues in this volume.

66. See Michael Naas, *Miracle and Machine: Jacques Derrida and the Two Sources of Religion, Science, and the Media* (New York: Fordham University Press, 2012).

67. Lauren Berlant, *Cruel Optimism* (Durham, NC: Duke University Press, 2011).

68. GGS, 1012.

69. Ibid., 668, 325. Furthermore, there is an immense testimonial literature on the reality of psychic powers (*ridd-sidh*), mystical and paranormal experiences, miraculous healings and healers—as well as the power of belief evidenced in

placebos. This counters affect theory's general orientation that affects cannot be controlled because we're animals.
70. See Steven Moore, ed., *Divinanimality: Animal Theory, Creaturely Theology* (New York: Fordham University Press, 2014), 16.
71. GGS, 722. Of course, this relates to a wider phenomenon of spirit-possession and channeling, though important distinctions remain.
72. Rousseau quickly adds what violence and horrors could have been avoided if someone had said, "Beware of listening to this impostor; you are lost if you forget that the fruits belong to all and the earth to no one!"
73. *Anatta-lakkhana Sutta: The Discourse on the Not-self Characteristic*, translated from the Pali by N. K. G. Mendis (https://www.accesstoinsight.org/tipitaka/sn/sn22/sn22.059.mend.html), accessed June 20, 2019.
74. "Yoga is the cessation of mind activities" (Yohanan Grinshpon, *Silence Unheard: Deathly Otherness in Patanjala-Yoga* [Albany: State University of New York Press, 2002], 97); "It (the Way) cannot be thought even if you think a hundred million times" (GGS, 1); "Tao can be talked about, but not the Eternal Tao. Names can be named, but not the Eternal Name" (Lao Tzu, *Tao Te Ching*, trans. John C. H. Wu [Boston: Shambhala, 1989], 3).
75. Or any hierarchically constructed pair: Hindu/Muslim, Brahmin/Dalit, citizen/immigrant. See Gyanendra Pandey, *A History of Prejudice: Race, Caste, and Difference in India and the United States* (Cambridge: Cambridge University Press, 2013).
76. See Ramon Grosfoguel, "Colonial Difference, Geopolitics of Knowledge, and Global Coloniality in the Modern/Colonial Capitalist World-System," *Review (Fernand Braudel Center)* 25, no. 3, Utopian Thinking (2002): 203–24.
77. John Caputo, "Beyond Sovereignty: Many Nations under the Weakness of God," *Soundings: An Interdisciplinary Journal* 89, no. 1–2 (2006): 1.
78. Note how Hardt and Negri distinguish between the people and the multitude by quoting Hobbes: "It is a great hindrance to civil government, especially monarchical, that men distinguish not enough between a people and a multitude. The people is somewhat that is one, having one will, and to whom one action may be attributed; none of these can be properly said of the multitude." See Michael Hardt and Antonio Negri, *Empire* (Cambridge, MA: Harvard University Press, 2000), 103. The hidden unwritable, self-organizing intelligence behind Whitman's and Yong's multitude is missed here.
79. Ibid., 90.
80. Ibid., 97.
81. Ibid., 70.

82. Ibid., 78.
83. Ibid., 82.
84. Within the Sikh tradition you see both freedoms (public and private) treated as one: earlier traditions sought only inner liberation by renouncing the world. Hence the choice between world renouncer (*buddha*) or a world-ruler (*cakkavattin*) foundation to Buddhism is rejected by the Sikh Gurus who saw the two as inseparable in the new ideal of the saint-as-sovereign (*sant-sipahi*).
85. Mary Evelyn Tucker, "A Communion of Subjects and a Multiplicity of Intelligences," in *A Communion of Subjects: Animals in Religion, Science, and Ethics*, ed. Paul Waldau and Kimberley Patton (New York: Columbia University Press, 2016), 646.
86. Ibid., 647.
87. Neil Roberts, *Freedom as Marronage* (Chicago: University of Chicago Press, 2015). Contrary to the so-called liberal origins of "freedom" located in the colonizers' enlightened visions, and based on the flight from slavery, "marronage" (marronnage, maroonage, maronage) re-locates freedom in the slave revolts, indicating a "liminal and transitional social space *between* slavery and freedom," where "people emerge *from* slavery *to* freedom." Though historically located, Roberts argues "marronage is a normative concept . . . [with] transhistorical utility" (Roberts, 3–4).
88. An Yountae, *The Decolonial Abyss: Mysticism and Cosmopolitics from the Ruins* (New York: Fordham University Press, 2016).
89. During Sikh–Mughal wars, a Sikh water carrier served water to all, including "enemy" Muslims. Upon being reported to the Sikh Guru, he was asked why? Bhai Kanhaiya said he sees God in everyone (mystical phenomenology). Pleased with this (nonrational, rather than irrational) answer, the Guru allowed him to continue. The nondual "oneness" being outlined here should not be confused with a general "New Age" conception of "oneness," as the former is political and works to uproot the ego, whereas the latter is often apolitical and affirms the ego in its desire for the "true self" measured by greater individual success and productivity. Furthermore, the GGS's focus on an existential praxis denies any and all "techniques of self-transformation" as each technique, be it yoga, breathing, or meditation, can become colonized by the ego; humility cannot become a goal of the ego (see Balbinder Singh Bhogal, "Sikhi(sm): Yoga and Meditation," in *Routledge Handbook of Yoga and Meditation Studies*, ed. Suzanne Newcombe and Karen O'Brien-Kop [London: Routledge, 2021], 226–40).
90. GGS, 383.

91. Ibid., 931.
92. Carl Schmitt, *Political Theology: Four Chapters on the Concept of the Political*, trans. George Schwab (Chicago: University of Chicago Press, 1985).
93. GGS, 20.
94. Ibid., 62.
95. Ibid., 74.

11. What Is Political about Political Islam?

MEHMET KARABELA

"Political Islam" became a catchphrase in academia from the 1980s onward, intensifying during the post–Cold War period in debates about Muslims and their political engagement. These debates revolved around the politicization of Islamic principles and doctrines aimed at bringing religion back into the public/political sphere for the purpose of capturing the secular state and making it Islamic. Over the first two decades of the twenty-first century, the term "political Islam" has been used interchangeably with "Islamic fundamentalism," "Islamic movements," "Islamic activism," "Islamic revivalism," "Islamic resurgence," "new religious politics," "radical Islam," and, most commonly, "Islamism."[1] Indeed, the list of vague and poorly defined terms for an already problematic concept does not end here. Employed by Muslim and non-Muslim scholars alike, many have used the words to marry Islam with "the political" (as opposed to "the religious"), whereas others, emphasizing the religion rather than the polity, have worked to keep the categories (Islam and politics) at arm's length.[2] Across a broad spectrum of opinion the reasoning behind this list of qualifiers implies several assumptions, among which are that political Islam is not "authentic Islam" and that politics in its "pure" Enlightenment and specifically Protestant sense cannot—or at least must not—be contaminated by religion.

In modern academic discourse, scholars justify their use of "political Islam" to emphasize its separation from Islam; that is, they separate it from religion and a faith community. Some justify their decision with the following formulations: Political Islam is too broad to define easily; or Islam is about a faith and a culture, whereas political Islam is about politics; or political Islam is composed of various social and activist movements; or it is made up of multiple contradictory ideologies that force it to remain clouded by vague abstractions. Whatever the usage, there remains a large array of political platforms and movements that do not fit neatly into any single box. Although scholars talk about nationalist Islamic movements whose claims are partly articulated by the modern concept of nation, especially in Kashmir, Palestine, Lebanon, and Chechnya,[3] transnational Islamist movements such as al-Qa'ida and ISIS have sought to replace the secular order of sovereign nation-states with a pan-Islamic state. Although scholars and political observers distinguish "jihadist militant" Islamists (e.g., Hamas and Hezbollah) from nonviolent Islamists (e.g., Turkey's AK Party or Tunisia's Ennahda) on the basis of whether they resort to ballots or bullets,[4] they still see "political Islam" subsuming politics and civil governance.

My objective in this chapter is to examine elements of the problematic dichotomy found in many discussions and usages of "political Islam," by exploring conceptual trends in modern scholarship on topics that are presented under the headings and variations of the term. My second objective is to investigate the concept of "the political" itself and how this relates to political Islam operating in a world of competing national interests. Modern scholarship refers to Islamic movements as "political Islam" because they are politically active (referring to religiously oriented political parties in Muslim societies), but none provides an adequate definition of what, in this context, "political" means or why acting *politically* requires a *religious* qualification. The modern scholar's approach to religious studies—treating the religious and the political as different categories—was inherited, in part, from post-Reformation German Lutheran academics and theologians,[5] who, minimizing the political element in religion, reflected the supposedly narrow, religious character of biblical theology at that time.[6] However, the hegemony of post-Reformation Protestant discourse in biblical theology has lost its significance in a "post-secular age,"[7] and so it is time to reassess this dominant "separationist definition" in the scholarship of political Islam.

Creating a new and more precise discourse will require reexamining previous scholarship and reconstructing the definition of "the political" in Islam. In this chapter, I suggest a revision of previous scholarship that separates the religious and the political, in an attempt to establish a new vantage point from which to imagine "the political" in Islam in terms of the larger, discursive realm of the humanities rather than from the standpoint of political science alone.

ITINERARY

First, I provide an account of the standard and dominant discourse in the scholarship of political Islam and the contemporary reformulations of it. Second, I attempt to clarify the meaning of "political" in political Islam. My point of departure is Carl Schmitt's *The Concept of the Political* and *Political Theology*. His analyses of political theory and discussions of sovereignty, the legitimacy of the state, the bases of constitutionality and their relationship to the rights and obligations of the individual—as well as his description of the purpose and scope of political power—have received renewed attention by social scientists and scholars of religious studies. For want of a better word, the Schmittian conception of "the political" clarifies some of the contradictions in the last generation of scholarship on political Islam, social movements, and political platforms in many parts of the Muslim world. Indeed, it raises the questions: What, if anything, is distinctive about Muslims when they enter politics as Muslims? And more generally: How do we situate Muslim political involvement within the problematic divide between religion and politics?

In order to clarify the relationship between the two categories, religion and politics, scholars such as Jürgen Habermas, Charles Taylor, John D. Caputo, José Casanova, and Talal Asad have redefined the term "secular" in the context of the "post-secular age"; however, I chose Schmitt's idea of political theology and the concept of the political as a framework for political Islam to illuminate the common structure that many theological and political concepts share. Neither Habermas, Taylor, nor others consider the question of theological concepts or religious structures informing the modern state structures. Nor do they treat the category of the political as something akin to the religious. Among them, Asad is the most influential scholar who considered the construction of the secular in the early modern period and the influence of this on modern Muslim societies. Asad mainly problematizes the secular/sacred dichotomy in his *Formations of the Secular* and argues that this dichotomy is simply the product of post-Reformation Europe. Schmitt, in *Political Theology*, shows how theology animates our politics by illustrating corresponding forms between theology and the modern theory of the State,[8] whereas Asad, by disagreeing with Schmitt, focuses on how this mutual co-implication of religion and politics produces different moral and political results, including a redefinition of religion.[9] Furthermore, in *The Concept of the Political*, Schmitt situates "enmity" (friend and enemy distinction) in relation to the "existential" quality of the politics and of the State and the main components of identity.[10] This is essential to the political Islam discussion; however, it is completely absent from Asad's work. Before considering Schmitt's concept of "the political," I first discuss the genealogy of the term "political Islam" and its semantic range in contemporary scholarship.

"POLITICAL ISLAM": PUTTING A NAME TO A CONUNDRUM

The collapse of the Ottoman Empire and the subsequent abolition of the Caliphate in 1924 saw Islam become the main point of reference for a variety of political activists and pan-Islamist movements.[11] During the Cold War, Muslim thinkers such as Sayyid Qutb (d. 1966), Abul A'la Mawdudi (d. 1979), Ayatollah Khomeini (d. 1989), and Ali Shariati (d. 1977) believed that Islam could provide a superior alternative form of governance to capitalism, represented by the United States, and socialism, represented by the former Soviet Union.[12] At the end of the Cold War, Francis Fukuyama responded to this "superior" Islamist alternative with his essay *The End of History* in which he argued that Western liberal democracy constituted the end of humanity's ideological evolution and its final form of governance.[13] Shortly thereafter, Samuel Huntington suggested an alternative political eschatology in *The Clash of Civilizations*. Huntington argued that although the end of the Cold War signaled the end of conflict within Western civilizations, a new era of intercivilizational or interreligious clashes would begin.[14]

Within this Cold War political setting and specifically in the aftermath of the 1979 Iranian Islamic Revolution, modern scholarship adopted the term "political Islam" to identify a distinctive form of Muslim politics, which referred to a political agenda that aimed at establishing an Islamic political order through a state agency. It is within the context of the intensification of the global decade of political Islam throughout the 1990s that French political scientist Olivier Roy claimed that "political Islam" had failed. Roy understands Islamist movements as a pendulum swinging between two opposites: a revolutionary pole (a top-down approach in which Islamization is realized through state power) and a reformist pole (a bottom-up approach where Islamization occurs through social and political movements).

Although both poles attempt to build an Islamic state by different methods, Roy argued that neither the top-down nor the bottom-up approach had been successful.[15] Consequently, the failure of political Islam gave birth to the formulation of a new discourse called post-Islamism propounded by Iranian sociologist Asef Bayat, who argued that an Islamism "from above" was no longer feasible. According to Bayat, post-Islamism focuses on rights, individual freedom, and plurality, not on duties; it signifies the emergence of a civil and a "nonpolitical" path to an Islamization project.[16] In light of Roy's work, Bayat's articulation has served as an analytical category for recent scholars, a kind of substitute for modernism in contemporary Muslim societies,[17] whereas Roy's has been understood as a historical category presenting Islamism as a political cul-de-sac.[18]

Within this context, several trends emerged in the writings of modern academics on political Islam, chiefly by political scientists and, to a lesser extent, sociologists and historians. Political science has dominated the scholarship on political Islam. This is one of the reasons that political Islam has been approached as a political phenomenon rather than a theological problem. In what follows, I highlight and assess the work of several political scientists and one sociologist (Bayat) to see how they distinguish political Islam as a separate and distinct entity from religious Islam. Specifically, I examine the ideas of Bassam Tibi and Mehdi Mozaffari as early classic examples of the "separationist discourse" and then show how this discourse took a different direction with Asef Bayat and Andrew March, resulting in no clear idea of what "political," "apolitical," or "nonpolitical" mean in the debate about political Islam.

SEPARATIONIST DISCOURSE: TIBI AND MOZAFFARI

Bassam Tibi, one of the early influential figures in the post–Cold War discourse on political Islam, calls for a radical separation between religious Islam and political Islam. In *Islamism and Islam*, Tibi defines Islam as a faith system in juxtaposition to Islamism, which politicizes the religion. Accordingly, Tibi classifies Islam as nonpolitical and Islamism as a totalitarian movement that exploits the symbols of Islam for political influence. In short, he believes Islamism is a body of thought that pursues "nonreligious ends," meaning political ends, whereas Islam is primarily focused on achieving "spiritual ends."[19]

Although for Tibi, "political Islam," "Islamism," and "Islamic religious fundamentalism" are different terms, they all denote the same phenomenon, one which involves the politicization of Islam in support of an Islamist world order known as "religion and state" (*din wa dawla*). However, Tibi makes a distinction between the institutional Islamists, who detach themselves from the use of violence and are willing to work peacefully through state institutions (e.g., the AK Party in Turkey) and the jihadist Islamists, who are committed to waging jihad as political violence.[20] In his understanding, Islamist religious fundamentalism is a modern political and sociocultural phenomenon, since he sees Islamist opposition to the prevailing Westphalian secular order of sovereign states as an expression of anti-globalism.[21] Therefore, Tibi sees political Islam as "modern" and something radically different from "traditional" religious Islam. However, his definition of political Islam is inextricably linked to its religious roots and underpinnings.

For Tibi, the many varieties of political Islam, such as jihadist and peaceful institutional Islamism, refer to the means they use—either participating in the institutions of civil society or waging an armed jihad—but not to their end goals. Tibi uses the writings of Sayyid Qutb, the father of modern Islamist theory, to show the ultimate goal of Islamism as a two-step strategy toward the Islamic ideal. The first step is to establish the divine order or sovereignty of God (*hakimiyya Allah*) throughout the Muslim world (*dar al-Islam*). After the establishment of the Islamic utopia in the Muslim world has become a reality, the second step—pursuing a global revolution of Islam in order to overcome the *jahiliyya* or pre-Islamic ignorance of the modern world—can take place. This refers to the vision of an Islamic revolution designed to lead to world peace under the strict conditions of the supremacy of Islam (*siyadat al-Islam*) over the entire globe.[22] From this Qutbian perspective, Tibi presents the "Islamic solution" or new world order as the unifying goal of all Islamic political movements, whether jihadist or moderate.

Another proponent of separationist discourse, Mehdi Mozaffari, analyzes political Islam following a common trend in modern scholarship, as many political scientists use the 1979 Iranian Revolution as the bedrock for Islamist political thinking. Accordingly, Mozaffari argues that after the Islamist revolution in Iran, European and North American scholars formulated a multitude of terms to grasp the "novelty" of the new era in the history of Islam. These terms produced in the aftermath of the Iranian Islamic revolution implied that this kind of Islam is quite different from other versions of Islam. Mozaffari is quite critical of the abstruseness associated with political Islam and asks the following question: "What precisely does this 'new' form of 'Islam' contain? The ambiguity remains almost complete."[23] Therefore, from the opening lines of his work, the reader may expect a concrete and tangible definition of political Islam. However, Mozaffari's definition is as complicated as the definitions he criticizes, although he does highlight the arbitrariness of the terminology associated with understanding and categorizing Islamist movements.

For Mozaffari, the concept of Islamism is composed of two elements: "Islam" and "ism." The former stands for a religion and a civilization with its specific history, and the latter indicates a non-Islamic, or to be more precise, Western suffix.[24] The composition of these two elements refers to a twofold construction composed of religion and ideology. In opposition to religion, Mozaffari defines ideology as a set of ideas by which human beings justify the ends and means of organized social action. By this definition, Islamism is different from Islam, because, as Mozaffari says, "Islamism is more than merely a 'religion' in the narrow sense of theological belief, private prayer and ritual worship, but also serves as a total way of life with guidance for political, economic and social behavior."[25] In other words, the goal of Islamism is the conquest of the world by any means, whereas Islam is more concerned with the conquest of the individual. Therefore, Mozaffari sees Islam in the narrow sense of theological belief, private prayer, and ritual worship.

The main thrust of the earlier separationist discourse discussed above (Tibi and Mozaffari) is based on two premises: First, Islamism pursues "nonreligious ends," which means political ends, whereas Islam focuses on achieving nonpolitical "spiritual growth"; and, second, religion is concerned with private prayer and spirituality, but not matters of the state. José Casanova summarizes this position as "privatization of religion" and sees "privatized religion" as a normative condition and a precondition for modern liberal democratic politics.[26] In the hands of liberalism, privatization thus becomes a useful tool to endorse the secularization thesis—religion's displacement from public life in modernity—while allowing for religion's ongoing vitality, albeit in privatized forms.

CONTEMPORARY REFORMULATIONS: BAYAT AND MARCH

The next generation of scholars has made some interventions in the discussion of political trends in Muslim societies to de-essentialize the Islamic or religious aspect of the phenomena they study. Asef Bayat makes a valid critique of such reductionism: As a sociologist, he understands "political Islam" as a diverse body of politically active social movements, each with independent goals and unique methods for attaining their desired goals. For Bayat, Islamism is differentiated and should not be reduced to the fixed and unique doctrine that is religious Islam. He makes a concerted effort to discard monolithic and totalizing narratives. Therefore, for Bayat, Islamism is not so much a religious or Islamic movement as it is a form of social activism.[27]

Bayat defines Islamic social activism as the "extra-ordinary religiosity of the Muslim population in modern times." By "extra-ordinary," he means extra-usual practices of active pious Muslims who aim to cause social change. Therefore, "active piety" refers to those Muslims who not only practice their religion but also preach it, inviting others to think and practice like them. In order to help illustrate Islamism as social activism, Bayat proposes the concept of "imagined solidarities."[28] He uses Iran's Reform Movement (*Jonbesh-e Eslah-talabi*) of the late 1990s under President Muhammad Khatami as a primary example of this imagined solidarity. He explains that this movement consisted of a broad combination of various political groupings, professional associations, student organizations, women's groups, and intellectual figures with diverse ideological and religious tendencies ranging from socially conservative clerics, to moderates, liberals, and seculars. Likewise, Bayat argues that even though the Iranian Revolution may have originated with radical clergy and liberal Islamic leaders, it was accomplished by very diverse social groups, including the secular middle class, workers, students, urban lower classes, ethnic minorities, and women. For Bayat, what binds these fluid and fragmented movements together into a cooperative unit both in the 1979 Iranian Revolution and the Reform Movement of the 1990s is the result of "their *imagining* commonality with others by imagined solidarities."[29]

Therefore, Bayat suggests seeing Islamism as social activism by providing a fairly detailed picture of the various constituencies that constitute Islamist ideologies working together with diverse non-Islamist apolitical groups. However, his answer for these fragmented groups' ultimate united front, which is "imagined solidarity," initially propounded by socially active Islamists who employed their "active piety," remains problematic. Bayat explains how this social activism can manifest in both a political sense, what he refers to as classic or traditional Islamism, and in an apolitical sense, what he describes as the active piety exemplified by the trends and movements in modern Islamic thought that center on individual freedom, rights, and plurality, which he calls *post-Islamism*. However, Bayat does not provide convincing examples of this "apolitical piety," nor does he explain why social movements are dissociated from political life so that they create extra-political spaces outside of state structures, such as social protest movements in the Middle East or the Iranian Green Movement.

In trying to define political Islam, Andrew March writes about how Islamism has become a major preoccupation for the whole world after 9/11. Like Bayat, March explains how contemporary Islamists differ not only in the purity of their ultimate goals but also about the means of reaching them. March provides the examples of political gradualists who are willing to work within corrupt un-Islamic political systems and radical revolutionaries who refuse to legitimize any institution that represents un-Islamic (*jahili*) political ideas and ideals. However, March distinguishes himself from the scholars discussed above by suggesting that the reason Islam has produced a political movement in modernity is because, for him, "there is something essentially political about Islam."[30] He refers to commonly used evidence for this view, such as the Prophet Muhammad's being a political and military leader who established Islam originally as a political entity, and Islam's historic inability to develop the institutional separation between church and a state out of which European secularism evolved.[31]

Therefore, March sees political Islam as the logical conclusion of a religion founded on the concept of *din wa dawla* (religion and state) clashing directly with the secularized world order. March notes that relegation of religious practice to a "personal and private" sphere is a "product of a historically situated eighteenth-century Christian conception of a privatized form of religion."[32] The entire Westphalian secular order of sovereign states was formulated by the eighteenth-century European Enlightenment thinkers who began to view theology as a hindrance to human intellectual development. By bringing this historical context, March gradually aims to present political Islam as a product of modern phenomena divorced from the authentic religious Islam.

Therefore, for March, Islamism is modern and not traditional because it was born in modernity, in a secularized world, but it seeks to transform the modern world order using its own religious tools and institutions. March goes so far as to compare modern Islamism to twentieth-century European fascism. He explains the striking similarities between the two movements, both of which are "based on the reaction to social dislocation and normative disorder."[33] He argues that both seek to integrate social classes into a national group on the grounds that true political conflict is between people and nations, not classes. Moreover, both groups make populist appeals to the dispossessed members of its community in a way that offers identity and culture instead of economic revolution. Although Islamists and fascists simultaneously attack nationalism, democracy, liberalism, Marxism, and capitalism, they still both contain a certain synthesis of other ideologies.[34]

Ironically, March refuses to see political Islam as the natural conclusion of Islam as a religion. March hints at this idea when he asserts that Islam is a political religion at its very core, but he still refuses to see these modern Islamist movements as being a part of religious Islam. However, March feels comfortable pointing out the various resemblances between modern political Islam and twentieth-century European fascism, since they are both the children of the modern age, so to speak. This persistence on dissociating political Islam from religious Islam, but rather seeing it as twentieth-century European fascism or totalitarianism or international communism or religious imperialism, has been a common trend among modern scholarship. Even though March identifies all the running themes within the historical development of Islam that gave grounding for political Islam to take its particular shape, he refrains from seeing political Islam as a form of religious Islam.

March criticizes Tibi's claim that "Islamism is not Islam" because for Tibi "Islamism is about political order, not faith."[35] March sees this simplistic dichotomy of Islamism versus Islam as a result of Tibi's reluctance to explore any premodern religious discussions of law and politics. March uses the writings of Sayyid Qutb as does Tibi, but in a different way in order to show the crucial relationship between law and politics. Qutb's writings emphasize how Islamic law is not only commanded to human beings by God, but it is also the law we would have naturally given to ourselves. In short, Qutb argues that Islam is by its very nature political "because it creates an egalitarian political society that frees humans from fear and domination to act on their natural goodness."[36] March's use of Sayyid Qutb's statements or observations about the relationship between Islamic law and society are strong evidence against Tibi's separationist discourse, but he maintains the gist of Tibi's idea: Islamism is not Islam as explained above.

On the one hand, March argues that political Islam or Islamic revivalism is the reaction to a modern Westphalian secular world order. On the other hand, he explains that religious Islam is more than narrow theological belief and private prayer, but rather is a way of life that is at odds with religious privatization in a secularized world. For March, the Muslim community's unwillingness to accept the status quo that has been forced upon it by colonization has allowed it to take shape as a modern political movement.[37] However, March fails to explain why he classifies these ideological movements in modern times as political Islam or Islamic revivalism separated from Islam in the religious sense. Nonetheless, this unclarity or confusion makes one thing quite obvious: "Political Islam" as a modern historical phenomenon is different from indigenous "religious Islam," according to March.

THE MISSING POLITICAL IN "POLITICAL ISLAM"

Given the intentions and objectives of the early users of the term "political Islam" and the contemporary reformulations of scholarly inquiry (explored above), how might Carl Schmitt's political theory advance an inquiry into the relationship between Islam and politics? Although it might be argued that Schmitt's writings are dated and no longer relevant to current political trends, his theories on religion and politics have attracted considerable interest in the late twentieth and early twenty-first century. In fact, his contributions to the debate on political theology, his critical sense of the fundamental problems of modern politics, and his critique of the ideas and institutions of liberal democracy make him one of the most interesting figures in contemporary political theory.

Schmitt's political writings provide a fresh perspective within the discourse on political Islam, which now teems with ambiguity. Schmitt was wary of the emerging liberalist thought that provides a Western-centric perspective of growing ideologies in areas of the world where liberalism has little influence. It is for this reason that critically evaluating and understanding political Islam through Schmitt's ideas offers a different approach to Islamic discourse.[38] So long as political Islam continues to be studied within the confines of Western liberalist discourse, it will remain ambiguous and opaque. Schmitt provides a different and, more importantly, a concrete interpretation of the "political" and "political theology"—a lens through which political Islam can be usefully viewed and understood. Schmitt's concept of "the political" can be used to reevaluate the relation of Islam to it.

The Concept of the Political begins with the assertion that all major concepts associated with human life (economics, religion, morality, aesthetics) rest upon categorical antitheses, such as rich/poor, beautiful/ugly, good/evil, fit/fat, and so on. The concept of "the political," he says, is derived from its own fundamental opposition—the distinction between friend and enemy. In an attempt to achieve state unity by defining the content of politics in opposition to the "other" or the enemy, Schmitt applies this distinction to the collective enemy. This "enemy" is any entity that represents a serious threat to or conflicts with one's own interests. Thus, to have a state, the political must have already existed, so that "the concept of the state presupposes the concept of the political." According to Schmitt, the definition of the political rests on its own ultimate distinctions—between friend and enemy—which are independent of any other distinction. These distinctions are real and physical, not metaphorical or symbolic.[39]

The basis of Schmitt's concept of the political assumes that Hobbes's "state of nature" is already a political arena by virtue of people assigning "friend" or "enemy" status to different groups, thus presenting the possibility of conflict. This leads to establishing an organized state that brings stability and security to each respective group so long as they are willing to fight to maintain its sovereignty. It is within the bounds of the state that Schmitt believes culture develops. He essentially equates "political nature" with "state of nature," where life is, in Hobbes's words, "nasty, brutish, and short," and this prompts people to seek safety by grouping together according to commonalities, such as language, religion, or customs.

It is these commonalities that bind groups together and enable them to identify "others" who are different. This "othering" is the first step toward the friend/enemy distinction. Once an "other" group is identified, it is not yet an enemy. "An enemy exists only when, at least potentially, one fighting collectivity of people confronts a similar collectivity."[40] This means that the enemy must not be a private enemy, competitor, or opponent, but rather an enemy of the collective, a *public* enemy.[41] Following the establishment of a public enemy, the extent to which the two groups are hostile determines how extreme the antagonism is. In Schmitt's concept of the political, it is the state which decides who is a friend and who an enemy. This raises the question: What is the state?

For Schmitt, the state is the specific entity of a people and represents the ultimate authority. This authority rests on the proposition that only the state can demand of its citizens or adherents a readiness to die. But again, the question arises: What defines the state as a political entity? For Schmitt, "the equation state = politics becomes erroneous and deceptive at exactly the moment when state and society penetrate each other. What had been up to that point affairs of state become thereby social matters, and, vice versa, what had been purely social matters become affairs of state—as must necessarily occur in a democratically organized unit."[42]

What Schmitt wishes to convey is that, in modern democratic societies, theoretically neutral domains (religion, culture, education, the economy, etc.) cease to be neutral. They have their own agendas, which invade the democratic state's function and decision-making process. The secularized notion that religion is a privatized area of worship far removed from political discourse perpetuates the stigma associated with countries in the Middle East and elsewhere that have religious principles embedded in their constitutions. The reality is that in modern democracies religion plays a role in modern political discourse.

For Schmitt, the friend/enemy distinction denotes the utmost degree of intensity of a union or separation, of an association or dissociation. The political enemy is not necessarily "morally evil or aesthetically ugly; he need not appear as an economic competitor, and it may even be advantageous to engage with him in business transactions. But he is, nevertheless, the other, the stranger; and it is sufficient for his nature that he is, in a specially intense way, existentially something different and alien, so that in the extreme case conflicts with him are possible."[43]

If "the political" is the ability of an authoritative body (i.e., the state) to determine its political friends and enemies, then to understand political Islam we must take a moment to recognize how this authoritative body would classify its friends and enemies. Because enemies exist only when one aggressive collectivity confronts another, the enemy is a public and not a personal enemy of the privatized sphere. Like the public enemy in the Qur'an (nonbelievers), the enemy for political Islam (based on the modern academic scholarship analyzed above) is the Westphalian secular political order and all those who wish to maintain or impose it. The consistent attempt by Islamists to challenge the moral legitimacy of the West aims to make their cause superior by claiming moral (i.e., religious) goals.

Since Islamism portrays secular society as the "other" with the intent of entering into conflict with them, this creates the friend/enemy distinction that, as Schmitt says, "simultaneously degrades the enemy into moral and other categories and is forced to make of him a monster that must not only be defeated but also utterly destroyed. In other words, he is an enemy who no longer must be compelled to retreat into his borders only."[44] Applying Schmitt's framework to modern Islamism is appropriate because by creating a distinction between the Muslim community (*ummah*) and the rest of humanity, Islamism advocates a dichotomous perspective of a world divided into collectives of friends and enemies (Muslims and non-Muslims), believers and unbelievers, the moral and immoral, and this justifies the use of force against them. Therefore, the friend/enemy distinction offers the possibility of conflict or war.

For Schmitt, however, conflict or war is neither the aim, nor the purpose, nor even the content of politics. It is an *ever-present possibility*, "the leading presupposition which determines in a characteristic way human action and thinking and thereby creates a specifically political behavior."[45] Schmitt shows how a religious community can become a political entity once that community demands that its adherents engage in war. Politics, therefore, cannot be defined by a separate "political" substance, but rather derives its energy from the intensity of its association with people, whose motives can be religious, national, ethnic, cultural, or economic. It is this proposition that separates Schmitt's understanding of the political from the modern understanding of it, where politics is a separate entity distant from all privatized religious endeavors. It is this understanding that has made it so challenging for contemporary academia to define and to place political Islam accurately. Nevertheless, we should clarify that being "political" is not necessarily negative. Only recently has the political nature of religious affiliation had a negative connotation, an unintended consequence of the post-Enlightenment yearning for separation of church and state.

For Schmitt, then, identity is relational, and the affirmation of a difference serves as the condition for the existence of every identity. For example, the Islamist pursuit of differentiating itself from the "other," either the West or non-Islamists, bolsters the Islamist identity against what they are "not." In other words, the determination of an "other" plays the role of a "constitutive outside," and identity is formed by what it is not—in this case, the "other." According to Schmitt, there is an "us" only because there is a "them." Despite attempts by modern liberalists to quell the distinction, the possibility of the us/them relation becoming a friend/enemy relation is an ever-present reality. The potential friend/enemy paradigm, like turning on a switch, becomes a reality when our enemies ("they," "them," or "others") threaten us.

This turning on of the switch occurs when the other is no longer considered merely as different but as the negation of "us." Any type of social structure has the potential to fall into a friend/enemy relation. For example, churches are predominant in religion, society in economics, but the state is predominant in politics. Yet for Schmitt the "political" is not an autonomous domain equivalent to other domains. It is, rather, the existential basis that determines whether domains should reach the point of "the political." In other words, Islam as a religion, like any other religion, is not exclusively theological when it distinguishes between "friend" and "enemy," swinging between the religious and the political. In the same vein, once a religious group, such as Islamists, forms a friend/enemy dichotomy with an outside group, their identity changes into a political one.

As I stated earlier in this chapter, I demonstrate how the dichotomy in modern scholarship between the political and religious domains, as separate and distinct entities, remains problematic, in theory and in practice. I illustrate how the confusion associated with understanding and analyzing political Islamic ideologies lies in the fact that they have been observed only through the narrow lens of liberalism, in which religion and politics are like oil and water, refusing to mix. Using the writings of Carl Schmitt, I explain how political actions and motives can be reduced to a friend/enemy distinction, which denotes a degree of intensity of a union or separation or of an association and dissociation. Thus, the legitimacy of a political entity, in the final analysis, lies in its authority to demand of its citizens the readiness to die. This entity need not be a nation-state. Every religious, moral, economic, ethical, or other phenomenon can transform into a political entity if it can group human beings effectively as friend or enemy. For Schmitt, a religious community that wages wars against members of other religious communities or other states is already more than a religious community: It is a political entity.

In *Political Theology: Four New Chapters on the Concept of Sovereignty*, Paul W. Kahn presents dying "for America" in war as "the ultimate self-sacrifice," echoing Schmitt's concept of exception.[46] From Kahn's perspective, an American dying in combat is a political act, as he or she dies from friend-enemy warfare, but it is also conceptually religious, representing the ultimate sacrifice for a divinized America.[47] Just as God is the ultimate force around which His community of believers (*ummah*) forms, America becomes the ultimate binding force of its citizens (nationalism/patriotism). Instead of dying for God as a Muslim, the citizen dies for America as an American. When a member of the US armed forces hears, "Thank you for serving our great Nation and families," he or she becomes a political/public servant little different from any other public official—except that this duty is performed in harm's way multiple times. Just as a Muslim does not die an ideal martyr confronting a private enemy but only when he or she confronts a public enemy, the US soldier confronts a public enemy that is always political.

Based on Schmitt's understanding of "the political," Islam becomes political insofar as it demands of its adherents a readiness to die. A Muslim does not self-sacrifice to God, but *for* God in the act of martyrdom, just as an American does not self-sacrifice *to* America (private) but *for* America (public). Political Islam, therefore, extends the religious realm, the result of a community's uncompromising insistence on God's exclusive legislative and normative sovereignty, grounded in the revelations of the Qur'an. From this perspective, the friend/enemy distinction within Islam is palpable because the nature and creation of the Muslim community throughout history *is* political, where "public" enemies are either internal (the Sunni-Shi'ite divide) or external (nonbelievers or idol worshippers).[48]

At the height of the Cold War, "political Islam" did not spontaneously arise from the Iranian Islamic Revolution as has often been suggested in earlier scholarship, instead, "the political" in Islam has always been there. In contemporary Muslim societies, the dichotomy between political and religious confounds scholarly inquiry because it fails to recognize "the political" in the Schmittian sense, as a dichotomy between "us" and "them." My conclusion, then, is that the separation between "political Islam" and "religious Islam" in modern scholarship is invalid because this discourse normatively determines what religion is and what it is not, in the belief that religion is exclusively a private, social and historical entity rather than a *potential* political one.

NOTES

Acknowledgments: I extend my heartfelt thanks to Ruth Chitiz, Clayton Crockett, Janet Darlington, and Ariel Salzmann for their substantial contributions and valuable feedback.

1. On this scholarship, see R. Hrair Dekmejian, *Islam in Revolution: Fundamentalism in the Arab World* (Syracuse, NY: Syracuse University Press, 1985); Bernard Lewis, *The Political Language of Islam* (Chicago: University of Chicago Press, 1988); Emmanuel Sivan, *Radical Islam: Medieval Theology and Modern Politics* (New Haven, CT: Yale University Press, 1990); Nazih Ayubi, *Political Islam: Religion and Politics on the Arab World* (London: Routledge, 1991); John L. Esposito, *Political Islam: Revolution, Radicalism, or Reform?* (Boulder, CO: Lynne Rienner, 1997); Bassam Tibi, *The Challenge of Fundamentalism: Political Islam and the New World Disorder* (Berkeley: University of California Press, 1998); Mansoor Moaddel and Kamran Talattof, eds., *Modernist and Fundamentalist Debates in Islam* (New York: Palgrave Macmillan, 2000); Salwa Ismail, *Rethinking Islamist Politics: Culture, the State and Islamism* (London: I. B. Tauris, 2003); Gilles Kepel, *The Roots of Radical Islam* (London: Saqi, 2005); Mary R. Habeck, *Knowing the Enemy: Jihadist Ideology and the War on Terror* (New Haven, CT: Yale University Press, 2006); Meghnad Desai, *Rethinking Islamism* (London: I. B. Tauris, 2007); Mohammed Ayoob, *The Many Faces of Political Islam: Religion and Politics in the Muslim World* (Ann Arbor: University of Michigan Press, 2008); Frédéric Volpi, *Political Islam Observed* (London: Hurst, 2010); John Calvert, *Sayyid Qutb and the Origins of Radical Islamism* (London: Hurst, 2010); Sayed Khatab, *Understanding Islamic Fundamentalism* (Cairo: American University in Cairo Press, 2011); and Daniel Lav, *Radical Islam and the Revival of Medieval Theology* (Cambridge: Cambridge University Press, 2012).

2. There are, however, a few critical studies that reconstruct the development of the term "political Islam" and the emergence of Islamism as a political discourse in the postcolonial context and during the Cold War period through leftist and postmodernist perspectives. These cannot be categorized as parts of the dominant paradigm on political Islam. See Armando Salvatore, *Islam and the Political Discourse of Modernity* (Reading, UK: Ithaca Press, 1997); Bobby Sayyid, *A Fundamental Fear: Eurocentrism and the Emergence of Islamism* (London: Zed Books, 1997); and Susan Buck-Morss, *Thinking Past Terror: Islamism and Critical Theory on the Left* (London: Verso, 2003). For a concise and up-to-date summary of Islam and politics in modern history, see Peter Mandeville, *Islam and Politics* (London: Routledge, 2014).

3. Mehdi Mozaffari, "What Is Islamism? History and Definition of a Concept," *Totalitarian Movements and Political Religions* 8, no. 1 (2007): 17–33.

4. See Bassam Tibi, "Political Islam as a Forum of Religious Fundamentalism and the Religionisation of Politics: Islamism and the Quest for a Remaking of the World," *Totalitarian Movements and Political Religions* 10, no. 2 (2009): 97–120; Christoph Schuck, "A Conceptual Framework of Sunni Islamism," *Politics,*

Religion & Ideology 14, no. 4 (2013): 485–506; and Haroon K. Ullah, *Vying for Allah's Vote: Understanding Islamic Parties, Political Violence, and Extremism in Pakistan* (Washington, DC: Georgetown University Press, 2014).

5. Throughout the seventeenth century, traditional German Lutheran theologians and scholars such as Daniel Clasen (1622–1678), Johann Heinrich Boecler (1611–1672), Michael Wendeler (1610–1671), and Daniel Morhof (1639–1691) argued that one had to maintain the strength of Christianity, spirituality, and religiosity against the opportunist "Catholic" Machiavellians and political elites (*politici* in Latin). Lutheran scholars were analyzing the concept of "political religion" from the early seventeenth century onward. Lutherans understood "political religion" not as a component of "reason of state," but as the political dimension and function of religion that the political elites were using as a tool for domination. Many Lutherans of the late seventeenth century saw this development as a dangerous form of politics. They believed religion must never be used to achieve political ends since religion contributes only to the spiritual good. Most prominent Islamists such as Sayyid Qutb, Abul A'la Mawdudi, Ayatollah Khomeini, Mahmoud Taleghani, and Ali Shariati during the Cold War period held the diametrically opposite opinion. For a summary of Daniel Clasen's thought, see Martin Mulsow, *Enlightenment Underground: Radical Germany, 1680–1720* (Charlottesville: University of Virginia Press, 2015). In my book *Islamic Thought through Protestant Eyes* (London: Routledge, 2021), I explore the post-Reformation Lutheran perception of Islamic thought and political religion.

6. German biblical scholarship, under the influence of Lutheran "Two Kingdoms Theology," has highlighted the "nonpolitical" character of the Christian Gospel, from the early seventeen century onward. This interpretation has contributed to the view that earlier Christianity was nonpolitical and spiritual, dominated by the eschatological expectation (end of the world) and thus free from worldly political and material concerns. Therefore, this view emphasized that the Christian religion is separate from politics. For a detailed examination of the Christian political thinking in the Bible, see Christopher Rowland, "Scripture," in *The Cambridge Companion to Christian Political Theology*, ed. Craig Hovey and Elizabeth Phillips (Cambridge: Cambridge University Press, 2015), 157–75.

7. Since around the turn of the century, the definition of "secular" has become intricate and convoluted. This has been the result of the resurgence of religion or the "triumph of religion" in the words of Jacques Lacan, within so-called secular societies. As a result, Jürgen Habermas, Charles Taylor, John D. Caputo, Jose Casanova, Talal Asad, and Hent de Vries have redefined the term "secular" and have proposed a postsecular model for understanding the relationship

between religion and democracy. Although they all agree on this issue, their postsecular models differ to varying degrees.

8. Carl Schmitt, *Political Theology: Four Chapters on the Concept of Sovereignty* (Cambridge, MA: MIT Press, 1985), 36–39.
9. Talal Asad, *Formations of the Secular: Christianity, Islam, Modernity* (Stanford, CA: Stanford University Press, 2003), 189–91.
10. Carl Schmitt, *The Concept of the Political* (Chicago: University of Chicago Press, 2007), 27.
11. For a review of the recent scholarship on Ottoman Islamist thinkers, see Mehmet Karabela, "Islamist Thinkers in the Late Ottoman Empire and Early Turkish Republic," *Insight Turkey* 19, no. 1 (2017): 225–27.
12. On Islam and politics, see their respective works available in English translation: *The Sayyid Qutb Reader*, trans. Albert Bergesen (London: Routledge, 2008); Abul A'la Mawdudi, *Human Rights in Islam* (Lahore: Islamic Publishing, 1976); Ayatollah Khomeini, *Islam and Revolution*, trans. Hamid Algar (London: Kegan Paul, 1985); and Ali Shariati, *Marxism and Other Western Fallacies*, trans. R. Campbell (Berkeley, CA: Mizan Press, 1980).
13. Francis Fukuyama, "End of History?" *National Interest* 16 (Summer 1989): 3–18. For Muslim critiques of the "end of history" thesis, see Ali A. Mazrui, "Islam and the End of History," *American Journal of Islamic Social Sciences* 10, no. 4 (1993): 512–35; and Abdelwahab El-Affendi, "Islam and the Future of Dissent after the 'End of History,'" *Futures* 31 (1999): 191–204.
14. Samuel Huntington, "The Clash of Civilizations?" *Foreign Affairs* 72, no. 3 (1993): 22–49.
15. Olivier Roy, *The Failure of Political Islam* (Cambridge, MA: Harvard University Press, 1994), 1–27.
16. Asef Bayat, *Post-Islamism: The Changing Faces of Political Islam* (Oxford: Oxford University Press, 2013), 7–34.
17. Following in the footsteps of Asef Bayat, Mojtaba Mahdavi sees Islamism as a reaction to "the economic and ecological violence of neo-liberalism" and post-Islamism as a Muslim modernism. See Mojtaba Mahdavi, "Muslims and Modernities: From Islamism to Post-Islamism?" *Religious Studies and Theology* 32, no. 1 (2013): 57–71.
18. As part of my quest, Forough Jahanbakhsh and I launched an international conference at Queen's University in Canada in 2015 on the religious and political transformations in modern Muslim societies. The conference, titled "Islamism and Post-Islamism: Religious and Political Transformations in Muslim Societies," brought together established scholars from around North America and the globe to discuss the changing faces of political Islam and its implications for the

continued validity of post-Islamism in contemporary scholarship raised by Roy and Bayat. The significance of the conference comes from the fact that it was a reconsideration of the ongoing relevance of post-Islamism as a project and as a historical condition in the wake of Arab Spring and ISIS. For a summary of the conference, see Mehmet Karabela and Brenna Drummond, "A Distinctive Form of Muslim Politics," *Turkish Review*, 5/4 (2015): 349–352.

19. Bassam Tibi, *Islamism and Islam* (New Haven, CT: Yale University Press, 2012), 7–17.
20. Tibi, "Political Islam as a Forum of Religious Fundamentalism," 99–100.
21. Ibid., 107–8.
22. Ibid., 105–7.
23. Mozaffari, "What Is Islamism?" 18–20.
24. Ibid., 21.
25. Ibid., 22.
26. José Casanova, "Rethinking Secularization: A Global Comparative Perspective," *Hedgehog Review* 8, no. 1–2 (2006): 14.
27. Asef Bayat, "Islamism and Social Movement Theory," *Third World Quarterly* 26, no. 6 (2005): 891–908.
28. Ibid., 894–95.
29. Ibid., 900–901.
30. Andrew March, "Political Islam: Theory," *Annual Review of Political Science* 18 (2014): 105.
31. Ibid., 106–7.
32. Ibid., 105–6.
33. Ibid., 107–8.
34. Ibid., 108.
35. Ibid.
36. Ibid.
37. Ibid., 108–17.
38. There is also literature on the reception of Schmitt in the Muslim world. See Joshua Ralston, "Political Theology in Arabic," *Political Theology* 19, no. 7 (2018): 549–52. For the use of Schmitt in the postrevolutionary Iranian context, see Milad Odabaei, "The Outside (*Kharij*) of Tradition in the Aftermath of the Revolution: Carl Schmitt and Islamic Knowledge in Postrevolutionary Iran," *Comparative Studies of South Asia, Africa and the Middle East* 39, no. 2 (2019): 296–311; and for different interpretations of political theology in the Indian context, see SherAli Tareen, "Competing Political Theologies: Intra-Muslim Polemics on the Limits of Prophetic Intercession," *Political Theology* 12, no. 3 (2011): 418–43.
39. Schmitt, *The Concept of the Political*, 19–27.

40. Ibid., 28.
41. In his later work, Derrida engages and critiques Schmitt at length by questioning the sovereignty in the Schmittian sense and the opposition of friend and enemy as Schmitt defines it. For Derrida's critique, see his *The Politics of Friendship* (London: Verso, 2006); *Rogues: Two Essays on Reason* (Stanford, CA: Stanford University Press, 2005); and *The Beast and the Sovereign*, 2 vols. (Chicago: University of Chicago Press, 2010). Also see Jacob Taubes's critique of Schmitt's friend-enemy distinction, *The Political Theology of Paul* (Stanford, CA: Stanford University Press, 2003).
42. Schmitt, *The Concept of the Political*, 22.
43. Ibid., 26–27.
44. Ibid., 36.
45. Ibid., 34.
46. Paul W. Kahn, *Political Theology: Four New Chapters on the Concept of Sovereignty* (New York: Columbia University Press, 2011), 7.
47. Ibid., 22–27.
48. I do not consider Islam as being universally unified by the idea of one collective friend-enemy split and do not minimize internal differences in Islam such as the well-known Sunni and Shi'ite division, among many others. In this chapter, so far, I have focused on the external enemy (public enemy) as the sign of "the political" and chiefly on the friend-enemy paradigm. However, a different type of enemy, what I would call the internal enemy, is the less studied question. To illustrate, an individual who transgresses against the state or religious community by committing a crime or sin, transgresses not only against another, which is a private "enemy," but also against a state or religious community, thus making the lawbreaker a public enemy of the State or God. Therefore, I think internal enemy is an interesting development in the concept of the political as it transforms an "expected friend" into a public enemy despite belonging to the same community. The idea of the enemy within is certainly an interesting one since it locates the "potential enemy" not just in the public sphere, but within the individual, or the inner circle, or within a community. I will elaborate on the category of the enemy within in my future work.

PART V

❧ From Genocide toward a Sacred Politics

12. #BlackLivesMatter and Sacred Politics

SETH GAITERS

The fight to save your life is a spiritual fight.
—PATRISSE KHAN-CULLORS

"Black Lives Matter." In many ways the racial justice movement that has taken off through this phrase has been considered different or even "more secular" than racial justice struggles in the middle of the twentieth century. This in a large way is because of its ambiguous relationship with "the Black church," unlike a certain ecclesial centering of the Civil Rights Movement, albeit there are many complex and diverse ways that religion animates the movement that many overlook. I believe the sacred is a good discourse to use in getting at this religious animation of moods, impulses, practices, and languages in the Black Lives Matter Movement. In fact, movement actors' embrace and utilization of sacred language signifies deep sensibilities of and commitments to a certain religious spirit or mood animating their practices signifying something more. Exploring this language permits passage into an exploration of the complex ways religion inspirits this Black-led movement. This essay involves a broad consideration of a theoretics of the sacred, which is operative in the Black Lives Matter Movement. I also approach this briefly by way of a close reading[1] of Patrisse Khan-Cullors's life narrative—*When They Call You a Terrorist: A Black Lives Matter Memoir*.[2] Khan-Cullors is one of the three women[3] who helped create and catalyze the movement. I consider her life narrative as synecdochical of a broader radical sacrality at play in this Black-led political movement.

I am finding that the vector of the sacred, within the movement, announces another horizon altogether than that which is projected by mainstream discourse about the movement in US popular culture, whether on formally religious or secular terms. In turn, my rhetorical deployment of the term *sacred* is meant to open up an analytical space that is not a reinscription of any binary, but pragmatically gets at a language and experience amid Black Lives Matter activists and organizers of seeing the world, especially Black life, as suffused with sacred meaning. What I am thinking of here in terms of what is sacred is evident in the expression of certain values, practices, and patterns of meaningfulness in the sacred language of activist memoirists—in this case Khan-Cullors—that names a fundamental commitment to realize a new world where the last will be first and the first will be last. At times it shows up enlivening religious traditions—as in the tranquillity and liberation of worship services—and at other times it shows up inspiring what many commonly think of as secular—such as in the turbulence of street protests demanding justice and liberation. For Khan-Cullors it is the source of the Divine, of Spirit, spiritual connection, or even "the divine-right mix of stardust" which inspires her passionate struggles for racial justice. And as a source of "otherwise possibilities"[4] it is not reducible or restricted to formally religious or strictly secular realms, but straddling them exceeds the horizon of their management/policing being always already something more than forms or systems of domination and definition.

A BRIEF HISTORY OF BLACK LIVES MATTER

In this essay, I refer to the Black Lives Matter Movement (also known as the Movement for Black Lives) by the abbreviations BLMM or M4BL. BLMM is one of the most influential Black-centered social movements of the post–civil rights era. It is recognized around the globe for Black liberation from state-sanctioned violence and an unjust criminal justice system operating at the expense of Black communities. BLMM was catalyzed by way of a radical response to anti-Black police and vigilante violence in the United States. In 2012 this movement was triggered in the raw consternation and reaction of Black folk to the public execution of Trayvon Martin and the acquittal of his killer (George Zimmerman) in 2013. In the public outcry to this horrific moment the BLMM began as a social media hashtag—#BlackLivesMatter[5]—in an act of Black care to love the living and memorialize the dead. Through this movement Black folk found "a[nother] way to hold onto . . . care," an ethic which Christina Sharpe says is "a way to feel and to feel for and with, a way to tend to the living and the dying."[6] An intramural concern of and for Black lives "in the wake" of state-imposed regimes of surveillance and anti-Black violence.

When Alicia Garza refused to be numbed by and desensitized to the public lynching of Trayvon Martin and the acquittal of his killer, she responded with a love note to Black people. She responded with care. She wrote, "Black people. I love you. I love us. Our lives matter."[7] In this kairotic moment the Black Lives Matter project emerged as a "love note"[8] to Black people. "[Black Lives Matter] was created out of a profound sense of Black love," says Opal Tometi. "We wanted to affirm to our people that we love one another, and that no matter how many times we hear about the extrajudicial killing of a community member, we would mourn, and affirm the value of their life."[9] In reply to Garza's Facebook post, Patrisse Khan-Cullors put a hashtag in front of Black Lives Matter—#BlackLivesMatter—helping to build community and bind together a Movement of love. With the assistance of Opal Tometi building out a digital platform this hashtag then transmogrified into a slogan and war cry penetrating the public consciousness to ubiquitous proportions[10] on par with previous phrases in the Black Freedom Struggle—"Black Power," "Freedom Now," "Black Is Beautiful," "I Am a Man," "We Shall Overcome," and so on. Then in 2014 following the public lynching of Mike Brown and the rebellions of Ferguson that ensued, what many outliers were still marking as a "moment" to soon blow over, swelled into a movement of global proportions.

Though these three women—Opal Tometi, Alicia Garza, and Patrisse Khan-Cullors—are credited by many as co-founders or catalyzers of the BLMM, and are reputed as the originators of the #BlackLivesMatter social media campaign against anti-Black racism and state violence, the reach of the M4BL extends far beyond their reach, and the fight does not begin or end with them alone. Though a single movement, it is a many-splendored thing. As the civil rights movement was referred to as a single movement aimed at increasing Black citizenship rights, even though it was a "disjointed collection of different activists, organizations, and groups with different goals, strategies, and politics," so too the BLMM with its own disjointedness and different aims, politics, activists, groups, and organizations is referred to as a single movement revolving around ending disproportionate police violence against Black people. And so, in a similar way, the heterogeneity and complexity of this contemporary movement of Black-led mass struggle transcends being pinned down to personalities alone. According to historian and activist Barbara Ransby, "The slogan [Black Lives Matter] has evolved into the battle cry of this generation of Black youth activists," and "there is hardly a person in the United States who has not heard the now ubiquitous phrase."[11] Such a rallying cry brought together a new younger generation of activists—largely Black millennial activists—who were already hard at work in their own various grassroots organizations. But now a national coalition of locally based grassroots justice organizations came together under the rubric of M4BL.[12] Nevertheless, this hashtag and the historical elements from which it emerged are a pivot, in fact a *kairos* moment, from which renewed consciousness in the Black Freedom Struggle and a new movement have broken through bellowing "Black Lives Matter!" for a new generation.

MISSING THE SACRED IN BLACK LIVES MATTER

Helpful and insightful examinations of the M4BL from well-regarded scholars are emerging. By way of critical histories the BLMM is being given cultural, intellectual, and historical context by skilled scholars—such as Angela Davis (in *Freedom Is a Constant Struggle: Ferguson, Palestine, and the Foundations of a Movement*), Eddie Glaude (in *Democracy in Black: How Race Still Enslaves the American Soul,* and in various lectures),[13] Barbara Ransby (in *Making All Black Lives Matter: Reimagining Freedom in the 21st Century*), Keeanga-Yamahtta Taylor (in *From #BlackLivesMatter to Black Liberation*), and others—mapping its unique framework and infrastructure. There is difficulty in documenting and analyzing this history, since as Marc Anthony Neal mentions, it is "a moving history,"[14] a history that is still being written. And yet to do such critical work is important and thoroughly political, since it represents a movement that has been and is still being problematized in US popular culture. Divisively, it is rendered problematic in media coverage— a coverage that reflects views held by the (white) American public (read: mainstream)—and thereby necessarily sparks controversy. For instance, on theological grounds M4BL is caricatured as "more secular" than the civil rights movement—from a perceived American Christian "norm," particularly by the (Christian) Right—as a way of politically marginalizing its efforts/ aims and articulating a rationale for managing/policing it as terrorist/

extremist. In this sense, secularizing BLMM is a discursive way of managing/policing it, and rendering it problematic.[15] It is here around the question of race a split is still being imagined in between the political and the theological. And here this "political" is read as the "secular." BLMM marks a particular ambiguity and "waywardness"[16] some seek to control since it is not religion proper, nor a proper religion, and neither is it merely reducible to what here is understood as secular. Yet pulsating from it is a radical impulse, that though unintelligible in US popular culture continually announces another horizon of sacrality and religiosity altogether.

Josef Sorett notes that the BLMM is perceived by many as "unorthodox," "heresy," "heterodoxy," a "decline" morally, and cast "as a break from the black past and . . . a full departure from 'the black church.'"[17] Being named "secular" in this instance is anti-Black and is a code for a colonial practice of policing/governmentality. It operates upon a metaphysical dualism as its foundation, is racialized, patriarchalized, classed, and de-sacralized; it works as a discourse of colonization that bell hooks would describe as "white supremacist capitalist patriarchy."[18] It bespeaks a secularism entwined in whiteness, with its core anti-Black and dualistic thinking, that is erected on a project of purity reminiscent of phantasmal racial categories and the governance of master/settler-colonial practices of enslavement to manage/police what is racially deemed as "other" in the margins. Now unveiling this imperial pedagogy, projected as secularity, is what Shelley Fisher Fishkin calls the "interrogation of whiteness."[19]

As an example consider Bruce Ashford, a leading white evangelical and conservative scholar, who perceives "BLM is rooted in the soil of secular ideology" and positioned "to overthrow the Judeo-Christian theological and moral foundations upon which our society has rested historically."[20] He marks for us a type of religious policing, of the Right, that represses the radical political theological dimensions of the movement—as secular, anti-Christian, and anti-American. Ashford demonstrates for us the threat that is created by the ambiguity of this Black sacrality, that is found in the BLMM. The violence of Ashford's imperial theological conformity works to erase the sacrality, and the ambiguity and legibility of the BLMM, which is disorienting to the present political order. To shed light on this radical sacral political space requires more listening than speaking, feeling than touching, and more seeing than representing, which are things that the governing powers of the present political order are unwilling to voluntarily do.

And yet from the Left there has also been a type of secular policing, perhaps unwittingly, repressing the larger aims of the movement and therefore not strong enough to unsettle a coloniality of religion and politics in US public culture. From the Left, many otherwise astute scholars have interpreted the movement in merely secular terms, and doing so, as Vincent Lloyd points out, they have ignored "organizers' spiritual language."[21] But it is important to listen to organizers' spiritual language because it marks a spiritual or a sacred metaphysic, and even a sacred or theological imaginary from which they are doing their work. I argue that such a secularizing reductionism does not adequately represent the BLMM, nor adequately contend with problematic racial representations of it in popular US culture. What many times are overlooked are the ways in which lurking within representations of the BLMM's "moving history," in both academe and popular culture, is also a history of secularism that is entangled with whiteness working to shape our understanding of the Black Freedom Struggle while forgetting Black sacred politics.[22] Thus the religious and spiritual language, practices, and sensibilities of activists circulating throughout this social movement of Black-led mass struggle are repressed and overlooked.

I propose, however, that we explore spiritual and religious practices as cultural and political practices, since spiritual and religious practices themselves cannot be understood apart from a certain cultural and political repertoire. According to Sylvia Wynter, every cultural practice is rooted in an ethnocentrism.[23] There exists a group logic in contemporary Western ethnocentrism that implicitly accepts the opposition between the sacred and the secular, or the political and the theological. Therefore, as there is no noncultural spiritual practice, there is no nonspiritual cultural practice in this Black social movement. Religion is a complex field and not an additive; we should be viewing religion in terms of the entire social praxis—art, culture, organizing, protest politics, and so on—of the BLMM. There is a story that messily brings together the sacred and the secular, that narrates the religious in the M4BL seamlessly, as a singular story. There is a radical sacred politics, a Black sacred politics fundamental to the racial justice struggles of the BLMM.

MEMOIR-IZING THE SACRED IN BLACK LIVES MATTER

Paying attention to the practices, ideas, and rhetoric of this racial justice movement, by thinking with its participants, forces us to confront a creative interplay going on where the boundaries between culture, politics, and religion are blurred, and we are entangled within the nexus of Blackness, protest, and the sacred. For these reasons one source that I have turned to (alongside social media feeds and manifestos) includes memoirs and/or life narratives, which are emerging within and around the M4BL. These texts allow me a way of thinking with activists and organizers, as I myself am thinking through spirit, spirituality, sacredness. Connecting spirituality up with activism can uncover religious formations rendered illegible underneath a secular regime. Letters are a fitting site for the traditions of imagining otherwise to take flight. Black critical thought happens within Black literature, and there is a historical relationship between Black letters and Black social movements. Black letters have oftentimes been one of the only places for Black imaginations to take flight conjuring up a new world. They give the reader liberty to take flight into the otherwise with their imagination, without capturing their imagination within rigid definitions, norms, and protocols of this present world.

Vincent Lloyd reminds us that "the exclusion or management of religion prompts us to remember the potency of what is excluded or managed.... [This is because] remembering the religious ... points to traditions of imagining otherwise."[24] Traditions of the sacred offer alternatives to a secular regime, where the imagination takes flight. Unmanaged and uncaptured by a modern secularized episteme, within this movement is a pedagogy of the sacred, a Black sacred politics, a Black religious political tradition of imagining otherwise. This site of knowledge production and energy has been a critical site for Black social justice movements, and here the M4BL is also presenting alternatives to the regimes of the state, and resisting them.

Memoirs are extremely useful sources for historicizing, documenting, and analyzing this movement from the bottom up.[25] Memoirs offer insight into the subjectivity of participants of the movement, as well as the BLMM at large. The rhetorical effectiveness of memoirs enables what Charles Griffin notes as the confluence of "self-definition and social advocacy." In other words, "the author's life story demonstrates the plausibility of enacting the movement's ideology at the level of the individual, while the movement's 'story' provides a backdrop against which the author can achieve a meaningful form of self-definition."[26] So if the self is imagined or defined within the frame of the sacred, so too are all social and political possibilities. The otherwise is found in the coupling of sacred imaginary and sacred subjectivity, even as a counter-public, and the sacred imaginary informs that imagination of what is possible in the world. Furthermore, with regard to how social movement authors intend to use their life-writings, scholars "have analyzed how memoirs, autobiographies, and life stories have been produced as part of an effort to generate further mobilization in . . . [the] social movement."[27] Life "narratives [are] strategic tools for social movements,"[28] and also for understanding them. Memoirs, and other forms of life writing, have been produced in Black social movements as a way of pushing up against illegibility, erasures, silences. In the M4BL, it is evident that these Black letters are being similarly utilized as tools in narrating and reimagining Black life. As in previous eras, their life writings are being used as counternarratives advancing particular ideologies useful in the Black Freedom Struggle. And of interest to me are the fundamental ways in which sacred rhetoric and a sacred imaginary are used in this process. Memoirists' utilization and modification of the language of the sacred for political and spiritual purposes in the fight for Black lives is critical for them.

"STARDUST!" NOT A "TERRORIST!"

This brings me to a brief consideration of Patrisse Khan-Cullors. In 2018 she released her memoir *When They Call You a Terrorist: A Black Lives Matter Memoir*, which recorded not only her own life but also perhaps an "autohistory"[29] of Black Lives Matter. She narrates her life story as entangled with and in some fashion reflective of a larger collective history of which she is a part. In this life narrative she wants the reader to see and take seriously the religious language of the sacred that she employs, and thereby the ways in which a sacred imaginary fundamentally informs her life and Black Lives Matter. Her engagement in examining her life serves as a concomitant examination of Black Lives Matter, offering insight into the BLMM, and it is "a call to action to change the culture that declares innocent Black life expendable." The reader is led to infer this synecdochic technique especially considering that the life narrative of Khan-Cullors is titled *A Black Lives Matter Memoir* and not merely *A Patrisse Khan-Cullors Memoir*. Though she is one person, and the Movement is broad in its diversity and many-splendored, she is proposing her narrative as somehow representative of the larger BLMM and to some extent what it means to be Black in America. Thus, on account of this, her life is to be taken as presenting a window into

Black Lives Matter, promoting what Michael A. Chaney might call "new kinds of seeing"[30] the BLMM.

There is a certain sacred literary labor, I propose, that she is involved in to shape in the reader a certain kind of seeing, which is a reimagining of Black Lives Matter. She has a stake in the reader seeing the sacredness of Black Lives Matter, as opposed to seeing terrorism. She admits that "the accusation of being labeled a terrorist is devastating,"[31] because it is dehumanizing. Her life narrative vocalizes a reality and another mode of being, which Charles Long would say not only "moves us beyond conquest, enslavement, and exploitation" but also moves us into a new understanding that recovers the "sensibility which lies at the heart of a religious attitude," illegible and inaudible to the protocols of whiteness.[32] It is her attempt to move us beyond "controlling narratives"[33] used to police/manage her subjectivity and fight for justice, and then move us into the movement. She exposes a sacrality that is beyond a way of thinking and seeing the world that is entangled with whiteness, and refuses the silences and erasures that distort her image and the image of Black Lives Matter. The sacred imaginary and sacred subjectivity through which she speaks provide a frame for illuminating her humanity, Black lives, and that of the BLMM. The ways in which she deploys religious language and ideas, as she represents her life, BLMM, and constructs her identity in *A Black Lives Matter Memoir*, has the potential to "overcom[e] cultural stereotypes, reductions, and essentialist collapses"[34] that she exposes in *When They Call You a Terrorist*. The visual field within the misnomer (*Terrorist*) is established within a hegemony of the state and an anti-Black discourse of US popular culture, which sees the BLMM as "Black Identity Extremists."[35] In confronting the inhumanity of "being labeled a terrorist by the state,"[36] she employs religious language and ideas as soft weapons of deconstruction, talking back to a hegemonic culture of whiteness. She labors to change and reconstruct the meaning of the movement as one imbued with a radical sacrality that is for too many left illegible or repressed.

She titles the introduction to her memoir "We Are Stardust." And as an entryway into this life narrative, through the introduction, she walks us through a sacred theoretic which refuses the dehumanizing statecraft that labels her and Black Lives Matter as terrorist. Along with co-author asha bandele, she focuses on our bodies—the bodies labeled/managed/policed as terrorist—and claims that the very atoms and molecules in our bodies are traceable to the crucibles in the centers of stars that once upon a time exploded into gas clouds. And those gas clouds formed other stars and those stars possessed the *divine-right mix* of properties needed to create not only planets, including our own, but also people, including us, me and her . . . we are in the universe . . . [and] the universe is in us . . . we, human beings, are literally made out of *stardust*.[37] (Emphasis added.)

Quoting Sonia Sanchez, Khan-Cullors claims to "write to keep in contact with our ancestors and to spread truth to people."[38] And as this quote finds its place in the introduction as its opening epigraph, in a literary act of juxtaposition she parallels the titular claim—"We Are Stardust"—with her "ancestors." She identifies herself as the

> the thirteenth-generation and progeny of a people who survived the hulls of slave ships, survived the chains, the whips, the months laying in their own shit and piss. The human beings legislated as not human beings who watched their names, their languages, their *Goddesses* and *Gods*, the arc of their dances and beats of their songs, the majesty of their dreams, their very families snatched up and stolen, disassembled and discarded, and despite this built language and honored *God* and created movement and upheld love. What could they be but *stardust*, these people who refused to die, who refused to accept the idea that their lives did not matter, that their children's lives did not matter?[39] (Emphasis added.)

Khan-Cullors creatively associates this "divine-right mix" with the creativity or vitality, and the resistance, in fact the humanity, of the ancestors from whom she has descended. Their survival of "slave ships," "chains," "whips," neglect, terror, all manner of precarity and abjection, and their willingness to still build "language," "honor God," create "movement," and uphold "love" despite the devastating violence to their lives and bodies is due to a union with the divine. It is this celestial content—"Stardust"—and sacred subjectivity which is the only explanation for the radical refusal to die and accept the idea that their lives did not matter. She marks a way of being in the world, in her Black ancestry, Ashon Crawley would say is grounded in abolition as the radical "refusal of violence and violation as a way of life" and "whiteness as the acceptance of violence and violation as a way of life."[40] For this reason this constant emergence of abolition, of radical refusal and the enduring fight/courage-to-be from the ground of her people's existence, she says, is "deeply spiritual."[41] As she contends elsewhere, "The fight to save your life is a spiritual fight." These Black people "snatched up and stolen" left "laying in their own shit and piss" refused the conditions they were condemned to endure, since in their bodies there is a "divine-right mix" traceable to the crucibles in the center of stars. A crucible anterior to the crucible of white supremacy and anti-Blackness for her is constitutive of their bodily existence. She points to an existence prompted by the initiative of the "divine-right mix" that is both in and of the universe, and of the divine. Though this radical existence is shaped by and inseparable from an ongoing history of anti-Blackness—"the hulls of slave ships" and their brutal aftermath—it is prior to and always already more than anti-Blackness.[42] This "stardust" though intimately tied to an ongoing history of anti-Black racism is never reducible to it. This is "stardust." It refuses, it resists, it fights, it escapes, it abolishes, it emancipates, it loves, it dances, it lives, it celebrates, it honors, it speaks, it sings, it dances, it dreams, and through Black life, Black lives, the persistent history of Black social life, its effulgence continues to shine. And it is not terrorist. She goes further:

> The members of our movement are called terrorists.
> We—me, Alicia Garza, and Opal Tometi—the
> three
> women who founded Black Lives Matter, are called, terrorists.
> We, the people.
> We are not
> terrorists.
> I am not a terrorist.
> I am Patrisse Marie Khan-Cullors Brignac.
> I am a survivor.
> I am *stardust*.[43]

This claim to being "stardust" provokes reflection that is all together religious and political. It is political-theological, and an act of resistance by an appeal to what is transcendent—the divine—and uncaptured/unmanaged/unpoliced by this world. "These people who refused to die, who refused to accept the idea that their lives did not matter, that their children's lives did not matter." She declares, over and against being called a terrorist, "The members of our movement. . . . We—me, Alicia Garza, and Opal Tometi—the three women who founded Black Lives Matter. . . . We the people . . . survivor[s] . . . [are] stardust."

Through this sacred politics, this political theology, she reimagines herself and her people aright, and not as terrorists, but as survivors and stardust. She reclaims a Black radical theological imaginary wed to a radical politic for Black freedom. N. Fadeke Castor calls this a "spiritual epistemology,"[44] and M. Jacqui Alexander "pedagogies of the Sacred."[45] Both Castor and Alexander show us that such sacred subjectivity (as "stardust") arises out of the intimate relationship with divinity which is the substratum for this knowledge and understanding. Khan-Cullors's language marks a self-knowledge that is deeply sacred and transcendent. It is an intimate knowledge that is transcendent, allowing her to think otherwise, beyond this world. It is a divine and spiritual knowledge, a sacred politics informing her fight for social justice, that quoting Jafari Allen, has the potential "to break down parts of the scaffolding of oppression."[46]

And so the question of whether or not this is religious is the thinner question. Black religious life is there. Spirituality is there. Theology is there. A sacred imaginary is there. But the thicker question is, "What is she doing with this?" It is hard to use religion in a transformative way, with the manner that all of these different critical voices are coming at her in popular culture, but still she is carefully navigating to show her use of religion in a politically transformative way. For her this question is the minefield that she is navigating, with people deadening or overlooking her intentionality and spirituality. Confronting this matter is central to her doing the work that she is doing in the fight for Black lives, as a part of the M4BL. For again, this fight for her is a "spiritual fight."

She knows that when she claims the radical religious register of the civil rights movement people (in the mainstream US public culture) say she is not supposed to be angry or enraged, and that she is supposed to be respectable and resigned, be led by clerics, led by men, to be of one of the Abrahamic traditions (principally Christianity), to be heterosexual, and so on. So through literary creativity she has to go about claiming the radical religious register in a different way. She must demonstrate the synchronicity of spirituality and social justice in the sacred. Through her life she must narrativize the structure, the spirit, and the mood of Black sacred politics in ways that prove useful to the Black Freedom Struggle. She wants to be heard and the movement to be properly understood, but there are these dead ends that she has to navigate around. She has to illuminate an alternative spirituality and alternative religiosity that is not resigned, which is a Black sacred politics that she knows is already in the trajectory of the civil rights movement and Black religious political protest. She's laboring to signal this creatively. One must look at what she is signaling. She cannot just say outright that she is the heir of the Rev. Dr. Martin Luther King Jr., in a simple manner and that's it, because it's a dead end in the ears of a white conservative audience that has colonized a popular understanding of Christianity, of the civil rights movement, of religion, and of politics in the popular culture. The creativity here that she is navigating with and around is ingenious and inventive.

So in an effort to accomplish this, in the text she creatively summons a symphony of sacred witnesses: Sonia Sanchez, Toni Morrison, James Baldwin, Audre Lorde, Octavia Butler, Lucille Clifton, Malcolm X, Harriet Tubman, Rev. Starsky D. Wilson, St. John's United Church of Christ, an altar call (to which she responds), sermons (she listen to or gives), bell hooks and Cornel West as mentors, gospel music and Christian hymns (she listens to), faith, hope, love, spirit, healing, joy; she reverentially invokes God, Jesus (of the Gospels), the Ancestors, Martin Luther King Jr., the civil rights movement; she mentions scholarly expertise from studying the Abrahamic traditions, majoring in the study of religion at UCLA, being an ordained minister—as both a leader within and practitioner of Ifá—presiding over weddings, offering multiple eulogies, and multiple prayers for justice; she also both critiques and rehearses Scripture, and more.

A sacred imaginary and sacred subjectivity are linked as a counter-public in the artfulness of this text. Her sacred imaginary and self-knowledge of sacred subjectivity informs that imagination of what is possible for her and Black Lives Matter, which is a world where Black lives matter and the first are last and the last first. She is speaking directly to the manner that Black Lives Matter has been misrepresented and its image distorted, even as she has been misrepresented and her image distorted. Rhetorically, she claims spirituality in a way that is genuine yet palatable for popular consumption and those who think she is anti-Christian, anti–civil rights, and anti-King, and so on, even though she reverently sees that she is in the same Black radical tradition of struggle as King and all of her ancestors that struggled before her. Khan-Cullors's theoretics of the sacred becomes a theoretics of movement building that is full of promiscuous solidarities. In other words, she woos others who "should not" be together at an affective level, through her sacred theoretics, in order to build out as broadly as possible a coalition for the freedom, justice, and dignity of Black lives. The invocation of the sacred involves a certain affectivity in which she reaches for a transformation of the heart in those that slow down enough to read (or listen to) her life narrative. And she wants the reader to feel with her an existence of a cosmology and metaphysical reality, entirely different from the violence of Western metaphysical dualism, wherein all of life—and not just a privileged/powerful few—is suffused with the sacred. For her the sacred is not only a necessary tool for freedom and a language to employ, but it marks the very essence and ground of being in which she lives, moves, and has her being. It is here that she marks her "people's resilience, [which, she] think[s], is tied to their will to live, our will to survive, which is deeply spiritual. The fight to save your life is a spiritual fight."[47]

NOTES

The epigraph is from Hebah H. Farrag, "The Role of Spirit in the #BlackLivesMatter Movement: A Conversation with Activist and Artist Patrisse Cullors," *Religion Dispatches*, June 24, 2015, http://religiondispatches.org/the-role-of-spirit-in-the-blacklivesmatter-movement-a-conversation-with-activist-and-artist-patrisse-cullors/.

1. Because of space constraints my examination of Patrisse Khan-Cullors's memoir here is concise, but I deal more extensively with it in my dissertation.
2. Patrisse Khan-Cullors, *When They Call You a Terrorist: A Black Lives Matter Memoir* (New York: St. Martin's Press, 2017).
3. Alicia Garza, Opal Tometi, and Patrisse Khan-Cullors are considered co-founders/co-creators of #BlackLivesMatter.
4. Ashon T. Crawley, *Blackpentecostal Breath: The Aesthetics of Possibility* (New York: Fordham University Press, 2016).
5. Alicia Garza. "A Herstory of the #BlackLivesMatter Movement by Alicia Garza," *Feminist Wire*, Oct. 7, 2014, thefeministwire.com/2014/10/blacklivesmatter-2/.
6. Christina Sharpe, *In the Wake: on Blackness and Being* (Durham, NC: Duke University Press, 2016), 139n28.
7. Alicia Garza's Facebook post, July 13, 2013.

8. Alicia Garza says, "For us as women who are organizers, there's a way in which our hearts connect to each other and to a real deep love for our people. And a real deep love for those mamas who are just trying to make it work, who've got the bucket under the leaky roof but are figuring it out. So the project that we are building is a love note to our folks" (https://nplusonemag.com/online-only/online-only/a-love-note-to-our-folks/).
9. Jamilah King. "The Women Behind #Blacklivesmatter," *California Sunday Magazine*, April 22, 2016, stories.californiasunday.com/2015-03-01/black-lives-matter/.
10. "[Commentary] How Black Lives Matter Is Penetrating Pop Culture," BET.com, June 9, 2016, www.bet.com/celebrities/news/2016/06/09/how-black-lives-matter-is-penetrating-pop-culture.html.
11. Barbara Ransby, *Making All Black Lives Matter: Reimagining Freedom in the Twenty-First Century* (Oakland: University of California Press, 2018), 1.
12. https://policy.m4bl.org/.
13. Eddie Glaude, "Definition of Black Lives Matter." C-SPAN.org, C-Span Documentary, May 8, 2015, www.c-span.org/video/?c4631235%2Fdefinition-black-lives-matter.
14. Marc Anthony Neal, "Left of Black with Barbara Ransby," accessed October 5, 2018, https://www.youtube.com/watch?v=5Equ2nru0Fw.
15. We can go to Talal Asad for this (and not necessarily Carl Schmitt).
16. I am thinking of the way religion, race, and the state collude in governing ways to condemn "wayward lives" in Saidiya V. Hartman's, *Wayward Lives, Beautiful Experiments: Intimate Histories of Social Upheaval* (New York: W. W. Norton, 2019). This logic of governmentality is mediated through religious symbols against BLM.
17. Josef Sorett, "#BlackLivesMatter and the Heterodox History of Afro-Protestantism," https://tif.ssrc.org/2016/09/22/religion-secularism-and-black-lives-matter/.
18. bell hooks, *Writing beyond Race: Living Theory and Practice* (New York: Routledge, Taylor & Francis, 2013), 177: "Religion is important because it is there that many folks learn the western metaphysical dualism—the notion of world divided between the good and the bad, the chosen and the unchosen, the worthy and the unworthy, the black and the whites—that is the philosophical foundation for white supremacy and other forms of domination. As long as this thinking serves as the foundation for how most people think about life (in neat binaries) then it will be impossible to eradicate racism. White supremacist capitalist patriarchy thrives on the core dualistic thinking that is the foundation of all systems of domination."

19. Shelley Fisher Fishkin, "Interrogating 'Whiteness,' Complicating 'Blackness': Remapping American Culture," *American Quarterly* 47, no. 3 (1995): 428–66, www.jstor.org/stable/2713296.

20. Bruce Ashford, "#BlackLivesMatter (6): An Evangelical Evaluation of BLM," http://bruceashford.net/2017/blacklivesmatter-6-an-evangelical-evaluation-of-blm.

21. Vincent Lloyd. "MLK Day and the Emergence of the New 'Sacred Politics' (Vincent Lloyd)." *Political Theology Network*, February 5, 2019, politicaltheology.com/mlk-day-and-the-emergence-of-the-new-sacred-politics-vincent-lloyd/.

22. Erica R. Edward, "'Welcome Back to the Living': Resurrections of Martin Luther King Jr. in a Secular Age," in *Race and Secularism in America*, ed. Jonathon Samuel Kahn and Vincent William Lloyd (New York: Columbia University Press, 2016), 99–121.

23. Consider, Sylvia Wynter in, "The Re-Enchantment of Humanism: An Interview with Sylvia Wynter," *Small Axe* 8 (2000): 119–207.

24. Vincent Lloyd, "Managing Race, Managing Religion," in *Race and Secularism in America*, ed. Jonathon Samuel Kahn and Vincent William Lloyd (New York: Columbia University Press, 2016), 15.

25. N. Salvatore, "Biography and Social History: An Intimate Relationship" (electronic version), *Labour History*, no. 87 (2004): 187–92.

26. Charles J. G. Griffin, "'Movement as Motive': Self-Definition and Social Advocacy in Social Movement Autobiographies," *Western Journal of Communication* 64, no. 2 (2000): 148–49, doi:https://www.tandfonline.com/action/showCitFormats?doi=10.1080/10570310009374669.

27. G. Marche, "Political Memoirs and Intimate Confessions: Analysing Four US Gay Liberation/Gay Rights Militants' Memoirs," *Sexualities* 20, no. 8 (2017): 959–80, https://doi.org/10.1177/1363460716677036, 960; H. Lénárt-Cheng and D. Walker, "Using Life Stories for Social and Political Activism," *Biography* 34, no. 1 (2011): 141–79; M. V. Perkins, *Autobiography as Activism: Three Black Women of the Sixties* (Jackson: University Press of Mississippi, 2000); J. Taylor, "Rich Sensitivities: An Analysis of Conflict among Women in Feminist Memoir," *Canadian Review of Sociology/Revue Canadienne de Sociologie* 46, no. 2 (2000): 123–41; and M. Watson, *Lives of Their Own: Rhetorical Dimensions in Autobiographies of Women Activists* (Columbia: University of South Carolina Press, 1999).

28. Marche, 960.

29. Sidonie Smith and Julia Watson, *Reading Autobiography: A Guide for Interpreting Life Narratives* (Minneapolis: University of Minnesota Press, 2013), 270.

30. Michael A. Chaney, *Fugitive Vision: Slave Image and Black Identity in Antebellum Narrative* (Bloomington: Indiana University Press, 2008), 9.

31. Khan-Cullors, 7.
32. Charles H. Long, *Significations: Signs, Symbols and Images in the Interpretation of Religion* (Aurora, CO: Davies Group, 1995), 69.
33. Patricia Hill Collins, *Black Feminist Thought* (New York: Routledge, 2000), 69–96.
34. Chaney, 9.
35. Khaled A. Beydoun and Justin Hansford, "The F.B.I.'s Dangerous Crackdown on 'Black Identity Extremists,'" *New York Times*, November 15, 2017, www.nytimes.com/2017/11/15/opinion/black-identity-extremism-fbi-trump.html; https://assets.documentcloud.org/documents/4067711/BIE-Redacted.pdf.
36. Khan-Cullors, xii.
37. Ibid., 3–4.
38. Ibid., 3.
39. Ibid., 4–5.
40. Crawley, 6.
41. Christina Heatherton, "#BlackLivesMatter and Global Visions of Abolition: An Interview with Patrisse Cullors," in *Policing the Planet*, ed. Jordan T. Camp and Christina Heatherton (London: Verso Books, 2016), 40.
42. I'm here thinking through Calvin L. Warren, "Black Mysticism: Fred Moten's Phenomenology of (Black) Spirit," *Zeitschrift für Anglistik und Amerikanistik* 65, no. 2 (2017): 219–30; and Fred Moten, "Blackness and Nothingness (Mysticism in the Flesh)," *South Atlantic Quarterly* 112, no. 4 (2013): 737–80.
43. Khan-Cullors, 8. Emphasis added.
44. N. Fadeke Castor, *Spiritual Citizenship: Transnational Pathways from Black Power to Ifá in Trinidad* (Durham, NC: Duke University Press, 2017).
45. M. Jacqui Alexander, *Pedagogies of Crossing: Meditations on Feminism, Sexual Politics, Memory, and the Sacred* (Durham, NC: Duke University Press, 2006).
46. Jafari S. Allen, *¡Venceremos?: The Erotics of Black Self-Making in Cuba* (Durham, NC: Duke University Press, 2011), 95.
47. Farrag, "The Role of Spirit in the #BlackLivesMatter Movement," https://religiondispatches.org/the-role-of-spirit-in-the-blacklivesmatter-movement-a-conversation-with-activist-and-artist-patrisse-cullors/.

13. Genocide and the Sin of Identity

NOËLLE VAHANIAN

Sometimes, I wear an old, hand-knitted, wool sweater. My daughter calls it the "potato sweater." She thinks it makes me look like a brown potato. Obviously unflattering, the sweater is warm and comfortable nonetheless. It was my father's sweater. And when I put it on, I remember him and his warm hugs. I did not wash it for a long time after I retrieved it from the destined-to-the-Red-Cross pile of belongings. I have a few select other pieces of clothing, accessories, and personal items—as *they say*—that I hold on to: an equally warm and hand-knitted, elbow-worn and holey cardigan; several cashmere scarves; a handkerchief; a couple of button-down shirts; an old belt, several pipes, a tobacco pouch, a couple sets of gold cuff links, a couple of small Italian leather, fleur-de-lis–embossed, jewelry boxes; a Mont Blanc and a Parker fountain pen. I know that I am not alone in holding on to things that belonged to loved ones. I have a few other items from several other deceased loved ones as well: shirts, pens, pencils, earrings, necklaces, rings, and brooches. Sometimes I wear the jewelry, but the pens, I rarely touch, and I've never worn the shirts. They're tucked away, and occasionally I glance at them. Usually, when I try to reorganize my closet. Sometimes I try to see if I can still smell the person they belonged to, but I can't consciously detect them, though I tell myself that in some infinitesimal way, something remains of their person. I held on to an unopened pack of cheap brand cigarettes that belonged to my dissertation adviser for over fifteen years. I may have recently discarded the pack though I am not sure. I can't remember the brand, but it was a white pack with blue horizontal lines.

Maybe they were *Vantage*, or something like that. I still have one of his Zippo lighters. I keep it on my desk, in a lacquer box my father brought back to me from one of his trips to South Korea. My father's Mont Blanc and Parker fountain pens are also in that box. I have a small leather business card holder that belonged to a cousin who shot himself. I still use a kitchen appliance that belonged to my grandparents. It's at least thirty years old. Then there is also a preserved wildflower that was in my aunt's possession when she died of friendly fire in France in August of 1944. I am named after her. I also have her monogrammed table linens. She had these as part of her dowry.

But some of these artifacts tell another story too. This one, not only mine or personally related to mine. These artifacts tell the story of our identities, or rather, they reveal to us that our identities are foremost stories, and that even while these may be real, cut of the flesh of our becoming, they are also imagined: woven fabric of material histories, loose threads of unfinished journeys, tattered garments of lived experiences.

Who are we? Generic "we," genetic "we," homo sapiens or human "we," us versus them "we," Me Too "we," forlorn "we's."

As evidenced by the postmodern death of the unitary, self-same subject, its correlative culture wars between identity and identitarian politics, and the mass-scale, profit-making, marketing of genetic testing for genetic origins, it is clear that the question of the "we" has replaced that of the "I." In other words, when we ask ourselves the question "who am I?," "we" is the answer: 50 percent this, and 20 percent that, and 1 percent probability of this on the genetic stick. Or we have the instances of narcissistic nationalist "we's": Trump is real America à la Louis XIVth, "l'état, c'est moi"; or again, "Je suis Charlie" and "Me Too" advocacy we's. "We" is the new individual. If I want to be myself, I have to feel at ease in the "we," forget myself in some "we," conflate myself or even deny myself in the "we."

The potato sweater was hand-knitted by another aunt. A weave so evenly perfect, it looks woven on the factory loom. This aunt was the eldest of my father's two half-sisters. Their own father died of an illness, before the outset, in 1915, of the Armenian genocide within Ottoman Turkey. The family was from Kharput (Harpoot), an ancient Armenian citadel on a hill overlooking the Euphrates valley. Kharput, long before coming under Ottoman rule, had been part of the Iron Age Kingdom of Van, also known as Urartu, which spanned the biblical mountains of Ararat and which, in the sixth century BCE, came to be the great Kingdom of Armenia, overcoming Byzantine and Sassanid Persian invasions before succumbing to Seljuk rule at the end of the first millennium, after the battle of Manzikert, and until the Ottoman empire was declared.

At the height of the genocide, the two sisters were sent to or left with a Near East Relief orphanage, because it was the best way to care for them: Kharput, Istanbul, Corinth, Marseille. My grandparents entered France as refugees with a daughter said to be born in Yerevan, in 1921. The details are vague, and even vaguer now that they are all gone. My grandmother, with her youngest in her arms, went to find her daughters. She said: "I am married; this is your sister." Then she left them to become housemaids, until each found a husband. They accepted the first offer.

This "potato sweater" was made by a woman who, as a child, lived through a death march and witnessed atrocities. I know this, and because of this, because I conceive this—and only because I do—this knowledge is constitutive of my identity. I locate Kharput on a map. Today, it is known as Elazig.

It would be easy, perhaps, to forget all this. It might be for my own children. Their own identity will be no more than what they are able to encompass. They are culturally at home in twenty-first-century North America. There is no question of their "assimilation." However, there are many diaspora Armenians who strongly identify as such. Take, for instance, the recollection of French archaeologist Jean Lassus, who upon his arrival in Syria around 1930, for an excavation project at Antioch-on-the-Orontes, found himself in need of a lightweight suit. He was referred to a tailor named Serrafian. "Your name is Armenian," he remarked. "I am Armenian," replied the tailor. "Where were you born?" "In Damascus." "And your father?" "Also in Damascus." "And your grandfather?" "In Aleppo. And his father also." "Four generations? Then you are no longer Armenian, you are Syrian." "You cannot understand. You are French. You belong to one of these recent nations that have not had the time to constitute themselves into a race. We, Armenians, you see, we are descendants of Aram, who was at the Tower of Babel."[1]

• • •

I began with a personal story to posit two general premises: First, that identities are fundamentally imagined; and second, that the "we" authenticates the "I." These are well known and, for most readers here, also well understood. But perhaps, a bit like a bitter pill one swallows daily while pinching one's nose, like an obligatory ablution, or a wink and a nod, they haven't changed us in the way one would expect profound understanding and realization would. Although, this latter point, too, can be said to be well understood. But the manner in which one arrives at these insights is a lament and a protest. Now is not a novel argument and a novel insight, but a distinct, singular path tying loose ends in a grand knowledge. We can tie Christianity, empire, colonialism, modern subjectivity, and capitalism together in telling the big story of our global world since 1492. But by the sound of our most widespread contemporary discourses, genocide is a modern crime and an exception, rather than an underwritten rule alongside slavery, racism, exploitation, and the despoiling of the earth. Genocide does not simply belong to the underside of modernity, but modernity—loosely understood and representing the arc of history—has written genocide out of its understanding of its own progression, repressed it as it were, projected it outwardly as the sin of the others.

To say that identities are fundamentally imagined does not make them any less real. Though for the so-called modern thinker, the question of their veracity falls somewhere between what one calls "truth" as opposed to "myth." But, as a postmodern or post-postmodern thinker, invested in what some call "unlearning," the distinction carries, besides its metaphysical ghost, the slew of Eurocentric epistemic habits that relegate to the periphery or to oblivion those whose posture, experiences, or histories and knowledges cannot be grasped by that myopic lens, at least not without considerable injury. Serrafian sees himself as, imagines himself to be, conceives or knows himself as a descendant of the biblical Aram. This fact is really constitutive of his sense of identity. One might puzzle, incredulous, over his assuredness. One might wonder if he "really" believes this. One might suggest that the statement expresses a desire-to-no-end, or a theological desire, a desire for extraordinary ordinariness. Or, in a more conventional version, one might explain away this biblical fundamentalism as a survival mechanism. After all, proto-Armenians were sun-worshipping pagans before their conversion to Christianity in the year 301 of the Common Era, when Saint Gregory the illuminator is said to have convinced the Armenian king, Tigridates III, to adopt Christianity as a state religion. Paganism and Christianity coexisted peacefully, but in the interest of safeguarding Armenian identity, Mesrop

Mashtots, a medieval linguist, theologian, and statesman, invented, in the early fifth century, the Armenian alphabet and herewith translated the Bible from the Syriac into Armenian. According to his first biographer, Mashtots admonished all the children to recite the psalmic verse "Forget your people and your father's house" (Psalm 45:10 NIV) both, as a contemporary scholar suggests, in order to spread his invention and to force the adoption of the Bible as sole authentic witness of humanity's past.[2] However forced or brutal this conversion may have been, there is little doubt as to its unifying power in the face of constant invasions. And in this way, Serrafian identifies himself as a people of the Book, not merely because he is a Christian, but more fundamentally, for him, because he is Armenian, descended of Aram, "who was at the Tower of Babel."

Now, at least according to Flavius Josephus, first-century Roman-Jewish historian, as he retraces the history of the Jews, Aram, one of the five sons of Shem and grandson of Noah, was the ancestor of the Aramites, or Syrians. But Ul, one of Aram's sons, founded Armenia.[3] Besides all this, the name Aram also refers to one of the great patriarchs of Armenia and Arame is the name of the first known King of Urartu. In addition, at its greatest during the first century BCE, the kingdom of Armenia spanned from the Caucasus, to northwestern Iran, across Turkey, into Syria and Lebanon. Now Serrafian makes no mention of the Urartu kingdom or of the height of the kingdom of Armenia under King Tigranes the great. But one surmises in his answer to Lassus that his Armenianness is impossible to root out. He expresses this in a language that may make many of us uncomfortable, namely, in the language of race. It appears indelible, constitutive of his identity. So much so that in 1930, which, not incidentally to this story, is when the new Republic of Syria was founded while still remaining a French mandate as declared by the League of Nations after the partitioning of the Ottoman Empire, Serrafian felt more Armenian than Syrian.

We, therefore, come to the other side of this imaginary conception of identity with full force. Namely, the modern concept of nations, bounded geographically, administrated from center to periphery, and, in some form, the legacy of botched-up colonial enterprises. In my own imagination, Lassus, the Frenchman, at once pointing out the Armenian name and refusing its referent ("you have an Armenian name," / "You are no longer Armenian, you are Syrian"), commits the sin of whiteness, or more generally, the sin of identity: orientalizing ignorance couched in modern erudition, ready as he is to relegate the significance of Serrafian's name to the antiquities, the past, the premodern era; self-assured as he is in his modern sense of identity; oblivious as he may be, or to be sure, insensitive as he may be, to the silencing of history that his own remark and incredulity blindly reiterate and perform. The performative utterance, "You are no longer Armenian," comes with an assumption of authority, a sovereign subjectivity, like that of the judge pronouncing a legal union.

As for the second premise, that the "we" authenticates the "I": "We, Armenians" verifies Serrafian's answer that not only his name is Armenian. Lassus, however, sees Serrafian as a Syrian, according to the country of his birth, because he himself is a Frenchman, for whom nationality and citizenship are one and supplant ethnicity or race. It is by that logic that the 2018 soccer world-cup champions are French and can't be identified as African. It is also by that logic that the French refuse the concept of race and have recently stricken the word out of their constitution. Since race has no biological basis, race, therefore, does not exist. We are all equal before the law regardless of sex, origin, or religion, but not race, since race has no biological reality. For the French, to identify the soccer players as African is to call into question their being French on the basis of race. It is not only racist, it is also impossible. Thus Serrafian is a Syrian, and though his name is Armenian, he can't be one himself. This is, of course, a very modern and Cartesian conception of identity. Strip everything that can be doubted, leaves one with the only identity that can't be doubted, that of the Cartesian cogito qua universal human being. And yet that is also a fabulation, one that hides its coloniality, some might say, or otherwise puts the fact that, borrowing from Walter Mignolo, "I am where I think": my objective knowledge comes with a set of provincial a prioris.

For example, as others have shown extensively and convincingly already, Kant projects his cosmopolitan point of view for a teleological notion of progress horizontally when he attributes most natural talents and proclivities for development and progress to the white human race; Locke's natural rights serve the interests of the landed and of the captains of industry when property rights are given to the industrious who would ensure land is not laid to so-called waste as he remarked about America. More generally, the humanist ideal is deployed from the West to the periphery, the non-West, noncivilized world through various imperialisms and the institutions, governmental, economic, and educational that they impose. To be modern, one needs to trade local dress, languages, and customs for Western ones. And because modernity ushers in the secular age of autonomous reason freed from the corrupted ethos of Catholic Church authority, Christian scholasticism, and divinely ordained monarchic rulers, to be modern also requires two degrees of conversion: the adoption, first, of Christian values, essential to ensure the self-depredation of the heathen who then, in a second stage, must renounce even the possibility of a transformative conversion by virtue of faith, modern science having deemed him naturally inferior, more primitive, less rational than the cosmopolitan ideal. It is in this sense that, however Christian Serrafian's Armenian identity may be, it is the wrong kind of Christianity that has him beholden to holy lands and peoples. The real Christian will have abandoned his sacred history for a geography of the logo-map.[4]

What, then, is the significance of these two premises? Perhaps it is possible to say that Serrafian's sense of identity reveals a different sense of time. His appeal to sacred history harks back to a Messianic sense of time, where past and future are one in a providential present—a divinely ordained, but imminently precarious now. In alluding to a biblical chain of events, which has him descended of Aram, Serrafian writes himself into a sacred genealogy in a refusal of modern history that would erase him from its maps. It is also possible to say that Lassus's notion of identity is a product of modernity and of a different sense of time, one in which the new order has arrived, is realized; one in which the sovereign is the nation; one, finally, in which secular universalism confers equality and freedom to the citizen. Who wouldn't leap at a chance for independence, at the chance to write one's future? But the larger point, that identities are imagined, imagined ways we relate to one another, to a past or a future, to an ultimate concern, means that they are theological, born of an infinite desire to be rather than not, to be significant, wedded to an origin, or a purpose, to echo meaningfully across the universe. At the same time, because they are imagined, identities are precarious, fragile, and ever so corruptible. Conjured of maleficence or not, the modern secular humanism that, on the one hand, seems to have promoted yearnings for independence from colonial powers, has, on the other, made it all too easy to dismiss, forget, erase, silence, or simply relegate to the ash heap of history untold diversity.

My thesis is fairly simple and it goes something like this: Sin is self-deception; identity is a form of self-deception that ontologizes imagined realities at the expense of forgotten or unthinkable identities. The first premise, that identities are imagined, puts into perspective the second-nature reflex to accept the foundational myths of modern states. Developed slightly, the second premise emphasizes the political nature of the most existential question. It is in this way that the second premise, that the "we" authenticates the "I," helps us see genocide—"the intent to destroy, in whole or in part, a national, ethnical, racial or religious group, as such"—in a different light.[5] Not as the exception to the rule, but instead, as a rule, possibly instantiating the modern I, for it is by this rule that it makes no sense for Serrafian to call himself an Armenian. By this rule, Armenianness, like race, does not exist—never existed.

There are two things I don't wish to do in all the foregoing. First, I don't wish to suggest that genocide is only a modern crime. Though I would have to agree that modernity is genocidal in its essence—as in the essence of whiteness. Second, I don't wish to minimize genocide by "generalizing" it. I want to show instead that genocide is, like the dust settling in one's interior castle, sin at the heart of identity.

Finally, then, the language of sin signals a theological inheritance. This is not an uncomplicated affiliation. Neither can it be squarely denied—one could abstain from using the word in question—nor can it be unequivocally welcomed. A secular theology of language, nondogmatic, sans metaphysical horizon, becomes a way of thinking *in extremis* against the genocidal tide of a world order whose testament is the ash heap of history.

• • •

I opened the drawer to my bedside table and, under other knickknacks, glimpsed the old pack of cigarettes intact, right where I remember leaving it. *Basics*—that was the brand. I left it untouched and closed the drawer.

CLARIFICATION

Identities are imagined. This is not to deny their factuality or the fact of our material conditions and concrete experiences or our biology or physics and our temporality. This is not to deny that we have inheritance, provenance, vestiges of our past in our bones and cells, evidence—however faulty—of our "kind" in our features and skin coloring, mannerisms, and expressions that may betray our social upbringing or cultural appurtenance. No, identities are imagined because we conceive them. This notion is much like that of the famous existentialist who said that "existence precedes essence." So it is nothing new, though it may still be controversial. We know this, we understand this, but what have we done with this freedom? To what degree is this "we" relevant, if "we" is a provincial scholar? The nod and the wink.

This leads me to the second premise: The "we" authenticates the "I." Here, too, much like that famous existentialist, there is a sense in which one cannot be who one thinks they are unless the public agrees. This is why some, for instance, experience the shiftiness of the color line. But this is also why the "I" internalizes the "we" that the "I" belongs to: We Armenians, says Serrafian, the tailor from Syria, in response to the Frenchman who will not accept his being an Armenian from Syria. To give a current example, when Donald Trump says "make America great again," he implies a "we" that he is. This is not the same as saying: "Together, we can make America great again." No, he, in virtue of his presidency, of being elected, of getting his way, verifies America is great again since he is the "we," or claims to be or imagines himself to be middle America, let's call it.

Identities are imagined, not too unlike the religious illusion Freud spoke of, in that sense that we all partake in the making and glorifying, or shattering and shaming of identities, in the sense also that the "I" becomes a rule that we follow—what I must do to be true to the "I," whether or not the "I" is in the truth or cares about being true to anything but itself. "I" becomes sovereign or else it cannot be itself. For "I" to be itself, "I" must, as if, cross the same river twice. There is no way to do this other than in self-deception or in community, or in the self-deceptions, however beautiful and commanding, that are our communal identities: We will die for country, cause, love, greater good even when that good is a good for us only, or when country turns empire, or cause turns to greed. How else is it possible that the psychological narcissism of the leader fuels the pathological narcissism of the nation? Sociologists like to describe the ubiquitous us-versus-them dynamic precisely in pointing out the frailty of individual identity, its seeking sustenance in a social, larger community, and when that community suffers, is threatened, or somehow sees itself as in danger, that is fodder against those who are not complicit—or those who are perceived as traitors, enemies from within.

The "we" verifies them or denies our imagined identities in a game of self-deception writ large. I gave two examples: Serrafian's Armenianness, which is almost a hagiography, because it positions those who belong in biblical lineage with Aram and thus as provident, fulfilling prophecy, divinely ordained, and ineradicable—as in eternal, almost. The other example is that which is congruent with modernity, European modernity, and the birth of a nation. These two are incompatible in one sense. They are incompatible for the Frenchman, the archaeologist, the one who believes in science, history, and progress, and for whom there is no such thing as an Armenian born a Syrian. If you are born in Syria and your father too and your grandfather and so forth, how could you be anything but a Syrian, thinks Lassus the Frenchman, and so your last name is only a reminder of a past that no longer belongs to you. and it certainly is noticeable, like a mole or a growth, or an extra toe maybe. Here the violence is in some sense genocidal.

But the Armenian counters with the only language the Frenchman could understand, the language of race: The Armenian race descended of Ul, son of Shem, grandson of Noah, and so forth. It is easier to see the fabulation, the wish fulfillment here, because we are so accustomed to our modern sense of identity tied to nation and humanist ideals and real geographical borders that we guard fiercely. Hence my thesis: Sin is self-deception, is identity. This thesis does nothing to absolve the sin of whiteness, which I would regard as a menace to the whole ecosystem, to cultural diversity, with its hegemonic force, swallowing as its other those it rejects as its kind or ignoring altogether those it has denied, those it has not thought, those it has erased, not just forgotten—forcing all into a game of complicity in various degrees—forcing all to cross the same river again and again. Therefore, the sin of whiteness is the foremost exemplar of the sin of identity. While it is possible in theory to disentangle the former from the latter, in actuality, the latter must be reckoned with, else—like the Holocaust—it is mistaken for an exception.

Identities are imagined. And this most existential question is at the same time what opens me to the other—to the I am not that I want to be or want not to be, to the possibility of good, to the possibility of love, and also to sin—we come to it—to sin in duplicity. Perhaps it is true that this openness to the other is preontological in the Levinasian way. This openness would be a heteronomous theological imperative to love, not to kill, to infinite hospitality. Read this way, the theological would command a certain "allergy to identity"—the modern I or we—but also command respect for the other's identity—the Armenian—which spells a different universe.[6]

Perhaps it is true, but a secular theology of language, while it can conceive this possibility, cannot believe it. That is, for a secular theology of language, the preontological is at best a quasi-transcendental concept to help us think a better way into this world that is all that is the case—for we are all already in medias res. This is why I suggest we view the call or command or sense of infinite desire or lure for divine ordinariness not as heteronomous and pure, coming from a divine without, but instead as the experience of one's resistance to the order of a modern subjectivity, where "one" is neither "I" nor "we" but rather always coming to be and ceasing to be—a subject in process/on trial, a subject/superject—a rebellious no.

It will be objected that this appears to be a weak subject position that could only be worthwhile to adopt for anyone already in a privileged position—easier to give up power than to give up its possibility altogether. But I disagree with the premise that a rebellious no in its openness to the other—to its becoming—is weak. Take off the mask, I say (I do not mean this literally in terms of the COVID-19 pandemic), and consider the alternatives to what has become a theological behemoth: the sin of identity in its current historical instantiation and devolvement as the sin of whiteness. The point is not to succumb to the rule of nobody—whereby the "I" morphs and disappears into the general "we" of the dutiful and yet morally irresponsible and willfully ignorant ordinary everybody. The subject position has strength only vis-à-vis an object, like a master needing a servant. But like the right of the poor to think, the rebellious no resists predetermined interpretations. And like the will to power of the overman, the rebellious no agitates not in order to be, but to live, in creativity. But openness to the other does not mean one is so empty as to be void; it does not mean acceptance of all and crushing equalizer of good and bad. It means instead that "I" cannot hide behind a "we," that the "we" cannot hide behind a "flag," that a "flag" cannot hide behind a god. Does such a rebellious no have a voice? What does it mean to speak truth to power if not in one's own interior, and by the grace of a tomorrow, to feel the quiver of uncertainty and trepidation? Finally, on the issue of privilege: One can subversively play the game of everybody—smile gratefully at a demotion for still having a job. One can look and live as if one were saying "yes." Meanwhile, in that seeming passivity, one can very much be aware of the "no." This "no" is easier to drown than to hold on to. Privilege is this carefree passivity where one easily morphs into a "we" and feels aggrandized by this. One can know privilege in one place and not in another. But perhaps one can envisage a type of subjectivity for which this endless game of "in" or "out" will not hold. This, then, is what I mean to put forth as a different way of thinking our subjectivities.

It will also be objected that my view of identity generalizes and minimizes genocide. This, too, I reject and in the small space here allotted will now attempt to sketch an answer why, an answer to make my claim of a theological behemoth more apparent, as well as my claim that a rebellious no is a way to resist this behemoth as it lures us even in our guise.

JUSTIFICATION

If there are contemporary revisionist correctives to our current understanding of the birth of liberal democracies, international courts, and human rights, I focus, shortly, on the key concept of genocide, and on the originator of the term, not only to revise how we understand the term and our history, but to further exemplify the sin of identity. Samuel Moyn has shown how the concept of human dignity, when it first made its political appearance in the Universal Charter (1948) was not associated with secular humanist ideals, but was, instead, the progeny of the Catholic Church and the politicization of its moralism, and postwar, it was a tool against communism. He argues, to the contrary of many an assumption, that human rights discourse did not crystallize until the 1970s, only as a result of other failed utopias, while the earlier postwar manifestation of human rights was in fact an intended substitute for promises of self-determination made in the Atlantic Charter of 1941.[7] Similarly, Robert Meister suggests that human rights discourse is counterrevolutionary, creating a false sense of contending with and redressing a violent past while eluding social and economic inequity.[8] Both thinkers undo our mythology surrounding our understanding of the lessons of the Holocaust or the moral ground on which we place them and in which we write ourselves. Let me now add to their revisions.

The concept of genocide is a modern one. The word was coined in 1943 by the Polish lawyer Raphael Lemkin, who lost most of his family in the Holocaust for being Jewish. But he intended for the word to capture an age-old crime that had been going on with impunity. When on December 11, 1946, in a unanimous vote, the United Nations General Assembly approved its first resolution to criminalize genocide, the language of the text referring to the targeted groups was more open, listing, besides "other groups" in general, "political groups" in particular.[9] By 1948, when the final draft was adopted, the language referring to political groups had been dropped.[10] Although the Soviet Union was not alone in protesting the inclusion of political groups, "the Soviet representatives argued that the inclusion of political groups would not conform 'with the scientific definition of genocide, and would, in practice, distort the perspective in which the crime should be viewed.'"[11] Here, then, is one example of realpolitik influencing not only the course of the law but also how the crime of genocide is to be understood.

Another important example is that of the United States, which delayed ratification of the 1948 convention until 1988, but not without a Sovereignty Package: The United States cannot be implicated before an international court of justice for a crime under the genocide convention without its own consent, and the US Constitution has supremacy over international law with respect to specific provisions of the convention (for instance with regard to what constitutes mental harm, which it defines as entailing permanent impairment).

Both examples are significant, in addition to being examples of realpolitik, because they reveal that double standards are constitutive of the convention and its applicability. But to come nearer my earlier contention, beyond the synchronic view, they also illustrate how these interests permeate and taint the ideals motivating the law in the first place. In this way, what may on the surface appear as a hurdle of the political process, a hurdle that compromise overcomes, now looks more like a defect opening the law to questions of fairness. A keyhole view of history surrounding the drafting and ratification process of the convention does not show how universality hides provinciality, how a law under which all nations should be equal lacks a principle of fairness; it is obviously not made and agreed to behind a Rawlsian veil of ignorance.

Going back to my first premise: Identities are imagined and, once ontologized, are forms of self-deception at the expense of forgotten others. If this is true, it is possible that the convention in itself hides behind the universal "we"/modern "I" of its collective signatories, behind the deliberative process of preparation of a draft convention acceptable to several nations, and behind the US conditions for ratification, its whiteness, its anticommunist neoliberalism, its ethnocentrism, and its weakened integrity.

But what of the ideals motivating the law in the first place? Do they stem from a modern "I" / universal "we" that is just as ethnocentric and provincial? For this is a precise case in which a man coined a word in order to facilitate, indeed, compel, a legal process. What is more, it is not just the case of a lawyer who sought a word to name a crime; Raphael Lemkin decided to study law precisely because he realized that there was no legal mechanism to punish and prevent atrocities and the decimation of entire cultures. It is often pointed out, by himself included, that his interest for and concern with human atrocities began in childhood. Lemkin, born in 1900, grew up in a Polish Jewish family within the Russian empire, in a town that, today, belongs to Belarus and which lay, at the time, within the Pale of Settlement region, the only region in the Russian empire where Jews were allowed permanent residence.

By 1933, he had penned a draft law to prevent what he then called "barbarity" and "vandalism," the destruction of groups and of their culture.[12] As the second world war broke out and the Germans invaded Poland, Lemkin fled first to Lithuania, then Sweden, and finally he was granted asylum in the United States where he reached port of entry in 1941 and joined the law faculty at Duke. As he had done while in exile, he continued to inform on the Nazi crimes and began to lobby for action for years to come.

Here then is a man whose apparent secular humanism is assuredly Western European. That is, one imagines Lemkin endowed with a Kantian-like courage and with the Cartesian-like certainty that autonomous reason is able to provide a clear and distinct solution to an age-old problem, that the force of law is a categorical imperative, and that international law garners the legitimacy of universal reason. Lemkin's solution is, from this angle, that of the *European*-cosmopolitan intellectual.

But unlike Kantian cosmopolitanism, which would be the teleological outcome of universal history from the European point of view, Lemkin is aware and prizes cultural diversity. For one, this is already visible in his cause and his concern for what he terms "vandalism." John Docker points out that already in 1944, that is, with the inception of the term "genocide," when it first appeared in print in *Axis Rule in Occupied Europe*, Lemkin proposes that genocide has two phases, that the first entails destruction, but the second is, in his own words, "the imposition of the national pattern of the oppressor," or otherwise put, what Lemkin also calls "ethnocide" or "cultural genocide," which, as Docker points out, is now no longer understood only as an "act or event" but instead as a "process" that "describes and entwines genocide and settler-colonialism."[13] Docker also shows how, in later unpublished papers, Lemkin will refer to various genocidal forms and methods used against Native Americans by the Spanish in South America, or the English, the French, and the postcolonial Americans in North America and into the nineteenth century.[14]

Growing up on a farm as a Polish Jew in antisemitic Russia, forced to hide in a forest when the Germans confiscated his home during the first world war, living in exile since the Nazi invasion of Poland, losing most of his relatives in the Holocaust, and then also having to lobby Washington for his cause, these experiences assuredly contributed to a more complex view of humanity than the universal, one-world vision of modern cosmopolitanism. As Docker surmises, "For émigré intellectuals of the 1930s and '40s eighteenth-century traditions of cosmopolitanism and internationalism were being engulfed and destroyed by Nazism, which itself was the culmination of nineteenth-century nationalism and colonialism."[15]

If W. E. B. Du Bois defined the problem of his century as the problem of the color line, a problem which establishes that the condition of privilege—the possibility of the American dream—for those on one side of the line, is the oppression of those on the other side, the concept of genocide and the process of its criminalization are not color-blind; for, inevitably, both originate from a specific locus in history, one that sees modernization largely through a Eurocentric lens that is culturally blind to the importance of the Atlantic slave trade or of colonialism in the establishment of its economic power and cultural influence. At the same time, the inventor of the concept, whose idea it was to give the crime a proper name so as to prevent its impunity and who fought tirelessly to see the creation of an international Convention on the Prevention and Punishment of the Crime of Genocide, could be seen as the fruit of a different double-consciousness from the one Du Bois exposes, and this explains his enlarged view of humanity and his culturally plural view of the cosmopolitan ideal. But then it puzzles me that Lemkin who was so sensitive to the cultural aspect of genocide spoke against the 1951 *We Charge Genocide* petition before the UN to indict the US for police brutality, KKK lynching, and in general, lasting psychological violence through a hundred years of slavery, exploitation, rape, and oppression. He objected that African Americans enjoyed improved conditions, and one can surmise he felt theirs was a vibrant culture.[16] Forget how this culture is a rising phoenix. It is hard not to see his choice not to support the *We Charge Genocide* petition as a form of tunnel vision, even if we accept and perhaps precisely if we accept that he feared support would confuse and conflate the Genocide Convention with the Universal Declaration of Human Rights Convention or would divert from ongoing genocidal campaigns in Eastern Europe.[17] That is, even if we accept that discrimination is an individual rights issue or that the deprivation of said rights do not amount to the destruction of a national or ethnic character, what Lemkin seemed to refuse to think was that, in the case of African Americans, patterns of discrimination applied to an entire people and their culture.

The concept of genocide is a modern one. The problem, however, with the definition as it stands is that it compartmentalizes who we are as such: Genocide, it goes, is the intent to destroy in whole or in part a national ethnic, racial, or religious group. But whiteness is not a race; it is not simply a race; it is a religious, ethnic, national, and political—dare I say, a theological—behemoth, a leviathan. This is the UN's definition, not Lemkin's for whom the word's etymology, "race murder," is closer to Serrafian's understanding of race than to that of Lassus, as cultural and historical identity. For Lemkin, too, therefore, genocide does not necessarily imply the physical death of a group of people but rather includes acts of barbarity and vandalism. Once the term becomes a legal one to which nations must agree, it reproduces or is liable to reproduce the very violence that it is intended to prevent: The law effects a decision that is contrived, as if it were ever only a matter of eliminating a national or ethnic or religious people as such. If Lemkin agitated to maintain the singularity of the crime of genocide over against its conflation with individual human rights discourse—if he did not want the convention to be conflated with the Declaration of Human Rights, was it because he saw human rights as a way to placate the promise of true freedom from imperialism and colonialism with self-determination? Was it because human rights stood for what they would not deliver—social and economic justice—by focusing on violence directed at the human body, as Robert Meister might suggest?[18] Or was it because focus on these would obscure, indeed, erase, the violence of the "we"—the group—not against the "I"—the individual—but against other modes of rationalizing the actual, other imagined identities? But then the irony that this word "genocide" comes to signify an exception and mass murder in almost everybody's understanding. It is disconcerting too that even Lemkin himself can be seen as succumbing to the "national" pattern of the white European oppressor, and by extension, the very concept and law that he was so instrumental in creating becomes indeed a modern concept, but by now, I hope to have shown that whatever is meant by this term "modern," as in "modern nations" or "modern civilization" with its whitewashing effect or Eurocentric bias reveals that it is a pharmakon.

Thus, there are no innocents—the sin of identity is a given. There is no way to escape this condition, but to find a better way is not a capitulation. Finding a better way begins with acknowledging that every "I" seeks authentication in the "we," which "we" is internalized and imagined—as when Trump believes he is America.

A couple more things I should point out. At the beginning of the essay I misremember something along with memorializing what has been and still is denied. I misremember what happened to the pack of cigarettes and I misremember their brand. No doubt my personal story would be told differently at different times, but the difference isn't an erasure or denial. In the difference is a forgetting, an antithesis of genocidal denialism with always the same refrain, the same idea and the same exception.

NOTES

1. My translation. See Jean Lassus, *Souvenir d'un cobaye* (Colmar: Editions Alsatia, 1973).
2. See Jean-Pierre Mahé, "Un dieu Guerrier à la campagne: L'exemple du Vahagn arménien," in *Comptes rendus des séances de l'Académie des Inscriptions et des Belles-Lettres*, 138ᵉ année, N. 3, (1994): 779–804, doi: https://doi.org/10.3406/crai.1994.15407.
3. Flavius Josephus, *Of the Antiquities of the Jews*, in *The Genuine Works of Flavius Josephus, the Jewish Historian*, trans. William Whiston (London, Ont.: Attic Books, 2008). See book 1, chapter 6.
4. Benedict Anderson, *Imagined Communities* (New York: Verso Books, 2006), 175. "In London's imperial maps, British colonies were usually pink-red, French purple-blue, Dutch yellow-brown, and so on. Dyed this way, each colony appeared like a detachable piece of a jigsaw puzzle. As this 'jigsaw' effect became normal, each 'piece' could be wholly detached from its geographic context . . . pure sign, no longer compass to the world. . . . Instantly recognizable, everywhere visible, the logo-map penetrated deep into the popular imagination, forming a powerful emblem for the anticolonial nationalisms being born." The point is

interesting that this possible geographical envisioning as emblem without "names of rivers" or "neighbors," highly reproducible, becomes a powerful tool for anticolonial nationalisms.

5. See Article II of the Convention for the Prevention and Punishment of the Crime of Genocide adopted by the General Assembly of the United Nations in 1948.
6. I owe the phrase "allergy to identity" to Santiago Slabodsky.
7. See Samuel Moyn, *Human Rights and the Uses of History* (New York: Verso, 2017).
8. See Robert Meister. *After Evil: A Politics of Human Rights* (New York: Columbia University Press, 2012).
9. Samuel Totten and Paul Bartrop, *The Genocide Studies Reader* (New York: Routledge, 2009), 4. Bartrop and Totten quote extensively from Leo Kuper, *Genocide: Its Political Use in the Twentieth Century* (New Haven, CT: Yale University Press, 1981), 25–28.
10. Totten and Bartrop, *The Genocide Studies Reader*, 16–17.
11. Ibid., 4.
12. Ibid., 21.
13. Lemkin's words are cited in John Docker's paper "Raphaël Lemkin's History of Genocide and Colonialism," for the United States Holocaust Memorial, presented on February 28, 2004. Accessed online 5/30/2019 at https://www.ushmm.org/m/pdfs/20040316-docker-lemkin.pdf, but Lemkin's work is from chapter 9 of Raphaël Lemkin, *Axis Rule in Occupied Europe: Laws of Occupation, Analysis of Government, Proposal for Redress* (Clark, NJ: Lawbook Exchange, 2005), 79. This is the chapter in which Lemkin defines the word "genocide," although in the preface, we learn that the term was first coined in 1943. For the distinction between the articulation of genocide as process rather than as an event, see especially Docker's paper, p. 6, and in reference to cultural, biological, and other forms of settler-colonial genocide, 9–15.
14. Docker, "Raphaël Lemkin's History of Genocide and Colonialism," 9–15.
15. Ibid., 17.
16. Ibid., 64.
17. On Lemkin's view of the Universal Declaration of Human Rights, see Samantha Power, *"A Problem from Hell": America and the Age of Genocide* (New York: Harper Perennial, 2007), 74–76.
18. See Meister, *After Evil*.

14. Mystic S/Zong!

J. KAMERON CARTER

As such, she is a referent to that which is without determination . . . not because she was excluded, but because her non-value does not mean negation but nothingness—she is without the patriarchal norm and its value assignation. . . . Here she stands for the Thing (Kant's das Ding), or what elsewhere I name the sexual in the female colonial (slave and native) body. . . . A referent of the Thing [and] as a referent of the plenum, and hence outside the scene of determination, she refers to the undifferentiated abyss and the promise of dissolution of the forms of the subject. Female flesh ungendered, in the patriarchal economy, equals (0) nothing.
—DENISE FERREIRA DA SILVA, "Hacking the Subject"

The fact that silence presupposes words is what gives it this ironic twist. Without words there can be no silence, yet the sheer absence of words is not silence. Silence forces us to realize that our words, the units of our naming and recognition in the world, presuppose a reality which is prior to our naming and doing.
—CHARLES H. LONG, Significations

So perhaps ritual provides a way through the thicket of impossibles . . . / I am committed to retaining an ambivalence of the sacred object.
—M. NOURBESE PHILIP, "Wor(l)ds Interrupted"

BLACK RAPTURE

The above statements from Black feminist theorist Denise Ferreira da Silva, historian of religions Charles H. Long, and poet M. NourbeSe Philip situate the central task of this chapter. That task involves an engagement with Philip's poetry in such a way as to begin to bring into relief an understanding of Blackness as harboring a distinct notion of the sacred, what might be called Black radical sacrality. This is a notion of the sacred that moves in proximity to an understanding of Blackness in its nonreduction to identitarian logics of racially gendered thinking. I mobilize the notion of "rapture" as *parousia* to elucidate this. To orient readers to my use of this term in relationship to Ferreira da Silva, Long, Philip, and beyond just this chapter in relationship to a tradition of Black radical thought where the religious and the aesthetic operate in a kind of blurred indistinction, I want from the outset to provide something of a background for the notion of rapture as a concept from its appearance in the New Testament into how it was taken up in medieval Christian, particularly medieval women's, mysticism. This background will aid me in specifying my distinctive use of rapture as a conceptual tool for elucidating the poetics of Black thought, while also helping me frame my specific engagement with Canadian/Caribbean poet M. NourbeSe Philip, whose poem *Zong!* and its poetics constitute the central subject of this chapter.[1]

Within certain branches of American evangelicalism, rapture is an eschatological concept that points to an end-time event when Christian believers along with resurrected believers will rise "into the clouds, to meet the Lord in the air." So the understanding goes among such evangelical Christians. This is the notion behind the Pauline idea (see the New Testament's First Epistle to the Thessalonians 4:17) of an aerial gathering, a being "snatched" or otherwise "seized away" from the earth to meet Jesus Christ in the air to go to heaven as the end of days commences. Closely associated with this is the story of Jesus's postresurrection ascension into heaven, the *parousia* as recorded in the New Testament's Acts of the Apostles (1:1–10). Jesus's ascension inaugurates the events of Pentecost (see Acts 2) wherein Jesus's followers were to undergo their own kind of earthbound ascension, to be carried away beyond or beside or out of themselves into sociolinguistic madness. Such was their pentecostal ascension into a state of spirit possession to speak in tongues and engage in charitable works of care.[2]

But before one gets to the contemporary American evangelical uptake of New Testament ideas around rapture to fund an end-time, eschatology meant to orient a political theology of American religion, there was the significant Christian medieval taking up of the idea of rapture and the pentecostal notion of the *parousia*. Medieval ideas around rapture serve as a vital bridge between New Testament themes of rapture and modern-day, settler colonial or American evangelicalism. Specifically, it's medieval women's Christian (and often heretical) mysticism in its resonance, at least aspects of it, with what might be thought of as the mysticism of Blackness, that is important to the story I want to tell.

Here I call attention to the beguine mysticism of Marguerite Porete, the "nothingness" mysticism of Meister Eckhart (formulated, it is important to note, under the sway of Porete's mysticism), and the merriment or joy-mysticism of Margery Kempe in the later Middle Ages. Within their mysticisms, rapture is key, though theirs is a rapture that entails ravishment (with all the erotic and challenging gendered and sexuated connotations thereof).[3] Within Porete's and Eckhart's descriptions, in particular, of mystical transport, of being caught up in, united with, or otherwise seized by divine love (this is a mysticism that captivated such twentieth-century thinkers as Georges Bataille, Simone de Beauvoir, Luce Irigaray, and Jacques Lacan), something is revealed or disclosed about both deity and flesh alike. This revelation or disclosure, which is also a dis-en-closure, is, strictly speaking, apocalyptic (from the Greek verb *apokalupto*, meaning to disclose, unveil, or reveal). Under conditions of catastrophe something is unveiled that is irreducible to the catastrophe that is the natal occasion of what is disclosed. But what is the catastrophe? The catastrophic, metaphysically considered, concerns the subordination of existence in its variety and with all of its entangled messiness down to the being of language itself to an absolute or transcendental ground meant to anchor or otherwise stabilize it (as if existence needs anchorage or stabilization). That absolute ground has sometimes been conceived of as "God" (particularly in medieval theology and philosophy) and at other times "Man" (in modernity, particularly, in Enlightenment thought). Either way, whether existence is transcendentally subordinated to "God" or "Man," this metaphysical maneuver aims to curtail the physics or the fundamental aliveness of existence, the fundamental wildness and wilderness of existence, the being of language itself. This metaphysical catastrophe has a physical correlate. That is to say, materially considered, this curtailing of the physics or the fundamental aliveness of existence is part of a general ecological violence against the earth and against existing things. It is part of a protocol of property or the enclosure of the commons and extraction from the earth.[4]

Rapture mysticism transgresses this protocol of extraction, property, and enclosure. It interdicts the divination-extraction relay, and in so doing, transgresses the would-be stabilization of language and ecology that metaphysically anchors extraction. In transgressing this protocol, rapture mysticism unveils or discloses some other way of being manifest in surrender to the "open field" of language, as down the line poet Robert Duncan might have put it, manifest from the "infinite canvas" of existence, as Denise Ferreira da Silva might have put it, and given in a "practice of outside."[5] This other way of being signaled in rapture mysticism marks a sociality akin to quantum entanglement wherein difference is without separability.[6] Put differently, this other way of existence is love's social physics. Hence, rapture mysticism is a mysticism of love in which, as poet Alexis Pauline Gumbs says after Lauryn Hill, "everything is everything."[7]

The rapture or ecstatic transport revealed in love-mysticism indicates this alternate imagination of matter. More specifically, it discloses being-in-transport from or beyond, among other things, the normative, dyadic terms of the male-female body precisely by dwelling in flesh, that is, in the baseness of matter as fundamental, material condition. In this trajectory of mysticism, which includes Porete, Eckhart, and Kempe but also includes, as Jayna Brown has helped us understand, the Black radical utopian mysticism of Sojourner Truth, Jarena Lee, Zilpha Elaw, and others, rapture is an apocalyptic or revelatory "falling" where such falling is, in fact, a descending ascension, a being caught up in (the fall of) the flesh.[8] This fall releases one to the flesh beyond the bodily comportment of the individuated subject. Hence, this mysticism is not only apocalyptic (or discloses and dis-en-closes something) but is also apophatic (from the Greek word *apophasis*, which literally means "speaking away").[9] A key term in grappling with how mystical discourse works, *apophasis* is a mode of discourse that unsays itself by torquing itself or even turning back on itself, iteratively extending itself in ongoing-ness. Charles Long might figure this type of discourse, for him indicative of Black religion, under the geometrical sign of the ellipse or the imperfect or squashed circle and the literary figure of ellipsis.[10] Apophatic discourse, then, undoes itself precisely insofar as it is a discourse of incompletion. The knowing generated in apophatic discourse is one that undoes or unknows itself.

The upshot of this for what concerns us here is the following: Rapture mysticism proceeds, on the one hand, as a practice of bodily non-comportment.

It undoes or unsays the body as would-be coherent or singular entity tied to a would-be coherent, singular subject. On the other hand, rapture mysticism is a practice of passional existence or existence in spirit possession. Here neither the "I" nor language is one. In rapture, we have to do with a language of "no one," that "no one speaks," a language choreographed in maroonage and bound to the immanent and collective intensities of flesh, the flesh of the earth.[11] In this regard, rapture points to a socio-physics of flesh that is bound up with matter's immanent generativity or aliveness, its capacity at the most base or molecular level to proliferate life forms. That pulsating, generative aliveness is what I take Zakiyyah Iman Jackson to be getting at in her recent theorization of Black *mater* as matter(ing), as matter, as mat(t)er.[12] In effect, by thinking the *mater* of matter, Jackson's theorizing operates adjacent mysticisms (such as medieval rapture mysticisms) not premised on a statist metaphysics of the body as a figure of identitarian stability.

My interest is in this *mater*ial or rapture mysticism of the matter of the earth. I'm interested in how it invites an unsaying of the individuated body in the name of some other kind of we-ness, one that does not require a them-ness to stabilize its bordered and governmental us-ness. I'm reaching for a social physics of flesh that exceeds any statist We (the People . . .). The breakdown of bodily comportment or the dis/orientation given in rapture happens in the flesh's un/saying of the monogendered and sexuated order of being, for flesh questions the gendered and sexuated order of racial capitalism. Nathaniel Mackey's whatsaying poet-narrator might say that flesh "whatsays" or displaces the sense of a singularly sovereign, coherent self precisely by attending to that "hollowed . . . out, sophic not-ness . . . [of the] fractured masses."[13] Such attention entails attending as well to the hollowed out, sophic not-ness of words too. This doubled attention is at the center of Mackey's practice of the poem wherein he practices the poem apophatically. That is, he deploys words in a way that subverts the illusion of their representing a stable reality by having their ground transcendentally located in either "God" (as was the case, generally, for medieval writers with the notion of the Word of God) or "Man" (as is the case, generally, for moderns with the Word of Man). In saying that Mackey practices the poem apophatically I am indicating that the poem in his experimental working of the arts transgresses such transcendentalism.

When Mackey's poet-narrator conceives of words, worlds, and collectives (masses) as "hollowed out" it is precisely this transgression that is being enacted or tapped into. In this way, his poetics is spirit possessed. It is possessed of that inspirited or murmuring reality, the reality of the (Sur)Real, operative at the edge or over the ledge of any language regime. It is the conduit of an alternative that speaks itself in language. This murmur at the edge of any and every language regime is what Mackey has called, drawing on West African Dogon mythology, the "creaking of the word."[14] Such creaking, such murmuring points to an alternative beyond the imagination of a stabilizing God or a stabilizing Man as the metaphysical basis of the figure of the citizen-subject and of statist governance with its languages of jurisprudence or the letters of the law. In other words, Mackey's practice of the poem is juris-generative or generative of alternatives precisely at the scene of regulatory jurisprudence.[15] This is a juris-generative rapture poetics, we might say. It advances what Sora Han might called a poetics of Mu, where Mu itself is the first letter in an apophatic alphabet in flight from the Word via the flesh of words.[16] It is in this way that Mackey's poetics "hollows out" the Word via words by amplifying the creaking internal to words. What Mackey's poetics trades on, then, is the groundedness of a groundless and boundless outside within language itself, or rather, that is language as such. Language as an ecology of aliveness.

If Mackey's poetics of hollowed-out worlds of words as fallen, entangled flesh, operates like this, it also bespeaks Porete's (and Eckhart's Poretean) mysticism, which advances from raptured flesh. The raptured fallness of flesh here bespeaks a lost or fallen away fullness that ever aspires toward a union of love or love's entanglement enacted in unsaying a phallic order of gendered and sexuated being. This rupturing and rapturous mysticism of unsaying unsays, or in Mackey's sense apophatically "whatsays," an essentialist understanding of divinity; it unsays or whatsays "monogendered deity and monotonic gender relations between divine and human." In fact, it whatsays that very binary in the name of an alternate or third way. And finally, it unsays the mono(en)gendering of matter through the writing practices or the practices of study exemplified by such beguines as Porete but also by some male monks such as Eckhart.[17] This latter point is worth underscoring inasmuch as it comes especially to the fore in the case of Porete, who before her inquisitors burned her at the stake as a heretic (a witch?) they deemed her a "pseudowoman" (*pseudomulier*).[18]

In short, in rapture the annihilated soul signals its nonbeing as a formal subject. It ex-ists in the name of *ekstasis* or in ecstatic "Relation."[19] The enraptured aliveness of flesh signals an alternative understanding of matter in refusal of a contemporary medieval political theologizing of matter through logics of transubstantiation. Of the air but also and importantly more than air, ether (sometimes written as "æther"), that fifth element in medieval alchemy, is of this alternative understanding of matter. Beyond the elements of "earth," "wind," "fire," and "water," ether or what medieval alchemists called "quintessence" connotes "air" as the deeper condition of the terrestrial elements. Not as essence but as quintessence, ether allows the other elements to be composed, decomposed, mixed, and remixed in any number of unforeseen ways. Ether is what allows reality to the surreal presence of alternatives, other planes of existence. One might think of ether, then, as both aerial and base, matter's fundament, its groundless ground. Understood in this way, ether is matter's mythic mater, that which makes possible an infinite composition of the elements. Rapture in medieval women's mysticism is a function of mythic mat(t)er. As discourse, rapture is best understood as a poetics (to use my nomenclature) or as a hermetic practice, and esotericism (to use a medieval nomenclature more in keeping, again, with alchemy and with notions of ether). In other words, rapture in medieval women's mysticism of the sort that I am interested in is predicated on a metaphysics and mathematics of matter's (maternal) in-finitude, the ongoing capacity of matter in its finitude to proliferate, generate, and re-generate forms ad infinitum.

The claim I advance in what follows is that Philip's poetry—my attention here is on her arresting book-length poem *Zong!*, though what I'm about to say can be even more richly displayed across the three-poem sequence of *She Tries Her Tongue, Her Silence Softly Breaks*, *Looking for Livingstone: An Odyssey of Silence*, and *Zong!*—exemplifies Blackness under the aspect of material or, more strictly speaking, mater/nal rapture, that is, under the aspect of mat(t)er's dark energy or sociopoetic force. In *Zong!*, mat(t)er is mystical matrix, realm of mater(-nal) invention, zone of "nonbeing" that resounds in the poem's sacrificial cutting of language that spreads language's elements across the page, thus disclosing the page itself to be not of essence but quintessence (alchemy's fifth element), the æthereal element of mat(t)er. Through a poetics of the cut the page becomes infinite plane, spiritual plane, infinite canvas on which resounds mat(t)er's chant, even if the poem's chant speaks (out of) the grandiloquence of a Middle Passage Silence, even if that chant is a "theorizing from a void" whose nothingness surely isn't vacuous emptiness. This is a Black poetics of unsaying that apophatically arises in rapture and that announces a subjectivity that is amphibious and aerial, Black ethereal, of Black mater(nity). Such writing is Black mythography.

In titling this essay "Mystic S/Zong!" I mean to focus this point about Black rapture and thus bring Blackness into blurred view in the face of a monomythic whiteness that violently produces "the World" by taking Reason, Rationality, the Universal, and the like as its logos. "Mystic S/Zong!" claims mysticism and reclaims myth even as I unhinge the latter notion—myth—from notions of founding or stabilizing origins. That is to say, I want to remythify myth by remythifying matter beyond racial capitalist flattening, the flattening that Hortense J. Spillers has called "mythic time."[20] Matter's remythification is Black mat(t)er beyond the racially gendered and colonial sexuated mutilation of flesh. In short, I here engage *Zong!* as a mystic song, an esoteric and gnostic text that refers to Blackness not first and foremost through racial-capitalist categories but as signaling an alternative mythos, cosmology, and imagination of matter, not monomyth but mystic polymyth, we might say. *Zong!* displays this otherness, this mystery of differential entanglement.

Here is where recourse to Rudolph Otto, an important thinker in the history of religious discourse, might be helpful. Blackness signals, and I read *Zong!* as exemplifying something akin to what Otto famously called "the Holy" (*das Heilige*) or the experience of the unfathomable that underlies what has come to be called "religion."[21] "The Holy" was Otto's term for what he also understood as entirely, irreducibly "Wholly Other" (*das Andere*). This experience of what's Wholly Other Otto also spoke of using the Latin phrase *mysterium tremendum et fascinans* to indicate that being caught up in the vortex, as it were, of what is irreducibly Other and one's entanglement with such Otherness is to dwell in the experience of a mystery (*mysterium*) that is absolutely unapproachable and that thus induces awe if not terror, dread, and repulsion at a sense of being ravished or overpowered (*tremendum*). And yet in the maelstrom of awe there is affective wonder, charm, fascination, and even attraction (*fascinans*) in the face of the awful and awe-inspiring magnitude of irreducible mystery. An account of the mystery of what is Wholly Otto is the basis of the phenomenology of religion that Otto unfolds in his highly influential work of the early twentieth century, *The Idea of the Holy: An Inquiry in the Non-Rational Factor in the Idea of the Divine and Its Relation to the Rational* (1917).

What found no place in Otto's account of religious experience and what the recently deceased giant of Black religious thought Charles H. Long brought to it, is an account of the history of Blackness understood precisely as a history of Black (W)Hole-iness or a history of what is Wholly Other in the making of the World (of Man), what is Opaque to the World and thus what is beyond the World, beyond World conceived of as singular coherent entity. Signaling the Wholly Other, Blackness calls forth contemplation, theorization, or study (*theoria*) inasmuch as its irreducibility to the natal occasion of this World's Middle Passage genesis points to another plane of existence, an-other aliveness, other socialities of Relation. While being to be sure aesthetic, those socialities, I insist, are at once aesthetic and religious, religio-aesthetic, in the experience of Blackness. Or to sharpen the point, it is not so much the category of religion that I am insisting upon, a category that we know was born of coloniality and as part of the invention of the World (of Man), as it is a poetics of Black religion that is part and parcel of a poetics of Blackness, where Blackness poetically and poethically exceeds racism's (and thus racial) reductions.[22] The concern of a poetics of Black religion is not so much with Black religion in its varied, formal institutional expressions—be it the varieties of Afro-Christianity, the institutional "Black Church" and the varieties of churches that fall under this rubric, or the varieties of Africana religions that have arisen in our sojourn through modernity. Rather, a poetics of Black religion points to Blackness as poiēsis, that is, as inventions and experimental (re)makings of the social. I mean alternative ways of being-with—with the earth and thus each other. The emphasis on the social follows from *religio* as the Latin root of the word "religion." This root has the sense of "binding" or "coming together," which further implies some notion or practices of assembly that are irreducible to those modes of assembly that the polis legitimates or that are authorized within the terms of the political as we know it. Blackness is an ensemble and as such is an assembly—anassembly, anensemble.[23] It is given to us to study the sacrality of Black assembly, to meditate on its poetics of the social. That is, it is given to us to study the parareligious mystery of the Wholly Other sociality into which we are enraptured, the base or fundamental mat(t)er, the ethereal matrix of mater(nity) within which, to abuse St. Paul's language, "we live and move and have being (in the not-yet-ness of incompletion)" (Acts 17:28).[24]

BLACK MYTHOGRAPHY

An articulation of this is a tall order, one that I suspect I will fail at. My hope, however, is that my fall may be a happy, generative one. May I fall well in extending a conversation about the religiosity internal to Blackness, the religiosity that is a function of Black poiēsis. I lift off from Denise Ferreira da Silva's work in Black feminist theory to aid me in reading M. NourbeSe Philip's poethical enactment of the sacred in its base genre or version as Silence. The epigraph at the top of this essay gives something of a sense of the fecundity of her thought. I'm interested in Ferreira da Silva's notion of "The Thing" as denigrated in the Western philosophical tradition from Kant to Hegel, though partially liberated by Heidegger but nevertheless still incarcerated in his thought. More specifically, I'm interested in Ferreira da Silva's notion of "The Thing" as she indexes Thingliness as a locution for "the sexual in the colonial female (slave and native) body" of "a long line of unacceptable women" and as a locution for what she also speaks of under the rubric of "excess" by which she means the "un-measurable, noncalculable, in-determinable in spacetime" as the basis of "unlimited possibilities of unthinkable, uninformed matter."[25] This gets to the notion of Black mat(t)er that I have already been invoking. The (Black feminist) poethicist—in contrast to the philosopher or the theologian or the pessimist—engages in that radical praxis whose referent is Black *mater*, Black matter, *mater*-ial Blackness, which itself is a praxis, a poetics of sacrality without sacrifice or the need to make an offering of death to establish proper life. In this sense, the sacrality of which I speak is improper, given to impropriety, wayward with respect to property. The praxis, this impropriety, this darkened sacrality, this poetics, this poethics is a kind of sorcery. It is a conjure poetics, a poethics of spirit possession in flight or fugitive refusal of capitalist or propertied and propertizing self-possession. Black radical as Black feminist poethics is a praxis of refugitivity, Gayl Jones might say, that operates anagrammatically to the grammar of "phallic sovereignty" or the "patriarchform."[26] That movement in the break and in the wake of the ontotheological or the political-theological grammar of the patriarch-form announces a kind of unrepresentable un/grammar, a writing of nonknowing and unknowing that fissures the grammar of racial capitalism as a tyranny of the World and against the earth. This nonknowing and unknowing bespeaks what might be simply called "the alternative." That is to say, it bespeaks an alternative onto-epistemological horizon whose relationship to the machinery of the political theology of sovereignty is not oppositional but appositional to theology (or philosophy, for that matter). The Black (feminist) poethical alternative is what I've at one point called "paratheological" and that here I want to call "atheological," a term I both purloin from Georges Bataille and yet refunction through the dissidence and the dissonance, the nonsonance of Black radical sacrality.[27]

My claim in what follows is this: In M. NourbeSe Philip's engagement with the historical incidence of the slave ship *Zong* near the end of the eighteenth century (the throwing overboard of upwards of 150 cargoed Africans destined to be slaves in order to cash in on the insurance policy that insured the cargo), indeed, in the very writing of the poem called *Zong!* (importantly, written with an explanation point), which emerges in relation to the court-issued summary judgment meant to render a verdict on whether the owners of the slave ship bearing that name, in fact, had a legal case—in engaging this scene of death, Philip is neither the optimist nor the pessimist; she's a poethicist. More specifically, she's a theorist in the tradition of "the sexual in the female colonial (slave and native) body" of "a long line of unacceptable women" engaged in that "radical praxis" of the un/grammatical. The referent of her poetics is toward the (Black feminist) Thing; toward and of "the outside" even as the Black, and here I purloin from Fanon's purloining from Césaire, "is not" (*le negre n'est pas*). The Black is not (of the World). This Fanonian statement moves in relationship to Fanon's anxiety about the Black woman: "About the Black woman . . . we know nothing about her."[28] Fanon here speaks a truth that exceeds his patriarchal grasp: Black matter, dark matter, dark-Black mater indexes a no-Thing-ness that shifts our mode of knowing. Our onto-epistemic frames are pressed into an unknowing or a nonknowledge. It is this that the "thought from outside," which really is the thought of the unthinkable, which is really Black prayer as itself a mode of thinking, points to.[29] The outness of which I here speak is not of a transcendence that acquires a certain legibility in relation to an immanence that is its dialectical inside. No, this is an outside that is out from the outside, out from that Hegelian-like dialectic of inside-and-outside, of transcendence-and-immanence, that in an anti-Black way animates the text of modern thought.[30] The outer-Outside here and the inner-Inside too for that matter are of the "Black outdoors." Such Blackness as outness, the Black out, indexes a certain dwelling with the earth, a certain "avian subjectivity."[31] It indexes base or Black or dark mat(t)er. Given the impositions of the World (of Man, the patriarch-form) on top of the earth, Blackness's mode of existence is ecstatic, is rapture. A mode of spirit possession that itself is a kind of dispossession that exceeds the brutalizing dispossession that is bound up with racial capitalism's logics of possession, "the Black ecstatic" moves in relationship to the World internal to which is "voided" mat(t)er, what I earlier called ether, reservoir of indeterminate potentials or forms.[32] In the "Notanda" essay that accompanies the poem *Zong!*, Philip suggests another name for this oceanic and atmospheric, this hydro- and astro- and even cosmo-poetic and ethereal "void"; it is a maternal "matrix."[33] A zone of indeterminacy and im/possibility, the maternal matrix that generates *Zong!* as poem and even Philip herself as more and less than the poem's singular "author" is what Philip (and Charles Long with her; see again the epigraphs that head this chapter) also calls "Silence."[34] *Zong!*'s breaking, fragmenting, and mu-tilating of the legal words from the appellate court's summary judgment—"words meaning / more / than the world they / pointing at"—carry readers to "some ecstatic Elsewhere," breaking time's bind, to some ecstatic elsewhen, all under the provenance of some other cosmology.[35] No; some other cosmo*graphy*, some other mytho*graphy*. I propose that Philip's poetics must be understood as premised upon an alternative mythic imagination. It breaks the "mythic time" of racial capitalism, the time of whiteness understood as a civilization logic, neither in the name of secular rationality nor of a better, more inclusive humanism, for mythic time animates "the secular" and the Human as anti-Black onto-epistemic regimes. Rather, *Zong!* reclaims (poly)myth beyond (mono)myth in such a way that *Zong!* itself comes into view as remythifying Black life in the name of a poetics of "Black aliveness."[36] Such remythifying is precisely the work of Black myth, where the work of Black myth is the storifying, the poeticizing of subjectivity in mystic or dispossessed spirit possession. And even the word "subjectivity" in the last sentence I'm not quite satisfied with inasmuch as the "subjectivity" that I want to think about in its incompletion and hollowed-out not-ness, knottedness, and churchical entanglements with all things in their thingliness is not that of "the subject." I'm trying to talk about existence beyond propertied self-possession and the metaphysics the belief in such propertied self-possession presupposes. *Zong!* is this mystery. Of in-finity. Of the poetry of livingness as such. It is of the mysterious "geometry of Black female sexuality," to think with Evelyn Hammonds, this being the geometry of Black mat(t)er. Black mythography is, in other words, what I'm interested in—the poetics or writing of mat(t)er's sociality given in the vertiginous experience of a raptured dwelling with the baseness of the earth, rapture as fall from the World and the Word (of Man) to the earth of wor(l)ds.

Perhaps I can slow this down for a moment and say more about how I see Philip performing a Black feminist poetic or as a poethicist. I mentioned above that Philip's poem poeticizes in relation to the court-rendered summary judgment of the legal case that ensued in the aftermath of throwing overboard some of the cargo. In the legal archive, that summary judgment has come to be called the *Gregson v. Gilbert* legal text. What Philip, in effect, comes to understand is that this text is a graveyard. But even more, what she comes to grasp is that as legal text *Gregson v. Gilbert* is a World, if not "the World." That is, the legal text of *Gregson v. Gilbert* as a modern text is a grammar of the World. Its Words encode the World, where Word and World constitute each other as "Wor(l)d."[37] Here Wor(l)d is a textual, discursive, and organizing system constituted through and manifest at the level of the sentence. To be of the ontology of the Wor(l)d is to be sentenced to the sentence. We might say, therefore, that *Gregson v. Gilbert* is a text of "World Literature." A piece of literature, *Gregson v. Gilbert* is a novel of the World inside of which the cargo in being destined for the plantation or New World labor are "worlded" and "worded" or "grammaticalized." They are fated by virtue of the "Providence" of that World to being sentenced or "worded" into the Logos or rationality of what Hortense J. Spillers has called the "American Grammar Book," a World Grammar Book. In other words, they are thrown into a cosmology, thrown into the *mythos* of a *cosmos* whose *logos* speaks as a theos-logos, a discourse of "God."

The reading I am about to offer of *Zong!* is premised on Philip's, and even more on the poet's intuition of this. I put it this way because the poet both coincides with and exceeds Philip herself even as the poem coincides with and exceeds the poem *Zong!* itself. Moreover, not only does Philip intuit this, but the poem is committed to producing a diagnostic of the production of the World as precisely the production of what Ferreira da Silva has called the "patriarch-form" and how that form takes shape through a certain brutalizing of and passage through or resourcing of Blackness as a kind of energy field.[38] Harnessing that energy generates or helps produce the patriarch as a civilizational form, while the form violently sustains or reproduces itself through the power of Black labor. Through violence against Black *mater*, Blackness is harnessed, indeed, extracted from to generate the World (of Man) and impose it on top of the earth.[39] And finally, not only does Philip offer an analytic of the *Gregson v. Gilbert* legal case as a juris-theological text of "World Literature"; her poetry moves "silently," excessively, ecstatically through the grammar of the World or through the modern philosophical text—in this instance, the law that is the basis of the *Gregson v. Gilbert* summary judgment. In this ecstatically rapturous and contemplative poem, we find a breaking open of the law or the juris-theological grammar of the World. It operates to break (open) the Wor(l)d. It moves in the world of "the cut," the incision, the downbeat, or "the break" that is always already there in the broken law that breaks worlds.[40] In the vertigo of its mad and enchanted speech, *Zong!* exposes the violence of the very notion of the World (of the One) to a violent ante-*mater*-ial Outside. In this way, *Zong!* breaches cosmology (the cosmos or World, that is, of the Logos or Word) toward some other mythography or poetics. That is to say, Philip's poem thinks into and on the far side of ontology or the structuring problem of anti-Blackness and onto the terrain of cosmology and myth otherwise. Her practice, in other words, is mytho-graphic, esoteric, and sorcery-like. This is, to borrow from R. A. Judy, *"poīēsis* in black."[41]

In this way, Philip taps into agencies that exceed or are ecstatic from and beyond the Wor(l)d of Man. This is what I mean by *Black rapture*. The agencies *Zong!* taps into are "juris-generative" to the juris-theological grammar of *Gregson v. Gilbert* as a World text.[42] They are what goes unthought and unthinkable in and within the terms of the juris-theological, the theopolitical text of modern thought. I want to think about this as akin to what Fred Moten has provocatively called a "mysticism of the flesh" and what Aliyyah I. Abdur-Rahman has called "the Black ecstatic," the referent to which we might call following Zakiyyah Iman Jackson's Black feminist theorizing the nonposition of voided matter or the matter of the void, that "constitutive absence of standpoint" and standing in the World.[43] To think in this company of thinkers is to engage in a mode of knowing whose object (which really is not one) is the unthought and the unthinkable as such or what I earlier called *mysterium*, invoking a language from the field of religious studies; it is to take up the thought of the outside that generates ante-theological, theopoetic, or mythographic nonknowledge.

Zong! operates within this framework. As poem, it is resourced by the unthought and thus has the unthought and the unthinkable, the im/possible, as its referent beyond the World. Moreover, resourced by and a referent of the unthought, of the Thing, of "the sexual in the woman," and of a "long line of unacceptable women," *Zong!* as signaled by its exclamation point fissures the *Gregson v. Gilbert* legal text or the Logos, exposing what hydro- and astro- or quantum-poetically surrounds the Wor(l)d insofar as it bespeaks what has been called "the Surround."[44] This goes precisely to Philip's description of her poetic practice as in the tradition of "Sycorax," the ghostly figure who haunts Shakespeare's *The Tempest* and who freaks out Prospero, who himself is an instantiation of what Ferreira da Silva calls "the patriarch-form." *Zong!* thus stages a sycoraxian, a Black feminist, a Black mater-ial and mater-nal mysticism of the flesh that evinces a commitment to what Philip elsewhere calls the "ambivalence of the sacred object" and a commitment to a mode of living through World damage.[45] Such commitment is, alas, Black Faith. Here Philip's poetics of the sacred, which moves in the interval "not in between" poetry and Blackness, is a kind of field or horizon of sociopoetic forces that Sycorax-like roams the earth.[46] This field of forces Philip calls "Silence," which must be understood as absolutely not the equivalent to being silenced. There's a *mater*-iality to Silence as it unfolds across the itinerary of Philip's poetry. That's what has my attention and will not let me go. Additionally, I'm interested in how Philip's notion of Silence exerts atheological pressure on the racial and settler colonial production of the notion of World as a production of political theology.

I'd like to say one last thing briefly before getting to my direct engagement with *Zong!*. It again has to do with the title I've given to this meditation, "Mystic S/*Zong!*" What I here call attention to is the "S/Z" in the title. Yes, there is an echo here not just of Roland Barthes's *S/Z* but of Barthes's larger project of exposing the mythologies of the Book, of the Logos or the "sign," that found modernity. Barthes came to understand that myth empties the sign, filling it with an otherwise signified. He thus rendered the sign or the Word always incomplete and even in/finite. Myth, thus, concerns itself with a process that Charles H. Long, Barthes's contemporary, called "signification" and that Long saw as finding a certain sociohistorical elaboration in relation to the Middle Passage.[47] In keeping precisely with this, the "S/Z" of my title points to another contemporary reader of Barthes's on signs, signifying, and myth. Hortense Spillers also rerouted Barthes's insights (as well as French feminist *écriture*) by proposing that modernity is based on a mythology that through the Middle Passage racially sexuates matter (the production of property ownership) in the making of Man as a gendered and engendering system of signs.[48] This insight on Spillers's part, which is in keeping with Philip's poetic intuitions, leads Spillers to think Black culture on the basis of what she calls "countermyth."[49] Here again we find the refusal to cede the terrain of myth or be embarrassed by myth, an embarrassment that often shows up in Black studies as an embarrassment about "Black religion" if not about "African religion" or the Afro-Atlantic fetish (and the "nonrationality" and supposed "benightedness" they signify) in the name of the so-called empiricism of (Western) modernist "rationality" and humanism.[50] What Spillers calls the "countermyth" and what I'm calling Black mythography refuse such embarrassment. And so does Philip. The question, then, is, What myth does Blackness serially, ongoingly write or poeticize? Here again, I come back to "S/Z." The "S/Z" of the title "Mystic S/*Zong!*" speaks to a slide between the slave ship called *Zong* and what Philip understands as an illegible sound that does not, cannot properly show up in the grammars of (theo)politicality. To the extent that it shows, it does so as the improper, as impropriety, as riotous property, as a riot in refusal of property and propertization. It's about the riot, articulated in the chant of glossolalic "Blackpentecostal" madness.[51] *Zong!* sounds that impropriety, and that sound is the countermyth, the Black mythographic. More specifically, in *Zong!* the poet is a poet of the riot, her speech resounds the ongoing aliveness of the collective dead, the overboarded. This collective speech softly breaks the very law that serves as the logos of the legal judgment. Philip's poem, which we might think of as the collective speech of the dead in their aliveness is the non-speech of an illegible sound within law. It is a Song of Silence—a murmur in the law, a creaking of the law. The S of "S/Z" is murmuring or creaking Sound, Song, and Silence. There is, in other words, a sonic slide between Zong and Song, held together in *Zong!*, held between the wound and the blessing, between Middle Passage and the unfinishable horizon that we might simply call "Passage."[52] In this slide, this slipping and sliding, this gliding and riding, and struttin' and stridin', this beholding, what we have is a radical praxis of the sacred that moves as rapture in the rupture, as refugitive refusal of that genre or version of the sacred that animates Man and his World, that figure of sovereignty who drives the slave ship *Zong*.

With this in place we're positioned (enough) to appreciate more fully Philip's esoteric, her work as a kind of sycoraxian sorceress, as a Black feminist or mystic poethicist, a "S/Z" mythographer. To *Zong!* I now turn.

MYSTIC S/ZONG!

It is at this point that I want to engage in a reading of M. NourbeSe Philip's arresting poem *Zong!* as ritual performance of what I have started to think in this chapter. That is, it is here that I begin a consideration of *Zong!* as mythographic text and of its "author" as mystic and mythographic collective.

In *Zong!* Philip poetically engages with the events that took place on the slave ship *Zong* in 1781, when the ship's captain oversaw the throwing overboard of upwards of 150 Africans in order to preserve the ship's dwindling provisions as the ship made its way to Jamaica to deliver its "cargo."[53] Philip tells us that her poetic engagement with this incident is authorized by those thrown overboard from the ship. (More about this below.) The poem's presumption is that those thrown overboard, though left dead or interred in the ocean, as well as left dead or interred in the words of the summary judgment of the court case that unfolded in the wake of the *Zong* events, yet *live* (inside of) death. (The legal case is officially the *Gregson v. Gilbert* case. Gregson was the ship's owner; Gilbert was the insurance company insuring the ship's cargo.)[54] Limiting herself to the words, including the syllables and sounds making up the words, of the summary judgment, which she understands as a "colonial script," Philip commits malpractice (196). That is, with a view to recuperating what's been submerged or silenced within the law, what the law censors or proscribes in order to secure the world it prescribes, Philip "breaks and enters" the legal text and thus the law's fundamental *ratio* or logic (or *logos*), its guiding concept, to wit, the "human" (200).

It is vital to note that recuperate here does not mean "[to recover] the individual identities of the Zong slaves [or] their stories," nor does it mean "to transpose the elisions, silences, and disavowals of the Zong case into a coherent narrative,"[55] into a story subjected to the "ordering mechanism" of "grammar . . . the mechanism of force" (192). To do that would be "to do a second violence. To the experience, the memory—the re-membering."[56] Instead, Philip not-tells or rather un-tells the tale by "mutilating" the *Gregson v. Gilbert* court document. In her own words:

> As the fabric of African life and the lives of these men, women and children were mutilated . . . I murder the text, literally cut it into pieces,

castrating verbs, suffocating adjectives, murdering nouns, throwing articles, prepositions, conjunctions overboard, jettisoning adverbs: I separate subject from verb, verb from object—create semantic mayhem, until my hands bloodied, from so much killing and cutting, reach into the stinking, eviscerated innards, and like some seer, sangoma, or prophet who, having sacrificed an animal for signs and portents of a new life, or simply life, reads the untold story that tells itself by not telling. (193–94)

In this profound passage, Philip gives us to understand that her procedure of textual production enacts a "potentially generative . . . mystically inflected" textual violence against the mythic violence of the law.[57] "This is the axis on which the text of *Zong!* turns: censor and magician" (199). The former, mystically inflected textual violence enacts a kind of shamanic, Sycoraxian, and indeed daemonic release that is a fugitive release of life and breath from that juris-mythic embrace that would contain it.[58] This violence against violence, or this doubling of violence in which the poet's hands are blood-drenched from so much textual dismemberment for the sake of textual de- as re-composition, stages a sacrifice that through the remains releases what remains. The remains that ambivalently offer themselves and withhold something else, are an excess, the undercurrent of a disturbance. Unheld by state projects—in this case, by the slave ship of state—what remains is some primary or anterior, prereflective structure that historian of religions Charles Long identifies with "the archaic symbol." Irreducible to categorization, the archaic harbors inexhaustible possibilities that refuse to coalesce into full signification. Like an ideogram lying somewhere between experience and category, the archaic symbol is the reservoir of a spiritual universe. For this reason, it invites different and various types of thought. To "crawl back through history" so as to confront the archaic is to confront a fundamental, prereflective opacity that is anterior to ontology. Anticipating Philip, Long states that it is to confront "Silence" or the parasemiotic murmurings or disturbances within the reigning regime of meaning. Those murmurings, that creaking signals otherworldly potentials set in motion in the practice of language itself. Crawling back through history, then, is in the interest entering the open field of this Silence, this sacrality (without sacrifice), the black radical sacred.

This sacred-otherwise is what state projects can't have. What is withheld as unholdable, as nonpossessable, as fantastic, is nothing less than the opacity of the sacred (the moment of "Black religion"), where at this archaic level the sacred must not be understood in terms of ontotheological substance but rather in terms of an exorbitance or in terms of a useless expenditure that plunges the collective poet—signaled in the two names on the cover of the published book *Zong!* and also the collective dead channeled through the book's poet-author(s)—into a "semantic mayhem" that, as it were, compresses and expands space-time so that it "opens up," says Mandy Bloomfield in her provocative reading of *Zong!*, "channels of communication with ancestors."[59] So understood, *Zong!* is a sacred text, or a text that malpractices the sacred, a text whose protocol is sacrifice. However, this is not sacrifice in the sense often observed in institutional religion in its alliance with state power where sacrifice is done with the expectation of something, such as salvation, being returned so as to secure the present toward a certain future. Rather, it is not containable even by institutional religion, which can quell the dangerous energies of the sacred; sacrifice here bespeaks a radical negation of utilitarian production in the name of an insurgency of the nonproductive, in the name of an insurgency of the "sacred instant," in the name, finally, of what holding can't have and what having can't hold but that can get a hold of you. This is sacrifice akin to what Bataille might have been trying to get at: "[While] there is a specific motive behind every sacrifice: an abundant harvest, expiation, or any other logical objective; nonetheless, in one way or another, every sacrifice has its cause in the quest for a sacred instant that, for an instant, puts to rout the profane time in which prohibitions guarantee the possibility of life."[60]

Philip's renegade-cum-sacrificial poetics moves in this way. Convening insurgent intimacies or gatherings of spirit and, indeed, of soul, sacrifice here conjures a mode of existence that exceeds and agitates against modern modalities of the individuated self. This is sacrifice given to insovereign headlessness, a practice of what Fred Moten has recently and extensively elaborated as a "consent not to be a single being." Animating Blackness is sacrificial malpractice, an erotics of the sacred given in "differential inseparability."[61] Pointing to and performing this is *Zong!*'s spiritual accomplishment. Philip's poetic "ex-aqua-ing," rather than ex-huming, the remains of those interred in "their 'liquid graves'" (202) was a feat of sonic memory as much as it was a kind of shamanic ritual. More specifically, in breaking open the legal text *Zong!*'s collective poet finds therein a religious text of theopolitical purity that the collective poet then further breaks open. In breaking open the law (of the subject) she breaks open how we imagine the sacred, and in so doing exposes the juris-theological terms of order that structure the Middle Passage and colonial modernity. Intuitively understanding colonial modernity and its racial logics as ritually enacted (again, law and religion, as, effectively, a shared or transubstantiated ritual), the collective poet breaks open the juris-theological text so as to be swept into the eddies of an insurgent "Silence" (Philip's term), the Silence of another ceremony that somehow, some way is always already there. Nowhere.

Against this backdrop what starts to come into view is this: *Zong!* subtly engages the political theology, and specifically the ritual, ceremonial, and sacramental logics, that harnessed the sacred to the European project so as to underwrite the oceanic and legal internment of those thrown overboard from the slave ship *Zong* and that more broadly ground (racial) capitalism as a project of Western salvation. The European project entailed the would-be deanimation of matter so as to then commodify it or impose on it an equation of value. In fragmenting the words of the court-issued summary judgment surrounding the events that took place on that slave ship and utilizing those words to generate the poem that is *Zong!*, Philip malpractices or, adapting Denise Ferreira da Silva, "hacks the sacred" precisely insofar as the sacred comes to be transubstantiated into the "patriarch form" as an ontotheological form or grammar.[62] More specifically, in breaking open the legal text *Zong!*'s collective poet finds within it a religious text. Further still, the collective poet discovers the religious logics that inform the juris-religious text, making it a juris-sacramental text the fundamental presumption of which is the individual, self-possessed body (politic). Intuitively understanding colonial modernity and its racial logics as ritually enacted (law and religion as, effectively, a shared or transubstantiated ritual), the collective poet theorizes the juris-theological text, breaking it open in a bid to hear the noisy Silence of another ceremony that moves in an insurgent anteriority to the juris-theological terms of order that structure the Middle Passage and colonial modernity, doing so by way of the practice of another ceremony, an otherwise worldly ritual. This is the ritual of other worlds, other words, nowhere.

To elaborate with a bit more textual specificity what I mean, I would like to zero in on one part of *Zong!* In the section of the poem called "Ferrum" (from the Latin meaning "iron" or "chains"), we find a subtle and sophisticated engagement with the ceremonial and, more precisely, sacramental logics of Christian theology that anchored the violence of the *Zong* events and by extension the violence of the Middle Passage and modernity itself. In ex-aqua-ing the dead from the juris-theological text of the *Gregson v.*

Gilbert summary judgment, the *Zong!* collective poet-narrator splays the words of the legal text to generate a scene on board the slave ship *Zong* in which those buried in the hold seem to overhear the captain and the sailors on deck partaking in what seem to be the prayers and accompanying hymns of the Christian Eucharist. For convenience of reference, I have reproduced as Figure 1, the page of the poem that records the scene to which I refer. In traditional Christian theology and church practice, the Eucharist is the ceremony of eating bread and drinking wine as the body and blood of Jesus Christ. I want to suggest that the scene splayed across the page presents dense "evi / dence of a pa / st drow / ned in no / w . . ." (141, lines 1–2). The collective poet witnesses that this history violently "p / lay[s] on my bo / nes the son / g of bo / ne in b / one" (141, lines 2–3). Bone grating against bone, bone becomes a kind of tuning fork, a resonator. As bone rubs against bone as a bow rubs up against violin strings, a sound is heard, a song is played. What, we might ask, is the song that the collective poet hears playing on "my [collective] bo / nes"? The broken or splayed words that themselves approximate broken or splayed bones and that follow lines 2–3 suggest an answer. What plays on the poet's collective bones are fragments or pieces of words that are broken off and in this way echo the Requiem Mass or the Eucharistic Mass for the dead. This is a Mass replete with a long history of hymns and music offered in the context of funeral prayers, vespers offered for the repose of the soul or souls of one or more deceased persons.[63]

It is worth offering a few words on the Requiem Mass itself in order more fully to appreciate the political theology of the Middle Passage that *Zong!* poetically spots. The Requiem Mass draws on the Roman Missal, the liturgical book that contains the texts and rubrics for the celebration of the Mass in the Roman Catholic tradition. The Requiem Mass draws its name from the opening section of the Roman Catholic liturgical celebration of the Eucharist, which begins with the words *"Requiem aeternam dona eis, Domine"* ("Grant them [the dead] eternal rest, O Lord"). Interestingly, fragments of language drawn from the Requiem Mass for the dead are discerned within the language of the court-issued summary judgment of the *Gregson v. Gilbert* legal case and thus make an appearance in the "Ferrum" section of *Zong!* That is to say, in the anticolonial splaying of the legal case a ceremonial or sacramental song of terror is revealed. Thus *Zong!*'s citation of the sacrament of the Mass breaks open the law in order to reveal the summary judgment of the sovereign judges to be part of a semiotic or signifying

MYSTIC S/ZONG!

Figure 1. M. NourbeSe Philip and Setaey Adamu Boateng, *Zong!* (Middletown, CT: Wesleyan University Press, 2011), 141.

system or apparatus. Structuring this semiotic system is a relay between the ritual eating of bread and wine on the seas and another consumptive ritual, namely, the fundamental transformation or, more to the point, the transubstantiation into "Slaves" or "Negroes" of those whose bones are being broken as they are being held below deck as "cargo." This semiotic convergence of the ritual transubstantiation of bread into the body-proper of Christ as (the God-)Man and the transubstantiation of bone into sentient labor-power or Slave is an instance of what theologian Lauren Winner has recently called "the dangers of Christian practice" and of what we might also think of as the horrors of the sacred.[64] As an otherwise ritual of other worlds, *Zong!* witnesses to and is negotiating the horror of the right-hand, racial-capitalist sacred—capitalism's would-be reduction of the sacred to the god-terms of "property," "contract," and "law" through the eucharistic ceremony of the slave ship, the sacrament of the Middle Passage—even as what generates the poem or un/grounds its poetics is precisely the groundless or archaic Silence that gives rise to (Black) thought from the improvisational abyss of the im/possible. As a symbol of Silence, Blackness from the hold releases the imagination of the sacred. This is what makes Philip's poetics so provocative. In the anticolonial break of *Zong!*'s citation of the eucharistic Requiem Mass, in its broken "S/Zong," the poem itself is summoned or conjured as both a witness to the dead and to an ongoing "aliveness."[65] That is to say, in citationality's break (down) into enchanted re-citation, into insurgent chant, otherwise worlds re-sound or surge forth.

First consider *Zong!*'s broken re-citation of the Requiem Mass itself in "Ferrum." What resounds in *Zong!*'s recitation of the Requiem Mass is a song of the remains of the dead, "the son / g of bo / ne in b / one" and that beats "my bo / nes" (141, lines 3–4). That song of terror, sung in ecclesiastical Latin no less, draws from three sections of the Requiem Mass: the *"Sanctus, sanctus, sanctus"* section ("holy, holy, holy," referencing the triune God of the Christian faith), the *"Pie Jesu"* section ("Pious Jesus," referencing a vibrant Christology), and the *"Agnus Dei"* section ("Lamb of God," referencing a theology of salvation by atoning sacrifice). This is what *Zong!* re-cites, what its chant and dissident mode of enchantment "hacks" open.

The broader language of the last two sections, particularly in Andrew Lloyd Webber's version of the Requiem Mass, which seems to be the version *Zong!* inflects, is striking when heard in the context of the historical *Zong* events. In locating the terror of the slave ship *Zong* in relationship to the language in Webber's version of the Requiem Mass, the poem suggests an alignment between the murderous consumption of Black life and the sacrificial and ceremonially salvific consumption of Christ's flesh and blood in the form of the eucharistic Mass. I will say more about this in a moment. But, first, consider the specific language of the *"Pie Jesu"* and *"Agnus Dei"* sections of the Requiem song that *Zong!*'s collective poet discerns within the mix of words making up the *Gregson v. Gilbert* legal text and in a broken way recites in broken chant by fracturing them across the poem. Here's the language from the Webber version of the second and third sections, respectively, of the song of the Requiem Mass:

Pie Jesu,
Qui tollis peccata mundi,
Dona eis requiem.

Agnus Dei,
Qui tollis peccata mundi,
Dona eis requiem,
Sempiternam
Requiem.

[Pious Jesus,
Who takes away the sins of the world,
Give them rest.

Lamb of God,
Who takes away the sins of the world,
Give them rest,
Everlasting
Rest.]

The theology embedded in the lyric of the Requiem Mass suggests that notwithstanding the crisis at sea, with dwindling food and the imminent prospect of losing their lives, the mariners nevertheless hope for salvation in Christ. Eating the bread and drinking the wine of the Eucharist as Christ's flesh and blood gives the mariners assurance of bodily salvation, for in eating the host they become a corporation; they are drawn into Christ's never dying body (politic). That is to say, they are given the gift of bodily integrity and stability amid instability. They become, in other words, saved bodies. But what the poem also invites us to understand is how the ceremony of the Eucharist on the *Zong* ship discloses a ritual structure to the Black Atlantic itself, and thus a ritual structure to the forging of a racial-colonial modernity. The poem breaks open the legal text to disclose its liturgical horizon. This is the horizon that activates the body, or more precisely, that activates Christ's body (politic) as the European, enslaving body through exploitative consumption of the enslaved body. Christ's "real presence" through the event of the eucharistic ceremony on the slave ship enfolds or stands forth through and as the mariners. The ceremony of eating Christ's flesh so as to become a body (politic) grants the mariners assurance of bodily security, assurance of salvation. What I am trying to do here is take very seriously the imposition of liturgical, soteriological, and/as onto-colonial governance through the Middle Passage as the threshold of modern political economy, indeed, as the threshold of "Whiteness."

To this end, let's stay with this a just bit longer. The (re)production of Christ's body that the collective poet spots as part of the ritual of Middle Passage and that aligns the enslaving-colonizing mariners with Christ as symbolic guarantor of (white) life in the face of apocalyptic destruction is happening in tandem with another type of consumptive destruction: to wit, the ritualized consumption of what remains alive in the hold. These two consumptions are really one consumption, the second of which we also glimpse in *Zong!*'s "Ferrum" section. Indeed, we hear of this other Eucharist-like, ritual consumption from "one of the strongest 'voices,'" Philip tells us, "in the *Zong!* text [and] who appears to be white, male, and European" (204). Figured in the poem as both perpetrator and witness to the *Zong* events, this other voice often addresses, as if in a diary entry or in a letter, a love interest named "ruth" (clipped "t/ruth"?), who herself emerges as a presence in the *Zong!* text. She is figured as one who consoles the European male as he confesses the "sins" he has committed aboard the ship and over his participation in what has happened. In one of these moments of melancholic confession, the European subject confesses to being restless over what's happened on the ship. He uses language that strikingly echoes the eucharistic consumption discourse described above. However, the difference between the two languages of Eucharist-like consumption is that what's being eaten in this scene is not the bread and wine that is Christ's flesh but "negro meat":

in th / at insta / nce of s / in ... can s / it no mo / re cl / ams feed on we / eds weeds fe / ed on fle / sh we din / e on neg / ro me / at grow fa / t (164)

What finally comes into view now is this: the eucharistic consumption of Christ's flesh and blood moves in tandem with the consuming of Black flesh and life, "negro meat." This Janus-faced operation is the moment of the materially transubstantive production of whiteness as religion in and through "the willful expenditure of the Other in an imposing production of the self" in a gesture of consumption.[66] That is to say, by eucharistically ingesting Black flesh as a kind of negative resource, Man is animated, his body vampirically brought to life.

And yet what *Zong!* ultimately points to is how quite unstable this all is. Indeed, that instability registers as a kind of reverb or as the aftereffect of "an excessive and residual Otherness,"[67] of an insurgent "beyond,"[68] of an agitating Silence, that allows for the production of *Zong!* through "sacrificing" the legal text along with the individuated and propertied self it seeks to uphold. *Zong!*'s untelling of a story that cannot be told but must be told moves in the break of this doubled ritual of fleshly consumption. Indeed, in fracturing not only the legal text but the liturgy internal to the law to enact another ceremony, *Zong!* sacrifices sacrifice without recourse to and in refusal of salvation or a return to "real presence." In Moten's words, "Theory of blackness is theory of the surreal presence."[69] This is the dissident surrealism of "otherwise worlds."

I come back to the "Ferrum" section of the poem to display further what I am getting at here. The collective poet shushes her readers ("sh h / ca / n you he / ar the be / at?" [141, lines 4–5]), urging a quiet upon them so that the poem's auditors can hear what surges through the enchanted re-citation of the Requiem Mass. Such re-citation aims not so much to tell or know anything but to un/tell, and to un/know. This is a feat of engaging that nonknowledge that conditions the violence of theo-legal, which is theo-secular, knowledge. We are invited to overhear (and eventually overdub) a song of "ontotheological terror," the song that is the eucharistic sound of violence on the slave ship:[70] "*pie // je // su pi // e // jes / u sanctus sanctus // sanctus ag // nu // s dei ...*" (141, lines 5–8). As with the legal text, so too with the theological text buried within it—the collective poet splays the Mass to move through and move around its innards. That is to say, in paralleling her poetics between the Roman Missal as religious liturgy and *Gregson v. Gilbert* as legal liturgy, the poet-narrator discloses the transubstantiation of religion and law into one another as that which grounds the (slave ship of) state. This is all ground I have already covered. But what is new is this: In fracturing the already fractured Requiem Mass, the poet-narrator in fact hears some other broken song singing or resounding through it. This is the song of another world, the surreality of a "surreal presence." Not the trinitarian "sanctus sanctus sanctus" of the Christian eucharistic liturgy but what the collective poet calls a "sa / nctus to the s / ea," a sea liturgy:

> in / san / ctus there i / s san say / a sa / nctus for m / e a san / ctus to the s / ea . . . i / am we a / re their e / yes stare / see thin / gs we ne / ver wil / l let my s / tory my tal / e my g / est gift ri / se up in ti / me to sn / ap the sp / ine of tim / e . . . (141, lines 8–19)

Notice that in these lines, in the chant that is *Zong!*, being—the conjugated "is" of "to be"—is split open such that the "i" now dangles at the end of the line (see Figure 1, line 8), incoherently stranded from the "s" that starts on the next line (see Figure 1, line 9). Further along, and again, the "i" and the "am" of the Cartesian "i am" are set astray from each other (see Figure 1, lines 13 and 14). And, finally, from the end of what I have quoted above we hear that the untelling that is going on here moves, in the break and in the wake, we might say, of time understood as progress, the temporality of the subject. *Zong!*'s insurgency "sn / ap[s] the sp / ine of tim / e . . . ," thereby witnessing the space-time of nowhere.

This takes us back to my earlier elaboration of the problem of ontology and genesis or onto-genesis in the "Black Mythography" section of this chapter as I was thinking through the problem of "the World" and of "Worlding." We find in the "Ferrum" section of *Zong!* an understanding of the slave ship—which can be extended to the plantation and the racial state—as the ontotheological space-time of the present. More than that, we witness that the ontotheological space-time of the present is predicated on the consumption of the sacred—the conversion of wild potentialities into labor power. And yet by way of its fractured poetics of the exclamation point, *Zong!* releases the sacred through an ecstatics not of real presence but of the *surreal, subreal* presence, that affirmative space of capacious negation where Lauryn Hill said that everything's everything, everything's all mixed up. In this way, the poem moves with, and finally *through*, the slave ship Zong. It dwells with what hovers as "Silence" (Philip's term), an invisible universe, on the far side of the teleological principle of ontotheological "real" presence. *Zong!* is broke(n), surreally in the break of that real presence. By this I mean that *Zong!* is a Requiem of an-Other sort, a hemmed-in hymn whose notes gather a fugued, fractured, and fractal commune-ion, an undercommune-ion of the undercommons. The resonance of its dissonance indexes some other kind of congregational practice given in the dark churchicality of the sea.

All of this, Philip states or rather punctuates in the poem's titular exclamation point. Through a riotous poetics of Silence, *Zong!*'s exclamation point *ex-*claims or stands "out from" every property claim. It moves dispossessively or spirit-possessively through dispossession. *Zong!* breathes even if by gasping "towards some air."[71] It is the sociopoetic or pneumatic force of a writing that gasps for breath. This is a fractured spirit-writing, a pneumatography, as I mentioned earlier, that propels *Zong!* Indeed, such writing convenes an alternative sociality, a nowhere church that moves with and through disorder, with and through disordered breathing and poetic palpitations, in its extra-ceremonial splaying of words, letters, and sounds spread out or floating across the ocean of the page. The gaps in the poem are breathing pockets, pockets of poetic air for ongoing animacies of the earth, air pockets that mimic the gasps for breath of those thrown overboard. Temples of lung and air, those pockets are sanctuaries or un/held spaces of communion, gaps on the page repurposed as a kind of infinite canvas, an open field. We are in the midst of what Philip calls a "poetics of the fragment . . . driven pneumatically by the energy of the breath, the open spaces that then enfold the fragments," spaces that now constitute a surround, a universe that is not of this world, that is fugitive from the very notion of "World," but that is felt through the *precarity* of this world.[72] That feeling is a kind of nonknowledge of a universe given in the noise uprising, that revolution of the sacred in the revolt of Silence that surges through both the legal text and the liturgical text of the Requiem Mass—witnessing to what cannot be told . . . but *must* be told as an untelling. This is where Philip is pointing when she says that the spaces between words and within words on the pages of *Zong!* may be understood as "ga(s)ps, in-breathings, breathings-out, or a simple holding of the breath," and that these gaps and gasps or fractured, quantum spaces carry "the potential of a universe . . . given that each breath we take is a fragment of the larger breathing and breath [and respiration] of the universe" (39).

Even Philip herself, as "author" of *Zong!*, is no ordinary author, no ordinary authorial "I." Rather, I think of her as spirit-possessed beyond propertied self-possession. That is, she is possessed by the collective subject named "Setaey Adamu Boateng," whom Philip understands both as a figure of those deliberately thrown overboard from the *Zong* and as a figure of Sycorax, the healer-witch, obeah woman, and sorcerer from Shakespeare's *The Tempest* who contested the theo-political magic through which Prospero sought to harness the sacred to his project of gentrifying the Caribbean island of Shakespeare's text, to turn the Americas, indeed, the earth itself into his piece of real estate—into a (propertied) World. Philip's authorial "I" emerges as a cumulative, accumulating "we." Re-en-gendered by a Silence that precedes her and that breaks down the space-time of this world, the very notion of a sovereign, possessive author is fractured, exposed to what surges and hovers beyond. The authorial I fractures into a (Black feminist) malpracticed we, a Boateng-Sycoraxian we-ness that is an "I 'n I"-ness. In moving from the single I to a Rastafarian "I 'n I," this "I 'n I"-ness encodes a socio-sacrality that the ga(s)ping "language of Sycorax, whatever that may be," releases.[73] That release manifests as rapturous excess within the disordered linguistic breaks and conceptual brokenness of *Zong!* This rapturous excess points to a ceremony exceeding the ceremony of theo-politicality, a new "Ceremony of Souls" in which both the dead and the earth breathe through an otherwise we-ness, an alternate imaginary of the universe. This is a hydropoetics-become-cosmopoetics of the sacred, the Black radical sacred.[74] Which is but to say that *Zong!* sounds an under-ness—the underlife, the underworld. It re-sounds the subaquatic and the extraterrestrial, what's under the sea and of the heavens; the broken clusters of words and letters that index the sounds that remain at sea are also like stars dotting the cosmic heavens of an open page. As we "read" this strange text or are "read" by it and *into* it—experienced most powerfully when Philip *performs* the poem—we become party to an unspeakable underness, an unspeakable language of un-telling. This "mystical language of unsaying" is the language of a strange us-ness whose unspeakableness or illegibility within the terms of order registers the fragmented echo of an abyssal elsewhere and elsewhen whose sociality, indeed whose *religiosity* (if this is even the right term), must be thought on its own terms.

By invoking the notion of the religious I come to the final threshold of the reading I here propose of *Zong!* specifically and of the provocation of Philip's poetics more generally. What is the relationship of Philip's poetics, of Black poetics, to the religious? I can here offer only fleeting, fugitive thoughts on this topic as it is the subject of extended meditations elsewhere.[75] For now, I briefly call attention to the complexities around the very word *religio*, the Latinate origin of the modern lexeme "religion." Those complexities are both etymological and substantial. What are this word's roots? What significations might it host? What does it indicate about the world? And finally, for my specific purposes in this chapter, why invoke religion in relationship to the "aesthetic sociality" afoot in Philip's poetics?[76]

Of obscure etymology, from Cicero's use of the term around the beginning of the Roman Empire to signal scrupulous fidelity to the traditional cultus or to broad social obligations to its appearance in English around the 1200s as "religion" to reference a life bound by monastic orders, the meaning of this term has been notoriously slippery and difficult to pin down, and it is not my ambition to pin it down here.[77] Nevertheless, there is something to be said for what seems to be *religio*'s double etymological sense, going back, on the one hand, to re- + lego ("to choose, or go over again") and, on the other, to re + ligare ("to bind or reconnect"). With the latter sense particularly in mind, *religio* references obligations and thus the ties that bind a group, such as a family but quite often the polis, together. Divinity, ecology, and economy all inflect each other. What I take from this is that etymologically understood *religio* is ecological, a practice of the "we"-ing of and "we"-ing with nature and cosmos.

But we must go further. Not content to think religion only etymologically but also sociolinguistically, Cornelius Castoriadis, who is increasingly important to my own attempts to think the Middle Passage and thereby the confrontation with Black(ened) existence as itself a religious confrontation and event that has instituted our World, argues that as a human creation, religion is basically a social practice of encountering what is irreducibly or Wholly Other (to come back to language from the first section of this chapter), indeed of encountering what is Abyssal and then subjecting the Abyss to (en)closure.[78] As Castoriadis lays it out, this is all done as a societal feat. That is, it is done as part of how society not only determines itself but how that determination is predicated on refusing its own contingency. That is, society constitutes its supposed coherence precisely by disavowing that it is contingent on encounters with other social phenomena that are irreducibly other to it *and* internal within it. Otherness, in other words, is internal to the fabric of society though society is what it is precisely through a kind of refusal of its own dependence on or entanglement with other social phenomena that it cannot subsume or that are irreducibly other, which is to say, that are Wholly Other. That disavowal of contingency in the constitution of the thing called society amounts also to resisting the idea of the potential revisability or transformation of society in the face of ongoing contingency. In other words, the disavowal of societal contingency in the face of other social phenomena that are irreducible in their otherness amounts to a society that resists alternatives to itself and within itself. It amounts to resisting alteration. The unthinkableness of the social alternative, or of imaging anything like an alternative to society as currently determined or constituted, happens by foreclosing the Abyss that is within and marks existence as such. It is just at this point that things get quite interesting for thinking religion, for what Castoriadis proposes is that the moment of closure against the absolute otherness within existence is precisely what idolatry means and this too is precisely what religion is. That is to say, if the abyssal condition of existence itself signals that society is contingent (even when it denies as much), then society in fact institutes and maintains itself by foreclosing upon the radically contingent, the Abyssal, within itself. That would-be foreclosure produces a new imagination of the "other." This new other is no longer the Abyss that exposes the contingency and revisability of societies, the fact that things need not be this way. Rather, the Abyssal is refashioned into a stable "God," the Law of the One who from a transcendental realm now commands the perpetuation of the existing order. The commandment (of "God," or the Absolute, to put this in a Hegelian idiom, or of the "I am") is juris-generative of society. Sovereign law or the law of the sovereign forecloses on the Abyss, even as that foreclosure grounds the (often exclusionary) "we" of a given society (as in, for example, the constitutional "we" of "We the People . . ."). Insofar as society and its limited but now ontotheologically sanctioned "we" are instituted both through confronting Abyssal alternatives of Wholly Otherness and by subjecting the Wholly Other or the Abyss to closure, society and its "we" are religiously instituted by transcendent(al) and commanding Law.

What I have here all too quickly summarized is what Castoriadis calls "socially effective religion."[79] "Socially effective religion" occludes the abyss of many possible modes of existence in the name of the social imaginary-institution of the One, proper (way of sociopolitical) being. More still, socially effective religion names the ongoing work of ritualizing and re-ritualizing the imaginary institution of sanctioned society. In effect, socially effective religion, as Castoriadis elaborates it, both institutes and confirms the societal order through encountering and concealing the abyss of existence or, if I might risk a neologism, in resistance to the polypolitical in the name of the monopolitical. Or perhaps better still, socially effective religion is the concealment of an an-archy (that which is without *archē*) that said religion and the society it institutes negatively positions itself over against—as its Black matter, its Black *mater*, as ether—in order to establish (its) sovereignty, the reign of proper rule, of mon-archy (which of course can and contemporarily, I'd argue, does take as one of its possible forms liberal, settler colonial democracy or popular sovereignty). Concealing the abyssal by violently repressing anarchic, anticolonial potentials, by foreclosing what Charles H. Long once called "the new *archē*" that is un/given in Middle Passage, is what, according to Castoriadis, the religious institution of modern society may be understood as meaning and doing.[80] It is what W. E. B. Du Bois is getting at with with the phrase "the *religion* of whiteness," and it is certainly what I am trying to think about under the rubric *monomythic whiteness*.[81]

To come at this one more time before concluding this meditation, in concealing and thus trying to seal off the Abyss within existence, religion is both born or transubstantiated through the Middle Passage even as in the process of its own birth modern-colonial religion, or the religion of modernity, aims to contain the anarchic or alternative socialities or the Wholly Otherness of the we-ness and us-ness, the sycoraxian and anarchic Blackness in the void of the Middle Passage. I hope that it is clear that by "the Middle Passage" here I do not mean just that historical occurrence that one might archivally investigate, for in many respects the archive registers a metaphysical experiment that it also occludes. It registers a violence that it also wants to render absent. It does this by targeting the Abyss or the Wholly Otherness of the encounter of peoples and modes of living and even the earth and subjecting it to the commandment of colonial rule, producing within that rule "race" as a global and differential technology of social control. In this respect, slavery's archive, as Saidiya Hartman has taught, is a "scene of subjection" where in producing modern society, including the "we" of colonially gendered humanity, mat(t)er has been Blackened and foreclosed upon.[82]

My claim is that what Philip's poetics invites us to consider is not just the metaphysical violence of the law of the archive (i.e., the *Gregson v. Gilbert* legal document). Her poetics invites consideration of the metaphysics of Middle Passage as the metaphysics of Black(ened) mat(t)er and the sociality or the socio-physics thereof. Rather than foreclosing the abyssal, *Zong!* is generated of it, echoing a broken natality and wounded sociality or kinship. This is a poetics of the Middle Passage that considers the Middle Passage, then, as quantum (non-) event—as Plenum (Ferreira da Silva), as Void (Zakiyyah Iman Jackson)—that hosts indeterminate, in-finitely parareligious socialities marked by "difference without separability."[83] If *Zong!* experiments alternative we-ness from the hold, then Philip is mythographer of the alternative, pneumatographer of such parareligious we-ness, I 'n I-ness, s/he n' you-ness, them 'n us-ness, and so forth. Or, as Philip herself puts it in an arresting statement about the sociality of breath,

> When I perform *Zong!*, I allow the words and word clusters to breathe for I 'n I—for the we in us that we epigenetically carry within the memory of our cells. When I invite the audience to read with me, we collectively engage in breathing for the Other—for those who couldn't breathe—then
> can't now
> and, perhaps, won't be able to.
> In doing so we give them a second life
> I can't breathe;
>   I will breathe for you. (39)[84]

Yes, "I will breathe for you." But if we might dare add and extend this, "I breathe for you" as you, anteriorly, before the fact, through ether's medium, have also breathed for us.

This "ecstatic-aesthetic universality" is what "Mystic S/*Zong!*" breathes, chants, mythographically sounds.[85]

NOTES

1. M. NourbeSe Philip (and Setaey Adamu Boateng), *Zong!* (Middletown, CT: Wesleyan University Press, 2011).
2. For more on Acts, see Willie James Jennings, *Acts: A Theological Commentary on the Bible*, illustrated and unabridged (Louisville, KY: Westminster John Knox Press, 2017).
3. The following reflections on medieval Christian mysticism and its ongoing relevance have been shaped by and are in conversation with the following:

Meister Eckhart, *Meister Eckhart: The Essential Sermons, Commentaries, Treatises and Defense*, trans. Edmund Colledge and Bernard McGinn, new ed. (New York: Paulist Press, 1981); *Meister Eckhart: Teacher and Preacher*, ed. Bernard McGinn, 1st ed. (New York: Paulist Press, 1986); Meister Eckhart, *Wandering Joy: Meister Eckhart's Mystical Philosophy*, trans. Reiner Schürmann (Great Barrington, MA: Lindisfarne, 2001); Amy Hollywood, *Sensible Ecstasy: Mysticism, Sexual Difference, and the Demands of History* (Chicago: University of Chicago Press, 2002); Karma Lochrie, *Margery Kempe and Translations of the Flesh* (Philadelphia: University of Pennsylvania Press, 1994); Marguerite Porete, *Marguerite Porete: The Mirror of Simple Souls*, trans. Ellen Babinsky (New York: Paulist Press, 1993); Robert Wargo, *The Logic of Nothingness: A Study of Nishida Kitaro* (Honolulu: University of Hawai'i Press, 2005).

4. For more on the links between practices of divination and ecology and extraction, see Dan-El Padilla Peralta, "Ecology, Epistemology, and Divination in Cicero *De Divinatione* 1.90–94," *Arethusa* 51, no. 3 (2018): 237–67. I am also quite indebted to a conversation with R. A. Judy on this point.

5. Robert Duncan is a central poet associated with "open field" or open form poetry. Bruce Whiteman summarizes such poetry and poetics this way: "In open field poems, the poet is 'obedient' to language and the poem finds its own unique form in the act of writing." It is a mistake to understand open form poetry as formless. "Open form poetry is not formless at all (a complaint often raised by conservative critics and poets) but possesses the 'in-formation' of a musical composition." One sees this at work in Robert Duncan, *The Opening of the Field: Poetry*, rev. ed. (New York: New Directions, 1973). The reference to "infinite canvas" is from Denise Ferreira da Silva, "Toward a Black Feminist Poethics: The Quest(ion) of Blackness toward the End of the World," *Black Scholar* 44, no. 2 (2014): 81–97. Finally, "practice of outside" is a phrase Robin Blaser mobilizes to elaborate Jack Spicer's poetics. See Robin Blaser, "The Practice of Outside," in *The Fire: Collected Essays of Robin Blaser* (Berkeley: University of California Press, 2006), 113–63.

6. Denise Ferreira da Silva, "On Difference without Separability," in *Incerteza Viva: 32nd Bienal de São Paulo: 7 Sept–11 Dec 2016*, ed. Jochen Volz, Rjeille Isabella, and Júlia Rebouças (São Paulo: Fundaçao Bienal de São Paulo, 2016), 57–65.

7. Alexis Pauline Gumbs, *M Archive: After the End of the World* (Durham, NC: Duke University Press, 2018), 7.

8. Jayna Brown, *Black Utopias: Speculative Life and the Music of Other Worlds* (Durham, NC: Duke University Press, 2021).

9. On the apophatic as "unsaying" and "speaking away," see Michael A. Sells, *Mystical Languages of Unsaying* (Chicago: University of Chicago Press, 1994).

10. I explore this aspect of Long's thought in J. Kameron Carter, *The Anarchy of Black Religion: A Mystic Song* (Durham, NC: Duke University Press, forthcoming).
11. See Rachel Zolf, *No One's Witness: A Monstrous Poetics* (Durham, NC: Duke University Press, 2021), and fahima ife, *Maroon Choreography* (Durham, NC: Duke University Press, 2021).
12. Zakiyyah Iman Jackson, *Becoming Human: Matter and Meaning in an Antiblack World* (New York: NYU Press, 2020).
13. Nathaniel Mackey, *WHATSAID Serif* (San Francisco: City Lights, 2001), 23.
14. Nathaniel Mackey, *Paracritical Hinge: Essays, Talks, Notes, Interviews*, 1st ed. (Madison: University of Wisconsin Press, 2005), 208.
15. I address Mackey's practice of the poem as part of a wider theorization of Black religion in Carter, *Anarchy*.
16. See Sora Han, "Poetics of Mu," *Textual Practice* 34, no. 6 (2020): 921–48. I'm also in conversation with Han in her ongoing work that advances the theorization of Mu begun in this essay in which she extends engagements with Mackey and others.
17. Sells, 204.
18. Sells, 204.
19. Édouard Glissant, *Poetics of Relation*, trans. Betsy Wing (Ann Arbor: University of Michigan Press, 1997).
20. Hortense J. Spillers, "Mama's Baby, Papa's Maybe: An American Grammar Book," in *Black, White, and in Color: Essays on American Literature and Culture* (Chicago: University of Chicago Press, 2003), 66.
21. Rudolf Otto, *The Idea of the Holy: An Inquiry in the Non-Rational Factor in the Idea of the Divine and Its Relation to the Rational*, trans. John W. Harvey (New York: Oxford University Press, 1958). I cover some of this ground also in J. Kameron Carter, "Other Worlds, Nowhere (Or, the Sacred Otherwise)," in *Otherwise Worlds: Against Settler Colonialism and Anti-Blackness*, ed. Tiffany Lethabo King, Jenell Navarro, and Andrea Smith (Durham, NC: Duke University Press, 2020), 158–209.
22. The literature behind this claim of the coloniality of religion and the secular is vast. A few reference points are Gil Anidjar, "Secularism," *Critical Inquiry* 33, no. 1 (2006): 52–77; Gil Anidjar, *Blood: A Critique of Christianity* (New York: Columbia University Press, 2014); David Chidester, *Savage Systems: Colonialism and Comparative Religion in Southern Africa* (Charlottesville: University Press of Virginia, 1996); David Chidester, *Empire of Religion: Imperialism and Comparative Religion* (Chicago: University of Chicago Press, 2014); Jason Ananda Josephson, *The Invention of Religion in Japan* (Chicago: University of Chicago Press, 2012); Charles H. Long, *Significations: Signs, Symbols, and Images in the Interpretation of Religion*,

rev., Series in Philosophical and Cultural Studies in Religion (Aurora, CO: Davies Group, 1995); Jason Masuzawa, *The Invention of World Religions: Or, How European Universalism Was Preserved in the Language of Pluralism* (Chicago: University of Chicago Press, 2005); Sylvia Wynter, "Unsettling the Coloniality of Being/Power/Truth/Freedom: Towards the Human, After Man, Its Overrepresentation—An Argument," *CR: The New Centennial Review* 3, no. 3 (2003): 257–337; and Sylvia Wynter, "1492: A New World View," in *Race, Discourse, and the Origin of the Americas: A New World View*, ed. Vera Lawrence and Rex Nettleford (Washington, DC: Smithsonian Institution Press, 1995), 5–57.

23. On ensemble, see Fred Moten, *In the Break: The Aesthetics of the Black Radical Tradition* (Minneapolis: University of Minnesota Press, 2003).

24. For more on this approach to Black religion, see Carter, *Anarchy of Black Religion*.

25. Denise Ferreira da Silva, "Hacking the Subject: Black Feminism and Refusal beyond the Limits of Critique," *PhiloSOPHIA* 8, no. 1 (2018): 31, 21, and 28.

26. Gayl Jones, *Mosquito* (Boston: Beacon Press, 2000), 34; Hortense J. Spillers, "'The Permanent Obliquity of an In(pha)llibly Straight': In the Times of the Daughters and the Fathers," in *Black, White, and in Color: Essays on American Literature and Culture* (Chicago: University of Chicago Press, 2003), 234; Ferreira da Silva, "Hacking the Subject," 33.

27. J. Kameron Carter, "Paratheological Blackness," *South Atlantic Quarterly* 112, no. 4 (2013): 589–611. Bataille's "Atheological Summa" consists of Georges Bataille, *Guilty*, trans. Stuart Kendall (1944; Albany: State University of New York Press, 2011); Georges Bataille, *Inner Experience*, trans. Stuart Kendall (1954; Albany: State University of New York Press, 2014); and Georges Bataille, *On Nietzsche*, trans. Stuart Kendall, reprint ed. (1945; Albany: State University of New York Press, 2016). In reading Bataille, I've been greatly aided by Jeremy Biles, *Ecce Monstrum: Georges Bataille and the Sacrifice of Form* (New York: Fordham University Press, 2007); Jeremy Biles and Kent L. Brintnall, eds., *Negative Ecstasies: Georges Bataille and the Study of Religion* (New York: Fordham University Press, 2015); Hollywood, *Sensible Ecstasy*; and Amy Hollywood, "Mysticism and Catastrophe in Georges Bataille's Atheological Summa," in *Mystics: Presence and Aporia*, ed. Michael Kessler and Christian Sheppard (Chicago: University of Chicago Press, 2003), 161–87.

28. Frantz Fanon, *Black Skin, White Masks* (New York: Grove Press, 2008), 157.

29. See Maurice Blanchot, "Thought from Outside," in *Foucault/Blanchot: Maurice Blanchot: The Thought from Outside and Michel Foucault as I Imagine Him*, trans. Jeffrey Mehlman and Brian Massumi (New York: Zone Books, 1987). With the notion of "Black prayer" I certainly have in mind Fanon's invocation of his "final

prayer" at the end of *Black Skin, White Masks*. That very formulation suggests that the entirety of *Black Skin, White Masks* is a prayer. I also have in mind Andrew Prevot, *Thinking Prayer: Theology and Spirituality amid the Crises of Modernity* (Notre Dame, IN: University of Notre Dame Press, 2015). But ultimately, it again is Charles Long's arresting meditation on prayer, the hold of slave ships, and the birth of "Black religion" in the suspension that was/is the Middle Passage. See Charles H. Long, "Passage and Prayer: The Origin of Religion in the Atlantic World," in *Ellipsis . . . The Collected Writings of Charles H. Long*, ed. Charles H. Long (New York: Bloomsbury Academic, 2018), 279–84.

30. Zakiyyah Iman Jackson nicely shows how the immanence-transcendence dichotomy works in anti-Black ways. See, particularly, chapter 2 of *Becoming Human*.

31. I cannot thank Sora Han enough for a conversation in which we were talking about the politics of air and aeration and the notion of Tiffany Lethabo King's deployment of the notion of the amphibious in her work. It was in this conversation that Han rolled out this formulation. As for King, see Tiffany Lethabo King, *The Black Shoals: Offshore Formations of Black and Native Studies* (Durham, NC: Duke University Press, 2019).

32. Aliyyah I. Abdur-Rahman, "The Black Ecstatic," *GLQ: A Journal of Lesbian and Gay Studies* 24, no. 2 (2018): 343–65.

33. M. NourbeSe Philip, "Notanda," in M. NourbeSe Philip (and Setaey Adamu Boateng), *Zong!* (Middletown, CT: Wesleyan University Press, 2011), 200.

34. Philip, "Notanda," 191. *Zong!* culminates a meditation of Silence that arguably marks Philip's entire oeuvre. At a minimum, the titles of her prior two poetry collections indicate as much: M. NourbeSe Philip, *She Tries Her Tongue, Her Silence Softly Breaks* (Charlottetown: Gynergy Books/Ragweed Press, 1989), and M. NourbeSe Philip, *Looking for Livingstone: An Odyssey of Silence* (Stratford, Ont.: Mercury Press, 1991).

35. These are lines, again, from Mackey's poem "Song of the Andoumboulou: 20" inasmuch as they resonate with Philip's poetics on just the point I am making here. He too is a mythography. See Mackey, *WHATSAID Serif*, 22, 3.

36. Kevin Quashie, *Black Aliveness, or A Poetics of Being* (Durham, NC: Duke University Press, 2021).

37. M. NourbeSe Philip, "Wor(l)ds Interrupted: An Unhistory of the Kari Basin," *Jacket2*. Accessed October 9, 2016. http://jacket2.org/article/worlds-interrupted.

38. See, Ferreira da Silva, "Hacking the Subject."

39. See Saidiya Hartman, "The Belly of the World: A Note on Black Women's Labors," *Souls* 18, no. 1 (2016): 166–73, and Jackson, *Becoming Human*.

40. On this use of "the break" and "the cut," see Moten, *In the Break*.
41. R. A. Judy, *Sentient Flesh: Thinking in Disorder, Poiesis in Black* (Durham, NC: Duke University Press, 2020).
42. On juris-generativity, see Robert M. Cover, "Nomos and Narrative," in *Narrative, Violence, and the Law: The Essays of Robert Cover*, ed. Martha Minow, Michael Ryan, and Austin Sarat (Ann Arbor: University of Michigan Press, 1992), 95–172.
43. Fred Moten, "Blackness and Nothingness (Mysticism in the Flesh)," *South Atlantic Quarterly* 112, no. 4 (2013): 737–80; Abdur-Rahman, "The Black Ecstatic"; and Zakiyyah Iman Jackson, "'Theorizing in a Void': Sublimity, Matter, and Physics in Black Feminist Poetics," *South Atlantic Quarterly* 117, no. 3 (2018): 620.
44. Stefano Harney and Fred Moten, *The Undercommons: Fugitive Planning and Black Study* (New York: Minor Compositions, 2013).
45. Philip, "Wor(l)ds Interrupted."
46. On "not in between," see Fred Moten, *Black and Blur* (Durham, NC: Duke University Press, 2017), 1–27.
47. Long, *Significations*.
48. See Spillers, "Mama's Baby, Papa's Maybe," "Interstices," and "'The Permanent Obliquity of an In(pha)llibly Straight,'" each in Spillers, *Black, White, and in Color*.
49. Hortense J. Spillers, "Ellison's 'Usable Past': Toward a Theory of Myth," in *Black, White, and in Color*, 68–79.
50. In *Becoming Human* (see chapter 2 particularly), Jackson makes a similar point about an embarrassment about the religious in Black studies. In a conversation with her on September 17, 2020, she reinforced this point. I am grateful to be in conversation with, learning from, and thinking with Jackson.
51. Ashon T. Crawley, *Blackpentecostal Breath: The Aesthetics of Possibility* (New York: Fordham University Press, 2016).
52. Fred Moten, "Notes on Passage (The New International of Sovereign Feelings)," *Palimpsest: A Journal on Women, Gender, and the Black International* 3, no. 1 (2014): 51–74.
53. On the history of this incident, see James Walvin, *The Zong: A Massacre, the Law, and the End of Slavery* (New Haven, CT: Yale University Press, 2011), as well as Philip's essay, "Notanda," at the end of M. NourbeSe Philip (and Setaey Adamu Boateng), *Zong!* (Middletown, CT: Wesleyan, 2011). References to *Zong!* and to this essay will occur parenthetically within the chapter.
54. Philip reproduces the summary judgment of the court case as part of the back matter of *Zong!*
55. Mandy Bloomfield, *Archaeopoetics: Word, Image, History* (Tuscaloosa: University Alabama Press, 2016), 192.

56. M. NourbeSe Philip, *A Genealogy of Resistance: And Other Essays* (Toronto: Mercury Press, 1998), 116, as quoted in Bloomfield, 192.
57. Bloomfield, 201.
58. In the background of this interpretation of Philip's statement is Walter Benjamin, "Critique of Violence," in *Walter Benjamin: Selected Writings, Volume 1: 1913–1926*, ed. Marcus Bullock and Michael W. Jennings (Cambridge, MA: Belknap Press of Harvard University Press, 2004), 236–52; and Walter Benjamin, "Goethe's Elective Affinities," in *Walter Benjamin: Selected Writings, Volume 1: 1913–1926*, 297–360. Between these two crucial texts of the Benjaminian corpus is Benjamin's theorization of divine violence in contrast to mythic violence as well as, in relationship to this distinction, his crucial formulation of the notion of the "daemonic," which I'm aligning with Philip's notion of the shaman and by extension with her notion of ritual, glossolalia, and magic—all of which comes to a head with the ghostly, witchly figure of Sycorax, figure of the Black radical, Black feminist sacred. I develop this idea further in my book-in-progress, "Black Rapture." I am grateful to the work of Nijah Cunningham for first sending me down this Benjaminian course of investigation. See Nijah Cunningham, "The Resistance of the Lost Body," *Small Axe* 20, no. 1 (2016): 113–28.
59. Bloomfield, 201.
60. Georges Bataille, *Lascaux; or, The Birth of Art* (Lausanne: Skira, 1955), 39.
61. Fred Moten, *Stolen Life* (Durham, NC: Duke University Press, 2018), 244, thinking with Denise Ferreira da Silva. See Denise Ferreira da Silva, "On Difference without Separability."
62. Ferreira da Silva, "Hacking the Subject."
63. For more information about the Roman Catholic Requiem Mass, see Pietro Piacenza, "Masses of Requiem," *Catholic Encyclopedia*, vol. 12 (New York: Robert Appleton, 1911), http://www.newadvent.org/cathen/12776d.htm. I am grateful for email exchanges with Yale Divinity School professor Teresa Berger that have helped me think through the Requiem Mass.
64. Lauren F. Winner, *The Dangers of Christian Practice: On Wayward Gifts, Characteristic Damage, and Sin* (New Haven, CT: Yale University Press, 2018).
65. On aliveness, I am thinking with Quashie, *Black Aliveness*.
66. Lindon Barrett, *Blackness and Value: Seeing Double* (Cambridge: Cambridge University Press, 1999), 28. See also Kyla Wazana Tompkins, *Racial Indigestion: Eating Bodies in the 19th Century* (New York: NYU Press, 2012).
67. Barrett, 27.
68. On Wynter's "beyond," see Sylvia Wynter, "Black Metamorphosis: New Natives in a New World," Institute of the Black World Records, MG 502, Box 1, Schomburg Center for Research in Black Culture, n.d.; and Greg Thomas, "Sex/Sexuality

& Sylvia Wynter's 'Beyond . . .': Anti-Colonial Ideas in the 'Black Radical Tradition,'" *Journal of West Indian Literature* 10, no. 1/2 (2001): 92–118. I elaborate on Wynter's notion of "beyond" in J. Kameron Carter, "Black Malpractice (A Poetics of the Sacred)," *Social Text* 37, no. 2 (2019): 67–107.

69. Moten, *Stolen Life*, ix.
70. Here I am thinking with and extending Calvin Warren's account of anti-Blackness as "ontological terror" to surface the onto-*theological* architecture of that terror and yet think what hovers beyond, within, "not in between," as Moten with Wynter might say. See Calvin L. Warren, *Ontological Terror: Blackness, Nihilism, and Emancipation* (Durham, NC: Duke University Press, 2018).
71. Amy De'Ath and Fred Wah, eds., *Toward. Some. Air.: Remarks on Poetics* (Banff, Alberta: Banff Centre Press, 2015).
72. M. NourbeSe Philip, "The Ga(s)p," in *Poetics and Precarity*, ed. Myung Mi Kim and Cristanne Miller (Albany: State University of New York Press, 2018), 31–40. Further references are within the chapter.
73. M. NourbeSe Philip, "A Piece of Land Surrounded," in *A Genealogy of Resistance: And Other Essays* (Toronto: Mercury Press, 1998), 167.
74. I am thinking here with Joshua Bennett and Sarah Jane Cervenak. See Joshua Bennett, "Vomiting in the Dark: Towards a Black Hydropoetics," in *Ecopoetics: Essays in the Field*, ed. Angela Hume and Gillian Osborne (Iowa City: University of Iowa Press, 2018), 102–17; and Sarah Jane Cervenak, *Black Gathering: Art, Ecology, Ungiven Life* (Durham, NC: Duke University Press, 2021).
75. See Carter, *The Anarchy of Black Religion*, and my manuscript in progress, "Black Rapture: A Poetics of the Sacred."
76. On Black aesthetic sociality, see Laura Harris, *Experiments in Exile: C. L. R. James, Hélio Oiticica, and the Aesthetic Sociality of Blackness* (New York: Fordham University Press, 2018).
77. The literature on the complexities around *religio* is vast and growing. I have found quite useful the following: Carlin A. Barton and Daniel Boyarin. *Imagine No Religion: How Modern Abstractions Hide Ancient Realities* (New York: Fordham University Press, 2016); and Brent Nongbri, *Before Religion: A History of a Modern Concept* (New Haven, CT: Yale University Press, 2013).
78. My all too brief reflections on Castoriadis in this paragraph are in conversation with Cornelius Castoriadis, "Institution of Society and Religion," in *World in Fragments: Writings on Politics, Society, Psychoanalysis, and the Imagination*, trans. David Ames Curtis (Stanford, CA: Stanford University Press, 1997). I must also say that my reading of Castoriadis has been greatly assisted by Stathis Gourgouris, *The Perils of the One* (New York: Columbia University Press, 2019), 179–84.

79. Castoriadis, 325.
80. Long, *Ellipsis*, 186–88.
81. Emphasis mine. See, particularly, chapter 2 ("The Souls of White Folk") in W. E. B. Du Bois, *Voices From within the Veil* (Amherst, NY: Humanity Books, 2002). I develop the notion of mythic whiteness in my work in progress.
82. Saidiya V. Hartman, *Scenes of Subjection: Terror, Slavery, and Self-Making in Nineteenth-Century America* (New York: Oxford University Press, 1997); and Saidiya Hartman, "Venus in Two Acts," *Small Axe* 12, no. 2 (2008): 1–14.
83. Ferreira da Silva, "Toward a Black Feminist Poethics"; Ferreira da Silva, "Difference without Separability"; and Jackson, "Theorizing in a Void."
84. "I can't breathe" were the words of Eric Garner, said eleven times as he was in a chokehold before he died at the hands of the New York City police on July 17, 2014. They too were uttered by George Floyd, as a police officer stole his life on March 25, 2020, by putting his knee on his neck and pinning him to the ground. According to the *New York Times*, the phrase "I can't breathe" has been uttered at least seventy times. See Mike Baker et al., "Three Words. 70 Cases. The Tragic History of 'I Can't Breathe,'" *New York Times*, June 29, 2020, sec. U.S., https://www.nytimes.com/interactive/2020/06/28/us/i-cant-breathe-police-arrest.html.
85. See Daniel Benjamin, "On Ecstatic-Aesthetic Universality—In *Zong!*" *Small Axe* 23, no. 1 (2019): 17–34. What he calls ecstatic-aesthetic universality I here elaborate as a mythographic or dark churchical sociality.

ACKNOWLEDGMENTS

This volume had its origins in the proceedings of the Nineteenth Transdisciplinary Theological Colloquium, titled "Political Theology at the Edge: Collectivities of Crisis and Possibilities," and was held at Drew Theological School in Madison, New Jersey, March 29–31, 2019. Chapter 1, "The Anthropocene as Planetary Machine," was originally published in William Connolly, *Climate Machines, Fascist Drives, and Truth* (Duke University Press, 2019), as Chapter 2, "The Anthropocene as Abstract Machine." Republished here with permission of Duke University Press. With gratitude, the editors want to acknowledge everyone involved in the conference. The unstinting support of the Drew Theological School, and in particular of its deans, Dean Javier Viera and then-Dean Melanie Johnson-DeBaufre, has been crucial for these conferences. Catherine and Clayton would like to thank Andrea White above all, for her extraordinary work in co-organizing the event with us, without which it would not have been nearly as significant as it was. In addition to the colloquium participants whose essays appear in this volume, an extensive cast of further participants also enriched the program. The extraordinary respondents were Mary Keller, An Yountae, Joseph Harroff, Jeffrey W. Robbins, John Thatamanil, Melanie Johnson-DeBaufre, Shelley Dennis, Jea Sophia Oh, Beatrice Marovich, Santiago Slabodsky, Dhawn Martin, and Karen Bray. The student presenters also included Sarah O'Brien, O'neil Van Horn, Jermaine Ross, Alice Kim, Hunter Bragg, Stephen Keating, Desmond Coleman, Thurman Willison, Prabhsharanbir Singh, Lindsay Grass, and Michael Anderson. In addition, we want to extend profound thanks to Wren Hillis for his excellent organizing work leading up to and during the conference. Special gratitude is also due to Fordham University Press through two decades of TTC conferences and volumes, and above all, for their invaluable support of this volume in particular, to editors Richard Morrison and John Garza.

CONTRIBUTORS

GIL ANIDJAR teaches in the Department of Religion and the Department of Middle Eastern, South Asian, and African Studies at Columbia University. He is currently completing a manuscript titled *Sparta and Gaza: The Tradition of Destruction*; sections of it have been published here and there.

BALBINDER SINGH BHOGAL is a professor in religion and the holder of the Sardarni Kuljit Kaur Bindra Chair in Sikh Studies at Hofstra University, NY. His primary research interests are South Asian religions and cultures specializing in the Sikh tradition, particularly the Guru Granth Sahib, its philosophy and exegesis. Secondary research interests include critical theory, political mysticism, and decolonial, animal, and affect studies.

J. KAMERON CARTER is a professor of religious studies at Indiana University, Bloomington, where he has additional appointments in the English, Gender Studies, and African American and African Diaspora Studies departments. He is co-director of IU's Center for Religion and the Human. His work focuses on questions of race, empire, and ecology as matters of political theology and the sacred. Carter is the author of *Race: A Theological Account* (Oxford University Press, 2008), the editor of *Religion and the Futures of Blackness* (a special issue of *South Atlantic Quarterly*, 2013) as well as *The Matter of Black Religion: Thinking with Charles H. Long* (a special issue of the journal *American Religion*, 2021), and the author of the forthcoming book, *The Anarchy of Black Religion* (Duke University Press).

WILLIAM E. CONNOLLY is the Krieger-Eisenhower Professor at Johns Hopkins University, where he teaches political theory. His recent books include *The Fragility of Things* (2013), *Facing the Planetary* (2017), *Aspirational Fascism* (2017), and *Climate Machines, Fascist Drives and Truth* (2019). His new study, *Resounding Events: Adventures of an Academic from the Working Class*, will be published by Fordham University Press in 2022. In 2020 the Western Political Science Association named a new award The William E. Connolly Award to be awarded to the best conference paper in theory every year.

CLAYTON CROCKETT is a professor and the director of Religious Studies at the University of Central Arkansas. He is the author or editor of a number of books, including *Derrida After the End of Writing: Political Theology and New Materialism*, and a co-editor of *Doing Theology in the Age of Trump: A Critical Report on Christian Nationalism*. He is a fellow of Westar Institute's Seminar on God and the Human Future.

THE VERY REVEREND DR. KELLY BROWN DOUGLAS was named dean of the Episcopal Divinity School at Union Theological Seminary and professor of theology at Union in September 2017. She was named the Bill and Judith Moyers Chair in Theology in November 2019. She also serves as the canon theologian at the Washington National Cathedral and theologian in residence at Trinity Church Wall Street. Dean Douglas is widely published in national and international journals and other publications. Her groundbreaking and widely taught book *Sexuality and the Black Church: A Womanist Perspective* (1999) was the first to address the issue of homophobia within the Black church community. Her latest book, *Stand Your Ground: Black Bodies and the Justice of God* (2015), examines the challenges of a "Stand Your Ground" culture for the Black church.

SETH GAITERS is a doctoral candidate and interdisciplinary scholar at the Ohio State University investigating the intersection of religion, race, and politics in the Americas. He is especially concerned with the conjuncture of religion and progressive social movements in the history of Black communities in the United States. Seth's dissertation examines the religiosity of the Movement for Black Lives, popularly called the Black Lives Matter movement. His study of these matters is driven by religious studies, Black studies, American cultural studies, critical theory, and political theology; alongside methods of narrative and discourse analysis.

LISA GASSON-GARDNER is a PhD candidate in Theological and Philosophical Studies in Religion at Drew University. Her research interests include the status of truth in contemporary political discourse, ethnographic accounts of charismatic evangelical Christianity, radical theology, and political theology. She is a full-time instructor in the Department of Philosophy and Religious Studies at Middle Tennessee State University. Lisa is committed to dismantling white, cis, hetero, abled patriarchy everywhere.

WINFIELD GOODWIN is a doctoral student in philosophy of religion at Union Theological Seminary in the City of New York.

LAWRENCE E. HILLIS is a doctoral student at Drew University. Located within the department of Theological and Philosophical Studies in Religion, his transdisciplinary research focuses on the intersection of political theology, religion and economics, queer and affect theories, and childhood studies. Hillis is a candidate for ordination in the United Methodist Church and has received several awards and fellowships for his work pertaining to constructive theology and Wesleyan-Methodist studies.

MEHMET KARABELA teaches in the School of Religion and the Department of History at Queen's University in Kingston, Canada. He is the author of *Islamic Thought through Protestant Eyes* (Routledge, 2021) and *Mustafa Sabri Efendi* (Opsi Press, 2021). Karabela's articles and writings have also appeared in edited books and journals. He has taught courses on Islam, religion and democracy, political theology, and religion and politics in Muslim societies as well as seminars such as the European perception of Jews and Muslims during the Enlightenment and Muslims, Christians and Jews in the Ottoman Empire.

CATHERINE KELLER is a professor of constructive theology at the Theological School of Drew University. Her books include *Cloud of the Impossible: Negative Theology and Planetary Entanglements* (2014) and *Political Theology of the Earth: Our Planetary Emergency and the Struggle for a New Public* (2018).

MICHAEL NORTHCOTT is a professor of religion and ecology at the Indonesian Consortium of Religious Studies, Universitas Gadjah Mada, Yogyakarta, Indonesia (2019–), and emeritus professor of ethics at the University of Edinburgh (2018–). He was guest professor at the University of Heidelberg in 2018. His most recent books include *A Moral Climate: The Ethics of Global Warming* (2008), *A Political Theology of Climate Change* (2013), and *Place, Ecology and the Sacred: The Moral Geography of Sustainable Communities* (2015).

AUSTIN ROBERTS is a doctoral candidate at Drew University in the Graduate Division of Religion. His current research focuses on the intersections of political theology, process philosophy, and critical Anthropocene studies. He lives, works, and teaches in Northern California.

NOËLLE VAHANIAN is a professor of philosophy in the Social Justice and Civic Engagement program at Lebanon Valley College, in Annville, Pennsylvania. She is the author of *Language, Desire, and Theology: A Genealogy of the Will to Speak* (2003), *The Rebellious No: Variations on a Secular Theology of Language* (Fordham University Press, 2014), and co-author of *An Insurrectionist Manifesto: Four New Gospels for a Radical Politics* (2016). Her current research engages the problem of genocide and its relevance to philosophy of religion.

LARRY L. WELBORN is a professor of New Testament and early Christian literature at Fordham University in New York City and honorary professor of ancient history at Macquarie University in Sydney, Australia. Welborn holds an MAR from Yale Divinity School and a PhD from Vanderbilt University. Among his publications are *Politics and Rhetoric in the Corinthian Epistles* (1997), *Paul, the Fool of Christ* (2005), *An End to Enmity* (2011), *Paul's Summons to Messianic Life* (2015), and *The Young against the Old* (2018). Welborn is co-editor of Synkrisis, a series published by Yale University Press, and editor of the Paul in Critical Contexts series of Fortress Academic.

TRANSDISCIPLINARY THEOLOGICAL COLLOQUIA

Laurel Kearns and Catherine Keller, eds., *Ecospirit: Religions and Philosophies for the Earth*.

Virginia Burrus and Catherine Keller, eds., *Toward a Theology of Eros: Transfiguring Passion at the Limits of Discipline*.

Ada María Isasi-Díaz and Eduardo Mendieta, eds., *Decolonizing Epistemologies: Latina/o Theology and Philosophy*.

Stephen D. Moore and Mayra Rivera, eds., *Planetary Loves: Spivak, Postcoloniality, and Theology*.

Chris Boesel and Catherine Keller, eds., *Apophatic Bodies: Negative Theology, Incarnation, and Relationality*.

Chris Boesel and S. Wesley Ariarajah, eds., *Divine Multiplicity: Trinities, Diversities, and the Nature of Relation*.

Stephen D. Moore, ed., *Divinanimality: Animal Theory, Creaturely Theology*. Foreword by Laurel Kearns.

Melanie Johnson-DeBaufre, Catherine Keller, and Elias Ortega-Aponte, eds., *Common Goods: Economy, Ecology, and Political Theology*.

Catherine Keller and Mary-Jane Rubenstein, eds., *Entangled Worlds: Religion, Science, and New Materialisms*.

Kent L. Brintnall, Joseph A. Marchal, and Stephen D. Moore, eds., *Sexual Disorientations: Queer Temporalities, Affects, Theologies*.

Karen Bray and Stephen D. Moore, eds., *Religion, Emotion, Sensation: Affect Theories and Theologies*.

Clayton Crockett and Catherine Keller, eds., *Political Theology on Edge: Ruptures of Justice and Belief in the Anthropocene*.

www.ingramcontent.com/pod-product-compliance
Lightning Source LLC
Chambersburg PA
CBHW032027290426
44110CB00012B/703